Harriet Allsopp holds a PhD in Politics from Birkbeck, University of London. She is an expert on the Kurds of Syria and contributes analysis to private consultancies and governmental departments.

Harriet Allsopp

THE KURDS OF SYRIA

Political Parties and Identity in the Middle East

I.B. TAURIS

LONDON · NEW YORK

New paperback edition published in 2015 by
I.B.Tauris & Co Ltd
London • New York
www.ibtauris.com

First published in hardback in 2014 by I.B.Tauris & Co Ltd

ISBN: 978 1 78453 393 9
eISBN: 978 0 85773 970 4

A full CIP record for this book is available from the British Library
A full CIP record is available from the Library of Congress

Library of Congress Catalog Card Number: available

Typeset by Newgen Publishers, Chennai

CONTENTS

NOTE ON TRANSLITERATION

This book has employed texts and interviews, in four languages: Arabic, the Kurmanji dialect of Kurdish, French and English. For Arabic, as far as possible I have used a simplified system of transliteration based on that of the International Journal of Middle Eastern Studies. For Kurdish I generally have used the alphabet developed by Jaladat Bedirkhan, particularly for names of political organisations, in an attempt to represent them correctly. For the names of towns and villages in the Kurdish regions I have tried to use their Kurdish names, employing the same alphabet. Although most place names have been subject to arabisation and have had their names changed to Arabic ones, Kurds in Syria still refer to them by their former names and it is often the case that the Arabic name is not known locally. The same alphabet is used for names of some well-known people for ease of understanding, although the majority of names are transliterated from Arabic or appear in their most commonly used form.

MAP OF THE KURDISH AREAS
IN SYRIA

The Kurdish Areas of Syria

CURRENT SYRIAN KURDISH POLITICAL PARTIES

As of March 2014

Partîya Dêmokrat a Kurdî li Sûriyê (el-Partî)

al-Hizb al-Dimuqrati al-Kurdi fi Suriya (al-Parti)
Kurdish Democratic Party in Syria (The Party)
Head: Dr Abdul Hakim Bashar

Partîya Dêmokrat a Kurdî li Sûriyê (el-Partî)

al-Hizb al-Dimuqrati al-Kurdi fi Suriya (al-Parti)
Kurdish Democratic Party in Syria (The Party)
Head: Nusradin Ibrahim

Partîya Dêmokrat a Kurdî li Sûriyê

al-Hizb al-Dimuqrati al-Kurdi fi Suriya
Kurdish Democratic Party in Syria
Head: Dr Lezgin Muhammad Fakhri

Partîya Dêmokrat a Kurdî li Sûriyê

al-Hizb al-Dimuqrati al-Kurdi fi Suriya
Kurdish Democratic Party in Syria
Head: Abdul Karim Sako

Partîya Dêmokrat a Pêşverû a Kurdî li Sûriyê

al-Hizb al-Dimuqrati al-Taqadumi al-Kurdi fi Suriya
Kurdish Democratic Progressive Party in Syria
Head: Abdul Hamid Haj Darwish

Partîya Wekhevî ya Dêmokrat a Kurdî li Sûriyê
(formerly *Partîya Dêmokrata Pêşverû
a Kurdî li Sûriyê*)

Hizb al-Musawah al Dimoqrati al-Kurdi fi Suriya
Kurdish Democratic Equality Party in Syria
Head: Aziz Daoud

Partîya Yekîtî ya Dêmokrat a Kurd li Sûriyê

Hizb al-Wahida al-Dimuqrati al-Kurdi fi Suriya
Kurdish Democratic Union Party in Syria
Head: Muhidin Sheikh Ali. Previously led by Ismail Omar (also known as Ismail
    Amo) who passed away 18 October 2010.

Partîya Yekîtî ya Kurd li Sûriyê

Hizb al-Yekîtî al-Kurdi fi Suriya
Kurdish Union Party in Syria
Head: Leader elected for a three year term. The term of Ismail Hemi began in
    2010.

Partîya Çep a Kurdî li Sûriyê – Kongra

al-Hizb al-Yasari al-Kurdi fi Suriya – Kongres
Kurdish Left Party in Syria – Congress
Head: Muhammad Musa Muhammad

Partîya Çep a Kurdî li Sûriyê- Komîta Navendî

al-Hizb al-Yasari al-Kurdi fi Suriya – al-Lajnah al-Markaziyah
Kurdish Left Party in Syria – Central Committee
Head: Salih Gido

Partîya Welatperêz a Dêmokrat a Kurdî li Sûriyê

al-Hizb al-Watani al-Dimuqrati al-Kurdi fi Suriya

Kurdish Patriotic Democratic Party in Syria
Head: Tahir Sadun Safouk

Partîya Dêmokrat a Kurdî ya Sûrî (el-Sûrî)

al-Hizb al-Dimuqrati al-Kurdi al-Suriy
Syrian Kurdish Democratic Party
Head: Jamal M. Sheikh Baqi

Partîya Hevgirtina Gelê Kurd li Sûriyê

Hizb al-Itihad al-Sha'bi al-Kurd fi Suriya
Kurdish Popular Union Party in Syria
Head: Mustafa Rashid
(Now primarily existing in exile with only a few, if any, members in Syria.)

Şepêla Pêşerojê ya Kurdî li Sûriyê

Tiyar al-Mustaqbal al-Kurdi fi Suriya
Kurdish Future Movement in Syria
Head: Jangidar Muhammad

Şepêla Pêşerojê ya Kurdî li Sûriyê

Tiyar al-Mustaqbal al-Kurdi fi Suriya
Kurdish Future Movement in Syria
Head: Rezan Bahri Shaykhmus

Partîya Azadî ya Kurdi li Suriyê

Hizb Azadi al-Kurdi fi Suriya
Kurdish Freedom Party in Syria
Head: Mustafa Juma'a

Partîya Azadî ya Kurdi li Suryê

Hizb Azadi al-Kurdi fi Syriya
Kurdish Freedom Party in Syria
Head: Mustafa Oso

Partîya Yekîtî ya Dêmokrat (PYD)

Hizb al-Itihad al-Dimuqrati
Democratic Union Party
Head: Saleh Muslim and Asya Muhammad

Partîya Rêkeftina Dêmokrat a Kurdistani – Sûriyê

Hizb al-Wifaq al-Dimuqrati al-Kurdistani – Suriya
Kurdistan Democratic Concord Party – Syria
Head: Nash'at Muhammad (replaced Fawzi Shengal)

Partîya Yekîtî ya Kurdistani li Sûriyê

Hizb Yekiti al-Kurdstani fi Suriya
Kurdistan Union Party in Syria
Head: Omar Daoud

Partîya Dêmokrata Pêşverû a Kurdî li Sûriyê

al-Hizb al-Kurdi al-Dimuqrati al-Taqadumi fi Suriya – Harakat al-Islah
Kurdish Democratic Progressive Party in Syria – Reform Movement
Head: Faisal Yusef

COALITIONS OF PARTIES

(Listed in chronological order)

Pre-Uprising Coalitions

Hevbendi ya Dêmokrat a Kurdî li Sûriyê

al-Tahaluf al-Dimoqrati al-Kurdi fi Suriya
The Kurdish Democratic Alliance in Syria
Formed: 1992–2011
Including:
Partîya Dêmokrata Pêşverû a Kurdî li Sûriyê (Abdul Hamid Darwish)
Partîya Yekîtî ya Dêmokrat a Kurd li Sûriyê (Ismail Omar)
Partîya Dêmokrat a Kurdî li Sûriyê (Nusradin Ibrahim)
Partîya Çep a Kurdî li Sûriyê (Muhammad Musa)

Eniya Dêmokrat a Kurdî li Sûriyê

al-Jabhah al-Dimoqratiyah al-Kurdiyah fi Suriya
The Kurdish Democratic Front in Syria
Formed: 1996–2011
Including:
Partîya Dêmokrat a Kurdî li Sûriyê (el-Partî) (Dr Abdul Hakim Bashar)
Partîya Wekhevî Dêmokrat a Kurdî li Sûriyê (Aziz Daoud)
Partîya Welatperêz a Dêmokrat a Kurdî li Sûriyê (Tahir Safouk)

Komîta Tensîqê ya Kurdî

Lajnat al-Tansiq al-Kurdiyah
The Committee of Kurdish Coordination
Formed: 2006–2011
Including:
Partîya Azadî ya Kurd li Suriyê (Khayr al-Din Murad)

Partîya Yekîtî ya Kurd li Sûriyê (Ismail Hemi)
Şepêla Pêşerojê ya Kurdî li Sûriyê (Meshaal Temmo)

Encûmena Siyasî ya Kurdî li Sûriyê

al-Majlis al-Siyasi al-Kurdi fi Suriya
The Kurdish Political Council in Syria
Formed: 2009–2011
Including:
Partîya Dêmokrat a Kurdî li Sûriyê (el-Partî) (Dr Abdul Hakim Bashar)
Şepêla Pêşerojê ya Kurdî li Sûriyê (Meshaal Temmo)
Partîya Welatperêz a Dêmokrat a Kurdî li Sûriyê (Tahir Safouk)
Partîya Yekîtî ya Kurd li Sûriyê (Ismail Hemi)
Partîya Azadî ya Kurd li Suryê (Khayr al-Din Murad)
Partîya Çep a Kurdî li Sûriyê (Muhammad Musa)
Partîya Dêmokrat a Kurdî ya Sûrî (el-Sûrî) (Jamal Sheikh Baqi)
Partîya Wekhevî Dêmokrat a Kurdî li Sûriyê (Aziz Daoud)

Coalitions Formed During the Uprising

Encûmena Niştimanî ya Kurd li Sûriyê

al-Majlis al-Watani al-Kurdi fi Suriya
Kurdish National Council (KNC)
Formed: 26–27 October 2011, Qamishli
Including:
{In response to the changed political conditions in Syria after March 2011, the KNC replaced existing coalitions of parties. It initially united ten political parties and included Kurdish youth organisations and independent activists. By May 2012, the KNC included 16 Kurdish parties}:

Partîya Dêmokrata Pêşverû a Kurdî li Sûriyê (Abdul Hamid Darwish)
Partîya Yekîtî ya Dêmokrat a Kurd li Sûriyê (Sheikh Ali)
Partîya Dêmokrat a Kurdî li Sûriyê (Nusradin Ibrahim)
Partîya Dêmokrat a Kurdî li Sûriyê (el-Partî) (Dr Abdul Hakim Bashar)
Partîya Dêmokrat a Kurdî li Sûriyê (Abdul Rahman Aluji)
Partîya Welatperêz a Dêmokrat a Kurdî li Sûriyê (Tahir Safouk)
Partîya Yekîtî ya Kurd li Sûriyê (Ismail Hemi)
Partîya Azadî ya Kurd li Suryê (Mustafa Juma'a)
Partîya Azadî ya Kurd li Suryê (Mustafa Oso)
Partîya Çep a Kurdî li Sûriyê – Congress (Muhammad Musa)
Partîya Çep a Kurdî li Sûriyê – Central Committee (Salih Gido)
Partîya Dêmokrat a Kurdî ya Sûrî (el-Sûrî) (Jamal Sheikh Baqi)
Partîya Wekhevî Dêmokrat a Kurdî li Sûriyê (Aziz Daoud)
Partîya Yekîtî ya Kurdistani li Sûriyê (Omar Daoud)
Partîya Rêkeftina Dêmokrat a Kurdistani – Sûriyê (Nash'at Muhammad)
Partîya Dêmokrata Pêşverû a Kurdî li Sûriyê (Faisal Yusef)

Yekitiya Hezin Kurdî ya Dêmokrat li Sûriyê

Itihad al-Quwa al-Dimoqratiyah al-Kurdiyah fi Suriya
Union of Kurdish Democratic Forces in Syria
Formed: 2011, Syria
Including:
Şepêla Pêşerojê ya Kurdî li Sûriyê (Meshaal Temmo)
Partîya Hevgirtina Gelê Kurd li Sûriyê (Mustafa Rashid)
[*Partîya Yekîtî ya Kurdistani li Sûriyê**
Partîya Dêmokrat a Kurdî li Sûriyê, (Abdul Rahman Aluji)*
Partîya Rêkeftina Dêmokrat a Kurdistani – Sûriyê (Nash'at Muhammad)*]

---

*these three parties left the alliance to join the KNC in February 2012

Encûmena Gel ya Rojavayê Kurdistanê

al-Majiis al-Sha'b li Gharb Kurdistan
The Peoples Council of Western Kurdistan (PCWK)
Formed: 16 December 2011, Dêrîk, Syria
Including:
Partîya Yekîtî ya Dêmokrat (PYD)
Tevgera Civaka Demokratîk a Rojavayê Kurdistanê (Tev-Dem) (the Western Kurdistan Democratic Society Movement)
Yekîtiya Star (women's organisation)
Yekîtiya Ciwanen Şoreşger li Rojavayê Kurdistan (the Youth Movement of Western Kurdistan)
Saziya Malbaten Şehidan (the Union of the Families of Martyrs)
Saziya Perwerde û Ziman (the Education and Language Institution)

Desteya Bilind a Kurd li Sûriyê

al-Hiy'ah al-Kurdiyah al-'Uliya
The Supreme Kurdish Committee (SKC)
Formed: July 2012
Including:
The Kurdish National Council
The People's Council of Western Kurdistan

Hevgirtina Siyasî Demokratî ya Kurdî li Sûriyê

al-Itihad al-Siyasi al-Dimoqrati al-Kurdi fi Suriya
The Kurdish Political Democratic Union in Syria
Formed: 15 December 2012
Including:
Partîya Dêmokrat a Kurdî li Sûriyê (el-Partî) (Dr Abdul Hakim Bashar)
Partîya Azadî ya Kurd li Suriyê (Mustafa Juma'a)
Partîya Azadî ya Kurd li Suriyê (Mustafa Oso)
Partîya Yekîtî ya Kurd li Sûriyê (Ismail Hemi)

INTRODUCTION

In July 2012, Kurdish political parties took control of the majority of Kurdish towns and regions in the north of Syria. This control was made possible by a committee formed from most of the Syrian Kurdish political parties, which administered the areas and maintained borders and security. For the first time, these highly factionalised political organisations were attempting to take control of their fate. Their aim was both to secure their own position and to protect the Kurdish people in the midst of the wider crisis in Syria. This unprecedented situation was the result of the particular dynamics of the Syrian uprising, the internal machinations of Kurdish politics and a history of decades of state suppression of Kurdish identity and attempts to secure political representation.

When spontaneous protests began across Syria in March 2011 as a reaction to the government's arrest and torture of several school children in Deraa in southern Syria, the response of the ruling government was to suppress them by force. This fuelled further resentment of the regime and, in the wake of revolutions in Tunisia, Egypt and Libya, encouraged further protests. Decades of silence from the Syrian opposition and the Syrian people were broken. The events in Syria and the stark exposure of the regime's brutality towards its own people attracted the attention of the world to this previously opaque country – a police state, ruled oppressively under the ideological banner of Arab nationalism.

The Syrian uprising changed the operating conditions of the Kurdish political parties, initiating significant changes in Kurdish politics in Syria. During this uprising, the state withdrew from Kurdish areas enabling the Kurdish political organisations to emerge as a unified and cohesive body, intent on securing Kurdish rights. At the same time the Kurds were able to establish a form of self-rule in many areas and the Kurdish issue in Syria became internationally significant, particularly in regional affairs. Yet the regime continues to defend its rule and gains by the Kurds and their political organisations are fragile and affected by the political situation in Syria, the policy of the government, the interests of Turkey and by international relations. The outcome of the uprising and what will follow it remains unclear and the Kurdish position in Syria is still undetermined. Moreover, understanding the present position of the Kurdish political parties in Syria – the challenges that face them and their future role in the country – requires more than a simple analysis of their actions and decision-making during the Syrian uprising, much of which remains unclear. It demands also an examination of their political development in Syria, of the particular circumstances that led to their formation and of the political conditions of Ba'thist Syria that shaped their agenda and their relations to the Kurdish population, the Arab opposition and the state. In an attempt to provide an up-to-date and comprehensive account of Kurdish politics in Syria, the pages of this book tell the story of the Kurdish struggle to gain national rights and describe the path that led Kurdish political parties to seize control of Kurdish areas in July 2012.

The book focuses on how these parties themselves have managed to operate illegally in Syria since 1957. It looks at how they have tried to negotiate this terrain of illegality in their attempts to bring some change to the situation of the approximately three million Kurds who live there.[1] It is a case study of a nationalist political movement operating in a state in which the Kurdish identity itself has been criminalised and, therefore, politicised. It examines the development of a specifically Syrian Kurdish political movement, the role of the Kurdish political parties in Kurdish society and the causes and consequences of their extraordinary factionalism. And this story contains a conundrum. From historical information about the activities and operating environment of the existing political organisations, it would appear that, on the eve of the Syrian uprising, the Kurdish political movement was in the midst of a crisis of legitimacy. Kurdish political parties were seen to be ineffectual and out of touch with the majority of the Kurdish population they claimed to represent. This resulted from a complex combination of political, social and economic changes; of shifts in Kurdish, Syrian, regional and international relations; and of new developments within the Kurdish political parties themselves. Nevertheless, out of the uprising, the Kurdish political movement appeared to emerge as a cohesive and effective institution capable of self-government.

Kurdish politics is a wide, varied and very complicated subject, not least because the Kurds are divided between four Middle Eastern states, each with its own complex internal social, political and economic environments. Kurdish politics has developed differently in each of these states. Syria is no exception, and although the Kurdish population of this state is considerably smaller than that of Turkey, Iraq or Iran, the problems encountered by the Kurds at the hand of the state are equally significant. Their political movement, having historically eschewed armed struggle and having suffered from internal factionalism, must be analysed differently from those in other areas of 'Kurdistan'.[2] In Syria, the particular circumstances of both the Kurdish areas and the state as a whole, resulting from the division of the region after the Sykes–Picot Agreement of 1916, have given Kurdish politics there a significantly different path of development to that encountered in the other Kurdish areas.

The state has targeted the Kurds as a minority which it considers potentially threatening to the identity and security of Syria. Its arabisation programmes[3] have affected the Kurdish areas and the Kurdish people considerably and opposition to them forms the heart of Kurdish demands for justice in Syria and provides the *raison d'être* of the Kurdish political parties. The state's oppression of the Kurdish people has provided the framework for the demands, activities and rhetoric of their political parties. What is more, it has shaped the identity and political mandate of the parties and the manner in which they operate.

Historically, various aspects of the autocratic Syrian state have complicated the history of the party movement.[4] One of these is that most Kurdish politicians present the work of the Syrian Kurdish political parties as modernising, reformist and democratic and the nature of Kurdish society as embracing modern ideologies and practices in a manner they claim to be distinct from that of Arab society and of the government. Yet at the same time Kurdish parties have developed and operated within a society which continues to contain traditional forms of social organisation if not traditional economic and political ones. It is a society, economy and polity in transition. Barely 50 years have passed since the tribal structures inherited by the state of Syria, began to be eroded by various socio-economic and political changes within the borders of the Syrian state. In many ways, the tribal system, although diminished in power and authority, remains significant in Kurdish society and politics, especially among the older generations. Consequently, the tribe continues to be an important feature of Kurdish social and political organisation and one that Kurdish society is currently grappling with. This unique and intricate fusion between traditional and modern relations has given the politics that has arisen within Kurdish society in Syria a particular character.

Moreover, socio-economic and political change has occurred at differing rates in the different Kurdish areas in Syria. These areas have been subject to contrasting influences and dynamics. This factor complicates the story, making it difficult to generalise about Kurdish politics in Syria per se. The importance of these regional differences will be a thread running throughout this book.

The Kurdish populations' opinion about their political parties, together with popular participation in them, has also varied over time, changing in response to internal and external factors, and not in a particularly coherent manner. Assessing public opinion about and participation in illegal Kurdish political parties was extremely difficult in Syria, and it proved impossible to produce quantitative survey data on the questions which might be analytically useful. The subject of public opinion, however, is important and is addressed in this book, particularly in Chapter 7.

The time period studied in this book is necessarily extended, stretching from the beginning of the French mandate and the establishment of the Syrian state in 1920 up to 2012. Its focus, however, is contemporary Kurdish political organisation and this lengthy historical period is drawn upon in order to trace socio-economic and political change in Kurdish society and to demonstrate the related transitions in the form and content of Kurdish politics in Syria and in the parties' relations to the Kurdish population. The subject matter could also be dealt with on a large scale. But, in fact, it has been narrowed, in particular to exclude the question of religious influences on the political parties and the question of the involvement of Syrian Kurds in state institutions and political organisations. The nature of Syrian Kurdish society and politics indicates that these two areas are less representative of the politics of the Kurdish population than the political parties themselves. None of the Kurdish parties in Syria define themselves by reference to any religious identity or ideology, and few important Kurdish religious families have become involved in Kurdish nationalist organisations. They remain for the most part religious figures, social mediators and moral guides. Indeed, much of the younger generation has rejected Islam as the religion of their oppressors and has revived interests in 'traditionally' Kurdish faiths such as Yezidism and Zoroastrianism. There are, of course, Kurds who are assimilated to the Arab identity of the state and who have chosen to become members of the Ba'th party or of the security services. They are a minority, however, and do not seem to have been involved in any political organisation among the Kurdish communities themselves.

The political parties that are the focus of this book are those that trace back their origins to the first Syrian Kurdish political party formed in 1957. Very few Syrian Kurdish parties exist which are not part of this genealogy. The exceptions are the *Partîya Yekîtî ya Dêmokrat* (PYD) founded in 2003, and *Şepêla Pêşerojê* founded by Meshaal Temmo in 2005 along with their offshoots. These parties are important, particularly with respect to their popularity amongst Syrian Kurds and because of the alternative political perspectives that they have expounded and they have obviously played their part within the story of Kurdish politics in Syria. The parties of 1957, however, have more of a historical profile in Syria, and examination of them will do more to demonstrate the development and changes in Kurdish politics in Syria over time.

Definitions

Immediately, when dealing with the Kurds, with the area of 'Kurdistan' and with political parties under authoritarian regimes, definitional problems arise. In the various states in which Kurds form compact minorities, their national or ethnic identity has been denied or belittled. In Turkey, the Kurds were described as 'mountain Turks', and, in Syria, state officials have described the Kurds as Arabs of Kurdish origin, or Arab Kurds. There are no official statistics for the number of Kurds in Syria or in other Middle Eastern states and the criterion of who is or is not a Kurd is equally open to interpretation. I have not attempted to discuss in detail the various political, religious and familial relations that overlap with 'Kurdishness' in Syria or the degree of assimilation that has occurred. Rather I have concentrated on the Kurdish political parties in Syria and the Kurds as a collective group identified by the state as a pariah group. The name 'Kurdistan' is often given to the areas in which Kurds form a majority. Kurdish claims to territory, however, often extend beyond present Kurdish majority areas. Artificial demographic changes, resulting from the destruction of Kurdish villages, from forced migration from Kurdish regions, as well as the settlement of non-Kurds in majority Kurdish areas, are the basis of territorial claims beyond Kurdish majority areas. Wadi Jwaideh gives a graphic description of the extent of the area of Kurdistan.[5] For the purposes of this book, however, it is enough to say that 'Kurdistan' refers to the areas of Syria, Turkey, Iraq, Iran and the former Soviet Union in which the Kurds form a majority or to which they hold an historical claim, or both. Its use is not meant to have any political connotations. It is merely a means of simplifying discussion of a complex political and geographical entity.

The definition of greatest importance to this book, and to the contextualisation of the empirical material within it, is that of the 'political party' itself. This definition has altered over time, as the nature of the political party itself has varied and understandings of it have also changed. Indeed, definitions and conceptualisations of the political party vary considerably between analysts over time and according to geographical location and the system of political organisation within different states. The academic literature has been dominated by a definition of the party in the context of liberal democracies; in such conditions political parties and party systems have been seen as markers of political modernisation and the major organising institution of modern politics.[6] Nevertheless, the democratic transitions that have occurred in many previously autocratic, one-party states in Europe and South America since the 1980s have generated a broader definition which allows its application to institutions that might have otherwise fallen outside mainstream definitions of the party.

In the Middle East, in countries such as Syria, the party institution was adopted under colonialism and nurtured by foreign governments as a means of imposing a modern political system on newly formed countries and polities. With the failure of democracy to develop in the region, however, the emergence and multiplication of political parties has occurred under the control and supervision of autocratic leaders and dominant immovable ruling parties or monarchies. Consequently, in the context of the Middle East, particularly in Syria, classic definitions and conceptualisations of political parties commonly associated with elections and the electoral process often sit uncomfortably with the organisations classified as political parties in these states, and this raises questions about whether or not they can realistically be categorised as parties.

Syria is a one-party authoritarian state in which the organisations under examination, Kurdish political parties, are illegal. As such they cannot enter into elections or compete for power; they cannot achieve any representation within government, nor can they freely express the interests of the constituencies they seek to represent. Indeed, opposition parties across Syria have primarily practiced 'reactive activism'.[7] They have struggled against repression, harassment and co-option by the ruling government and against the very political framework in which they exist, with no real possibility of competing for power[8] or employing legitimate channels for expressing interests. In such a context, even the norms of what is a 'political' sphere, act, channel or venue are challenged.[9]

Despite the limitations on opposition and minority parties in the Middle East, however, the party institution remains the organisational form considered best suited for effective political expression[10] and for political participation and mobilisation.[11] As this book shows, the Syrian Kurdish organisations, defined by themselves as political parties and recognised as such by their constituencies, have undergone significant changes in the more than 50 years of their existence. Significant transformations have taken place within the make-up of the party leadership, membership and support bases and, with these transformations, many Kurdish parties in Syria moved even further away from mainstream definitions of the political party, in the sense that they failed to represent the interests of their constituencies and weakened their central roles in society prior to the outbreak of the Syrian uprising. Yet the Kurdish political parties in Syria and participation in them are clearly directed at influencing the state, although the interests they themselves represent have altered over time. They are identified as political parties amongst the Kurds in Syria and it is generally accepted that these organisations are political organisations and their definition as political parties is not widely questioned. The future development of the Syrian uprising may have substantial effects on the mandate of these parties and their ability to transform themselves into political parties more recognisable according to western definitions. But for the purpose of this book, the Kurdish political organisations which carry the title 'party' are referred to as political parties and more detailed scrutiny of their political identity must await future empirical research.

Researching the Subject

Writing this book involved a combination of using the existing academic literature to provide a context and then conducting research on the ground in Syria, including numerous interviews and the analysis of many political documents and processes. The literature employed has come from a number of different sources: academic literature and articles published by commercial publishers and sourced in England and in Syria; books in Arabic and Kurdish printed privately and distributed through networks of Kurdish activists and institutions in the UK, France, Germany and Syria; documents collected from political party representatives themselves and journals, articles, documents, news, opinions and responses to questions, in various languages; and other documents collected from the internet.

Published academic literature on the Syrian state and on the Kurds and Kurdistan has provided considerable and invaluable historical background material for this book. While there are several books on Syria, the Syrian Arab Ba'th Party and its rule in Syria, the subject of the Kurds and other ethnic and religious groups and underground political movements has received little academic attention. Concentrating for the most part on Syria's state structures, foreign policy and position within the Middle East and in international relations, most academic works on the country mention the Kurds only in passing. They are often mentioned early in the pages of works on Syria in descriptions of the ethnic make-up of the state and Syria's 'fragile mosaic' of ethnic and sectarian communities.[12] Some reference may be made to the exploitation or repression of the Kurds in Syria,[13] while other publications fail to mention the Syrian Kurds at all.[14] In most important works on Syria, no detailed analysis is given to the Kurds or to their political organisation, despite their importance to the historical development of the Syrian state, to Syrian domestic and regional politics and to understanding the identity of the state and Ba'th party and their vulnerabilities.

The neglect of the Kurds in academic studies of Syria is part of a wider overall weakness on the subject of Syrian internal affairs and the activities of the Syrian opposition prior to the uprising of 2011. This weakness is a reflection of the political circumstances in Syria and the difficulties of gaining access to information on such issues, described below. Authors dealing explicitly with the Syrian opposition and evaluating the ruling regime have had to accept the inevitable consequence of being denied visas to enter Syria. For an academic with a specialisation in Syria, the prospect of not being allowed access to her or his country of expertise has serious consequences for conducting future research and implications for the credibility of the findings of research conducted without fieldwork.[15] Since the Syrian opposition showed its public face during the Damascus Spring in 2000, things have changed little, although publications on Syria and Bashar al-Assad's rule have generally included sections on the Damascus Spring and the Syrian opposition.[16]

Academic publications on Kurdish issues are dominated by studies of the Kurds in Iraq and Turkey.[17] In many works, the Kurds of Syria, or the Kurdish presence in Syria is mentioned primarily in the context of the development of Kurdish nationalism amongst Kurds in Turkey (forced into exile in Syria following Atatürk's repression of Kurdish organisations) or in descriptions or examinations of Xoybûn.[18] Studies on the Syrian Kurds as a distinct subject group have, in some cases, been included in edited volumes or general histories of the Kurds. Often, however, these have been short chapters summarising the situation of the Syrian Kurds which are relegated to the final pages of the book, almost as an afterthought.[19] Although greater detail is included in more recent articles on the Syrian Kurds following changes in their situation after the Qamishli uprising of 2004, the general format for chapters on the Syrian Kurds has remained, for the most part, an all-embracing generalised summary of the subject, glossing over the complexities of the political movement.[20]

In 2005 my own work on the Kurds in Syria was published by the European Centre for Kurdish Studies in Berlin.[21] The study provided an historical overview of the political situation of the Kurds in Syria examined through the lens of human rights. In 2009, Jordi Tejel's book, *Syria's Kurds: History, Politics and Society*, was published. This was an important and widely distributed publication, in English, and provided a wide historical account and analysis of Kurdish society and politics in Syria. While both these books worked to fill the deep gap in the literature on the contemporary history of the Kurds in Syria, and both discuss the Kurdish political parties, neither of them described the parties in any real detail. After the start of the Syrian uprising and particularly after the Kurds seized control of Kurdish areas in Syria and began to be seen as critical players in the latest struggle for Syria, a number of reports discussing the various Kurdish political actors were published by organisations such as KurdWatch, the Henry Jackson Society and ORSAM. Until the time of writing, however, more detailed examination of Kurdish political parties in Syria remained limited to a few books written in Arabic by Syrian Kurds, published and distributed privately.

The realities of conducting research in a state such as Syria have not facilitated efforts to correct this shortage of published material,[22] and the dearth of literature is especially evident on subjects related to the period following the end of the French mandate, extending until today. Indeed, ever since the French mandate came to an end in 1946, the subject has been neglected. It attracted some renewed interest after the end of the Cold War, when the issues of minorities, human rights and political opposition began to be seen in a new light. Also, in the years following the Kurdish unrest that erupted in March 2004, when mass protests shattered state restrictions on the expression of dissent, a number of doctoral studies on the Kurds of Syria were produced in addition to several books, articles and reports.[23] But the existing published literature remained insufficient for the tasks of writing this book which required the collection of alternative material and information from within Kurdish communities, both in Syria and in exile. The political conditions in Syria had significant implications for the manner in which research for this book was conducted and also on the nature and accessibility of the sources employed.

As mentioned above, a few books on the Kurdish political movement in Syria have been published by independent private publishers in Syria, Iraq and Europe.[24] Generally these are written in Arabic and are not widely available. Consequently, the distribution of such material is often limited largely to those involved in the Kurdish political movement in Syria. Otherwise it has been necessary to seek out such publications, often from the authors themselves. The same has been true of Kurdish party documents and statements. Between 2002, when I first began conducting research on Kurdish politics in Syria, and the writing of this book, a decade later, I developed a large network of contacts. Through them, I was able to acquire personal copies of such books and documents. More recently, with the development of the internet in Syria, increased access there and the establishment of a number of Syrian Kurdish websites in Europe, news from the Kurdish regions in Syria has been more forthcoming and some Kurdish parties use email to disseminate their party papers and statements. Increasingly, articles and opinion pieces, and even some publications by Kurdish authors, are published online, facilitating access to such material.[25] Access to party documents remains particularly difficult due to the fact that many parties do not maintain websites or post such documents on them.

The archives in London and archive material from French sources have been useful in providing information on the Kurds and on Syria during the mandate period. Research in the Syrian national archives in Damascus, however, yielded few results. The absence of information on the Kurds and their political movement, even before the coming to power of the Ba'th Party in 1963, was conspicuous, despite some considerable political activity which took place. In addition, research in Syrian archives was not facilitated by the nature of Syrian bureaucracy and the research subject in question. It was often necessary, when dealing with government employees in the archives, to ask for information indirectly connected to the Kurdish issue rather than asking openly for the information sought, and any copying of documents had to be approved and overseen by the attentive director of the archive.

The events of March 2004 stimulated the interest of governments and institutions the world over in the political position of the Kurds of Syria, and gradually the subject has become a little more accessible to the outsider. With this, more historical information has become available. But objective information and analysis of Kurdish political organisation during the second half of the twentieth century and the first decade of the twenty-first, on which this book focuses, is less accessible. The core of the book is based on information obtained through interviews with Syrian Kurdish politicians, members of political parties, independent Kurdish political and cultural activists and laypersons, inside Syria and in Europe, as well as on unpublished political documents. Consequently, it depends on and presents previously unpublished material, while published literature has provided essential background information which provides a context from which to examine Kurdish political parties.

The scarcity of literature on Kurdish politics in Syria stems, in no small way, from the difficulties of attempting to gather information on the Kurds and in conducting research inside Ba'thist Syria. A feared and brutal authoritarian state in which the security services were granted extraordinary and far-reaching powers, Syria is a country whose internal affairs have been shrouded in secrecy, obscured by a wall of misinformation and internalised by a silenced population. Kurdish political organisation and activity is illegal in Syria, and the expression of Kurdish identity has regularly been treated by the state as a threat to its security, internal cohesion and legitimacy. Consequently, research on the Kurds of Syria has very rarely been officially permitted. The absence of permission to conduct such research inside Syria and unwanted attention to the researcher by Syrian security forces in the Kurdish areas are among the problems encountered. In addition, Syria is a state in which such politics is a taboo subject, in which the fear of informers dominates and in which the consequences of political dissent are very severe. Consequently, in my experience of research in Syria, it was not unusual to encounter rejection when seeking to interview people or failure to fulfil promises of information, even when I had been introduced through reliable sources or already had an established history of communications with the respondent. More than once, I was followed and questioned by *mukhabarat* (the Syrian intelligence services) about my presence in certain areas. As a result, some important information I expected to receive from respondents never materialised.

Conditions in Syria also give rise to the ethical problem that interviewing any individual or group in Syria about Kurdish politics exposes the interviewee to the risk of harassment and harm by the Syrian authorities. Despite this, the general lack of literature with which to engage has meant that much of the core information in this book is based on material gathered through such research and interviews in Syria and in Europe. I made fieldwork trips to Syria in 2002, 2006 and 2007. In spite of the difficulties in obtaining information on the Kurds in Syria, the wide network of contacts that I developed during this period yielded significant results and facilitated the collection of important information as yet unavailable to the general public, as well as unpublished and narrowly distributed privately published books, articles and Kurdish political party documents. I met with and interviewed a broad range of respondents from inside the political parties as well as outside them and from all sectors of Kurdish society. My interviewees included leaders of Kurdish political parties, members of their central committees and politburos, Kurdish intellectuals, authors, artists, journalists, lawyers and stateless Kurds, as well as tribal leaders, students and street vendors. Interviews were used to provide historical evidence through eye witness and expert accounts as well as to gauge opinion about the parties. Although I had questions on which to base my interviews, the content of interviews varied considerably between respondents according to their position, social status or area of expertise as well as being influenced by what they wanted to tell me and, in some cases, messages that they wished to convey to the outside world through my research. As well as the history of the political parties, their organisational structures, their activities and public opinion about them, interviews covered subjects such as Syrian nationality law, taxes, details of land ownership, tribal structures, the state school system, the Syrian security services, methods of interrogation, Syrian prisons and corruption. It was by gathering information on all these wide ranging and diverse subjects, that it was possible to describe and analyse the Kurdish political parties in Syria in the detail provided in this book.

Interviews in Syria were generally conducted in the homes of third parties, trusted by the interviewee, and in some cases in their own homes. Others, at the request of the interviewee, took place while walking through crowded streets in an effort to prevent any security personnel that might be observing them, or me, from listening to the conversation. On the occasions when I stayed in the homes of interviewees much information was gathered over the course of the stay. While time was set aside for more formal interviews, general conversation with the families and individuals accommodating me presented opportunities to dispose of structured interview techniques and allow my informants to talk at their leisure. Similarly, I met several interviewees on more than one occasion, allowing me to develop my relations with them, to earn their trust and to follow-up on issues raised and information presented in previous interviews which required further detail.

For each fieldtrip to Syria I had a general list of interview questions, based on the subject areas that I envisaged addressing. From these lists questions could be selected according to the identity and position of each interviewee. Naturally the expertise of interviewees, which ranged from political party leaders and intellectuals to street vendors and stateless Kurds, varied considerably. It was often the case that interviews were arranged by mutual connections, with very short notice, little information about the respondent and little time to prepare a formal set of questions. For the most part, therefore, my interview structures remained fairly flexible, open to change and to the character of the interviewee.

Most party leaders agreed to interviews being recorded. In some cases, however, when a translator was present, it was requested that the translator's voice not be recorded as a precaution in case the recordings were seized by the Syrian security services. Non-party interviewees generally preferred not to be recorded and in such cases detailed notes were taken and transcribed afterwards. Consequently the manner in which the interview was structured, conducted and recorded varied considerably from one person or group to the next and according to the setting.

In conducting any interview it was particularly important to take precautions against causing any harm to my informants. The research that I conducted inside Syria was done clandestinely and could have very serious consequences for anyone providing me with information. It was necessary to take steps to avoid the attention of Syrian security officials (the *mukhabarat*) so as not to draw attention to my interviewees. The identity of any interviewee was never revealed to any third party and even in my own notes they were coded. In addition, when transforming the material collected through interviews from raw material into this book, I have protected the identity of interviewees who wished to remain anonymous or who provided me with information that might be construed as sensitive by the Syrian authorities or by the political parties themselves.

While in Syria I tried to avoid having any negative effect on the Kurdish communities I entered into. For example, for the most part, I based myself in Damascus and travelled to the Kurdish areas for several limited periods to conduct interviews; I did not distribute any surveys to assess public opinion about the Kurdish political parties; I avoided prolonged periods of stay in certain areas where I knew that my presence would arouse the interest of the *mukhabarat*, I cut short visits if my presence was generating any untoward attention and I conducted many interviews at night. In this respect, it was often more straightforward to interview the leadership of the Kurdish political parties, who were already known to the Syrian authorities and are 'duty-bound' to publicise their cause as much as possible. Access to the general public and assessing public opinion was necessarily more difficult and the ethical issues involved were more pronounced. What is more, the parties themselves do not disclose information about their members and are naturally biased in their estimations of their strength compared with other Kurdish parties. As a result, examining what it is that attracts members to one party rather than another, and comprehending the exact character of the parties' power bases, were made more difficult. The privileged access that I had gained, however, to political party personnel, independent political and cultural activists and intellectuals meant that I was able to gain an unprecedented insight into the political parties' organisations, their history, activities, social functions and the way in which they were regarded within the Kurdish communities.

In the interpretation of my interview data I have tried to make allowances for any natural biases. I was aware that both party leaders and independent players in the political field might be influenced by the clandestine nature of the encounter. This might push them either towards secretiveness or towards an exaggeration of the facts or of their opinions – a heightened nationalism, for example or, in the case of the non-politicians, a more cynical appraisal of the political parties than they actually felt day to day. These are, of course, the problems of any attempt at empirical accounts of the world using informants or eyewitnesses, and, on the whole, I trusted the good faith of my respondents. I had built up my network of contacts carefully, checking, as far as I could, the reliability of each one. Furthermore, I verified the facts presented to me, where I could, by checking with other informants or seeking documentary support. Obviously, the clandestine nature of the research prevented any formal triangulation of method. I was confined to interview and document and any more direct observation on my part would have been out of the question. When canvassing the opinions of my non-party political respondents on the nature of the political parties and their leaders, I was aware that any summary of what I heard could only be suggestive of the current standing of the parties among the Syrian Kurdish population, discussed in Chapter 7. Such interviews, however, often confirmed my own general observations on and estimation of public opinion towards the parties that I had developed by spending time within Kurdish families and communities in Syria.

This book necessarily contains much historical information and description about social structures, socio-economic change and the development of politics amongst the Kurds in Syria. This is set within the context of the Syrian state. It takes a bottom-up approach, concentrating on the sub-state Kurdish society and politics rather than on how the Kurds fit into Syrian society or the politics of the state as a whole. Indeed, it is assumed that the reader has some prior knowledge of Syrian politics in order to avoid unnecessary description of the Syrian state. This allows for a greater concentration on the Kurdish political parties and Kurdish society in Syria. Moreover, as discussed above, there is a significant body of expert literature on Syrian politics which this book has drawn upon and to which the reader is directed for further examination. The place of the Kurds and Kurdish political organisation in the Syrian state context will be evident in what follows. Through approaching the subject in this manner it is hoped that this book will make a significant contribution to the literature on the Syrian state, which, much like the state itself, is somewhat dominated by the seizure of power by the Ba'th Party and its ruling regime.

In writing this book, I have drawn on all of the literature mentioned above, political documents, interviews and more. I have spent long periods of time in the Kurdish areas in Syria and outside it, piecing together a picture of the Kurdish political party movement in Syria. I have tried to present the complexities and details of the party movement in a manner that is accessible and clear to a non-specialist reader. This is not to say that I have attempted to answer all possible questions about Kurdish political parties in Syria and I am aware that this study is likely to raise more questions than I can possibly answer. Yet, it is a subject on which there is, up to now, only a limited amount of published information, and it is hoped that it will provide a more detailed and accurate account of the parties and their activities and their relation to the Kurdish communities in Syria than already exists. Naturally, this work is my own interpretation of the information I have collected and analysed over a period of more than a decade. I hope that it will stimulate debate and further academic research into Kurdish politics in Syria.

Organisation of the Book

The first chapter entitled 'The Kurdish Political Parties in Syria', provides an overview of Kurdish society, the Kurdish political parties and their position within the Syrian state. It provides an explanation of why Kurdish parties exist in Syria, looking at the state's policy towards the Kurds and the Kurdish regions and at Kurdish grievances against the state which form part of the rationale for a specifically Kurdish political movement in Syria. The general identity and politics of the parties is outlined and the question of how their illegality in Syria has affected their political mandate and operation is examined. The chapter provides a basis from which to abstract historically and examine the development of Kurdish party politics and their role in Kurdish society in the following chapters.

Chapter 2 examines the historical progress of Kurdish nationalism and politics among the Kurds in Syria. It traces the development of a specifically Syrian Kurdish polity up to the formation of the first Kurdish political party in Syria in 1957. Following this, the first part of Chapter 3 continues this historical analysis, looking at the founding and expansion of this Kurdish party and at the causes of its initial fragmentation. It continues in the second part with an assessment of the causes of factionalism within the party movement, showing how internal party dynamics, the Syrian government and foreign parties have all contributed to this aspect of the Kurdish political movement in Syria.

Chapters 4 and 5 examine the functions of the political parties in Kurdish society in Syria. Chapter 4 looks at the relations between the Kurdish political parties and the Syrian state under the Ba'th Party, focusing on how the parties attempted to address Kurdish grievances against the state. It does so through looking at the parties' efforts to mobilise the Kurdish population in social action against the state, the parties' relations with the Arab opposition in Syria and their relations with the Syrian authorities. Chapter 5 takes the social role of the parties as its subject, looking in turn at their roles in facilitating cultural expression and reproduction and in mediation in social problems. It explains how the parties act as agents of civil society amongst the Kurdish communities in Syria through the organisation of cultural events and groups and through their attempt to protect Kurdish society from the state. The ability of the party leaders to assume a role in mediation, normally associated with traditional leaderships led by tribal chiefs and sheikhs, is discussed, and, through this, the relationship between the party organisations and tribal networks is broached.

Chapter 6 constitutes a case within a case. It takes as its subject the approximately 300,000 Kurds in Syria who have been denied Syrian citizenship, known as the 'stateless Kurds'. It looks at the politics of this specific group of Kurds and assesses the relation of the political parties to them. The first half of this chapter outlines the condition of these Kurds from the Jazira region who are denied Syrian citizenship and consequently most of the rights associated with it. It describes how these Kurds became stateless in 1962 and how statelessness affects their daily lives. The second half examines the consequences of statelessness for these Kurds and the forms of political organisation that arise among them. It seeks to determine whether they have any particular forms of organisation among themselves, and what are their levels of political consciousness and their relations with the Kurdish political parties. I also examine the Kurdish migrant community of Zor Ava in the suburbs of Damascus, whose stateless population is approximately half of the total.

In Chapter 7, the relationship between the pre-uprising crisis in the Kurdish political parties and the rise in Kurdish national consciousness is discussed. Here the information contained in the preceding chapters is drawn together to show how the parties had disengaged from the population while, in the meantime, the Kurdish population in Syria had become more psychologically engaged with their national identity and politics than they had been for decades. In contrast to much of the literature on the Kurdish political movement produced in the years between the 2004 and 2011 uprisings, which declared the Kurdish movement to have entered into a new period of visibility, this chapter concludes that Kurdish political parties were facing a crisis of credibility among the Kurdish people, before the upheaval of the Syrian uprising transformed their political environment.

The Kurdish response to the Syrian uprising of 2011 is examined in the final chapter. It traces the political manoeuvrings of the Kurdish political parties in the first year of the uprising, and examines the events and processes that resulted in the Kurds making a bid to self-govern Kurdish areas. Through this it summarises the changes that the uprising has induced in the Kurdish political movement and offers a tentative analysis of the experience of Kurdish 'self-rule'.

This book was written in the midst of the Syrian uprising and covers the period up to and including the establishment of Kurdish control in Kurdish areas of Syria. It contains descriptions of political activity, of events, processes and transformations that occurred historically and also of those that were ongoing at the time of writing. The outcome of the years of uprising against the regime is unknown and the longevity of forms of local political organisation, conflicts and defences is subject to the influence of countless factors. The political situation in Syria and in each town, village or neighbourhood is in constant flux. Although the Syrian uprising has changed the face of Syria, the regime that dominated it and defined its politics and society for the past 50 years remains in place. Formal institutions of state as well as laws coexist with ad hoc local governance, lawlessness and new forms of domination. As a consequence, locating and placing descriptions of the politics of the Kurds and their political parties historically has been problematic. The nature, identity and state of their politics prior to the uprising remain applicable to the parties today. Their relations to the state and to the mechanisms of authoritarianism are altered, but are not forgone. Their political environment is in flux and the authoritarian rulers and/or political systems and ideologies that defined the Kurds as a threat to the state may remain central to whatever regime emerges from the quagmire that Syria has become. The historical circumstances that governed the political parties prior to the start of the uprising cannot as yet be assigned to history, despite the changes in their external and internal state during the course of the uprising. This is especially in light of the authoritarian nature of PYD rule in Kurdish areas and of Islamic governance in the Syrian interior.

Consequently, the accounts of Kurdish political organisations that are offered in this book are caught somewhere between historical fact and an uncertain future. Here, when describing the Kurdish situation in Syria and their political parties prior to the uprising, I often place descriptions of them in the present tense. The parties have not transformed to the extent that characteristics that defined them, or the policies, structures and prejudices that shaped them then, can be realistically allocated to the historical past. Indeed, the nature of Kurdish self government, controlled by the PYD, is reminiscent of Ba'th Party rule, if not, some say, more constraining or authoritarian. As the uprising continues further changes will alter the nature of Kurdish politics in Syria. With the turn of history and the future resolution of the conflict, the uncertain time horizons of this book may cause some confusion. It reflects, however, the state of flux in Syria and Kurdish politics there at the time of writing and to write it otherwise would be potentially misleading.

CHAPTER 1

THE KURDISH POLITICAL PARTIES IN SYRIA

In the seismic social and political change brought about by the Syrian uprising, one thing that has not changed is the sheer number of illegal Syrian Kurdish political parties; by the end of 2012 there were approximately 20 of them, and Kurdish sources suggested in March 2013 that this number may have doubled.[1] Of the 20 discussed in this book, all but three trace their origins back to what is considered to be the first Syrian Kurdish party in Syria, *Partîya Dêmokrat a Kurd li Sûriyê*,[2] founded on 14 June 1957. The stated aims of all the existing parties are fairly uniform. Some parties even have the same name and goals as each other, differing outwardly only in their leadership. This is the plurality of organisations which seek to represent the Kurdish population in Syria and which attempt to bring about some change in their fortunes. They strive for national and equal rights for the Kurds, an end to their oppression in Syria and a comprehensive and just solution to the Kurdish issue in the country.

Confronted with this number of political parties, the immediate questions that trouble most outside observers, and even Syrian Kurds themselves, are, first, why there are so many parties when all of them seem to be working for one end; second, what are the functions of these parties in Kurdish society when their illegality prevents them from entering the state electoral system; and third, what, if any, alternative power relations do they conceal? These central questions are addressed in later chapters, while this first one provides two starting points, one historical, providing a summary of the changing form of politics and political relations within Kurdish society during recent decades, the other more analytical, which examines various aspects of the social and economic relations that underlie Kurdish political parties.

From both these viewpoints the primary question is the position of the Kurds in relation to the Syrian state and to their organised form of politics (the Kurdish political parties) before the beginning of the Syrian uprising. Important changes in Kurdish politics have occurred during the course of the uprising, but in order to understand their significance as well as other aspects of the Kurdish position during the uprising, it is essential to look closely at their politics prior to its beginning, and this is done in three main sections. The first looks at the purpose of the Kurdish parties, tracing the development of Syrian identity and the state's policies towards the Kurds. The second describes the Kurdish parties themselves, providing an overview of their organisation, aims, ideology and activities as they were before the Syrian uprising. And the third section examines the strategies that the parties employed in negotiating their illegality in Ba'thist Syria – in particular, their use of networks of relations which are available to them.

To provide such an overview of pre-uprising Syria, it is useful to start with some historical explanation of Syria's political development and of state policies towards the Kurds. This should equip the reader with an understanding of the discrimination that the Kurdish population faces and the issues that delineate the identity of the Kurdish parties. It is also important to provide some explanation of how these parties operated and of the wider Syrian environment that shaped them. But detailed historical description of the complex political history of the Syrian state is avoided since it has been dealt with expertly in numerous existing academic works.

Why Kurdish Political Parties?

The Kurds

The number of Kurds in Syria is a matter of contention. The government's denial that the Kurds are indigenous to Syrian territory and its attempts to create a homogenous Arab identity for the state and its people have meant that, since the French mandate, no census in Syria has included any indication of ethnic identity. Most Kurdish sources put the number upward of 3 million, or between 12 and 15 per cent of the total Syrian population of 22 million. In contrast, the state offers no estimates at all. More conservative approximations put the number at about 1.5 million, or 8 per cent of the population.[3] The Kurdish areas of Syria are located in the north of the country, along the borders with Turkey and the Kurdistan Region of Iraq. The three main Kurdish regions in Syria are the Kurd Dagh[4] (Kurdish mountains) in the northwest; Kobanî, to the east of the Kurd Dagh; and the Jazira, which roughly corresponds to Hasaka province, in the northeast of Syria. In these regions Kurds grow up with the Kurmanji dialect of Kurdish[5] as their first language and do not start learning Arabic until they begin school, at about six years of age. There is also a large and ancient Kurdish community in Damascus, said to date back to Ottoman times, when Kurdish contingents were sent to Damascus to protect the pilgrimage route to Mecca,[6] and to the time of Salah al-Din Ayubi. This community is more integrated into Arab society and will often use Arabic as their first language. Large numbers of Kurds also live in other cities and regions such as Aleppo, Idlib, Hama, Homs and Latakia.

Geographically, the three main Kurdish areas are of economic and strategic importance to the state. They are among the most productive and resource-rich areas of land in the country. In Hasaka province about half of Syria's annual grain yield of 4 million tons is grown. Hasaka is also the origin of most of the country's approximately 385,000 barrels per day of crude oil[7] and 219 billion cubic feet per year of natural gas.[8] Kurdish areas lie on the fertile land between the Orontes, Euphrates and Tigris rivers and the Kurd Dagh area is famous for its olives, olive oil and subsidiary products. The region boasts more than 13 million olive trees. The border with Turkey is also a sensitive one. Turkey almost went to war with Syria in October 1998 over Syria's harbouring of *Partiya Karkerên Kurdistan* (the Kurdistan Workers' Party or PKK), which it used as a tool against Turkey's control over the water of the Euphrates.[9] Syria also maintains claims to Alexandretta/Hatay province, which was ceded to Turkey by the French in 1939. The Kurds have historically been used as pawns in inter-state politics and rivalries between Syria, Turkey, Iraq and Iran.

The presence of a national minority with a natural demographic extension into Turkish and Iraqi territory on these borders is an obvious cause of tension in Syria's relations with its Kurdish population. The government's fears of separatism are added to by the fact that the Jazira was not historically a natural part of former Greater Syria but part of Mesopotamia.[10] The Kurds retained much autonomy under the French, resisted centralisation under the early Arab mandate governments and in the late 1930s the Jazira was set to become a Kurdish–Christian mini-state[11] and the Kurd Dagh an autonomous unit under the joint leadership of the *aghawat* (traditional Kurdish landlords) and of a Naqshbandi religious group called the *Muroud*.[12] Consequently, the Kurds of the Jazira have been the objects of particularly oppressive policies since the early 1960s and the Syrian public has been encouraged to see the Jazira as potentially another Israel, with the Kurds as 'occupiers'.[13]

The development of Syrian identity and politics

The modern Syrian state was established in 1920 when the League of Nations granted France the mandate over Syria. Although the state existed in some form from 1918 to 1920 when it was ruled by Emir Faysal, its current borders were determined by the French occupation and international agreements made between 1920 and 1939. The people included within its borders were multi-confessional and multi-ethnic. During the rule of the Ottoman Empire, identity and political loyalties generally extended to both the fairly unobtrusive Ottoman state and to the local confessional, ethnic, tribal and kin groupings. Local power and authority were also secured from the same sources. It was only in 1920 that the Syrian territory became a political unit and then, under French divide-and-rule policies, semi-autonomous states were created within its borders.[14] Various religious, ethnic and status groups, however, began to compete for their share of power, both locally and in government.

After independence from France in 1946, Syria fell into a period of great political instability and was swung between martial and parliamentary rule by successive coups. The years of the French mandate and the immediate post-independence period in which a parliamentary system was established were dominated by the rule of urban and landed notables. The traditional Sunni leadership and merchant urban elites retained a vested interest in the system developed under the mandate, on which their positions and local power depended. This predicament had been achieved through a parliament dominated by the National Bloc and then the National Party. Increasingly the shallow legitimacy of the traditional political elites was eroded by their failure to contain or reverse the effects of colonialism, as Arab nationalist sentiment spread among the peasantry and became a popular force.[15] Developmentally the traditional leadership was seen as pro-Western, and the 'imposition of a liberal-capitalist model on a "semi-feudal" social system', a legacy of the colonial years, was producing economic instability, inflation and unemployment. Most of the negative impact of this was borne by the peasantry whereas the benefits of industrialisation were channelled to a small portion of the population.[16]

In this period the position of the state towards the Kurds was determined largely by the ethnic background of the particular leader and his position towards Arabism. Husni Za'im, who took power in 1949, was of Kurdish descent and relied heavily on the support of Kurdish and Circassian officers. Adib al-Shishakli, who ruled Syria between 1949 and 1954, was also of Kurdish descent.[17] He aimed, however, to establish a homogenous Arab Muslim state, setting in motion a number of decrees that restricted the use of the Kurdish language and enforced bans on Kurdish music and other expressions of Kurdish identity.[18]

Opposition to the system came from increasingly politicised Alawi and Druze reformists, independent farmers and from a peasants' movement led by Akram Hawrani.[19] Both capitalist and radical reformists opposed the maintenance of a status quo inimical to their interests.[20] The political arena began to fragment along regional lines dictated by the interests of merchant elites.[21]

As a result, communism and Arab nationalism became popular forces of political mobilisation, and mechanisms of contesting the power of the dominant elite and of integrating into the national community on an equal basis.[22] Parties such as the Syrian Communist Party (SCP), the Ba'th Party and the Socialist Union Party represented these interests. The concepts and systems of democracy and capitalism were increasingly tainted by their association with colonialism and imperialism both through experience and through increasingly popular socialist and Marxist–Leninist ideologies. The 'radicalisation' of Arab politics reached its heyday in the mid- to late-1950s, marked by the Baghdad Pact and intense inter-state competition among the 'radical' Arabist states and between them and the conservative monarchies.[23] Anti-Kurdish propaganda campaigns linked Kurdish nationalism to Zionism and Western imperialism, portraying Kurds as traitors and separatists. Kurdish officers were purged from the military and members of Kurdish political organisations were arrested and put on trial. Expressions of Kurdish cultural identity, including speaking the Kurdish language and playing Kurdish music, were forbidden, and recordings of music and Kurdish publications were seized by the Syrian authorities, while their owners and distributors were arrested.[24] With the rise of popular Arab nationalism, the Kurds also became targets of racist assaults, both by the regime and by the Arab public.[25]

In this period Syrian Kurdish political organisation began. The first Syrian Kurdish political party, *Partîya Dêmokrat a Kurd li Sûriyê*, advocated the liberation and unity of Kurdistan, the struggle against colonialism[26] and democracy in Syria.[27] Although formed clandestinely, the party operated relatively freely until 22 February 1958 when Syria entered into a shotgun marriage with Egypt, forming the United Arab Republic (UAR). In this period, all political parties were banned and the arabisation of the Kurdish areas began in earnest. The principles of Arab nationalism, championed by Nasserites and Ba'thists, dominated Syria's political and economic arenas and penetrated popular organisation. The Kurdish communities became targets of projects aimed at securing Syrian territory against separatism and external intrigue and guaranteeing the Arab character of the state and its people.

Syria's union with Egypt was not all that it seemed to be. In short, it was a last ditch attempt to protect the state and its government from the threat of coups originating from the domestic and external arenas.[28] Under the UAR Syria was subjugated to economic, social and political exploitation and domination by the Egyptian leader, Jamal Abdul Nasser. This period was particularly difficult for the nascent Syrian Kurdish political movement. In 1960, only three years after its founding, most of the leadership and a number of supporters of *Partîya Dêmokrat a Kurd li Sûriyê* were arrested. The arrests caused a number of cleavages to emerge in the ranks of the party inside the prison. The main differences centred on the strategy to be employed by those arrested when dealing with the authorities in prison and they would later become the main dividing line between the left and the right wings.

The UAR was brought to an end on 28 September 1961 by a right-wing putsch led by Lieut-Colonel Abd al-Karim Nahalawi, backed by Jordan, Saudi Arabia and Syria's 'disgruntled business community'.[29] A period of intense struggle occurred between the government of the day (composed of urban notables) and the Military Committee, and within the Military Committee between Ba'thists and Nasserites. The Ba'th Party finally seized power in 1963.

The Ba'th Party coup of 8 March 1963 grew out of a very broad anti-oligarchy alliance: the radicalised lower middle class, important elements of the officer corps, marginalised minorities and the peasantry mobilised through agrarian conflict. Syria was propelled into a 'populist revolution' by the radical socialist, Arabist, anti-imperialist ideology of the Ba'th, the development of a new middle class, the military, marginalised minority groups (especially the Alawis and the Druze) and the radicalised peasantry.[30] With the Ba'th Party coup the political and social character of the state and its power base were transformed. Young elites drawn from the military and from rural lower class backgrounds and the 'small-town intelligentsia' replaced the political elite that had dominated Syria almost continuously since its independence.[31]

The Ba'th Party was split by internal power struggles until 1970 when Hafiz al-Assad seized power in a coup, stripping the civilian section of the party of most of its powers.[32] Assad's Syria has been characterised, in stark comparison to the preceding years, by 'stability' and continuity. Many authors, members of the regime and ordinary citizens have praised Assad for bringing 'stability' to the country.[33] This has, however, been at great social and political cost. 'Stability' has been achieved by broadening the 'popular' base of the regime through corporatist institutions and an Arab nationalist identity, and by the severe suppression of opposition.

Under the Ba'th Party Syria became a one-party state. The state extended its control over society building new institutions and transforming old ones. The military and security services (the *mukhabarat*) were expanded and regulated, becoming the central pillars of the regime and its control of the society and the state. Under Hafiz al-Assad, the Ba'th Party's slogan, 'unity, freedom and socialism', soon lost its central meaning for the party. The name of the state was changed from the Syrian Republic to the Syrian *Arab* Republic in 1963. Assad capitalised on the Arab defeat by Israel in 1967 calling for greater Arab unity. The permanent state of war with Israel and emergency law[34] provided fuel for mass acceptance of Arab nationalism as the legitimising rhetoric of both the state and the regime. Arabism was enshrined in the constitution of 1973, which defined the state and its people as Arab, the Ba'th

Party as the ruling party of Syria, the goal of the 'revolution' as Arab unity. Accordingly, the state was defined as a temporary political unit that would eventually give way to a greater Arab union.[35]

With that the oppression of the Kurds was enshrined in the central institutions that defined Syrian identity – the constitution, the law, and the political system. These institutions have remained more or less unchanged during the history of Ba'thist rule in Syria, the constitution only being amended once in the year 2000 to lower the minimum age of the president, allowing Bashar al-Assad to inherit his father's seat at the age of 34.[36] Then, on 27 February 2012, almost one year into the uprising, a new constitution was adopted. The limited changes within it aimed at appeasing the Syrian opposition and demonstrating the regime's willingness to implement reforms and to liberalise. The new constitution had no effect on the Kurdish issue in Syria, maintaining the Arab identity of the state and its citizens.

The Kurds have been excluded from participation in the state unless they do so as Syrian Arabs; this would be considered by many to be a compromise of national identity. Since the 1960s, the Kurds and Kurdish identity have been treated as a threat to the state, its territorial integrity and security. Rather than accommodating the Kurds, the government either alienated them or attempted to forcibly assimilate them to the Arab identity of the state. On the one hand Syrian officials claimed that the Kurds were not native to Syria but were illegal migrants from Turkey whose presence in Syria threatened the Arab identity of the state. This provided the rationale of many policies implemented from the 1960s until the time of writing. On the other hand, state officials have described the Kurds as Arabs of Kurdish origin, or Arab Kurds, and have restricted the use of the Kurdish language and other expressions of Kurdish culture and identity.

The rationale of state policy towards the Kurds is exemplified by the writings of two officials in Hasaka province. After the secessionist coup of 1961 the Kurds remained subject to great pressure from the government and regional officials. The memoirs of Sa'id al-Sayyid, former governor of Hasaka province and pronounced Arab nationalist, and the report written by the Ba'thist Lieutenant and head of security of Hasaka province in 1963, Muhammad Talab Hilal, are two examples of the official position towards the Kurds in this era.[37] Both described the Kurds in the region as alien infiltrators, intent on conspiring to annex parts of Syria and proclaim independence and thereby endangering the Arab character of the province. Hilal's secret document for dealing with the Kurds of the Jazira, *Dirasah 'an Muhafazat al-Jazirah min al-Nawahi al-Qawmiyah, al-Ijtima'iyah, al-Siyasiyah*,[38] was an attack on the Kurds, detailing the perceived threat that they posed for Syria and comparing them to Zionist settlers. The study outlined a 12-point plan for dealing with the Kurds of the Jazira region.[39] Although never official policy, the conditions for the Kurds in Syria and their repression by the regime, outlined below, bear a good deal of similarity to Hilal's proposals.

The policies and projects implemented in the 1960s and 1970s aided forced assimilation of the Kurds to the Arab identity of the state and removed them from their land. Known as 'arabisation', this unofficial policy was continued by Hafiz and Bashar al-Assad through discriminatory decrees, regulations and state institutions. Thus, the government attempted to influence the demography of the Kurdish regions in favour of Arabs and to undermine Kurdish identity and presence in Syria, with devastating and continuing effects for the Kurdish population. The Kurds have generally resisted assimilation and arabisation, from the grassroots level. Nevertheless, state policy has had a material and negative effect on Kurdish population figures in Syria, the density of Kurdish habitation, the physical character of the land, as well as Kurdish culture and national identity itself.

Arabisation

Until after the start of the Syrian uprising in 2011 there were more than 300,000 Kurds in Syria who were completely stateless and denied rights associated with Syrian citizenship.[40] Thousands remain stateless despite a presidential decree in April 2011 granting some the right to apply for naturalisation. Their statelessness was a consequence of an official census conducted in 1962, the results of which have had continuing and worsening effects as statelessness was inherited by generation after generation of Kurds. Statelessness has inflicted severe poverty, discrimination and other hardships upon this group of Kurds. The conditions they live under and the way this has affected their politics is discussed in detail in Chapter 6. Here is just a brief outline of how this situation came about and its part in the arabisation of the Kurdish areas.

In 1962 an official census was conducted in the predominantly Kurdish province of Hasaka, in just one day. The government claimed that a large number of Kurds had entered Syria illegally and obtained Syrian identity documents. They hoped to identify these illegal immigrants by demanding that all inhabitants of the region provide proof of residency prior to 1945. On the day of the census, many participants could not provide the required proof; many were away from home and others chose not to participate, hoping to avoid military conscription and government taxes.[41] The Kurds of the region were the only ones affected by the census, and between 120,000 and 150,000 were stripped of Syrian citizenship and registered as *ajanib* (foreigners). There is a second category of stateless Kurds, those who are not registered at all and who are known as the *maktumiin* (concealed/unregistered people). Those who did not take part in the census became *maktumiin*. Later, the number of unregistered Kurds grew considerably because the state has not recognised the marriages of many stateless Kurds.

The stateless Kurds are denied most rights associated with citizenship. They cannot own or even rent property; they cannot hold a passport or Syrian identity document; they are disenfranchised and cannot be employed in the public sphere. Consequently, both *ajanib* and *maktumiin* Kurds are subjected to daily discrimination and encounter obstacles to living a normal life. Identity documents are required for everything in Syria, from internal state travel to obtaining employment, state benefits and subsidies; and from renting a property to renting a room in a hotel. They are needed for what would normally be routine identity inspections but which become, without the standard papers, humiliating and lengthy processes of identity confirmation and security checks.

The Syrian government's claim that the Kurds whose citizenship was removed were 'foreign infiltrators' is undermined by the fact that it made no apparent attempt to repatriate any of these Kurds. Instead these Kurds have been economically, politically and socially marginalised and subject to daily discrimination and hardship. The official purpose of the census is also undermined by the removal of citizenship from a great number people who could, and still can, prove residency in Syria prior to 1945, including a number of well-known political and military figures in Syria whose right to Syrian identity and contribution to Syrian history has never been questioned.

Kurdish land and culture have also been subject to arabisation since the 1960s. In the same region of Hasaka, arabisation changed the demography of the area in favour of Arabs. In 1965 a *cordon sanitaire*, between 10 and 15 kilometres deep and running 275 kilometres along the Syrian–Turkish border, was planned. Known as the Arab Belt, or *al-Hizam al-'Arabi*, implementation of the plan began in the 1970s when the state began to move Arabs into the region from the Euphrates River basin. To accommodate these Arabs and reduce the Kurdish population in the region the state attempted to remove the inhabitants of more than 450 Kurdish villages along the border with Turkey and Iraq. The Kurdish villagers resisted removal, but the authorities continued to move Arabs into this area, housing them in 34 specially constructed villages along the Syrian–Turkish border and providing them with arms.

Land reforms were applied more generally across the Jazira, breaking up large Kurdish estates and redistributing land among the *falahiin* (peasants). Kurdish sources, however, claim that the Kurdish *falahiin* who worked these lands were excluded from the redistribution programme and the land was transferred to Arabs resettled in the area by the state. Kurdish sources suggest that through agrarian reforms conducted in the Jazira region alone, the state expropriated 6,552,700 acres of land from Kurdish farmers.[42] According to

Salah Bedr al-Din, former secretary of the Kurdish party *Partîya Hevgirtina Gelê Kurd li Sûrîye*[43] this constituted as much as 43 per cent of the total land seized by the government in all Syria.[44]

The other Kurdish areas of Efrîn and Kobanî ('Ayn al-'Arab) have not been immune to the land reforms and arabisation policies either. Although the Arab Belt policy was never applied to these Kurdish regions, Kurdish land owners in Efrîn had large areas of land expropriated by the state. In this area land was redistributed amongst local peasants, and hence, the area remained predominantly Kurdish. It is reported that either side of Kobanî Kurds have been prevented from purchasing land or properties and from setting up businesses in the towns of Jarablus and Tel Abyad.[45] Kurdish sources believe that this is a deliberate attempt to divide the Kurdish areas and towns within Syria from each other by establishing Arab majority areas between them, such as between Efrîn and Kobanî, and between Kobanî and Serê Kaniyê (Ras al-'Ayn).[46] It is also reported that unsuccessful attempts were made to arabise Kobanî town itself through the redistribution of Kurdish lands into Arab hands.[47]

Similarly, Kurds claim that the land within a 25 kilometre deep strip along the border with Turkey in the area of Kobanî and north of Efrîn, has extraordinary security regulations applying to it.[48] In addition, since 1964 Hasaka province in its entirety has been defined as a border area, despite the fact that the distance from Hasaka city to the nearest border is 80 kilometres.[49] Before 2008, Syrian law prohibited the 'establishment, transfer, modification or acquirement of any right to land in a border region or its use for rent or other commercial purpose for a period of more than three years in the name of or for the benefit of an individual or legal entity…unless prior permission is given' by the Ministry of the Interior. This law, Statute 41 of 26 October 2004, restricted the acquisition of undeveloped land in the border regions but did not extend it to inner-city areas intended for development.[50]

In October 2008 Presidential Decree 49 was published. The decree replaced Statue 41 and tightened and extended regulations on land ownership and acquisition in Syria's border regions.[51] The new decree meant that any alteration of land titles, whether for agricultural or urban development or whether previously occupied or vacant, required permission from the Ministry of the Interior. Under this decree permission was only granted on the recommendation of the Ministry of Municipal Affairs,[52] also taking into account the opinion of the Ministry of Defence and the Political Security Directorate in Damascus. Ultimately, this meant that final decisions on issuing licences to sell, buy, rent or develop property rested on political considerations. Kurds, being subject to suspicions of separatism and disloyalty, were routinely disadvantaged by this process. One effect of the decree was to restrict and remove the right of hundreds of Kurdish farmers to farm land which they previously occupied and to prevent the sale and development of urban sites. It was reported by Kurdish sources that, in accordance with the provisions of Decree 49, 580 Kurdish peasants from Dêrîk (Malikiya) area had their names removed from lists held by the Directorate of Agricultural Reform in Hasaka that previously guaranteed their right to farm land in the region.[53] The decree also had a significant effect on cities such as Qamishli, where construction and real estate were economically important.

While Decree 49 was applicable to areas inhabited by Arabs as well as those inhabited by Kurds, in practice the effects of the decree landed heavily upon the Kurdish population concentrated along the Turkish–Syrian border, and particularly those in Hasaka province. In non-Kurdish border areas permission was said to be granted without complication within about three to four months. In comparison, in Hasaka province, permission was granted in only a few cases, and evidence suggested that there was also a bias in favour of Arab and Christian applicants over Kurdish ones. In Efrîn, Kurds were generally granted permission only after considerable delays; Kurds considered politically active encounted greater difficulties obtaining permission, as did Arabs selling land to Kurdish buyers.[54]

As part of its effort to prevent Kurdish involvement in the Syrian uprising, Bashar al-Assad repealed Decree 49 within the first few months of the uprising. All these policies affecting the demography of the Kurdish areas, however, have had long-term economic as well as social ramifications for the Kurdish population. Added to this, the Kurds in Syria face an intensity of cultural discrimination that restricts the very expression of Kurdish identity. By defining the Kurdish population in Syria as a threat to the territorial integrity and security of the state and through the state's apparent attempts to weaken the Kurdish presence in northern Syria, Kurdish culture has been politicised and expression of it is often deemed a political crime. Many Kurdish cultural activities have been made illegal by the Ba'th Party government. They have been monitored and heavily policed or restricted in ways that make their practice illegal. It is not legal either to teach or to learn Kurmanji Kurdish or to speak Kurdish in the work place and in other specified public places. Kurdish music has been periodically banned and confiscated.[55] The restrictions on the use of the Kurdish language have had consequences for the legality of and ability to perform and sing Kurdish music and songs. Organisers of Kurdish festivals or weddings must have permission from the regional political security branch and permission is frequently granted only with signed agreements that Kurdish singing will not take place.[56] It is illegal to possess, read or distribute written material about Kurdish history or politics.

The Kurds are not mentioned anywhere in Syrian text books despite their contributions to Syrian history.[57] This absence from Syrian history has been supported by government decrees changing the names of Kurdish towns, villages, farms and historical sites to Arabic.[58] Many Kurdish businesses have been ordered to change their names because they were Kurdish or made reference to Kurdish national symbols.[59] It is even necessary to get security clearance to name a child with a Kurdish name in Hasaka province, and it is reported by Kurdish sources that several Kurds have been expelled from university on account of their names.[60] In school children are taught that they are Arabs. Several interviewees recounted that any objection was met with corporal punishment.[61]

For the Kurdish population in Syria, artificial demographic change, the elimination of the Kurdish character of the land and people and the denial of the Kurdish existence in Syria defines their relations with the state. This discrimination is seen by the majority of Kurds as a threat to the presence of the Kurds in Syria and their ability and freedom to express their Kurdish identity. This threat to Kurdish national and ethnic identity and historical presence in Syria provides the fundamental purpose of the Syrian Kurdish political parties. These specific circumstances, as well as the general absence of democratic institutions and political process in Syria, provided the context for Kurdish political party activity and contributed to the rationale for the parties' existence.

Identity and Politics

Party organisation, aims and ideology

Kurdish political activity in Syria has always been illegal. Despite this, there were at least 20 Kurdish political parties in Syria at the time of writing, all involved in attempts to put forward Kurdish demands and represent this section of Syrian society. Their general aims include bringing an end to the discrimination against the Kurds, the reversal of policies and laws damaging to Kurdish rights, securing political, cultural and social rights for Kurds and the democratic reform of the Syrian state.[62] Defined by Kurdish identity, the political parties are generally nationalist, although the strength and character of this nationalism has varied between them. Since the various parties' aims are in many ways similar, the Kurdish parties are examined here as a group rather than individually. The individual identities of various parties are examined further in Chapter 3, when looking more at the history, development and fragmentation of Kurdish political organisation in Syria.

As with many other opposition parties and organisations in Syria, the illegal Kurdish parties have been tacitly tolerated by the government and permitted to exist, providing that they do not cross certain unwritten 'red lines' limiting their conduct. For example, they have been tolerated so long as their activities remain controlled and covert and so long as they do not profess support for a Kurdish state in any form, advocate revolution or regime change within Syria, develop a mobilised and active mass support base or form a cohesive unified Kurdish political body. Nonetheless, their activities are continuously monitored, restricted and suppressed by the security apparatus and political activists are regularly arrested.

All parties, bar the *Partîya Yekîtî ya Dêmokrat* (PYD), are organised in the form of the Communist party, with a pyramidal structure and members operating in secret cells. The smallest unit of the party structure is the cell (about three to five people). Each cell is represented by one member in the local committee. Each local committee is then represented in a regional committee, which is in turn represented in the central committee and the politburo. The party is headed either by a secretary-general or a president.[63] One party that claims to differ from this centralised power structure is the *Partîya Yekîtî ya Dêmokrat Kurd li Sûriyê* (*Yekîtî ya Dêmokrat*), which has decentralised its organisational power and voting to the regional branches in an attempt to construct a more democratic party structure.[64] The basic shape of the party, however, is the same. This hierarchical structure, and secrecy of membership guaranteed by it, are reflections more of the circumstances under which they were formed and operate than of their ideology and political leaning. Incidentally, this party structure makes judging the strength of support for the various parties very difficult. Membership numbers are only known by the top ranks of the party and this information is secret.[65] Interviews conducted before the start of the Syrian uprising, however, suggest that no party had more than 5,000 actual members, while some had as little as 50.

Party membership is open to all Kurds over the age of 18 who are introduced to the party and have a 'good reputation'. They must agree to the principles set out in the party programme and obey party orders.[66] Generally, it takes at least one full year for someone to become a member. During this time the applicant must demonstrate knowledge of the party programme and a commitment to the party. About six months after being introduced to the party, potential members join a cell for a probationary period, after which their commitment, relations with other members, activities and loyalty will be reviewed before she or he is nominated by at least two people within the party and then voted in as a full member.[67] *Yekîtî ya Dêmokrat* also requires their new members to introduce five new people to the party.[68] All parties provide training for their intended members and this concentrates on education in the Kurdish language, along with history, particularly the movement's political history, and the party programme. Throughout this period of education the potential members maintain contact with the party and party cells are required to spread party propaganda and attract others to the party.

Since their establishment, the parties' mandates and activities have concentrated on cultural issues and on bringing an end to the oppression of the Kurds in Syria and obtaining national and human rights for them. As nationalist parties, they have sought to preserve, maintain and reproduce Kurdish culture and national identity, distinguishing it from that of Arabs and Turks, and to shield it from arabisation. At the same time they have attempted to establish a legal platform for Kurdish cultural activities and practices by attempting to change state policy towards the Kurds. They seek the reversal of the arabisation policies applied to the Kurdish areas of Syria, democratisation of the Syrian political system, respect for human rights and the development of Kurdish–Arab relations. The solution to the Kurdish question in Syria is connected firmly to political reform in Syria itself, as well as to Kurdish collective political mobilisation and action with specifically Kurdish aims. No party has called for armed resistance or a Kurdish revolution.[69] Democratisation, however, was understood as necessarily entailing the end of one-party rule in Syria as well as political pluralism and constitutional change.

Before the start of the Syrian uprising, the main differences on the political spectrum (from right to left) depended on definitions of the Syrian Kurds and understandings of their place in Syria. The right wing demanded only minimal cultural rights and equal citizenship for the Kurds, describing them as an ethnic minority within Syria.[70] It prioritised the Syrian identity over a pan-Kurdish national one. In comparison, the left wing described the Kurds as a nation in Syria, living in their historic land,[71] called for constitutional recognition of this status and attached more importance than the right wing to the trans-state Kurdish national issue. Up to now, none of the parties has called for the establishment of a Kurdish state. Whether this is a pragmatic policy choice made in response to Syrian authoritarianism and the limits imposed by international relations or whether they do not even secretly support the establishment of a state is impossible to discern from party publications. Individuals commonly express a desire for a Kurdish state but it is clear at present that independence for Kurdistan is not on the parties' agendas. Many parties have sought constitutional national recognition of the Kurds as a second nation in Syria and political representation as Kurds. They have also emphasised the need for the liberation of the Kurdish nation backed by a just solution to the wider Kurdish question.[72] Prior to the start of the Syrian uprising in 2011, only a small minority of parties called for Kurdish 'self-determination within Syria',[73] while the majority restricted their demands to minority and national rights for the Kurds.[74]

Activities

The Kurdish political movement in Syria has been relatively non-confrontational towards the Syrian government and the Kurds have never engaged in armed conflict, as they have in Turkey, Iraq and Iran. Even during the Syrian uprising, Kurdish groups have avoided conflict with the regime, preferring to protect the Kurdish areas and people from the worst effects of the uprising. The aims of the parties have been translated into two main forms of activity. On the one hand, many party activities are directed towards the Kurdish population and the preservation and reproduction of Kurdish culture and national identity against the state's arabisation policies. By these means the parties have played an important historical role in imagining an idea of the nation and disseminating it among the Kurdish population. On the other hand, the parties have sought to instigate change in the political system and to affect the make-up of the Syrian state. Since the commencement of Syrian Kurdish party politics the condition of illegality in which the parties have had to operate in Syria has led them to concentrate a large portion of their activities on the former of these two strategies.

The earlier description of the state's policies towards the Kurds showed that the Syrian state makes no clear distinction between its attitude to the cultural and the political in its policies towards explicitly Kurdish activities. The state is itself complicit in defining Kurdish cultural activity as political by treating Kurds and expressions of their identity as a threat to the state. This means it is complicated to examine Kurdish politics as a purely political phenomenon, and culture as a purely cultural one. This complex inter-relation is seen in all aspects of the state's response to illegal Kurdish activity, cultural or political.

As illegal organisations, the Kurdish parties have operated primarily in a private sphere not normally associated with political party activity in democratic states. This has limited their political mandate in ways that define and alter their behaviour as political parties. Excluded from the public sphere and from participation in public affairs and denied even a platform for legal Kurdish cultural expression in Syria, the agenda of these parties has, to a large extent, been dominated by cultural and educational duties. The cultural dimension of their politics, however, has also been used as a strategy to confront the government. From the beginnings of the Kurdish national movement in Syria during the French mandate, education and the advancement of the Kurdish nation within Syria has been seen as a strategy of confronting oppressors. Kurdish nationalists in Syria sought to distinguish the Kurds culturally and to establish them as a community that could not be arabised or overlooked economically or socially, in the same way as they have been politically.

With the establishment of the first Kurdish political party in Syria, *Partîya Dêmokrat a Kurd li Sûriyê*, in 1957, the political parties assumed this role. Their strategy included teaching the Kurdish language and history, organising the Kurdish Newroz (New Year) festival, weddings and other cultural events, running sports clubs and sponsoring teams and promoting the development of Kurdish literature. Through such activities the parties have played a part in both protecting Kurdish culture and in reproducing and stimulating nationalist sentiment among the Kurdish population. In addition, representatives of the parties also claim that they have had an important social role, providing social support for the elderly, sick and other dependents and functioning as mediating bodies between conflicting individuals or groups within the party or local communities.[75] The party programme of *Partîya Yekîtî ya Kurd li Sûriyê* places great importance on the party role in developing Kurdish society and civil society organisations as well as having a role in diversifying the local economy as a means of promoting greater Kurdish self-sufficiency in Syria.

Teaching the Kurdish language privately in Kurdish homes in the towns and villages is described as a means of reducing Kurdish language illiteracy and ensuring that the daily use of Kurmanji in the Kurdish regions is not negatively affected by state discrimination against the Kurds and the restrictions placed on the use of their language.[76] Publishing and distributing Kurdish literature and folklore, as well as political material, has been an activity commonly associated with the parties. Yet, due to strict rules on printing, publishing and distribution of printed material,[77] party papers and most other Kurdish publications are printed outside Syria, primarily in Lebanon, Iraqi Kurdistan or are distributed in Europe via the internet. These party papers promote the party programme, present party communiqués and announce activities. They report on cultural issues, current events and developments in other areas of Kurdistan, in Syria more generally and on international issues that bear upon the situation of the Kurds.

The more visible political activities that directly engage with the public sphere have been limited and rare. The absence of open dialogue between the parties and the regime has reflected the fear that people have of the pervasive security services and the perceived danger of arrest for such activities. The main actions of the parties in this area have been lobbying and protests, such as demonstrations, writing letters to the president highlighting concerns, expressing opposition to policies or protesting the arrests of individuals and petitioning for their release.

Actions such as these have usually been connected to particular occasions, such as Kurdish and Syrian national holidays or anniversaries like that of the 1962 Hasaka Census. At these times, groups of Kurds demonstrate outside the Syrian parliament in Damascus demanding the return of citizenship to the stateless Kurds. Attaching demonstrations to regular events reduces the confrontational character of the act. Despite this, demonstrations are frequently forcibly dispersed by the police and organisers and participants are arrested. Kurdish political activists are commonly dealt with by the security services and have faced charges connected to separatism and inciting sectarian strife. For example, in the year 2002 on International Human Rights Day (10 December), approximately 150 members of *Partîya Yekîtî ya Kurd li Sûriyê* demonstrated peacefully outside the Syrian parliament. Following the demonstration two members of the *Yekîtî* leadership, Marwan Othman and Hasan Salih, were arrested by the security services.[78] The two party representatives were held in prison where they were tortured, then tried at the beginning of the year 2004 by the Supreme State Security Court (SSSC). The judicial proceedings were condemned as grossly unjust by Amnesty International. They were charged with membership of an illegal organisation and with inciting sectarian strife.[79] On the 22 February 2004, the two were released from prison.[80]

Before the year 2000, organised public protests by Kurds were virtually unknown and, until March 2004, demonstrations remained infrequent and small. All this, however, was to change. On 12 March, in response to the killing of a number of Kurds at the football stadium in Qamishli, Kurds across Syria spontaneously took to the streets and maintained mass demonstrations for more than one week, despite the entry of the military into the Kurdish areas, further killings and mass arrests. The number of demonstrations and public actions increased noticeably following the events of March 2004, despite the regular arrest of organisers and participants and the forced dispersion of the protesters. This implied that there was a greater willingness on the part of the parties and the Kurdish people to risk involvement in actions which were directed against the state and which forced the Kurdish issue into the public sphere.

One of the main factors explaining this increase in visibility of the parties, and in the Kurdish people generally, is the gradual reorientation of dissent round the human rights discourse after the end of the Cold War, and particularly following the international interventions in Iraq (1990), Yugoslavia (1995) and Kosovo (1999). This caused cultural issues to become much more potent political concerns. This change was accompanied by a belief that international organisations and foreign governmental institutions had a duty to protect persecuted groups. Consequently, the idea that systematic abuses of human rights could not be sustained in the present climate without international intervention in some form convinced the Kurdish people and parties in Syria to take greater risks to achieve their higher aims. Another important change was the establishment of the no-fly zone in northern Iraq in 1991 and the formation of the Kurdistan Regional Government in that region. This placed the Kurdish issue on the international agenda and gave the Kurds an unprecedented degree of independence and political leverage. The gradual development of Kurdish autonomy in northern Iraq over the following decade stimulated the idea that rewards for Kurdish efforts there would be felt across Kurdistan. Another factor was the intervention in Iraq in March 2003 and the fall of the Ba'th Party regime in April 2003; these events made the prospect of liberation from authoritarianism a more realistic goal. The similarity of the Ba'th regime in Iraq to that in Syria and increasingly aggressive United States rhetoric towards Syria placed Assad's regime under greater international and domestic pressure to reform. All these changes were reinforced by the subsequent official recognition of the Kurds as a national group in Iraq, of the Kurdistan Regional Government, of Kurdish as an official language and of Kurdish cultural and national rights in the Interim Constitution, adopted on 8 March 2004. These events heightened the belief that Kurdish fortunes were changing and that the benefits would also be felt in the other areas of Kurdistan.

Although questions about the future of Iraq and the status of the Kurdish areas remained, the events in Iraq added to Kurdish confidence in Syria by defining the Kurds as equal participants in the state and as a recognised people and nation rather than as the persecuted subjects of a dictatorship. Ultimately, the election of Jalal Talabani as president of Iraq and Masoud Barzani as president of Iraqi Kurdistan in 2005 coupled with international pressure on the Syrian government to reform influenced Kurdish political confidence in Syria significantly and convinced much of the Kurdish community that the times were changing in their favour.

Although the mass demonstrations of March 2004 were spontaneous and not instigated by the Kurdish parties, they deserve some description here because they are indicative of the stage of popular Kurdish politics in Syria on the eve of the Syrian uprising and represent an important turning point in the Kurdish political movement. Following the events of March 2004, political mobilisation of the Kurdish population was at the highest it had ever been in Syria. For the Kurds the events of March 2004 have been characterised as an 'uprising';[81] they have been inscribed in Syrian Kurdish history and adopted as symbolic capital by Kurdish nationalists. The uprising continues to be celebrated as a triumph for the Kurdish movement and the deaths of an estimated 36 Kurds are commemorated as a symbol of the state persecution of the Kurdish population. The exact implications of the events for the political parties are examined over the course of the following chapters. The details of the occurrences are recounted here both as part of the description of Kurdish political activity and as an example of the state's position toward the Kurds in Syria.

The March 2004 'uprising'

On the 12 March 2004 at about one o'clock in the afternoon, as spectators assembled for a football match in the Qamishli stadium, fighting broke out between Arabs from Dayr al-Zur and Kurds from Qamishli. The Kurdish media reported that the supporters of the *Futuwwa* team from Dayr al-Zur, a renowned Ba'thist and pro-Saddam Hussein city, marched through the centre of the city *en masse* before entering the football stadium armed with knives shouting and bearing pro-Saddam and anti-Kurdish placards.[82] Arab accounts report that Kurdish supporters chanted slogans in support of the Kurdish leaders in Iraq and US President George Bush, provoking the Arab supporters. It is reported that, as the two sides clashed, the Mayor of Qamishli ordered security forces into the stadium and surrounding areas and gave permission to them to fire on the crowds.[83] An estimated seven Kurds were killed inside the stadium and a radio report broadcast at the time indicated that this included three children, though this was later found to be false.[84]

That night demonstrations and rumours of a massacre in Qamishli spread across the Kurdish cities of Amudê, Dêrîk, Hasaka and Serê Kaniyê (Ras al-'Ain) in the north-east of Syria and into the capital, Damascus. Many government buildings were attacked and burned, including the Ba'th Party Headquarters in Qamishli. For the first time ever, statues and portraits of the late President Hafiz al-Assad were destroyed by protestors. Government forces clashed with Kurdish civilians and used lethal force against them, killing and injuring several Kurds. The Governor of Hasaka province ordered tanks and helicopters into Qamishli, people were ordered off the streets and a curfew was imposed on the city. The following day, as the bodies of Kurds killed the day before were carried through the streets of Qamishli by a crowd of almost 100,000, police opened fire on the crowds. An estimated five marchers were killed. The wounded were initially taken to both public and private hospitals in Qamishli, but emergency vehicles with police escorts quickly moved them to national hospitals where they were identified and kept under guard.[85] Both the families of the wounded and doctors objected to the transfers and the hospitals were ill-equipped to cope with the numbers injured. A large number of the wounded deliberately avoided hospitalisation because of fears that they would be arrested.[86]

By nightfall, reports indicated that a further six Kurds had been killed in Dayr al-Zur, three in Damascus, and a 16-year-old boy (Hasan Nouri) killed and more than 80 injured in the Kurdish town of Dêrîk. Over the following days, reports of mass demonstrations, clashes with Syrian security forces and the killing, injury and arrests of Kurds were appearing from all Kurdish areas in Syria and Kurdish businesses and residences were being attacked by groups of Arabs.[87] Unconfirmed reports suggested that security forces tolerated this vandalism and looting to a large extent, even participating in burning public buildings, and that the government armed Arab tribes to aid the suppression of the unrest.[88]

In Damascus, on the evening of 12 March, demonstrations were held by Kurdish students in Damascus University. Further demonstrations were held almost every day while the unrest continued and hundreds of Kurds were arrested.[89] On 18 March dozens of Kurds were expelled from the university for reasons such as committing acts that violated the college and residencies, distributing leaflets or participating in political acts.[90]

Calm was imposed on the Kurdish regions by the deployment of the military in and between Kurdish towns and villages, along with heavy policing and curfews. Rather than encouraging a Kurdish uprising, the Kurdish parties also called for calm in a bid to limit the loss of lives and the inevitable state repression that would follow. The end of the demonstrations was followed by the arrest of approximately two thousand Kurds across Syria, many of them minors. In the year after the disturbances, arrests of Kurds for involvement in the events of March 2004 continued.

Despite differences in accounts of the events between Kurdish, Arab and independent sources, a number of irregularities in the security presence at the football match and the conduct of security forces in attempting to disperse the crowds are apparent. It is normal procedure for law enforcement squads to be present at such occasions and for routine security procedures to be undertaken. There were no such forces or procedures undertaken within the stadium in Qamishli, so when fighting erupted it quickly escalated.[91] It was reported by Kurdish sources that Syrian security personnel who were summoned by the Mayor of Qamishli when the clashes started, joined the *Futuwwa* team supporters in attacking the Kurds. The security forces used live ammunition, including particularly dangerous shrapnel bullets[92] against those in the stadium and against protestors in the following days. The use of live rounds on this occasion was extraordinary and disproportionate. For similar incidents, tear gas and water hoses are typically employed to disperse crowds and only in extreme instances would rubber bullets be used.[93]

Although the protests were brought to an end, the significance of the Kurdish question to the Syrian state was clearly demonstrated. Following the events of March 2004, the state made some conciliatory gestures towards accommodating the Kurds, suggesting that citizenship would be returned to 20,000 Kurds and referring to the Kurds as a nation and as an important part of the fabric of Syrian society and history.[94] No practical moves, however, were made and the government continued, and even stepped-up, its suppression of both Kurdish political and cultural activities.

This form of spontaneous mobilisation was repeated with the disappearance of the liberal Naqshbandi cleric, Sheikh Ma'shouq Khaznawi, in May 2005 and again with the discovery of his tortured body in June 2005. The demonstrations of May and June 2005 were heralded by some as a 'second uprising'.[95] In this case, however, protests were largely confined to Hasaka province. Although the mobilisation of the Kurdish people on these occasions was a consequence of crises rather than a result of a call for action by the Kurdish parties, these events arguably represented a new stage in Kurdish political activity in Syria. Analysts commented on a reawakening of the Kurds in Syria,[96] a new visibility of Kurdish protest[97] and a rediscovery of the Syrian Kurdish issue by outside observers.[98] Mobilisation outside periods of crisis, however, remains fraught with difficulties and the counter actions of the Syrian authorities have been effective in quelling Kurdish activities and reminding the political parties and the population of the harsh consequences of crossing the state's 'red lines'.

The dynamics of the relations between the government, the Kurdish parties and the Kurdish population throughout this period also highlighted discrepancies between popular expectations of the parties and what they were able, or prepared, to deliver. This friction between the Kurdish population and the parties following March 2004 is returned to in Chapter 7, where the implications of these events to the political movement are examined further. While the Kurdish political movement had, indeed, appeared to have entered a new, significant era following the events of March 2004, the particular characteristics of this era will be discussed in the final chapters. In expectation of this, and of the discussion of the functions of the parties and their factionalism, the final part of this chapter looks at the ways in which the parties negotiate their illegality in Syria and how they rely on alternative avenues of applying pressure to the regime that do not depend on mass mobilisation.

The Negotiation of Illegality

As well as altering the parties' political mandates in the ways described in the previous section, the illegality of the Syrian Kurdish political parties has had further consequences for their identity, operation and the methods they employ in confronting the government. It has presented them with unique challenges and obstacles to the tasks of representing the Kurds and bringing about a change in their situation.

In order to operate in Syria and confront the state, the parties employ extensive networks of relations to negotiate their illegality. These networks can be divided spatially between those inside Syria, that are formed across Kurdistan and those that take place in the international arena. In what follows each level is introduced in turn. The first level, that within Syria, is also examined in more detail in Chapter 4 as a beginning to the observation of the functions of the parties. As will be seen, these relations have affected Kurdish politics in ways which have both opened and restricted the opportunities available to them.

Syrian domestic relations

Until the beginning of the Syrian uprising, the Kurdish parties' most immediate concerns related to gaining state recognition of the existence of the Kurdish nation in Syria rather than to speculation about the political situation that might follow such recognition.[99] The pursuit of this aim, however, depended on some form of dialogue or interaction with the government and in Syria *wasta* (the Arabic term for networks of patronage and mediation) has been essential to gaining access to and negotiation with the regime. Access to *wasta* was in turn limited by the illegality of their activities. Political prudence remains almost essential to party survival in Syria, especially considering that all party actions, relations and the movements of party representatives are believed to be monitored by Syrian security services. As a result, and as explained above, direct confrontations of the regime have been rare and party activities are more commonly directed towards the private sphere. Meetings between Kurdish party and government representatives are rare, unofficial, and their occurrence and content is subject to the political climate in Syria and its international relations. After the events of 2004 and 2005 the dialogue between the state and the parties was intensified. Negotiations, however, concentrated on the issue of the stateless Kurds with which the state had begun to engage.

The fact that there have been so many different political parties independently attempting to represent the Kurdish population of Syria has naturally presented further difficulties in confronting the regime, forming relations with the other elements of the Syrian opposition and cooperating as a Kurdish front within it. Relations with other opposition parties and organisations in Syria, however, were cultivated as a means of strengthening the movement and of placing the Kurdish issue on the Syrian national agenda. It appears obvious that real democratisation of the Syrian political system could only be achieved with the cooperation and participation of all elements within the Syrian opposition. The Arab opposition could not form a democratic state without the recognition of the existence of the Kurdish minority within it. Nor could the Kurdish political parties extend their authority over Arab majority areas. At the same time, attempts to gain control of the Kurdish regions could be interpreted as attempts to form a separate government by the majority of the Syrian Arab population. Consequently, for both the Arab and Kurdish political parties and reformists, the development of cooperative relations in the quest for democratic reform of the state is essential. That said, for the Kurdish parties, the cultivation of these relations has often involved compromising nationalist ideals and political objectives in order to accommodate the nationalist criteria of the Arab opposition.

The Damascus Declaration for National Democratic Change of October 2005 is one such example. The Declaration was drawn up and signed by a number of Arab intellectuals, businessmen, opposition parties and by the majority of Kurdish political parties.[100] The text of the Declaration expressed only the minimum demands of the Kurdish population and political parties, mentioning only the extension of equal rights to the Kurds and the return of citizenship to the stateless Kurds, while including specifications about the Arab character of the nation and the state.[101] Despite this, only three Kurdish parties refused to sign it.[102] For the others, it was seen as a starting point and framework for working with the Arab opposition and something that would potentially help to address Kurdish problems in Syria and aid Kurdish participation in democratic reform and eventually in state government. Cooperation between Arab and Kurdish political parties and independents, within the framework of the Damascus Declaration, continued until October 2011. Several Arab signatories and advocates of the Declaration were arrested in the years following its publication. No Kurdish party leader, however, was arrested for involvement in the Declaration. It is possible that this was a deliberate strategy employed by the Syrian government to further undermine the legitimacy of the Kurdish political parties amongst members of the Arab opposition and of the Damascus Declaration within the Kurdish communities in Syria.

Kurdish national relations (the PKK, the KDP and the PUK)

Because of the limitations on the means of negotiating illegality within Syria and due to their natural affinity with the Kurdish national movements in Turkey and Iraq, these wider Kurdish movements have also become a means of furthering Kurdish interests indirectly and of gaining nationalist capital by fostering relations with them. Despite the fact that all these movements are defined by their respective state structures, it has commonly been anticipated that advances in the Kurdish question in Iraq or Turkey would have beneficial effects in Syria too. As a result, Kurds in Syria directed much of their attention and efforts towards Kurdish political parties and movements outside Syria. Not all of the effects of these relations, however, have had positive effects on the Kurdish political movement in Syria.

For example, in 1980 Abdullah Öcalan, and with him, the Kurdistan Workers' Party (PKK), entered Syria with the aid of local Kurds. Abdullah Öcalan and PKK units remained in Syria until he was expelled by the Syrian authorities in 1998. It was widely believed that the Syrian government had given the party unofficial sanctuary. They did not attempt to expel the PKK or stop its activities in Syria and the party maintained offices in several Syrian towns. Officially, however, the government denied that Öcalan was in the country and sent him temporarily to Lebanon where the PKK established training camps in the Baqaa Valley. For Syria, the presence of the PKK on its territory became a geopolitical tool and a means of applying pressure to Turkey. The PKK acted as a balance to the leverage over Syria that Turkey possessed through its control over the Euphrates water flows. At the same time Turkey's control over the Euphrates waters was used to pressure Syria concerning the operation of the PKK from its territory.

Initially the organisation's militant politics and armed resistance received widespread support among the Kurds of Syria, and it recruited widely among the Kurdish youth there. The organisation dominated over Syrian Kurdish political organisations and the local Kurdish population contributed services, money and manpower to the PKK struggle against Turkey.[103] The PKK drew thousands of Syrian Kurds to its ranks in the 1980s. The large numbers are reflected in reports that approximately 7,000–10,000 Syrian Kurds who joined the ranks of the PKK were killed in combat against Turkey or remained missing from Syria.[104] Syrian Kurdish sources suggested that joining the military wing of the PKK became a substitute for official Syrian military service in Syria. This is because some Kurds who joined the PKK, and some who died fighting for the PKK, never received an official summons to perform compulsory military service, suggesting that the Syrian authorities were informed of the names of Syrian Kurds in the party and that serving in it was in practice a substitute for state military service.[105]

During the 1990s criticism grew of PKK tactics, ideology, its relations to the Syrian government and its local activities. Relations worsened in 1996, when in an interview Abdullah Öcalan suggested that most of the Kurds of Syria were refugees and migrants from Turkey and that they would benefit from returning there.[106] While many Kurds in Syria continued to support this organisation, all the Syrian Kurdish political parties disassociated themselves from the PKK. After the PKK was expelled from Syria in 1998 the party operated clandestinely and its main bases outside Turkey were moved to Iraq. Support for the PKK was, in general, transferred to parties formed after 2003 which are based in Syria and identified themselves as Syrian Kurdish parties but which adopted the same ideology and organisational structures as the PKK.[107]

The PKK presence in Syria and the loyalty of much of the Syrian Kurdish community to this political party was, in many ways, detrimental to the Kurdish movement in Syria. Syrian Kurdish issues were swamped by Turkish Kurdish issues and, rather than aiding the Kurds of Syria, the PKK activities and relations with the Syrian government contributed to maintaining the suppression of the Syrian Kurds and Kurdish politics. In 2003, a new party named *Partîya Yekîtî ya Dêmokrat* (the PYD), which boasted ideological affinity with the PKK, was established in Syria. Although it categorically denied any organisational connections to the PKK, the party was a member of the *Koma Civakên Kurdistan* (KCK) or the Union of Communities in Kurdistan, an umbrella organisation founded by Öcalan, and led by the Kurdistan People's Congress (*Kongra-Gel*), which serves as the group's legislature and includes the PKK.

Early on in the Syrian uprising, after the Turkish government broke its relations with Assad's regime and began to call for Assad to step down, allegations that the regime was supporting the PKK resurfaced. In Syria, the PYD was accused of organisational affiliation with the PKK by both the Turkish government and elements of the Arab opposition. Together with the PYD push to gain control in Kurdish areas, these allegations threatened to destabilise Kurdish attempts to unify the Kurdish political movement. The strong assertions and reiterations of the PYD that it was neither connected to the PKK nor supported by the Syrian government, as well as its popularity with many Kurds, established it as a serious competitor to the bloc of Kurdish parties that formed the Kurdish National Council (KNC) in October 2011. Even the suggestion of affiliation to the PKK, however, was used to justify opposition by Turkey and elements of the Syrian Arab opposition to meeting Kurdish demands in Syria. While PYD officials sought the fall of the regime, amongst Syrian Kurds questions remained about the party's political affiliations. Many Kurds remained convinced that the PYD had some form of agreement with the regime and deplored the negative impression that the party gave to the wider Kurdish political movement.

The Kurdistan Democratic Party (KDP) and the Patriotic Union of Kurdistan (PUK) both maintain official offices in Syria which have served as an important diplomatic aid to the development of Iraqi Kurdistan. The PUK itself was established in Syria in 1974 and had good relations with the Syrian authorities. PUK officials suggested that the Kurdish areas in Syria were subordinate to the Kurdish struggles in its other areas.[108] Its image as a left-wing party and its relations with Palestinian and other similar organisations strengthened its links to Damascus, while the KDP was often regarded as more reactionary and conservative due to past relations with the USA.[109]

Inadvertently, the Kurdish uprisings in Iraq and the presence of the Iraqi Kurdish parties in Syria have also served to divert the attention of Syrian Kurds away from their own oppression. Although the KDP and the PUK never conducted their politics or recruited amongst the Syrian population, as the PKK did, the strength of the Iraqi Kurdish leadership, combined with the Syrian Kurds' historical support for the Kurdish political movement in Iraq, meant that their presence in Syria worked to further weaken the endogenous Kurdish movement in Syria. In the absence of any endogenous armed resistance movement and with no political leader capable of commanding the loyalty of the Syrian Kurdish population, the Kurds of Syria lent much support and manpower to the Kurdish struggles in northern Iraq and to the KDP and the PUK, as they did with the PKK, and acted as a communications and supply route out of Iraq.

Both the KDP and the PUK adopted a policy of non-interference in the domestic affairs of neighbouring states. The strength and standing of the KDP and PUK across Kurdistan mean that events in Iraq and Turkey naturally have some impact on the political aspirations of the Syrian Kurds. As indicated above, events in Iraq from 2003 and renewed international pressure on Syria stimulated Kurdish aspirations in Syria. With this came renewed suppression of manifestations of Kurdish identity and the activities of political parties. Intervention by Iraqi Kurdish leaders on behalf of the Syrian Kurds, however, was not forthcoming. Since the start of the Syrian uprising, the KDP has been acting as a mediator between various Kurdish political alliances and encouraging unity within the political movement. Syrian Kurds have been given training by KDP *peshmerga* in the Kurdistan Region. Yet, while the regime remains in place, the party preserves its official policy of non-interference.

The dominance of these other Kurdish political parties over Syrian Kurdish politics has also contributed to the factionalism among the parties. Kurdish politics in Syria have been somewhat overshadowed by those of Iraq and Turkey. Most Kurds in Syria profess some form of loyalty to one or other of the KDP, PUK or PKK. The Syrian government has actively encouraged this external allegiance and diversion of attention by allowing these political parties to operate in Syria. One of the consequences of this predicament is that Kurdish party politics in Iraq and Turkey, and divisions within the parties, has often been reflected in the Kurdish politics of Syria. Relations exist between *Partîya Dêmokrat a Kurdî li Sûriyê (el-Partî)* of Dr Abdul Hakim Bashar and the KDP in Iraq[110] and between *Partîya Dêmokrat a Pêşverû a Kurdî li Sûriyê* of Abdul Hamid Darwish and the PUK of Iraq. The party programmes and their policies reflect those in Iraqi Kurdistan. Many party leaders interviewed stressed that since the beginning of the 1990s, many other Kurdish parties in Syria had reoriented their political activities and focus on Syria itself and away from pan-national Kurdish issues and the parties in Iraq or Turkey. Alliances between parties within Syria, fractures within them and funding, however, continue to be coloured by relations with the parties of Iraqi Kurdistan.

International relations

Beyond this, the Kurdish parties of Syria are all represented in Europe and the USA. The parties have the same organisational structures and programmes, but they operate legally and have alternative channels of political action open to them. The same form of political activity takes place as in Syria. Demonstrations, lobbying and social and cultural activities in the private sphere all define Kurdish party activity in the diaspora. Outside Syria, however, the need for this relates to the conditions of absence and/or exile from Kurdistan, rather than to state restrictions on cultural practices and persecution of individuals and communities for expressing Kurdish identity.

In the diaspora, relations with Western institutions and organisations become a means of pressuring the Syrian state and, therefore, negotiating their illegality and applying indirect pressure to the Syrian regime. Prior to the start of the Syrian uprising, however, interactions with Western governments and organisations were still underdeveloped and efforts to correct this were hampered by a number of obstacles. Besides the complexities of foreign policy decision making in Europe and America, the lack of unity among the Kurdish parties in Syria prevented the party branches in the diaspora from effectively exploiting the democratic channels open to them. The large number of parties meant that there was no real representative body that these state institutions and international organisations could turn to. And relations with Western governments, frowned upon by the Syrian government,[111] were avoided by the parties in Syria. Consequently, the ability of the party representative in the diaspora to develop relations was also hindered by the parties' efforts to avoid crossing the government's 'red-lines'.

Numerous attempts to establish umbrella organisations through which to unite the Kurdish voice or to replace the existing political parties have resulted in adding further names to the list of parties and organisations existing in Europe. On the eve of the Syrian uprising, Syrian Kurdish politics, even in the diaspora, was characterised by internal and inter-party disputes which undermined their potential political strength both inside and outside Syria.

How Distinctive Are Kurdish Parties in Syria?

After Bashar al-Assad came to power in Syria, some conciliatory gestures were made towards the Kurds, but nothing came of them. The promulgation of Decree 49 allowing *ajanib* Kurds in Syria to apply for citizenship did not provide a solution to the problem. Even if citizenship was returned to all those affected by the census of 1962, the parties and people are clear that this alone is not a solution to the Kurdish question in Syria. A solution, acceptable to all Kurdish political parties in Syria, could only be achieved by a constitutional reform which removes the specifications about the racial and national identity of the state and its people, recognises the Kurds as a national minority in Syria with guaranteed national rights, removes the clause that defines the Ba'th Party as the ruling party in Syria and allows other political parties to exist and operate outside the PNF.

The ruling regime managed to maintain a stable equilibrium for more than 40 years, avoiding political reform and challenges to its grip on state power despite the presence of many illegal and underground opposition groups and despite the Kurds. These opposition groups have all been suppressed by promises of reforms on the one hand, and clamp-downs on expressions of dissent, culture and national identity on the other. By fuelling distrust among all people, by fomenting dissent within and between political groups and by keeping people in fear of the consequences of dissent, the regime continues to dominate Syrian politics and economics and has penetrated deep into the heart of Syrian society.

It is clear that the Kurdish political parties operate under extremely difficult circumstances, which are not conducive to their unity. The use of networks inside Syria, within Kurdistan and internationally is a strategy employed to negotiate their illegality and to advance the Kurdish cause in Syria. Due to the complexities of international, national, state and sub-state politics, these same relations can also act as impediments to this aim. The combined interests of actors with which they relate (be they of other Syrian Kurdish parties, parent parties, other Kurdish parties, governments or organisations) have actually hindered their ability to negotiate their parties' illegal state and exert pressure, directly or indirectly, on the regime of Syria.

While events in Syria such as the March 2004 uprising and the demonstrations about the disappearance and death of Sheikh Khaznawi in May 2005, showed that the Kurdish population were united and able to act in unison, the Kurdish political parties in Syria failed to reflect this. Until the Syrian uprising provided conditions that necessitated some form of unity, the parties were divided. The political, social and economic conditions in Syria and those which were special to the Kurds gave rise to a particular form and dynamic of political activity in which party illegality meant that modest political and cultural activities dominated Kurdish politics in Syria.

While a brief overview of the political parties' activities in Syria gives the impression that the Kurdish political parties are broadly similar, the true nature of the various political parties and the real differences between them will only be seen when, and if, their untested policies are put into practice. Alternatively, it is possible to dig beneath the surface of Kurdish politics in Syria and examine the functions of the parties, their factionalism and socio-economic foundations. Their relations to Kurdish society to tribal structures, religious organisations and class can be used to expose the dynamics of their politics and to understand and explain the complexities of social and political relations in Kurdish society in Syria. Before that, however, an historical diversion is necessary to contextualise and comprehend the development of the Syrian Kurdish political movement, its content and later fragmentation.

CHAPTER 2

THE BIRTH OF A SYRIAN KURDISH POLITY, 1920–1957

The Kurds in Syria and of the other areas of Kurdistan have been faced with the difficult task of organising political nationalist resistance against attempts to deny their ethnic identity within a particularly complex setting. Kurdish national identity is a pan-state phenomenon and Kurdish nationalism began life without the obstacles of fixed international borders, sovereignty and the inter-state rivalries that split Kurdish territory. The area of Kurdistan is, today, divided between four Middle Eastern states as well as former Soviet territories, all with complex internal political dynamics and where state identity is connected to ethnic, national and/or religious identities. The development of Kurdish nationalism and Kurdish identity has been challenged by the division of the Kurds and what this means for pan-Kurdish nationalism and political organisation within each state. The Kurds of each area have had to adapt political organisation to differing political and physical environments while maintaining an idea and an ideal of the whole Kurdish nation. Consequently, each area of Kurdistan has developed its own political identity and its own forms of nationalist organisation.

This chapter looks back historically to examine the development of Kurdish politics in Syria. It looks at how a specifically Syrian Kurdish political identity was formed and at what led to the establishment of the first Kurdish political party in 1957. This is done through examining Kurdish political organisations that developed within the state of Syria after its establishment in 1920. Necessarily, some idea of the politics that preceded it is important for understanding the development of Kurdish nationalism and a Syrian Kurdish polity, but the examples used here do not extend further back than the nineteenth century. Accordingly, this chapter looks first at the conditions in Syria at the time of the establishment of the Syrian state and at the stage of development of Kurdish nationalism in the region. From there, it traces the development of Kurdish nationalism and politics in Syria. It looks in particular at the political structure and leadership in four distinct organisations which involved the Kurds and which existed before the establishment of the first Kurdish political party: i) Xoybûn, ii) the Kurdish–Christian autonomist movement of 1937, iii) the Muroud and iv) the Syrian Communist Party (SCP).[1] These four organisations are connected to specific developments within the whole Kurdistan region, in the country of Syria and in the Kurdish areas of Syria. Examining them in the context of changes in regional and local socio-economic and political conditions reveals that a specifically Syrian Kurdish politics did not begin as an organised phenomenon until well after Syrian independence.

The Development of Kurdish Nationalism

The end of the Ottoman era

At the point at which Syria became a state, Kurdish identity was already well established; the Kurds had defended it for centuries from foreign governments and invasions. Some have traced actual examples of Kurdish nationalism back to the sixteenth century in the poetry and writings of Sharaf Khan Bitlisi (finished in 1596) and to the seventeenth-century poet, Ahmed i Khani.[2] These persuasive examples are held by Kurdish nationalists as proof of the existence of a distinct Kurdish nation and a desire for a Kurdish state that dates back centuries. Such examples of written and oral historiography pronounce upon the uniqueness of Kurdish identity and demonstrate persistent attempts to defend and protect this identity, along with Kurdish culture and territory, from central governments. Certainly, the Kurds were participants in a rich and complex history of great civilizations, empires, principalities and tribes.

According to Robert Olsen, modern Kurdish nationalism developed in four stages. The first was marked by the rise to power of the sheikhs in the wake of the nineteenth-century collapse of the Kurdish principalities. Under the Ottoman state, Kurdistan was divided into principalities that enjoyed a large degree of autonomy.[3] During the reign of Sultan Mahmud II (1808–1839), however, attempts were made to break the power of the Kurdish *mîrs* (princes) and centralise state authority.[4] The policy was continued by Sultan Mahmud's son and successor, Abdulmecid (1839–1861)[5] and further eroded any remaining power or autonomy in the Kurdish regions. With the interference of the state in the affairs of the *mîrs* and the threat that this posed to them, the first wars for Kurdish unity and independence were fought. The last principality, of Mîr Bedirkhan Beg of Bohtan, fell in 1846. In its wake, tribal politics re-emerged and within the lawlessness that followed the leadership of the sheikhs came to the fore. Fears of Armenian ascendancy in the

Kurdish regions and resistance to further reforms within the Ottoman state led to the emergence of one such leader, Sheikh Ubaydallah of Nehri, head of the Naqshbandi Sufi order, who rebelled in 1880, demanding an independent Kurdistan.[6]

The second stage in the progress of Kurdish nationalism, the formation of the *Hamidiye* regiments (1891–1914), might also be described as a regression rather than a development. Olsen characterises it as the latter because the *Hamidiye* concentrated power and authority in Kurdish hands and gave many Kurds military training and expertise.[7] The third stage was that of the establishment of public Kurdish nationalist organisations. These were organisations founded by Kurdish intellectuals, primarily the sons of *mîrs* and sheikhs who lived in exile in Istanbul and Europe. They came into conflict with the Young Turk government which took power in 1908 and under which the Kurdish organisations were closed. Kurdish nationalist organisation was then put on hold until after World War I. But Kurdish organisations were revived and several attempts were made to secure the position of the Kurds within the great power politics of this era centring on designs to carve up the Ottoman state. The fourth and final stage in Olsen's schema was the Sheikh Said Rebellion of 1925 which was the first large scale Kurdish rebellion.[8] Tribal and religious leaders joined forces to confront Atatürk's army; the rebellion was defeated, however, and thousands of Kurds fled across the border into Mandate Syria.

At the time that French authority over Syria was granted by the League of Nations in 1920, Kurdish nationalism was in Olsen's third stage of development, characterised by the Kurdish urban intellectuals, whose role is examined further below. The remnants of tribal politics still haunted Kurdish socio-economic relations, in some areas more strongly than in others. Within Syrian territory there were significant disparities in the strength of tribal relations between the different Kurdish areas. In the Kurd Dagh, the last tribal war had ended in 1850 and until the establishment of the Syrian state the region remained predominantly peaceful and was occupied by the French between 1918 and 1920 with relative ease.[9] In the Jazira region, tribal orientation and organisation was much stronger and politics was primarily concerned with local tribal issues. The French met most resistance in this region, into which they made slow and painful inroads between 1920 and 1929. Interstate power politics, particularly those between France and Turkey, were reflected in local Kurdish politics and the tribes exploited these international dynamics, feeding rivalries and extending the life of traditional politics among the Kurds of the Jazira. The local tribes and exiles from Turkey who had fled the repressions of the Sheikh Said rebellion allied themselves with the French or resisted their rule according to tribal conflicts; some even made alliances with the Turkish government and fought against the French in order to secure their interests against local foes and to gain land and authority in the new Turkish state. The majority sided with the French following the Turkish suppression of the Sheikh Said rebellion but Turkish offers of amnesty and land[10] induced others to return to Turkish soil and fight French forces from across the border.[11] As a consequence, the Jazira region was not brought fully under French control until 1930.

A declining tribal system was replaced by a new landed aristocracy whose power and authority was based on monetary possessions and land ownership. Kurdish society in northern Syria was largely agricultural and landlords often owned areas encompassing more than 20 villages.[12] Large landowners preserved semi-feudal relations with peasants within their area of domination.[13] While providing land and seeds to farmers, the landlord, or *agha*, would extract taxes and expenses from the harvest's profits as well as any money lent (with interest), returning as little as one-quarter of the remaining profit to the farmer.[14] This remained the case until the land reforms of the 1950s and 1960s broke their hold on power. These '*aghawat*' (landlords) assumed social, economic and political leadership in the Kurdish regions and their position was, for the most part, hereditary.

Until the 1950s local politics was the domain of the local *agha*. Most evenings the men of the village would gather in the home or special room of the *agha* to discuss local issues and politics of state that affected the region. Anyone absent from the meeting without good reason would be punished, often serving time in the *agha*'s prison. The *agha* was landlord, representative of the village, or a number of villages, and often had a seat on the local council. It was only these village heads and large landowners who engaged with the state or with local councils. Accounts of local inhabitants, however, reveal that village infrastructure was largely developed and built by the people themselves and at their own expense without support from the *aghawat*.[15]

The French Mandate

It was not until after Syria became independent in 1946 that the politics of the Kurds in Syria began to accommodate the division of Kurdistan between Syria, Iraq, Turkey and Iran and the former Soviet Union in their political organisation. The French mandate had no great immediate impact on the Kurdish areas. The Kurds had little sense of being part of or belonging to a larger Syrian state and identity. Their lives continued to be defined by their tribes and land, far from the centres of power and economic heartlands of the Syrian state. Kurds continued to cross between Turkey, Iraq and Syria as if there were no border.

Soured relations between France and Turkey made securing Syria's northern borders necessary, spurring French infiltration of the Kurdish areas.

The French courted the Kurdish *aghawat* and tribal leaders to facilitate their occupation of the northern regions. The Kurdish leaders' relations with the French colonial powers were somewhat mixed. Several tribes supported the French. These were mostly Christians or Kurdish leaders whose local power had depended on the decentralised administration of the pre-1908 Ottoman authorities.[16] Their political stance towards the French authorities reflected their desire to maintain their positions and, as a result, the status quo. Others aligned with Arab tribes or religious movements which rejected French rule over Syria and supported the anti-colonial and Syrian independence movements of the 1930s.[17] Others also allied with Turkey which, as mentioned above, offered land and arms in exchange for support with fighting the French in the contested border regions.[18]

The French 'divide-and-rule' policy in Syria supported the existing social and political order in Damascus which was characterised by decentralised power and the domination of Sunni urban notables and established merchant families. At the same time, the French authorities hoped to extend their rule by limiting the power of the dominant groups. They also tried to stem the rise of Arab nationalism in Syria by nurturing the autonomy of minority groups. French rule over Syria relied on *Les Troupes Spéciales de Levant* which drew heavily from the minority groups in Syria, including Kurdish, Alawi, Druze and Christian communities, and pitted them against each other.[19] The Kurds were recruited into the military in great numbers and were used to police the Arab population.[20] The use of the Kurds and other minority groups in the defence of the colonial powers and their occupation of Syria contributed to tarnishing the Kurdish reputation in the minds of the Sunni Arab majority and both caused and exacerbated ethnic and communal tensions in the new political unit of Syria.[21] The Syrian Arab population began to regard the Kurds as a 'suspect group'[22] and, as the previous chapter showed, the dynamics of this policy still have a bearing on Syria's domestic communal relations today.

It was in this environment that the Kurdish nationalist political movement in Syria began. In the beginning, however, the main orchestrators of this movement were not Kurds native to the Kurdish areas encompassed by Syria, but Kurds who had fled from repression by the government of the Turkish Republic. These Kurdish leaders, full of grievances against the new Turkish state, began to organise both culturally and politically within Syria under the banner of Kurdish nationalism.

The Kurds Organise

Modern and public Kurdish nationalist organisation was developed under the tutelage of the Kurdish elite, who were mostly intellectuals educated and resident in Istanbul or Europe, and who had adopted Western concepts of nationalism. Their form of Kurdish nationalism was characterised by Robert Olsen's third stage of development. It grew from simple Kurdish associations and cultural organisations with no grand political agenda during the reign of Ottoman Caliphate into a political movement that confronted the new Turkish nationalist regime and its intolerance of expressions of Kurdish identity. It developed alongside Armenian and Arab nationalisms and in response to the Turkish nationalist ideology that threatened its existence. The Bedirkhans were pioneers of the Kurdish nationalist movement in Syria and the construction of Kurdish national identity,[23] and their work has had important ramifications for the development of Kurdish politics in Syria which continue to be relevant to this day.

The Bedirkhan brothers

Although the Bedirkhan brothers[24] were not solely responsible for the start and development of Kurdish politics in Syria, nor were they involved in the specifically Syrian Kurdish political party movement that developed in the 1950s, they deserve some attention here. It was arguably their pioneering efforts, their work for Kurdish autonomy and their contribution to the Kurdish cultural revival that determined the future course of the development of Kurdish political nationalism in Syria. Their interpretations of Kurdish culture and identity and their strategies for its revival and development were later incorporated by the Kurdish political parties in Syria into their mandates.

The brothers Jaladat Ali, Kamuran and Sureya Bedirkhan, were sons of Mîr Emin Ali Bedirkhan (1851–1926)[25] and grandsons of Mîr Bedirkhan Beg of Bohtan, the last Kurdish prince to resist abolition by the Ottoman sultans. All three were involved in Kurdish nationalist and political organisation in Mandate Syria. The Bedirkhan family had won its fame through its apparent justness and its resistance to the centralising efforts of the Ottoman state, both of which have been enshrined in Kurdish nationalist mythology and symbolism.[26] At the beginning of the twentieth century such Kurdish exiles, mainly notables and landed aristocracy, living in the capital and centre of Ottoman government, Istanbul, were influenced both by Ottoman identity and the idea of Ottomanism as well as by European ideas of national identity, sovereignty and self-determination. These two strands of thought co-existed and were not exclusive, allowing criticism of the Sultan for policies in Kurdistan while maintaining loyalty to the state and caliphate.[27] Emin Ali, Jaladat and Kamuran Bedirkhan were responsible for and involved in a number of Kurdish associations and organisations under the Ottoman

Empire. The first public Kurdish nationalist organisation was founded in 1908 in Istanbul by Emin Ali Bedirkhan, General Mohammad Sherif Pasha, Sheikh Said Abdul Qadir of Nehri (son of Sheikh Ubaydallah), Ahmed Zulkefl Pasha, a Baban from Sulaymaniya and others. The principal actors of this group were all working in high posts in the Ottoman administration. Under the name *Kurdistan Ta'ali ve Teraqi Cemiyati* (Society for the Rise and Progress of Kurdistan), the organisation produced a newspaper, *Kürt Teavün ve Terakki Gazetesi*, which focused on Kurdish history and literature. The society was also involved in opening a number of schools for Kurdish children in Istanbul in which the Kurdish language was taught.[28]

A number of other Kurdish organisations were established in the following years.[29] The organisations of this time were primarily cultural and social, focusing on the development of the Kurdish areas, with a mandate that included addressing the underdevelopment of the areas and the low levels of literacy. They also encouraged Kurdish national unity as a means of overcoming tribal rivalries and addressing Kurdish–Armenian land disputes. At this stage, however, they sought government support to address these issues without demanding special political rights for the Kurds.[30] The majority of the Kurdish leaders of this era, including intellectuals, sheikhs and tribal chieftains, considered themselves primarily Ottoman subjects, but qualified their support for the Ottoman unionists with specifications about their own Kurdish identity and supported a liberal, decentralised Ottoman state. They sought to strengthen their distinct ethnic identity and develop the Kurdish areas and people while maintaining the privileges that the state secured for them.

Following the Young Turk Revolution and the development of an essentialist Turkish nationalism, *Kurdistan Ta'ali ve Teraqi Cemiyati* was closed down by the Young Turks who 'saw no advantage in allowing the Kurds to organise'.[31] All Kurdish organisations were made illegal and those which did not close down operated outside the law. In this period the Bedirkhan brothers made contact with the traditional leadership in the Kurdish areas, rousing opposition to the ruling Committee of Union and Progress (CUP) and promoting the idea of Kurdish autonomy. The experience of World War I triggered new cooperation between the urban intellectuals and rural tribesmen and the armistice of 31 October 1918 marked the resurgence of Kurdish nationalist activity.[32] *Kurdistan Ta'ali ve Teraqi Cemiyati* was reactivated in 1918 under the name *Kurdistan Ta'ali Cemiyati* (the Society for the Rise of Kurdistan) and involved members of the eastern tribes in addition to the urban educated nationalists. Many other organisations were revived or established in this period; Kurdish nationalist organisation flourished and several bids for independence were made.

The division of Kurdistan

After the fall of the Ottoman Empire, and as the intentions of the Great Powers to divide the spoils of World War I between them became clear, many Kurdish tribal leaders and intellectuals alike made attempts to secure their interests and gain some form of autonomy or independence for the Kurds. Delegations representing Kurdish nationalist organisations were sent to conferences around the world, petitioning for Kurdish rights to self-determination.[33] Rebellions, negotiations and petitions for autonomy, organised by leaders of tribes, sheikhs and intellectuals, punctuated this era of Kurdish history. Although promised autonomy for a considerable part of 'Kurdistan' in the Treaty of Sèvres in 1920,[34] changes in the balance of power in the region, colonial interests and great power politics meant that the Kurds were excluded from the subsequent Treaty of Lausanne which replaced Sèvres in 1923. The Kurds were divided between five different states, two of them, Iraq and Syria, being particularly fragile political entities over which the British and French were granted mandate authority.

As the power of the new nationalist Turkish government expanded and Atatürk turned his attention to dealing with the Kurdish areas, Kurdish nationalist movements, as well as tribal forces which had attempted to secure their interests against the government, came under increasing pressure. In a deliberate attempt to rid Turkey of Kurdish nationalism and dissent, Atatürk initiated a number of policies designed to drive Kurdish inhabitants out of the region. These policies included a military campaign in the Kurdish regions which forced thousands to flee over the border to the Syrian Jazira and beyond.[35] Several rebellions erupted in the Kurdish regions over the next few years, the most famous and large scale being the Sheikh Said Revolt of 1925. The suppression of the revolt was brutal: land was destroyed, villages burned, Kurds were deported and harassed by the Turkish authorities.[36] Sheikh Said and most of the leaders of the rebellion were hanged on 29 June. The Kurdish nationalist leadership came under attack and were forced to escape across the borders, to areas of Kurdistan or countries out of Atatürk's reach. The Bedirkhan brothers fled the new Turkish state, Jaladat Ali Bedirkhan moving to Syria in 1931 after first fleeing to Egypt and then Iraq. Rejected by the British, he found refuge in Syria where he stayed until he died in 1951.

Syria was the recipient of many members of Turkey's Kurdish nationalist and traditional leadership. This included Kurds such as Emin Ali Bedirkhan, his sons Jaladat Ali (1893–1951), Kamuran (1895–1978) and Sureya Bedirkhan (1883–1938), who had been involved in Kurdish cultural and political activities under the Ottoman Empire, Ihsan Nouri Pahsa (1893–1976) who was to lead the Ararat Revolt, and both Akram Jamil Pasha (1891–1974) and Qadri

Jamil Pasha (1892–1973), as well as Kurdish intellectuals such as Osman Sabri (1905–1993). While in Syria, these Kurdish exiles continued efforts to promote Kurdish culture and organise the Kurds against the Turkish government. The Bedirkhan brothers renewed their struggle for Kurdish independence and unity and Jaladat Bedirkhan was one of the founding members of the Xoybûn League,[37] the first Kurdish political organisation seeking independence for Kurdistan and bringing together Kurdish leaders from all areas of Kurdistan.

Kurdish Political Organisation in Syria

The foregoing section summarises the stage of development of Kurdish nationalism and its political context when the Syrian state was formed. By the end of the suppression of the Sheikh Said rebellion, all previously existing Kurdish political organisation had been crushed by Atatürk and, needless to say, no Kurdish political organisation with a Kurdish nationalist agenda existed, at that time, within the state of Syria. The political organisations that were to develop within the Kurdish communities in Syria after the division of Kurdistan were mostly defined by local conditions and interests. Although this is true, these organisations nearly always included some form of adhesion to Kurdish identity and developed some form of Kurdish agenda. This may have been due to one of a number of causes – the development of the Kurdish nationalist agenda, the locality and membership of the organisations, a reaction to the new political developments in the region and the realities of state sovereignty – or some combination of these.

It is generally accepted that early Kurdish nationalist political organisation in Syria involved primarily Kurdish exiles from the new Turkish Republic.[38] Certainly, it was the Turkish government which posed a direct threat to the Kurds within its territory and efforts to organise the Kurds in Syria politically began with an organisation formed to confront the Turkish government. Nationalists and activists, both tribal and intellectual, who had fled persecution by the Turkish government, continued their endeavours from the safety of Syrian territory. These exiles made connections between various tribal and religious leaders in Syria and Iraq and proposed the organisation of the Kurdish leadership into one united organisation with the aim of confronting the Turkish forces militarily and establishing an independent Kurdish state.

Xoybûn[39] and its aftermath

The efforts of Kurdish exiles culminated in the establishment of the Xoybûn League in 1927. The committee which came together for its formal establishment in Lebanon[40] was made up of Kurdish intellectuals, leaders of tribes, sheikhs and rebel fighters from Turkey, Syria and Iraq.[41] The group set out to unite the Kurdish movement around a single aim: to unify their political efforts and turn their struggle towards Turkey and the liberation of the Kurds from Turkish 'claws'.[42] At this point in time, the Turkish government was seen as the primary 'enemy' of the Kurds. The Arab governments that would later threaten the Kurdish identity and existence had not yet been established in Syria or Iraq and the mandate authorities were seen as temporary authorities that maintained a decentralised state. In order to cultivate the new relations that Kurdish nationalists had developed with the French and British mandate authorities, the founding principles of Xoybûn specified that the efforts of the organisation should be directed towards Turkey and not towards Kurdish political gains in any part of Syria, Iraq or Iran. In fact, policy specified that relations with the governments of these countries should be developed, that in Iraq and Syria the rights granted to the Kurdish people by the mandate authorities were sufficient and that no demands for other political rights should be made of these governments.[43] Although not suppressing Kurdish cultural expression, the French authorities resisted granting any specific cultural or political rights to the Kurds and played the Kurdish card as they saw fit.

Xoybûn brought together traditional and modern elements of Kurdish society in a common struggle. This potentially contradictory equation was reflected in the discourse of the organisation, particularly so in the oath that all members had to take:

> I do hereby swear on my honour and religion that from the date of my signing this promise, for a period of two years, I will not use arms against any Kurd unless an attack is made by him on my life and honour or upon the lives and honour of those for whose safety I am responsible by family or national obligation. I will postpone until the expiration of these two years, all blood feuds and other disputes, and do my utmost to prevent bloodshed among two Kurds on private matters. Any Kurd who attempts to contravene this undertaking is regarded a traitor of his nation, and the murder of every traitor is a duty.[44]

The symbol of the party included an ear of wheat and a quill on either side of a dagger[45] representing the traditional attachment of the Kurds to the land and the modern reformist endeavours of the Kurdish intellectuals, united in armed struggle. While the accommodation of these two sectors of Kurdish society was novel and in many ways ground-breaking, according to Muhammad Mulla Ahmed, author of *The Xoybûn Association and Kurdish–Armenian Relations*, the organisation continued to be composed of and reflect the interests of the large landowners and the bourgeoisie.[46] Consequently, the organisation had little real connection to the Kurdish masses who, in the absence of a peasants' movement or any champion of their rights, continued to be subject to semi-feudal master–servant relations with landlords and tribal chiefs within the organisation. It would take significant socio-economic change in the Kurdish regions to politicise the peasantry and the breaking of the power of the landlords and traditional leadership to widen the appeal of Kurdish nationalist and political organisation.

The most significant role of Xoybûn was its involvement in the planning and execution of the Ararat (or Agrî Dagh) revolt[47] which took place in Turkey between 1928 and 1931. The organisation aimed to coordinate the Kurdish movements in Syria, Turkey and Iraq to support Kurdish rebels in the Ararat region and attack key Turkish military posts within Turkish territory. In the Kurdish National Congress, in which the idea for the organisation was discussed, Kurd Ava at Agrî Dagh was declared the capital of Kurdistan. At the founding meeting in Beirut, Ihsan Nouri Pasha was declared supreme commander of the Kurdish forces at Agrî Dagh. In 1928 he initiated the revolt leading his men to Mount Ararat and set up a mini Kurdish proto-state which flew the Kurdish flag and had thousands of trained and armed forces and supply depots.[48]

With the beginning of the Ararat revolt in 1928 and under pressure from Turkey, the French and the British imposed heavy restrictions on those involved in Xoybûn.[49] The Turkish authorities made attempts at conciliation with the Kurdish forces. No settlement was reached, however, and in 1930 the Turkish authorities' began a military campaign against the Kurdish rebels, surrounding Mount Ararat from all sides. On 15 June, Kurdish nationalist forces launched counter-offensives in many areas, which diverted Turkish forces so that the army was forced to abandon its offensive against Agrî Dagh. In the same month, Jaladat Bedirkhan held a meeting in his home in which Kurdish chiefs participated. A plan of action was devised which involved the infiltration of Kurdish groups into Turkish territory at three points along the border with Syria. The participation of the Syrian Xoybûn groups in the revolt would serve to precipitate a new Kurdish revolt in a region other than Ararat, using tribal relations and mobilisation on both sides of the border.[50] The diversionary attack was planned for the night of 3 August. Faced with the might of the Turkish forces, which now included the air force, a number of Kurds defected and returned to Syria. The effect of the Kurdish attack was limited and, despite Jaladat's determination to take Midat and help ignite a wider rebellion through the areas of Diyarbakir, Bohtan and Mardin, the Kurdish chiefs all withdrew to Syria between 5 and 7 August. Following the attempted revolt, the French authorities took further measures to remove the chiefs of Xoybûn from the Kurdish regions of Syria. The sons of Jamil

Pasha, Hajo Agha and his sons were removed to Dayr al-Zur and then to Damascus; Jaladat and Kamuran Bedirkhan, Mamduh Salim and Hratch Papazian (Armenian) were forbidden from entering the regions east of the Euphrates. Mustafa and Bozan ibn Shahin were placed under house arrest in Aleppo, the sons of Ibrahim Pasha were removed to Hasaka and Qadour Beg, Rasoul Agha and Sami Bey al-Milliye were exiled to Dayr al-Zur.[51] Several villages were placed under surveillance and/or disarmed.

The failure of the Ararat Revolt shook the nascent Kurdish movement and threw Xoybûn and its method into question.[52] Many participants lost hope in the organisation, including its president, Jaladat Bedirkhan. Jaladat concluded that what the Kurds lacked was intellect and understanding and a complete political consciousness and that, therefore, success in their struggle was impossible.[53] Accordingly, he resigned from Xoybûn and launched a cultural movement, turning his attention once again to the propagation of culture and learning among the Kurds. Armed revolt as a tactic was abandoned in favour of this cultural approach, using Kurdish culture and tradition as a path to enlightenment and as a method of confronting the oppressors. Strengthening Kurdish belonging to the community or national group was to be achieved through the restoration of the Kurdish language, the revival of Kurdish literature, the development of education in Kurdish history and language, all of which were obtainable despite the setbacks encountered in their military efforts. This task of modernising and 'civilising' the Kurdish people and establishing them as a political body fell to the Kurdish intellectuals who launched a form of cultural renaissance[54] that would define the Kurdish movement and Kurdish national identity in Syria until the present day.

Until 1930, there was no formal education system in the Kurdish areas of Syria. In fact, in the absence of state education, most of the population was illiterate. The few who received an education did so under Sufi mullahs in their homes or learnt the Quran in Quranic schools that existed in some of the Kurdish villages.[55] This literary and religious education, however, taught the Arabic language rather than Kurdish. Generally, Kurdish intellectuals were also employing Arabic, Turkish or Persian as their medium of expression and, when writing in Kurdish, used the Arabic script. Consequently, the Kurdish community lacked both a literary tradition in the Kurdish language and a written record of the myths and cultural tradition of the Kurdish communities. What did exist among the Kurdish population was a rich oral tradition of popular literature, folklore, myths and songs. Until today, this oral tradition remains strong among the Kurds and much of the traditional history and stories continue to exist in the minds, songs and tales of the older generation, many of whom remain illiterate with only a basic knowledge of Arabic.[56]

The Kurdish nationalist intellectuals saw a situation in which the dominating cultures of the Turks, Arabs or Persians would envelop and consume the Kurdish identity and feared that, without concerted effort, the Kurdish language would fade away with the domination of official state languages over the then weak and deficient Kurdish vernacular. Consequently, they sought to revive and modernise it and spread the use of the Kurdish alphabet developed by Jaladat Bedirkhan in 1919, which used the Latin script. Through this they hoped that the language would become a medium for writing and reading among the Kurdish population and would develop generally through this literary use. They also sought to establish the Kurds as a modern civilised population by 'Westernising' them through education and intellectual endeavours. The result of this would be the cultural ascendancy of the Kurds over sections of the population with numerical superiority and political dominance.

With the aid of the French authorities in Syria, a number of journals were launched by Jaladat Ali and Kamuran Bedirkhan in this period, the first being *Hawar* (The Calling, published between 1932 and 1935 and again between 1941 and 1943) which concentrated on propagation of the Kurdish alphabet and the development of grammar as well as the publication of Kurdish classics, folklore, and historical and ethnographic studies. In fact until 1941, the bi-monthly journal was written using the Arabic script and French. But from 1942, *Hawar* and another monthly journal named *Ronahî* (meaning Light, published from 1 April 1942 to 1945),[57] employed the Kurdish alphabet. Both of these journals were distributed in Syria and smuggled out to Turkey. Through them the Kurdish alphabet was spread and became the medium for publication for Kurds in Turkey.[58] Being cultural in content, these journals formed a basis for the development of Kurdish national identity in Syria and beyond. Today, the journals and their founders continue to be revered and considered central to Kurdish national patrimony.

The fact remained that this was an intellectual effort and that the majority of the Kurdish population (notably the peasantry and women) was largely unaffected by modernist notions of national identity associated with the nation-state. The growing criticism of feudal relations led many Kurds to become involved in politics and to identify with communist and religious movements rather than applying themselves directly to the Kurdish national cause. But the close-knit nature of Kurdish society, the experience of repression by the Turkish authorities and the dissemination of information among the Kurds helped to stimulate Kurdish political consciousness in Syria and aided understanding of the consequences of the division of Kurdistan and the need to secure Kurdish rights.

Even after the Ararat revolt and the securing of the Syrian–Turkish borders in the 1930s, Kurdish national identity remained a shared identity which spanned the new state borders that divided Kurdistan. Xoybûn and its involvement in the Ararat revolt reflected and confirmed this identity.

In retrospect Xoybûn has been charged with being defined by the Turkish state and ignoring the Kurds of other areas.[59] It is true that the map of the Kurdish state that Xoybûn envisaged did not include Kurdish areas in Syria. The situation was such, however, that Kurdish identity and land was under threat from the new Turkish state and the organisation was dependent on the tacit support of the mandate authorities. The division of Kurdistan was not an accepted reality. The Kurds, under the French and British mandates in the fledgling states of Syria and Iraq, did not experience suppression or denial of their culture or identity. With time, these same borders created new realities for the Kurdish people, the political space in each state impacting differently in each section of Kurdistan and so exposing the Kurdish people to new political socio-economic dynamics and new political factions. Consequently, the political organisation of the Kurds in each state was forced to adapt to the politics of sovereignty, bounded territory and centralised administration. After the failure of Xoybûn, the move to Syrian Kurdish nationalist political organisation was not immediate. It was followed by a withdrawal of Kurdish nationalist intellectuals to the cultural sphere and the development of more local organisations and movements in which Kurdish identity was more coincidental or secondary to the interests of the traditional leadership.

The Kurdish–Christian autonomist movement

Another political movement which involved the Kurds in the Jazira was the Kurdish–Christian autonomist movement of 1937. Before this, a number of demands for independence and autonomy had been made by various Kurdish leaders in the 1920s. For example, the deputy Nouri Kandi from the Kurd Dagh demanded autonomy for all Kurdish majority areas along the Syrian–Turkish borders while warning of the potentially harmful consequences of Arab nationalism to French interests in the areas; tribes allied to the Alaedin tribes from the Barazi confederation made similar demands; and Jarablus leaders demanded autonomy for their region of control only.[60] According to Jordi Tejel, these petitions for autonomy demonstrate the desires of these leaders to become local support for the French authorities rather than a desire to obtain political and cultural rights for the Kurds of these areas.[61] Particularly with regard to the first two petitions mentioned, however, it may be possible that nationalist aims were framed within rhetoric designed to appease the French authorities and secure Kurdish interests. With the arrival and settlement of Kurdish exiles from Turkey, a petition for Kurdish autonomy was made which included specifications about the introduction of Kurdish as an official language in the Kurdish regions, the replacement of Arab functionaries in the regions with Kurds, the formation of a Kurdish regiment charged with guarding Syria's northern borders and aid to facilitate the settlement of Kurdish refugees in Hasaka province.[62] This reflected the work of the Kurdish émigrés, their intellectual background and nationalist ideology. The French rejected the proposal, yet existing conflict within the French administration between the civil and intelligence services provided opportunities for the Kurds of the Jazira region to pursue their interests. Captain Pierre Terrier of the intelligence services, in particular, understood the potential of the Kurds in the colonisation of the Jazira and the resolution of border disputes with Turkey. He devised a plan to counter demands for Kurdish independence or autonomy for all the Kurdish regions in Syria, by instructing local Kurdish leaders to concentrate efforts on the Jazira region where autonomy was a possibility. The plan involved the nomination of Kurdish functionaries in the Jazira, the formation of a Kurdish–Christian battalion within the French *Troupes*, the foundation of a Kurdish class in the Arab College for Higher Education in Damascus, Kurdish night classes in Beirut, permission to publish the journal *Hawar* and the granting of identity documents to Kurdish refugees. All of the above were introduced between 1928 and 1936.[63]

The Kurdish–Christian alliance and petition for autonomy of 1937 was a reaction to the Franco-Syrian Treaty of 1936, in which the French agreed in principle to Syrian independence and the establishment of an Arab nationalist central government in Damascus, and which, in effect, ended French–Kurdish relations. The French need for protégées in the region was removed, threatening the position and interests of rural based Kurdish tribal leaders and urban Christian notables previously supported by the French in exchange for securing the Jazira against Turkish interests. The disturbances began when French officials supportive of local leaders were replaced with Syrians from outside the Jazira. Encouraged by the local French officials, several prominent figures in the region began demanding that, as a minimum, officials appointed in the Jazira region should be from among the population there.[64] Kurds resorted to violence when these demands were ignored and officials from outside the area were appointed in Hasaka in June 1937.

The leadership of the movement repeatedly petitioned the mandate powers and the government, demanding economic and administrative decentralisation of the Jazira under the protection of France and administration of the area by local Kurds and Christians. As the movement developed, Arab nationalists declared *jihad* against the Christians.[65] Tensions then mounted between local Kurds and Christian autonomists on the one side and local nationalists who were supported by the central Arabist government, on the other. The Arab nationalist government had begun to encourage Arab Syrians from the areas of Aleppo, Hama and Homs to move into the Jazira in an attempt to consolidate the Arab character of the area. At the same time, local officials who supported autonomy for the Jazira, that is Kurds and

Christians, were fired from their jobs and replaced with Sunni Arabs loyal to the central government.[66]

In August 1937 the Christian quarter of the town of Amudê was attacked by supporters of the pan-Islamic campaign and Christians were massacred.[67] The French suppressed the unrest using aerial bombardment and re-established direct control over the Jazira. This temporarily increased the autonomy of the area from the central government and the French allowed the establishment of a number of Kurdish social and cultural organisations and clubs.[68] The mandate powers began to encourage the Christians to secure their survival in Syria through cooperation with the Sunni Arab government. But minority rights were not secured by the French mandate power itself and the French, no longer dependent on the Kurdish population of the area for security, abandoned their local protégées.

The Kurdish actors involved in the autonomous movement were predominantly tribal figures and large land owners. For example, the most prominent members of the movement were Hasan Hajo Agha, Qaddur Beg and Khalil Beg Ibrahim Pasha – all landlords and tribal leaders who had become close allies with the French authorities. Hajo Agha was chief of the Haverkan tribal confederation and one of the first Kurdish exiles to be settled in the Jazira.[69] After his submission to the French in 1926, Hajo Agha became their most reliable and privileged supporter in the Jazira and an enemy of Turkey.[70] Qaddur Beg was the former Qaimmaqam of Nesibin. He had his own militia created in 1924, which fought the French and was proprietor of the left bank of the Jag Jag River, including the land that Qamishli now occupies. He became the Syrian deputy for the Jazira in 1936 when he ran in legislative elections in the region and was elected along with Khalil Beg Ibrahim Pasha and Said Ishaq.[71] Khalil Beg Ibrahim Pasha was head of the Milli tribe. What is more, since their Christian allies were predominantly urban-based, their alliance allowed the extension of their influence into the region's cities rather than only rural areas. For the Christians, the alliance allowed them to maintain control of local affairs and ensure their future in Jazira as a religious minority.[72]

The impact of this movement on the Kurdish nationalist organisation was mixed. The movement itself and French support in some respects thwarted the development of Kurdish political organisation and national unity within Syria. The decision to concentrate efforts for autonomy on the Jazira, as the Terrier Plan encouraged them to do, had a lasting negative effect on the cohesion of the Kurdish regions in Syria. As the French negotiated administrative centralisation in Syria and calls from all areas for Kurdish autonomy were heard, the opportunity for effective Kurdish cooperation across the Kurdish regions in Syria presented itself. Yet the concentration of these Kurdish tribal leaders on autonomy in the Jazira alone worked to weaken attempts to build a united Kurdish identity and polity in Syria, establishing divisions between the three Kurdish regions and their social and political development. In addition, rivalries between local Kurdish tribes were reflected in whether a leader allied himself with the autonomists or with the Syrian nationalists' Damascus alliance,[73] reproducing tensions and discord within Kurdish society in the Jazira. At the same time, a French mandate report suggested that in this period Kurdish autonomists were collaborating with Kurds across the border in Turkey to create an autonomous entity in the Jazira, reunify it into Kurdistan and proclaim an independent state.[74]

Calls for autonomy from the region continued until the French left in 1946, but the impact of this movement on Kurdish politics was primarily local.[75] It advanced Kurdish nationalist politics in the area, enlightening the population to some of the potential effects of the centralised Arab government on the area and on local power relations. It is nearly impossible to say, however, how broad an impact nationalism had on the peasantry in the area, as at this time tribal relations dominated and dictated political allegiances.

The Muroud[76]

In the Kurd Dagh, Xoybûn had been relatively weak due to the absence of Kurdish exiles from Turkey; these were concentrated in the Jazira region and in Damascus. Despite calls for autonomy from the area, (such as that of Nouri Kandi cited above) the opportunity for a sustained autonomous movement was thwarted by the French authorities and local politics. In this area, socio-economic transformations in the second half of the nineteenth century had left only a few tribal families with any real power. Others were in decline, if not ruined already. In their place a new landed aristocracy developed which owed its power and influence to possession of land and material prosperity rather than to military strength or number of followers as in the case of the ancient tribal chiefs. The presence of these families and the rapid disintegration of tribal relations gave the Kurd Dagh a significantly different political and socio-economic character from other Kurdish areas.[77] Peasants were not tied by tribal loyalties to their landlords, giving rise to very diverse socio-economic relations between landlords and tenants and an increasing awareness of the potential for political action among the peasantry.

Among the Kurds generally, religious leaders offered some alternative to the local *aghawat* as sources of support and leadership. In the Kurd Dagh region, however, this was not the case. The big religious groups were not well represented. The Qadiri Sufi order was represented by only one sheikh. The Rifa'i order consisted of approximately one hundred people, led by Sheikh Abdul Hanan from Balut village. For the Naqshbandi, Sheikh Ahmed Lam'a came seasonally from Damascus to preach in the area around Azaz. The Kurd Dagh also contained the lowest number of mosques in Syria and religious rules and practices were not widely followed.[78] Yet it was in the Kurd Dagh in the 1930s that a movement arose, led by a Naqshbandi sheikh, which was religious in its identity and gained wide support from the local population.

The popularity and success of the *Muroud* in the Kurd Dagh is explained more by local socio-economic conditions than by the religious character of the movement. The *Muroud* was a religious and a social movement, and also a struggle against the oppression of the feudal landlords. It later fought against the French mandate authorities in the region as part of the Syrian independence movement.[79] Aside from Roger Lescot (the French orientalist and diplomat) and a few local Kurdish intellectuals and nationalists,[80] this organisation has attracted little academic or other attention despite its significant popularity and impact in the region and its contribution to the Syrian independence movement. The *Muroud* succeeded in changing some social practices amongst the inhabitants of the Kurd Dagh, for example, minimising the dowry in marriage contracts.[81] Its involvement in and contribution to Kurdish nationalism and political organisation, however, was at most minimal.

The *Muroud* was led by the Naqshbandi sheikh, Ibrahim Khalil. Ibrahim Khalil came to Syria in 1925, where he studied religious science in Damascus and Homs. His ethnic identification, whether Turkish or Kurdish, is not clear but his family originally came from the western area of the Kurd Dagh. He grew up with his father in Ottoman Turkey, and Ibrahim Khalil was in both the Ottoman army and that of the New Turkish Republic. While in the latter, he was involved in the suppression of the Sheikh Said rebellion in 1925, suggesting that he had little interest in Kurdish nationalism. But he spoke both Turkish and Kurdish and his poetry expressed identification with the Kurdish nation.[82]

Ibrahim Khalil arrived in the Kurd Dagh region in 1929, residing in Derswan, under the patronage of Fa'iq Agha of the Sheikh Ismail Zade family, through whom he obtained Syrian identity documents and became a powerful and influential man in the region, both among the people there and with the French authorities. He began as a teacher of the Quran, instructing the children of Derswan and those of the *aghawat*. His experience of the *aghawat* – their lack of devotion, their indulgence in alcohol and oppression of the peasantry – induced him to leave Derswan for Nebi Houri.[83] There, through his sermons, he gained a number of followers including Hanif Arab, Ali Ghalib, Rashid Ibo and his brothers and several others from among the religious community and the peasantry. The group formed an organisation with a formal leadership and programme, Ibrahim Khalil assuming the position of the president, Sheikh Hanif Arab the post of civil and religious affairs, Rashid Ibo that of deputy to Sheikh Ibrahim Khalil and head of the military branch of the organisation.[84]

The goals of the organisation were religious, social and, some say, national. They aimed to promote the proper following of Islam according to the Naqshbandi tradition (abstention from drinking alcohol, smoking, gambling and the rest) and from 1936 they directed their struggle against the French occupation of Syria. The majority of its adherents were from the peasantry and deprived classes from the northern areas of Bilbil and Rajo, territory of the Bayan and Sheikhan tribes, where the hold of the large landowners was comparatively weak. South of this area the *aghawat* were able to curb the expansion of the *Muroud*.[85] Some of the *aghawat*, however, supported the *Muroud*, although for diverse reasons: some provided aid in exchange for the protection of their interests (such as the leaders of the Shakak tribe, Kor Rashid and the Haj Omar family in Derswan). Others sought to gain support in elections (such as Husni Awni, leader of the Sheikhan, who was elected to the Syrian parliament as deputy to the Kurd Dagh in 1936 with the support of the *Muroud*). Yet others used it to strengthen their position in rivalries and conflicts between families. This was especially true for those who had disputes with Sheikh Ismail Zade, who turned against the movement. The *Muroud* also gained popular support pioneering the rights of the peasants against the interests of the *aghawat* by off-setting debts, working for the restitution of land to those from whom it had been unjustly taken, and such like. To this end, the group organised isolated attacks of banditry, mostly under the command of Rashid Ibo, against large landlords who did not patronise the organisation. The family of Sheikh Ismail Zade felt that their interests and their position in the region were threatened by the *Muroud* and roused the French authorities against Sheikh Ibrahim Khalil, who was arrested in July 1931 and charged with inciting unrest in the border areas.[86]

By 1936 the *Muroud* had turned its attention to anti-colonial activities in the Kurd Dagh. This change in focus was partly the result of relations it had developed with the National Bloc. Also, the French were seen to be complicit in maintaining relations of domination in their support for the landed *aghawat* in the area. The positions of the *aghawat* were bolstered by the French and the maintenance of these relations ensured that the *aghawat* preserved certain privileges and benefits at the expense of the peasantry. In 1936 the *Muroud* began an armed uprising in the region against the French, known locally as 'the Kurd Dagh revolution', which lasted until 1940.

Towards the end of 1936 the majority of the *aghawat* began to comprehend that it was in their interests to group together in order to confront the *Muroud*. Local power politics, however, as well as personal rivalries, thwarted efforts to unite this class and each family continued to defend its own territories and honour without the aid of neighbours or relatives. Indeed, according to Roger Lescot, to some extent the *Muroud–aghawat* conflict mirrored that between the Bayan and Sheikhan tribes: the *Muroud* being represented in much greater numbers among the Sheikhan than the Bayan tribes.[87]

By 1939 the influence of the *Muroud* had spread east to within three kilometres of Azaz where French intelligence services were based. The French amassed its forces and using tanks and the air force struck against *Muroud* strongholds in the northern border areas, destroying villages and sending adherents, their families and other local residents fleeing across the border into Turkey. Some returned only after the French issued a general pardon to the civilians after several months. Others returned only after the withdrawal of the French forces.[88] Following this, the power and presence of the *Muroud* in the Kurd Dagh declined until the withdrawal of the French in 1946 removed their primary purpose. Sheikh Ibrahim Khalil and other supporters attempted to revive the organisation, beginning with a number of raids across the border in 1940. The Turkish authorities removed the Sheikh to the Turkish interior and provided him with agricultural land. Nothing was heard of him after that, but the *Muroud* in the Kurd Dagh remained loyal to him until his death in 1952.[89]

Khalil Rashid Ibrahim, son of Rashid Ibo, claimed that despite their religious orientation and the direction of their struggle against the French, the *Muroud* did have an implicit Kurdish nationalist aim. He claimed that in a meeting of the *Muroud*, Ibrahim Khalil announced that if the Kurd Dagh fell under the power of the *Muroud* then the group would ask for autonomy akin to that granted to Iskanderoun/Hatay province. The French response to this was that it would be considered, provided that all the leaders of the Kurd Dagh were in agreement.[90] This meeting prompted the Sheikh to meet with the Kurdish leadership in the region. But no agreement between the *aghawat* and the *Muroud* was reached and, consequently, no autonomy was granted in the area. It is unclear whether this bid for autonomy was actually informed by nationalist tendencies or an interest in securing power in the regions. Indeed, it appears that no efforts were made by the leaders of the *Muroud* to contact nationalist leaders among the Kurds in Syria, suggesting that the latter explanation is more feasible.

Clearly, in this case, the immediate interests of the local *aghawat* and the disagreement between them and the *Muroud* outweighed any nationalist current that might have existed in the Kurd Dagh. In comparison with the Kurdish–Christian movement in the Jazira (a struggle for autonomy in which interests were located largely in preserving existing power bases and controlling local territory), the motivations underpinning the *Muroud* movement were to change the status quo. In relation to local peasant–*aghawat* relations, they sought to expose and break relations of domination. In the wider Syrian sphere, they joined forces with the Syrian nationalist and the independence movement of Ibrahim Hananu in an attempt to remove French influence in the region. The motivation of this group was that of liberation from oppression with the oppressors defined as the ruling classes and the colonial powers. In contrast, Kurdish nationalism at this point was for the most part dominated by the intellectual elite and landed aristocracy.

The two movements described above illustrate the disparities in interests between the ruling classes and the peasantry among the Kurds and between the Kurdish areas in Syria. In the absence of a centralised threat to the Kurdish identity and territories in Syria, these immediate local interests were played out through relations with the French authorities. Kurdish nationalism remained predominantly the domain of the Kurdish intellectuals and, until the 1950s, found its expression not in political but in cultural organisation.

The Syrian Communist Party

Given the limited access to education in the Kurdish areas and the proliferation of illiteracy at that time, it is probable that the Kurdish cultural renaissance initiated by the Kurdish intellectuals failed to reach the majority of the population.[91] The practical effect of the *Muroud* on relations between the *aghawat* and the peasantry in the Kurd Dagh had been limited and the former remained exploitative and oppressive. The *aghawat* took large percentages of crops, commanded villages, and dominated any politics that took place among the population.

Although the socio-economic conditions in the Kurdish regions during the 1920s and 1930s gave rise to a greater awareness among the peasants of their economic circumstances and their relation to their feudal masters, the issue of exploitation had not been addressed by the Kurdish nationalist movement and would not be until the establishment of the Kurdish political parties in the late 1950s. The leadership of Xoybûn and the Kurdish–Christian autonomous movement were not prepared to champion peasants' rights. Nor were intellectuals prepared to champion their rights within Xoybûn because of their desire to incorporate and unite both the modern and traditional leaderships within the Kurdish communities. Consequently, the Kurdish intellectuals with modern reformist and Westernising ideals were not able to confront the *aghawat* or tribal leaders on the subject of usurpation and exploitation. It has already been noted that the composition and character of Xoybûn confirmed existing and traditional socio-economic relations. Xoybûn's committee members originated from the Karput–Bitlis–Botan triangle and, consequently, its activities and membership were concentrated in the east of Syria, particularly in the Jazira area where the majority of exiles from Turkey were settled. The Kurdish–Christian movement also defended the interests of the traditional Kurdish leaders and landowners in the Jazira.

At the same time, Kurdish nationalism was central to this movement and it promoted the Kurdish identity of the region and connected it with certain rights of self-determination. While the *Muroud* did champion peasants' rights, its focus on freedom from exploitation meant that it became absorbed into the Syrian independence movement against the French and its influence waned with the withdrawal of the French forces in 1946. Kurdish nationalism was not a driving force behind this organisation and it did little to spread Kurdish nationalism among the peasantry.

The withdrawal of the French in 1946 and the introduction of mechanised agriculture brought considerable socio-economic upheaval to the Kurdish regions. Syria entered into a period of transition in which various social, religious and political groups wrestled for power.[92] New social classes emerged which were linked to the Syrian state system. At the same time the traditional elite and notables lost much of their power base as colonial interests and French patronage were removed. Developments in agriculture and the introduction of mechanised farming added to the marginalisation and unemployment of large numbers of farm labourers.

On the Kurdish national front, several significant developments had occurred in the Kurdish areas of Iraq and Iran. In the early 1940s Mulla Mustafa Barzani led an uprising against Baghdad. After its failure he retreated to Iran where he and his soldiers played an integral part in the formation, organisation and defence of the Mahabad Republic, founded in January 1946. The Kurdistan Democratic Party was founded in Iran in 1945 and in Iraq in 1946. The symbolic importance of these developments to the Kurdish nationalist movement in Syria cannot be overstated. Both Barzani's rebellion, however, and the life of the Republic were short lived. After Barzani's flight to the Soviet Union and the assassination of Qazi Muhammad in 1947, Kurdish political activists in Syria held little hope or enthusiasm for fresh political endeavours. The Kurdish political movement had lost its momentum and the French withdrawal had robbed the Bedirkhans of financial support for their cultural endeavours. Consequently, a vacuum in political and nationalist leadership among the Kurds developed at the same time as a large number of disaffected workers became more politicised.

So it was that towards the end of the 1940's many Kurds turned to the Syrian Communist Party (SCP) as their political outlet. The Communist Party, which was formed in 1927, was led by a Kurd, Khalid Bakdash. The party became particularly popular in the Kurd Dagh where socio-economic change towards capitalist ownership had already sparked tensions and conflicts between the peasantry and the *aghawat*. The Communist Party's doctrine of equality, peasants' rights and the redistribution of wealth found a welcome audience among the peasantry, Kurdish reformists and intellectuals.[93] The support that the Soviet Union gave to Mulla Mustafa Barzani after his time in exile there may also have been a factor influencing the Kurdish attraction to the Communist Party.

The Syrian Communist Party attracted Kurdish personalities such as Cigerxwin,[94] Muhammad Fakhri, Rashid Hamo and Shawkat Na'san. The poet Cigerxwin from the Jazira was largely responsible for recruiting Kurds from the Jazira to the party in 1950 and, through his contacts with the secret Kurdish Cultural Association in the Kurd Dagh,[95] he promoted the party amongst the Kurds of this region also. In 1952 Rashid Hamo and Shawkat Na'san joined the Party and established the first communist organisation in Efrîn. The influence of the party spread quickly among the poor peasantry in the region and, in general, it gained more support in the Kurd Dagh than in either Kobanî or the Jazira. The party attracted supporters and members from different sectors of Kurdish society, including the Xocê Xilalka, the Imam of Xilalka village mosque, who, during his ten years as village Imam, was also a member of the Communist Party. In 1953 the party established a peasants' union in the region to defend their rights.[96]

From all accounts, it appears that, for many Kurds, their incentives for joining the party were based on Kurdish national interests and a leftist leaning rather than on class interests or a belief in the communist utopia. But, to a large degree, these interests coincided. The Kurds watched socialist liberation movements with interest and, like so many other leftist and liberation movements of this time, they adopted Marxist–Leninist ideologies and communist party organisation as a vehicle for achieving emancipation, equality and justice for the Kurdish people. Indeed, it was presumed that within the ranks of the Communist Party the Kurds could realise national rights that were otherwise unobtainable.[97] The fact that the leader of the party himself, Khalid Bakdash, was a Kurd gave substance to these beliefs and communist and socialist ideology became the general ideology of the Kurdish resistance politics of this era. The success of the Communist Party among the Kurds of the Kurd Dagh is also explained by the relatively more developed economy of the Efrîn region, the absence of tribal influence in the region and the established class of landowners. Also, the class character of the earlier *Muroud* movement meant that peasants and the lower classes were, to some extent, already politicised or at least already had some experience of political organisation.

The basic communist premise that essentialism and nationalism could be avoided naturally meant that the Kurdish presence in the party and the characterisation of this party as a 'Kurdish party' sat uncomfortably with its internationalist ideology and also threatened its popularity among Arabs in Syria. As a result, the party adopted an official position against the recognition of Kurdish national rights in Syria. In the second half of the 1950s a significant number of Kurds left the ranks of the Communist Party when they found the party to be reluctant to support this cause or to use the Kurdish language in their publications which were written in the Jazira in both Arabic and Armenian.[98]

The party revealed an anti-Kurdish nationalist trend when nationalist members of the party such as Cigerxwin, Muhammad Fakhri and Rashid Hamo petitioned the party to print party publications in the Kurdish language so that it could be better understood by local inhabitants. Instead the party began to restrict Kurdish cultural publications such as the 'Denge Jotkar', supervised by Cigerxwin, and 'Alif Baa', which was a Kurdish language book by Osman Sabri. These publications were regarded as examples of a 'bourgeois Kurdish nationalist culture' in the ranks of the party.[99] According to Kurdish sources, Communist Party representatives in the Jazira area used the excuse that reading and writing in Kurdish was limited and that suitable typewriters were not available.[100] Fakhri and Cigerxwin contributed funds for the project and began writing in Kurdish for the party. Kurdish sources, however, claim that the leadership of the Jazira branch made no effort to pass their request to the central leadership. Differences grew from this point causing Fakhri and Cigerxwin to resign. They were followed by many others in the Jazira.[101] Simultaneously, in the Kurd Dagh, Rashid Hamo's attempts were met with the rapid convening of a party trial. He was accused of publishing and disseminating bourgeois nationalist ideas and of assuming the role of representative of the Kurdish people within the party. It was suggested to him that the Kurds were incapable of being communist. The trial concluded that Rashid Hamo should immediately cease all party activities and the decision was published in the party paper, *al-Nour*. Many other Kurds resigned from the party in protest about the charges against Rashid Hamo and about what was considered to be a chauvinist trend within the party.[102] Following Hamo's expulsion from the party, its presence in the Kurd Dagh steadily declined, leaving, once again, a political vacuum in the region.

While the Syrian Kurdish love affair with the Communist Party was relatively short lived, it had a lasting effect on the Kurds and on their political movement in Syria. First, the Communist Party provided many Kurdish nationalists with the political experience necessary for continuing the nationalist movement within the framework of a political party, and it has had an enduring impact upon the structure and organisation of Kurdish party politics in Syria. Second, it brought together Kurds from both the Kurd Dagh and the Jazira. Third, the Communist Party actually contributed to learning and education in the Kurd Dagh region by sending hundreds of students to Socialist countries on scholarships. Fourth, a significant sector of the Kurdish political parties maintained a commitment to socialism, communism and Marxism–Leninism. Like other nationalist and liberation movements across the world at this time, the rhetoric of equality and liberation of the oppressed provided the Kurds with a framework for the expression of their political demands and interests.

Experience within the Communist Party brought Kurdish nationalists from the Kurd Dagh and the Jazira together into one organisation in which they appeared to have cooperated in attempting to secure Kurdish rights within the framework of the party. Until this point in the history of Kurdish nationalist organisation in Syria, it seems that these areas remained largely independent of each other in their nationalist activities and endeavours, despite some attempts to bridge them.[103] In the years following the Kurdish withdrawal from the Communist Party, attempts were made to form new organisations and political parties, such as the class-based *Azadî* (Freedom), established in the spring of 1958 by Cegerxwin, Fakhri and others from the Jazira who had left the Communist Party.[104] *Azadî*, however, was an organisation of the Jazira region, and it was only with the establishment of *Partîya Dêmokrat a Kurd li Sûriyê* in 1957 that the political and nationalist leadership of all areas of Syria and all Kurdish communities came together within one organisation.

Meanwhile, in the state and regional arenas, Arab nationalism was growing stronger and stronger. The removal of the military dictatorship of Adib al-Shishakli in 1954, the restoration of civilian government followed by democratic Syrian parliamentary elections saw the Syrian leftist movement gain unprecedented parliamentary power. The Arab Ba'th Party won 22 seats,[105] and Khalid Bakdash won a seat for the Syrian Communist Party for the first time in the history of the party. The rise of the left in Syrian national politics caused anxiety among the ruling circles in Iraq, Turkey and Iran and increased pressure on Syria to commit to regional Arabist alliances.

In the face of the growing strength and popularity of Arab nationalism and its incorporation into state policy there was an obvious need for a party representative of Kurdish interests in Syria. In 1956, this led a number of Kurdish activists to come together in support of a project to establish a Kurdish political party in Syria. A year later, on 14 June 1957, the foundation of the first Syrian Kurdish political party was announced.

Towards a Syrian Kurdish Political Organisation

This chapter focused on the four main Kurdish political organisations of the period: Xoybûn, the Kurdish–Christian autonomist movement of 1937, the *Muroud* and the Syrian Communist Party. It has described their purposes, the key actors and interests that drove them and has looked at their contribution to the development of Kurdish nationalist organisation in Syria. Xoybûn was explicitly nationalist and was a military organisation, but it had a limited following and represented the Kurdish elite and bourgeoisie.

While also nationalist in essence, the Kurdish–Christian movement too was motivated by tribal interests and the desire to protect power and privileges from changes to the political organisation of the Syrian state, in particular, the centralisation of government. The *Muroud* represented an altogether different sector of society and had more interest in challenging the status quo than maintaining it. It reflected mounting tensions between the peasants and the *aghawat* but became connected to the Syrian nationalist and anti-colonial movement rather than to Kurdish nationalism. Finally, the Communist Party was the first political party to attract Kurdish representation from all Kurdish areas in Syria. The motivations for joining the party were both Kurdish nationalism and the quest for social equality. It was believed that a solution to the Kurdish question could be found within this party and that exploitative socio-economic relations in Kurdish society should be challenged. In an increasingly hostile Arabist state, interest in obtaining national rights outweighed the more general quest for social equality, and faith in the party's ability to deliver these rights turned out to be unfounded. The Kurds were left still seeking political representation that could incorporate their nationalist interests.

The political organisations that preceded the establishment of *Partîya Dêmokrat a Kurd li Sûriyê* were diverse in character and in the motivation that drove the actors involved. All but the Communist Party displayed a tendency towards local organisation and, even this party's particular strength in the Kurd Dagh reflected local socio-economic conditions. This localisation of Kurdish politics in Syria came at a time when Kurdish nationalism had been gaining pace and revolts had been attracting wider participation. This apparent retreat from nationalist organisation can be put down to a number of factors. In the first place, the Kurdish nationalist movement had received a number of heavy blows such as the brutal suppression of the Sheikh Said rebellion and the Ararat revolt. Armed resistance and rebellion as a strategy for achieving Kurdish goals was rejected and existing organisations were left defeated and abandoned. No doubt this had a negative effect on participation in Kurdish nationalist organisation. Moreover, on the question of the creation of the Syrian state, Kurdish society was still defined primarily by relations to the local community and leadership was predominantly either tribal and/or connected to the Ottoman state. While Kurdish nationalism had spread considerably, the idea of the Kurdish state was not sufficient to rouse and unite the Kurdish population, particularly the tribes, into one political organisation, in the absence of any real prospect of achieving that state and securing their interests within it. A further cause was the concentration of exiles, nationalists and political activists in the Jazira and the coincidence of nationalist goals with the interests of exiled tribal leaders meant that this area witnessed more nationalist organisation than either the Kurd Dagh or Kobanî. Organisation occurred among the exiles themselves who rallied against the Turkish state, due in part to personal grievances. Little attempt was made to involve the Kurds of other areas within Syria. Things were made worse by the French divide-and-rule policy which worked to foment divisions between the Kurdish areas. The French did not deal with the Kurds as a single group but as separate regions, applying different policies to different areas. This worked to exacerbate socio-economic and developmental differences between the regions. Finally, physical differences between the Kurdish areas failed to further unite nationalist organisations, while unequal levels of socio-economic development meant that differences in political and social interests arose, adding to existing disparities.

Attempts to unite the Kurds of Syria around a common aim of securing the Kurds' rights to express their identity, practice their culture and represent themselves politically within the Syrian state were only made after Syria became independent in 1946. At this point the interests of the Kurds in Syria as a group began to be threatened by the rise of both Arab nationalism and the central Syrian government. The attraction of the Kurds to the Syrian Communist Party and their attempt to find political representation within it mark a significant change in the way many Kurds understood their position in Syria and in Kurdistan. A shift had begun: away from organising as pan-Kurdish nationalists, while identifying with local interests, and towards conceptualising the Kurds in Syria as an independent polity in need of its own political representation. The first Syrian Kurdish political party was formed in 1957 and from this point forward, political parties would become the main form of political organisation for the Kurds in Syria.

CHAPTER 3

KURDISH POLITICAL
PARTIES, 1957–2011

On the eve of the Syrian uprising there were more than 15 established Kurdish political parties in Syria. Party divisions increased during the 1990s, and the following decade saw the establishment of more new parties in Syria than in any other since the establishment of the first Kurdish party in 1957. Added to this, in the latter part of the 'noughties', a number of other parties were formed, most of which were crushed by the Syrian authorities or failed due to internal organisational problems. The Kurdish party movement became a source of confusion for most onlookers since many parties had the same names and were only distinguishable by their leader.

Having examined the formation of a specifically Syrian Kurdish polity, this chapter looks in more detail at the first Syrian Kurdish political party in Syria and seeks to clarify and explain the identities and predicament of the various political parties that have grown from it, exploring especially the causes of factionalism within the party movement. Moving on historically from the previous chapter, the first section of this one traces the historical development of the Kurdish political party movement in Syria. It looks at the first political party formed in 1957, its leadership, the early divisions within the party and the creation and definition of the political spectrum as it applies to Kurdish politics in Syria. It would not make very interesting or enlightening reading to provide an historical account of every split of a political party from 1957 until 2011, of which there have been at least 11.[1] So the historical narrative of the first section is discontinued in favour of examining the divisions of the parties through their causes. This second section of this chapter looks in turn at the ideology and political programmes, the personalities and the external political dynamics, to see how these three factors have caused disunity within the ranks of the parties. Following this, a brief look at attempts to unite the political movement in the period before the start of the Syrian uprising reveals not a simplification of the political movement but further complication.

Amid the sea of political parties it is possible to distinguish five that have been said to be stronger and command more and wider support than the others. Those parties are: *Partîya Dêmokrat a Kurdî li Sûriyê (el-Partî)*, of Dr Abdul Hakim Bashar, *Partîya Yekîtî ya Dêmokrat a Kurd li Sûriyê*, of Sheikh Ali, (formerly Ismail Omar),[2] *Partîya Yekîtî ya Kurd li Sûriyê*, currently led by Ismail Hemi, *Partîya Azadî ya Kurd li Suryê*, led by Mustafa Juma'a[3] and *Partîya Dêmokrat a Pêşverû a Kurdî li Sûriyê* of Abdul Hamid Darwish. These parties feature more in this chapter than the others, although reference to other parties and their leaders is made where appropriate. Through this examination, the political parties themselves and their driving forces will, it is hoped, become less opaque and inaccessible to the outsider, and it will become possible to draw some conclusions, however tentative, about the real nature of Kurdish politics in Syria and the substance of the political parties.

The Establishment and Division of the First Kurdish Party

The Kurdish Syrian polity found its first organised political outlet with the formation of *Partîya Dêmokrat a Kurd li Sûriyê* in 1957. For all intents and purposes *Partîya Dêmokrat a Kurd li Sûriyê* is considered to be the original Kurdish political party in Syria and it is this to which nearly all of today's political parties trace their origins.[4] As the previous chapter demonstrated, Kurdish nationalism in Syria had been developed primarily by exiled Kurdish intellectuals. It was seen how Syria had become a seat of dissemination of Kurdish nationalism and attempts to form a united political movement to resist Turkey's oppression of the Kurds. The failure of the Ararat Revolt and the innate divisions within Xoybûn, between the traditional and modern leadership, resulted in an impasse in the Kurdish movement in both Syria and Iraq until after the withdrawal of the Mandate authorities. As the French withdrew, leaving in their wake a centralised Arab government and no guarantees for the protection of the minority groups that they had previously supported, the Kurds in Syria were left cut off from the main body of Kurdistan and without any political representation in an increasingly Arab nationalist and unstable Syrian state. As Arab nationalism developed into a popular movement, the Kurdish identity came increasingly under threat and the need for political representation and organisation ever more pressing.

The separation between the Kurdish areas of Turkey, Iraq and Syria and the realities of the border also encouraged the Kurds of Syria to organise within the boundaries of the Syrian state. In Iran and Iraq Kurdish political parties defined by the sovereign state were formed in 1945 and 1946 respectively.[5] While familial and tribal connections across the border persisted and national identity continued to be defined by the whole area and people of Kurdistan, attempts to organise the Kurds internationally were abandoned. The processes of state formation and socio-economic and political modernisation had changed the way in which Kurds understood their position within the international state system.

In Syria, under the French mandate and following the French withdrawal, Kurdish intellectuals continued their efforts to develop and revive Kurdish national consciousness, culture and identity. Kurds based in *Hayy al-Akrad* (the Kurdish quarter) in Damascus[6] had a considerable impact on Kurdish national consciousness in this period, publishing journals and opening a number of clubs and societies, such as *Nadi Kurdistan* (the Kurdistan Club) which sought to spread the Kurdish national spirit amongst the Kurdish youth,[7] and *Nadi Salah al-Din* which aimed at raising the status of Kurds in the Middle East region.[8] It was Osman Sabri, resident in Damascus, who first proposed the establishment of a Syrian Kurdish political party.

In the mid-1950s, Osman Sabri, Abdul Hamid Darwish (then a student in Damascus), his cousin Majid Haj Darwish and uncle Muhammad Salih Haj Darwish and their friend Khadir Farhan 'Issa, formed a literary organisation called *Jam'aiyah Ihiya' al-Thaqafah al-Kurdiyah*[9] which aimed at spreading learning and writing in Kurdish.[10] The organisation published a journal called *Derda Ma* (Our Suffering). According to Abdul Hamid Darwish, the journal provoked criticism from the Syrian Communist Party, which called for the withdrawal of Kurdish party members, Majid Darwish and Khadir Farhan from the organisation. The issue led to the collapse of the organisation and in the summer of 1956 Osman Sabri put the idea of establishing a Kurdish political party to Abdul Hamid Darwish. Sabri began to draft a political programme in the Kurdish language, in consultation with Jalal Talabani, who was living in Damascus in exile from Iraq, and with Dr Nur al-Din Zaza.[11] Armed with a draft of the party programme, Sabri and Darwish set about forming a central committee which would also include leftist Kurds resident in the Kurdish regions. The draft was shown to Hamza Nouiran[12] who was invited to join Sabri and Darwish in the leadership of the party on condition that he leave the Communist Party, which he duly did. Sabri, who was well acquainted with Rashid Hamo, contacted him about the proposal and Hamo proposed translating the programme into Arabic. Hamo himself approached Muhammad Ali Khoja, Khalil Muhammad and Shawkat Hanan, all from the Kurd Dagh, encouraging them to join the organisation's leadership. Sheikh Muhammad 'Issa Mulla Mahmoud also joined the leadership, according to his grandson, at the same time as Hamza Nouiran.[13] Though there is some disagreement about his involvement in the party, his grandson, Jamal Sheikh Baqi, has said that the involvement of Sheikh Muhammad 'Issa was kept secret at this time due to the fact that the religious community opposed the nationalist movement.[14] Against this, Muhammad Mulla Ahmed, who conducted interviews with Osman Sabri, Abdul Hamid Darwish, Rashid Hamo and Shawkat Hanan, recalled that each of them stated that they did not remember the sheikh being a member of the central committee or being one of the founders of the party.[15] By all accounts, however, it is clear that he played a central role in the leadership.

On 14 June 1957 these Kurdish intellectuals and political activists came together once again in the first Party Congress.[16] On this date they formed a united Kurdish political party that sought to represent the interests of all Kurds in Syria and which would place them on a par with the Kurds in Iraqi Kurdistan and Iran. Osman Sabri was the secretary of the party and in 1958 Dr Nur al-Din Zaza became the party's first president. The leadership further expanded when two other Kurdish political organisations in the Jazira joined with the party. The first of these was *Jam'aiya Wahidat al-Shabab al-Dimoqratiyin al-Akrad* (the Organisation of United Democratic Kurdish Youth). It had been founded in 1952 in Qamishli by Muhammad Mulla Ahmed, Abd al-Aziz Ali Abdu, Sami Mulla Ahmad Nami, and Darwish Mulla Sulaiman.[17] With their inclusion within the party the support base among the Kurds of the Jazira grew considerably. The second party that joined was *Azadî* (Freedom) which had been established in the spring of 1958 by Cigerxwin, Muhammad Fakhri and others who had left the Syrian Communist Party. It is said that the party wanted a leading position in *Partîya Dêmokrat a Kurd li Sûriyê*, but that the leadership refused, saying that each person should join individually. The issue created a division within *Azadî* and one group, including Cigerxwin and Fakhri, joined *Partîya Dêmokrat a Kurd li Sûriyê* in the summer of 1958. Cigerxwin became a member of the Central Committee and Fakhri a member of the Regional Committee. The other group maintained the former *Azadî* party, but it dissolved when it became clear that they could not compete with *Partîya Dêmokrat a Kurd li Sûriyê*.[18]

The programme of the original party is an area of contention among those who were involved and those who have inherited knowledge and information about the party through their own party ranks or family members. According to Muhammad Mulla Ahmed[19] all the members of the leadership agreed to Sabri's original political programme, which included in it the slogan 'freedom and unity for Kurdistan'.[20] In contrast, Abdul Hamid Darwish recounts that the phrase in question was not included in the programme until 1959 and was then removed from the programme in 1963.[21] Similarly, while most contend that the original name of the party was *Partîya Dêmokrat a Kurdistan a Sûriyê*, or the Kurdistan Democratic Party of Syria and that it was changed to *Partîya Dêmokrat a Kurd li Sûriyê* in the following years, Jamal Sheikh Baqi, leader of *Partîya Dêmokrat a Kurdî ya Sûrî (el-Sûrî)*, insisted that the word '*Kurdistan*' was included in the name of the party when Zaza became its president in 1958 in order to attract people to the party, and that originally it read '*Kurd*' or Kurdish, without mentioning 'Kurdistan'.[22] Another account tells us that the word Kurdistan was only included at the beginning of 1960 at the insistence of Jalal Talabani[23] and that Osman Sabri opposed its inclusion in the name. Supporting this, Muhammad Rashid recounts that Sabri opposed its inclusion because it would be impossible to defend such a position against the state.[24] Whatever the truth about the exact language used in the party slogan and name, it is clear that it was an important point of tension between the leaders of the party and that it was instrumental in causing the first division within party ranks in 1965 which is discussed in the following section.

While the initiative to establish the party came from Kurdish intellectuals resident in *Hayy al-Akrad* in Damascus, where many of those who had been involved in Xoybûn lived,[25] the central committee formed between 1956 and 1958 included Kurds from all Kurdish regions in Syria. The leadership of the party brought together liberal religious leaders such as Muhammad 'Issa Mulla Mahmoud, former members and sympathisers of Xoybûn such as Nur al-Din Zaza and Osman Sabri, former members of the Communist Party such as Rashid Hamo, intellectuals, poets and writers, such as Qedrîcan and Cegirxwen; students, teachers and labourers, all committed to Kurdish nationalism and political action. The majority of the leadership were leftist in their politics and, if not committed to ideologies such as Marxism, did not object to this inclination.[26]

In the first two years the party concentrated its efforts on expanding the support base of the party and uniting the political leadership in Syria. Under pressure from the KDP in Iraq to form a party representative of all sectors of society, including the traditional Kurdish leadership in Syria, the party established connections with the more conservative elements of Kurdish society. The leadership attempted to draw the *aghawat* and tribal leadership (known as *beys* or *begs*) into the party organisation. In September 1958, the first meeting with the traditional Kurdish leadership was held in Aleppo, where it was agreed that Hasan Hajo Agha would become an honorary president of the party and a new joint committee representing both the party leadership and the beys would be formed.[27] In another meeting between members of the party leadership and Qadri Beg Jamil Pasha, Akram Beg Jamil Pasha, Jamil Hajo and Arif Abbas (all Kurdish tribal leaders), points of the programme were discussed and three main directives were agreed upon i) the freedom and unity of Kurdistan, ii) opposition to colonialism and iii) the struggle for democracy in Syria.

While some members of the party leadership courted the tribal leadership[28] and sought to pass control of the organisation to them, the party in general continued its progressive and leftist tendencies which often conflicted with tribal interests. With the recruitment of the Kurdish *agahwat* and beys, the party incorporated contradictory political ideologies and interests. Kurdish nationalism became the unifying ideology and rhetoric of the party as it worked towards gaining rights for the Kurdish people. Through its nationalist message, in its early years the party attracted more than 30,000 members and thousands more supporters from across the Kurdish regions of Syria and from all sectors of society. The Kurdish nobility began to compete to gain connections with and to support the party as a route to winning honour within the local Kurdish communities. But with the spread of the party organisation and its popularity, animosity towards the party and the Kurds also grew. The Syrian Communist Party in particular launched attacks against the party as its power base amongst the Syrian Kurds was eroded.[29] The party came under pressure from other political parties in Syria and from the government of the United Arab Republic, formed in 1958. As the need for representation and organised opposition to the arabist policies of the government rose, so pressure on the leadership to define their position in relation to the state intensified and the unity of the Kurdish political leadership was beginning to be tested.

The development of differences within the leadership

The contradictory mix of conservative traditional leaders with reformist intellectuals within the leadership after 1958 soon developed into competition for control over the party organisation with the beys placing individuals within the ranks of the party to represent their interests and attempting to by-pass the central committee.[30] The party branch in Dêrîk was a case in point. Here problems between the beys and the regional and central committees developed to the point that the central committee took a decision to close the branch on 14 July 1960 and establish a new leadership committee in the area excluding representatives of the beys.[31] It appears that the tribal leadership saw in the organisation a means of promoting and securing their own interests in the Kurdish regions and of gaining popularity and control. It was not long, however, before the party's leadership and supporters became the targets of an official state drive to eradicate Kurdish political organisation in Syria and to gain control over the Kurdish population and regions. In 1958 and 1959 several members of the leadership were arrested and interrogated, including Hamza Nouiran, Rashid Hamo, Shawkat Hanan and Osman Sabri. The pressure on the organisation led some of the leadership to seek refuge in Iraqi Kurdistan.[32] In 1959 the government of the UAR announced that it intended to hold elections in Syria. A meeting of the Kurdish leadership revealed a difference of opinion between the tribal leaders and the political leadership of the party. The beys thought it necessary to participate in the elections and to develop relations with the authorities, whereas other members of the leadership saw no benefit from participation as long as the government was unable to meet the party's demands. The party boycotted the elections and by doing so exacerbated tensions between the party leadership and the beys. It also made their opposition to the government public.[33]

Further tensions within the party surfaced in the summer of 1960 when all political parties were banned and the Kurdish party and the Kurdish people in general came under increased pressure from the government. General Abd al-Hamid Saraj launched the 'Great Campaign' against the Kurds which began on 12 August 1960 and in which more than 5,000 members and supporters of the party were arrested, including the majority of the party leadership. Of those arrested, 32, including Osman Sabri, Nur al-Din Zaza and Rashid Hamo from the central committee, Muhammad Neyo, Majid Hajo and Muhammad Mulla Ahmed and other members of the leadership, were imprisoned in Mezze military prison in Damascus, facing charges of separatism, racial incitement and membership of an illegal political party.[34] It is reported that while awaiting trial Dr Zaza urged the other prisoners not to mention that the party sought unity and freedom for Kurdistan, stating that Kurdistan was but a 'dream' and the Kurds a minority in Syria rather than a nation.[35] Ahmed claims that Osman Sabri refused on the grounds that this was among the essential aims of the party, that the Kurdish nation was their purpose and its members should stand by and fight for what they had agreed on. This disagreement was the basis of the two blocs that formed within the party leadership over the few months that the prisoners awaited trial and attempted to reach an agreement on their statements. The outcome was that the group of Sabri decided not to make a statement and remain true to the party programme, and that Zaza suggested forming a new central committee from among the prisoners. His suggestion, however, included appointing non-party personalities to the committee which was unacceptable to Osman Sabri. Similar disagreements followed and the situation ended without a resolution of the differences between Sabri and Zaza. Instead, the party suffered from divisions within its central committee, between these two[36] and also between party members and non-party people among those arrested. These differences continued to affect the party and developed into ideological differences following the eventual release of the leadership from prison.

With the arrest of the party leadership Kurdish tribal leaders were quick to distance themselves from the party and deny any connection to it. The party organisations in the Kurd Dagh and Aleppo had been subject to a devastating wave of arrests, 120 members and supporters in the first day, as a consequence of confessions and information extracted by torture. In the

Jazira the organisation had not been discovered because the leadership had been forewarned about the impending crackdown and members had taken measures to avoid arrest. Over the following 18 months in which the leadership were detained, Abdul Hamid Darwish kept the party going. He is said to have suggested that Sheikh Muhammad 'Issa Mulla Mahmoud become temporary secretary of the party and together they agreed to add a further two provisional members to the central committee. They were Sa'idallah Ibo and Mulla Abd al-Farid Abdallah. They remained within the leadership until February 1962 after the detainees had been released and the first party conference was convened in which a new committee was elected. Dr Zaza left the party in 1962,[37] but the basic fault lines that had developed between the groups of Zaza and Sabri continued to affect the party, and in 1965 it divided into two groupings based on the same factions that had formed in prison.

This first division of the party stemmed not only from these personal and ideological differences but was influenced heavily by events in Iraqi Kurdistan. The Syrian Kurdish party followed the lead of the KDP Iraq of Mustafa Barzani, despite the fact that its political agenda was defined by the Syrian state. The party worked to support Barzani after his return from exile in the Soviet Union in 1958. Kurds from among the leadership of the party in Iraqi Kurdistan, Muhammad Ali Khoja and Cigerxwin, worked in the Kurdistan Radio in Baghdad. After the Kurdish revolt against Abd al-Karim Qassim[38] began in 1961, Khoja became responsible for groups of peshmerga. *Partîya Dêmokrat a Kurd li Sûriyê* acted as a communications channel for Iraqi Kurdistan, sending news of the revolution of 1961 to the international community and facilitating communications with the area, recruiting Syrian Kurds to join the revolution and raising funds.[39] Differences within the party leadership between the left and right wing, however, continued to affect the party and when the KDP Iraq split between the conservative Barzani faction and the Marxist Talabani faction in 1964, the Syrian party soon followed suit. With this division a political spectrum began to form within the Kurdish party movement in Syria.

Within the KDP of Iraq, internal ideological differences between Mulla Mustafa Barzani and Jalal Talabani in 1964 had led Ibrahim Ahmed and Talabani to be expelled from the party, and to form the KDP-Politburo (later becoming the PUK). Shadowing this division within the KDP, the Syrian party formally divided in 1965; but the division between left and right was not straightforward. *Partîya Dêmokrat a Kurd li Sûriyê (Çep)*[40] of Osman Sabri and Mulla Muhammad Neyo, reflected the opinion of the left and viewed the Kurds as a second nation in Syria, but was closer to the conservative Barzani.[41] On the right, *Partîya Dêmokrat a Kurd li Sûriyê (Rast)*[42] led by Abdul Hamid Darwish[43] considered the Kurds a minority in Syria. Darwish's party continues to have good relations with the PUK[44] and until after the start of the Syrian uprising, advocated a minimalist political agenda. Abdul Hamid Darwish, although inclined towards Marxism in his youth is certainly not a leftist and is generally considered to represent the far right in Syrian Kurdish politics. Nevertheless, Darwish joined the Marxist camp of Talabani who had been his schoolmate[45] and although Darwish may not have shared the same ideological conviction as Jalal Talabani, relations between the two parties were close and involved mutual support. Indeed, the PUK supported Darwish's statements about the Kurds of Syria being a minority group in Syria and dismissed them as a less important relative of the Kurds in Iraq. This helped attempts to preserve good relations with the Syrian authorities.[46]

In 1970, Mustafa Barzani himself intervened in Syrian Kurdish politics in order to attempt a reconciliation between the left and the right. The congress was held in Iraqi Kurdistan and was attended by the majority of the leadership of both sides in the dispute. No agreement was reached and, instead, the result was the formation of a third party under the leadership of a Kurdish notable, Daham Miro,[47] which united conservative leaders and remained loyal to Barzani. Thus, the conservative nationalist social strata came to be represented by the political centre, allied to the KDP of Iraq, and which remained committed to Kurdish nationalism and the definition of the Kurds as a national group in Syria. Although it has been subject to at least four internal divisions, this party, *Partîya Dêmokrat a Kurdî li Sûriyê* (*el-Partî*), now led by Dr Abdul Hakim Bashar, remains the stronghold of the conservative nationalists and one of the larger Kurdish parties in Syria.

As a result of these divisions, the left and right in Syrian Kurdish politics came to be defined more by position towards the state than by socio-economic group, although social groupings coincided with positions towards the state to a large degree. The right defined the Kurds as a minority in Syria while the left defined the Kurds as a national group living within their historic homeland and demanded constitutional recognition of the Kurds as a second nation in Syria. It is interesting to note that, for the most part, the conservative group, consisting of notables and religious leaders, and landowners and professionals, considered its interests would be best met by the development of some form of Kurdish autonomy from central government as defined by *el-Partî*. This indicates that the nationalist interests of this group outweighed any interests in preserving the status quo and that social status remains largely a product of local and traditional power and economic relations rather than a development based on relations with the state authorities.

Since 1970 the parties have steadily divided due to both internal and external factors, a process which will become clear in the second half of this chapter. Naturally, ideological and policy disagreements have caused divisions over the years. Prior to the start of the Syrian uprising, however, fundamentals of political aims, ideology and method varied only marginally between parties.[48] The main demands of the parties included i) ending oppression of the Kurds in Syria, ii) securing political and cultural rights for the Kurds and democracy for Syria and iii) the abolition of the state of emergency and any racially motivated laws or projects against the Kurdish people. Yet the character of Syrian politics (illegality, constant surveillance by the security services and a lack of incentive to stay within a party) has allowed subtle differences in method and political agenda to widen into almost unbridgeable fissures within the Kurdish political party movement.

The Causes of Factionalism and the Formation of New Parties

The causes of divisions within Kurdish political parties have been fairly diverse, relating to internal party dynamics, personalities of the leadership and so on, as well as to external factors such as the intrigues of the Syrian security services, involvement of Kurdish parties of other areas of Kurdistan, or changes in international relations. Some explanations of party divisions might involve all the causes mentioned here, while in other cases, it is clear that explanations that allege ideological differences simply hide personal ones. Indeed, in some cases it is unclear exactly why the parties divided when they did. Yet the divisions have all occurred within the context of illegal existence in an authoritarian state, under constant surveillance and intrigue, and subordination to external Kurdish political parties.

As a result of the organisational structure of the political parties – a pyramidal structure based on that of the Communist party with the leadership occupying the pinnacle and secret cells forming the base – all divisions have begun within the leadership of the party and have spread downwards. The secrecy of membership and absence of communication between cells prevents any dissent from within the base affecting the leadership and also prevents democratic resolution of differences and problems within the party. Therefore, the discussion of the causes of divisions within parties concerns the ranks of the leadership such as the President or Secretary-General and the Politburo and the Central Committee rather than the lower sections of the parties.

Policy, method and ideology

As seen in the previous section, the initial split in the Kurdish political movement formed a left and a right wing based on three premises. First, the position of the party towards ideas of Kurdish independence and the definition of the Kurdish political identity in Syria: that is, whether the

Kurds are a minority in Syria or a national group living within their historic land; second, these disagreements over nationalist demands translated into ideological differences between the two parties, split between the leftist-socialist and conservative camps; finally, the closeness of relations with either Barzani's KDP or Jalal Talabani's PUK mirrored, if ambiguously, the distinction between left and right. This latter distinction characterised the initial division in *Partîya Dêmokrat a Kurdî li Sûriyê*. At this stage, however, it did not follow ideological inclinations but personal allegiances. With the further division of the Kurdish political movement, political alliances and support from the Iraqi Kurdish political parties began more closely to reflect ideological leanings, with the left party (*Partîya Çep*) in the 1970s receiving support from the PUK to the extent that it followed the PUK's lead. Yet personal allegiances and enmities continued to be reflected in political alliances.

When *el-Partî* was formed in 1970, it filled the centre position on the political spectrum, representing Barzani supporters and a conservative social strata, typified by the tribal leadership and families that had been connected to Xoybûn, but which sought greater concessions from the state than the right wing did and defined the Kurds as a national group living in their historic land. The positions of the three parties, although varying ideologically and particularly on relations to the state and the degree of adherence to Kurdish nationalism, were all defined by nationalist aims and simple mainstream ideological tendencies that limited their politics to Kurdish issues. In 1973 this changed. One member of the leadership of the left party, Salah Bedr al-Din, convinced the party to adopt Marxism–Leninism as the official party ideology, distinguishing the party from those of the right, left and centre. This moved the Kurdish political movement into a new situation, exposing it to attack and criticism from across the political field once more.[49] The Syrian Communist Party, particularly the Kurds within it, again began to view the Kurdish left as a competitor in the Kurdish regions.[50] Meanwhile, making a connection between the Kurdish political movement and communism, conservative Arab and Islamist groups began to regard the Kurdish left with suspicion. The criticism and condemnation of the ideological move did not stop there. Kurdish nationalists defined the adoption of Marxism–Leninism as a departure from the demands for Kurdish national rights in Syria. The result was a split within the Kurdish movement itself.[51]

The left began to expand its political horizons and adopt positions on international affairs using the rhetoric of liberation and emancipation that started to put it at odds with the centre and right wing and with the Syrian regime. Sheikh Ali[53] attributed the division within *el-Partî* in 1981, (when he and Haval Ahmed, founders of *Partîya Kar a Kurd li Sûriyê*,[54] were in the politburo) to disagreements about policy towards external political forces.

He described Kamal Ahmed, then the leader of *el-Partî*, as unclear about the party position on matters such as anti-democratic policies of Khomeini's Iran which Sheikh Ali and his comrades within the party condemned.[55] They believed that the parties should adopt positions on matters of foreign policy, particularly those relating to the Kurdish issue.

Between 1975 and 1990 the number of parties in the left and centre of the political spectrum grew dramatically while on the right, the party of Abdul Hamid Darwish did not experience its first, and only, division until 1992. The left saw the formation of several parties distinguishing themselves through the adoption of 'socialist', 'workers', 'union' or 'left' in their party names.[56] Other parties retained the same names, the factions distinguishable only by their leaders. Several reasons have been put forward as causes of the greater fragmentation of the left and centre than that of the right. A primary one has been that the official adoption of Marxism–Leninism by the Kurdish political movement caused a number of more religiously minded individuals and groups of cadre within the party to split off due to their association of Marxism with atheism. In addition to this, there has been a general inability to respect the opinions of others within the parties and, as a consequence, differences in ideology or opinion on party policy have led to the formation of hostile blocs within the leadership which eventually split into separate parties. Indeed, the left is more open to ideological distinctions and variations on policy than the right wing, where there is little room for manoeuvre. In a state such as Syria, the right is closer to the state, which is a position that the majority of Kurdish nationalists are keen not to be associated with. The frequent marginalisation of opposition parties within the Syrian state means that they often turn passive, thus provoking the more militant individuals and groups within the parties to seek greater party opposition towards state policies and more activity within Kurdish societies. A final factor is that new parties are developed to renew interest of the youth in Kurdish politics and to attract support from this sector of society. The right is on the whole unattractive to the politicised nationalist Kurdish youth and represents the interests of traditionally orientated families that seek to preserve their interests through seeking a solution to the Kurdish question in Syria while in other ways preserving the status quo.

During the late 1970s and through the 1980s, there was a reorientation of Syrian Kurdish politics towards the Syrian state. The domination of *el-Partî*, its connections to the KDP and what was believed to be subservience to the commands of Mustafa Barzani and Masoud Barzani led many within the higher ranks of the party to seek independence from controls and restrictions imposed by the KDP Iraq. The party's need of external channels of communications and support against Saddam Hussein meant that the KDP avoided antagonising the Syrian authorities or interfering in its internal affairs.[57]

Consequently, while supporting *el-Partî* financially, the KDP did little to support their political demands in Syria. Sheikh Ali formed *Partîya Kar a Kurd li Sûriyê* in 1981 and Sheikh Baqi formed *Partîya Dêmokrat a Kurdî ya Sûrî (el-Sûrî)* in 1975. In 1989 *Partîya Palên Kurdî li Sûriyê*[58] was formed. Each of these parties stressed the need for independence from the Kurdish parties of Iraqi Kurdistan, for the definition of the Kurdish people in Syria as part of the Syrian state and people and for building relations with the Arab opposition. Each party defined its policy in relation to the Syrian state and favoured the development of relations with all democratic Kurdish political organisations rather than dependence on one of them.[59]

'Soft' policy towards the state and the Syrian security services has also been a matter of contention within parties.[60] For Abdul Hamid Darwish, leader of *Partîya Dêmokrat a Pêşverû a Kurdî li Sûriyê*, it is a position that has distinguished his party from the rest and has allowed him certain privileges and protection from the state. Relations with the security services in Hasaka province put him in a position in which he was able to mediate between the Kurdish population or political parties and the state and allowed him to act as unappointed representation for the Kurdish parties towards the state. But for other parties and leaders, relations with the state authorities work against them. For example, in 1978 a new political party was formed calling itself *Partîya Sosyalista Kurdî li Sûriyê*, (the Kurdish Socialist Party in Syria) led by Salih Gido. Gido's alleged relations with the Syrian regime tainted his reputation so that when the party joined with another small party, *Partîya Çep a Kurdî li Sûiryê* of Muhammad Musa, the union did not work to the advantage of *Partîya Çep* and it is suggested that the party became weaker as a result of the union.[61] This was also a factor in the division within the politburo of Abdul Hamid Darwish's *Partîya Peşveru*, when Aziz Daoud, Rashid Hamo and Tahir Safouk split off in 1992.[62] Aziz Daoud was more critical of state policy towards the Kurds than Darwish. Other factors, however, were at work in this division, namely personal differences between Rashid Hamo and Darwish and organisational issues which went back to the 1980s. There was little ideological difference between the politics of the two resulting parties, each retaining the same name until May 2008 when Aziz Daoud changed the name of his party to *Partîya Wekhevî Dêmokrat a Kurdî li Sûriyê* or *Hizb al-Musawah al Dimoqrati al-Kurdi* (the Kurdish Democratic Equality Party in Syria). Indeed, Aziz Daoud was considered the father of *Peşveru* ideology before its division, characterising the party as democratic-liberalist.[63]

Most party divisions have involved only minor policy and ideological differences, if any. The fact that many parties are virtually indistinguishable in policy from the one that they split from, implies that personal differences or external involvement played more important roles in causing the divisions. Adding to the confusion over party identity, each time *el-Partî* divided each side retained the party name. Some changed their name after some years,[64] another merged with other parties and individuals forming *Partîya Yekbûn Kurdî Sûriyê* in 1990. This party, in turn, changed its name in 1993 to *Partîya Yekîtî ya Dêmokrat a Kurdî li Sûriyê* then split in 1998 adding *Partîya Yekîtî ya Kurd li Sûriyê* to the list of parties in Syria. Today there are four parties calling themselves *Partîya Dêmokrat a Kurdî li Sûriyê*, one led by Dr Abdul Hakim Bashar (until 2008 by Nazir Mustafa) and which has representation in all Kurdish areas and has undisputed connections with the KDP in Iraqi Kurdistan; another is led by Nusradin Ibrahim and is said to be small and local; the third was formed in 2007 and was led by Abdul Rahman Aluji and made several unsuccessful attempts to unite with that of Dr Abdul Hakim Bashar. This last party split after the death of Abdul Rahman Aluji on 24 May 2012. The question of leadership caused the party to split in October 2012. Until 2005 there were two parties called *Partîya Çep a Kurdî li Sûriyê* and until May 2008 there were two named *Pêşverû*.[65]

Since the end of the Cold War ideological concerns have not affected the parties so much. Party rhetoric and behaviour has reflected the reorientation of dissent around the issue of human rights and democracy – one of the consequences of the fall of communism. The Kurdish political movement in Syria has witnessed a greater concentration on building relations with other democratic forces inside and outside Syria and a commitment to nationalist liberalism, and gradual democratic reform. The decline in ideological distinctions, however, has not freed the Kurdish political movement from further fragmentation. On the contrary, between 1990 and 2000 seven splits and four party mergers occurred, and between March 2004 and 2010 at least seven attempts to establish new Kurdish political parties were made.[66] There is little information available on these new parties but they seem to represent a significant departure from the norm established within the Kurdish political party movement.

At least one of them (*Harakah Huriyah Kurdistan*, The Kurdistan Freedom Movement) formed after the Qamishli uprising of 2004, employed arms to attempt to address the Kurdish issue in Syria. By the name of this party alone it is clear that its objectives involved the liberation of the whole area of Kurdistan. Due to the militant nature of the organisation, its pan-Kurdish identity and its operation outside the framework established by the political parties that trace their history to *Partîya Dêmokrat a Kurd li Sûriyê*, this new party came under heavy pressure from the regime. In September 2008 many of their leadership were arrested in connection to an attack on a Syrian police station in which two policemen were killed.[67] Another party, *Yekîtîya Azadî ya Qamişlo*,[68] adopted strong language against the Syrian regime, referring to the killing of three Kurds as a 'massacre' by 'state terrorists'. They also spoke of 'dictator Bashar' and dismissed the Ba'th Party as fascist.[69] Such language was not employed in the publications of any of the other political parties, even the more militant ones such as *Yekîtî*. Party rhetoric is generally restricted to referring to the policies of the regime as chauvinistic and racially motivated. While information on these alternative political groups is scarce and some have ceased to operate after being crushed by the government or have disintegrated due to internal organisational difficulties, it appears that they were not closely connected to the main body of Kurdish political parties. Their appearance is associated with the aftermath of the Qamishli uprising of March 2004[70] and reflects the anger and frustration of the Kurdish youth not only with the Syrian government but also with the existing Kurdish political movement.

Personality

As in many Middle Eastern countries, and in Syria itself, the leader occupies a position that commands respect and is something to be coveted and held onto. Kurdish politics in Syria has developed against the background of the notion of the eternal and charismatic leader and the legacy of tribal organisation. The absence of democracy and democratic institutions and processes in Syria has contributed to a culture of reverence of leadership and of hereditary succession. Indeed, the personality of leaders is pivotal to party strength and support. Despite this there is not one Kurdish party in Syria or one charismatic leader comparable to figures, such as Mulla Mustafa or Masoud Barzani, Jalal Talabani or Abdullah Öcalan, capable of commanding the support of the Kurdish population inside and outside their particular regions of influence. The reasons for this are several. During the history of the Kurdish political movement in Syria there has been no indigenous armed struggle through which a leader has established control over an armed resistance, commanded the support of the population and come to embody the idea of resistance and Kurdish national liberation. The existence of such leaders and armed movements in Iraq and Turkey has led Kurds in Syria to lend support and political allegiance to the leaders of these other areas of Kurdistan. This is particularly true in areas where the continuation and extension of tribal relations across the borders into these areas has encouraged those in Syria to follow the political allegiances of relations and traditional leaders across the border. Also, the illegality of the parties has prevented any leader from gaining political capital, prestige and support through party activities or electoral processes. The result is an absence of strong political leadership among the Syrian Kurds.

In Syria it has been particularly difficult for a party leader to obtain wide popular support within the Kurdish communities. Consequently, many party leaders have relied heavily on the support within their family, tribe or region to obtain recognition and prestige as well as funding. Indeed, there are a number of parties which are very small, which depend almost solely on the relatives of the leader (such as *Partîya Çep* of Muhammad Musa), or on a group of loyal individuals (such as *Pêşverû* of Aziz Daoud).[71] The scope and spread of such parties is often limited regionally. Muhammad Musa and his brother, who is also in the leadership, have support and respect within Dirbasiye. Jamal Sheikh Baqi's party, *al-Surî*, has been limited to Kurds in Damascus although it has some support in his home town of Dirbasiye, where the family is well known and esteemed. Similarly, before he joined with others in forming *Yekbûn* (*al-Wahida*) in 1990, Sheikh Ali's party, *Partîya Kar* was confined to the Kurd Dagh region.[72] His position as Secretary General of *Yekîtî ya Dêmokrat*, second to the president Ismail Omar until his death in 2010, allowed this party to extend its reach and firmly establish itself in the Kurd Dagh region.

Considering the importance of the leader to the party's identity and support, the process of appointing a leader to a party and his specific requirements should be mentioned here. The details of the appointment process, however, are vague. This is a result of the nature of Kurdish politics in Syria and the fact that most parties are formed by the leaders themselves and the majority change their leadership only when an existing leader passes away. It appears that in some parties, at least in the past, the leader was appointed directly without election.[73] Interviews with Sheikh Ali revealed that one reason for his split from *el-Partî* in 1981 was the absence of democracy within the party leadership.[74] If it is clear that a change of leadership must occur due to the ill health of the leader or some other circumstance, a new leader is often primed to take over office.[75] Agreement to his appointment is confirmed within the party congress where his appointment is put to the vote.[76] According to *Yekîtî ya Dêmokrat* party leaders, there are certain requirements of prospective heads of Kurdish parties. They should have spent at least ten years in the party, have a sound knowledge of the Kurdish language, including reading and writing, have a good reputation, if possible have a university education and be voted into leadership by a party congress.[77] Although there is no official specification about gender, there has never been a woman in the leadership of any Syrian Kurdish political party, other than the PYD. Whether or not the election process is truly democratic is unclear simply because the leadership rarely changes and, therefore, the process is seldom tested. The exception is *Yekîtî*. The term of the Secretary-General is fixed at four years and the position rotates within the party leadership. From 1998 to 2002 Abdul Baqi Yousef was secretary general, followed by Hasan Salih (2002–2006) then Fuad Aliko (2006–2010). On 9 April 2010 Ismail Hemi (former member of the political committee of the party) became Secretary-General of *Yekîtî*. By all accounts, with the exception of *Yekîtî*, it appears that the majority of leaders are self-appointed and eternal. They are groomed to take over leadership, or in some cases, they assume the leadership by hereditary succession.

Interviews confirm that an important cause of party splits is that there is little scope for advancement inside the party. Although party congresses normally include election processes, the advancement of an alternative leader is likely to cause a split in the party rather than to initiate a democratic election process. In the spirit of Middle Eastern politics and hereditary leadership, Abdul Hamid Darwish, in his advanced years, was reported to be grooming his son to take over leadership of his party.[78]

The illegality of the parties is also a reason why personal differences easily cause divisions within the party ranks. As with other proscribed parties in Syria, the absence of incentives to remain within a given party causes fragility within the ranks. Illegality means that there is neither electoral competition with other parties nor an established path for achieving representation within government. Even if a party has secret relations with the government, these are unofficial and may act as a disincentive rather than an incentive for others to remain in the party.[79] Illegality has also led to policy compromises by the parties in order to protect their existence and to defend the Kurdish people from counter-measures taken by the regime. Consequently, what results is a clear softening of political demands and lowering of party activities. The question of unilateral political disarmament is examined in the next chapter. It is enough to say here that it is also a cause of divisions within the party ranks, particularly when the left-wing elements in the leadership of the movement attempt to intensify their opposition to the regime's policies towards the Kurdish people. This usually results in a split in the party leadership when the radical suggestions are rejected by the existing party leader.

The fact that the parties have an uncertain future often means that prominent individuals are inclined to work independently or in small groups. It could be argued on a functional, rather than a psychological level, that as a survival technique, smaller and dispersed parties are less likely to be destroyed, because they are less threatening than a united front. The evidence suggests that the fragmented state of the Kurdish political body is not a deliberate and conscious strategy of the parties; nonetheless only a factionalised body could have survived the political environment in Syria.

In the event that a member of the leadership of a party breaks off to form an alternative one, the leader will usually be supported, both organisationally and financially, by other individuals or groups from within the leadership of the party or outside it.[80] How much of such support comes from family sources is not entirely clear but interviews suggest that family relations do not dominate party alliances or party formation. Several examples were given to support this conjecture, although the same evidence suggests that family connections are, or were, relatively common within the political movement:

In 1975 Yousef Dibo who was in the politburo of *Hevgirtin*, opposed his cousin, Salah Bedr al-Din, who was at the time Secretary General of the party. The incident resulted in Dibo's expulsion from the party on charges of betraying the nation.[81] In the same year Sheikh Muhammad Baqi left his brother Sheikh Muhammad 'Issa Mulla Mahmoud, who was considered a pivotal member of the Kurdish nationalist leadership and one of the founders of the first Kurdish political party in Syria. Both Baqi and 'Issa were in the leadership of *el-Partî*. Baqi's faction formed the *el-Surî* party, which since 1997 has been led by Baqi's son, Jamal Sheikh Baqi. Although it has been assumed that succession to party leadership followed traditional hereditary forms, Jamal Sheikh Baqi claimed that the need for change of leadership was discussed with Sheikh Muhammad Baqi during the seventh party congress, and although Sheikh Baqi did not wish to surrender his position as party Secretary, he accepted the decision of the majority and the leadership changed without the division of the party.[82] In this case Muhammad Sheikh Baqi retired from work in politics.

Another example is that of the division that occurred within the ranks of *Partîya Çep* in 1982. *Partîya Çep* divided, with one side retaining the name and the other calling itself *Partîya Palên Kurdî li Sûriyê*. 'Ismet Sieda was the Secretary General of *Partîya Çep*, while his nephew, Sabghatallah Sieda, was Secretary General of *Partîya Palên* and his other nephew, Abdulbaset Sieda, was a member of the leadership.[83] While all these examples demonstrate that family relations do not prevent political differences from causing divisions within the ranks of the party leadership, they also show that family relations have been a fairly common phenomenon within the leadership of the Kurdish parties and that certain families have been particularly prominent.

It has also been suggested by non-party informants that family or local problems may be played out in the ranks of the parties. If one side in such a conflict is connected to a particular political party, the other side may join or collude with a local rival party, either to gain support for his position or to attempt to resolve the issue. In this way a personal or private conflict becomes a political matter and can lead to the formation of factions in the political parties.[84] Family problems may also play a role in causing or exacerbating existing political differences within or between political parties.

The culture of reverence for leadership, the limitations on advancement within political parties caused by Syrian government repression and the lack of democratic processes within the parties mean that differences and divisions occur easily. The orientation of Kurdish politics around the personality of one leader also contributes to the formation of blocs within party organisations. The higher ranks of the leadership tend to be surrounded by individuals loyal to the leader rather than to the particular policies or ideology of the party, which in any case vary only slightly from one party to another. Consequently, when differences arise between two or more members of the leadership, these networks of loyal individuals come into effect and blocs form within the party itself.

External influences (Syria, Kurdistan and International)

The external influences that contribute to divisions within the parties can be divided into three further sub-sections: those within Syria, those originating from other areas of Kurdistan and those influenced by international relations and the politics and experience of the diaspora.

Within Syria the government and the security services are the main actors that directly or indirectly influence developments inside the political parties. Although the parties are illegal, the regime and the security services are well informed about their activities, their internal dynamics and about their leadership. The fact that the Kurdish parties exist and operate in an authoritarian state such as Syria implies that the parties receive a certain amount of tacit tolerance from the regime. Their existence and activities are of course monitored and they have in the past been warned and advised to alter their behaviour if they are seen to be crossing the unwritten 'red lines' that divide acceptable from non-acceptable behaviour by the parties. Non-compliance with these boundaries set by the regime is normally met with arrest and detention.

Party leaders and non-party people alike are adamant that the *mukhabarat* have infiltrated party ranks and instigated problems within the leadership and that some parties were actually formed by government agencies. It is believed that the *mukhabarat* has offered support to individuals to establish new parties and encourage dissent within party ranks. The *mukhabarat* are known to have eyes everywhere and to have informants within the Kurdish communities and within the parties. In some cases informants have been well known to the Kurdish communities and to the political parties. One party leader commented that 'in the daytime they work for the security services, but by night they are our people',[85] illustrating the complexity of the relationship between the Syrian security services and Kurdish political parties.

Informants are often recruited after being arrested. Individuals arrested in relation to political 'crimes', such as involvement with a political party, or displaying Kurdish nationalist symbols, or attending a Kurdish cultural event, are commonly released from detention only after signing a declaration that they will report on political activities within their local Kurdish community or that they will refrain from all political activity. Declarations by the detainee are also commonly extracted through torture supplemented by threats against family members. The alternatives to cooperation involve harsh punishment for crimes deemed to be treasonous and threatening to the security of the state as well as the carrying out of the threats to relatives. As a result, the individual, once released, has little choice but to fulfil his obligation to inform the security services for fear of further arrest, black-listing, problems for the family and exclusion from any state employment. Additionally, difficult economic circumstances have driven individuals to act as informants, supplementing low incomes with payments for information. While Kurds have been found within the Ba'th Party and the security services, it is rarely a commitment to the regime or concerns about threats to state security emanating from Kurdish communities that induces a Kurdish individual to inform on his community. Rather it is a response to threats from the security services themselves or a result of economic hardship.

The division and fragmentation of the Kurdish party movement has, of course, been beneficial to the regime rather than to the Syrian Kurdish political parties, although, consequentially, it has facilitated their existence. While there has been little real competition between the Kurdish parties in Syria, the divisions between them have ensured that there is a certain dis-cord among them and that much party attention has been spent on futile attempts to unite against other parties or to unite factions of the Kurdish movement in different umbrella organisations.[86] The fact that leadership is revered and coveted prevents the dissolution of parties in favour of a united and representative organisation. The party leadership, also, has operated with the understanding that a united movement would not be tolerated by the regime. Consequently, no one leader gains the support and respect necessary to dominate the national movement, and so the Kurdish people never achieve coherent and effective representation and the movement never gains enough support to challenge state policies towards the Kurds effectively.

In addition to pressures and intrigues originating from inside the Syrian state, the Kurdish parties are also affected by factors related to their national identity and the extension of the nation beyond the borders of Syria. As shown above, the Kurdish parties of the other areas of Kurdistan, in particu-lar the KDP and PUK in Iraq and the PKK of Turkey, have been important factors in the fragmentation of Kurdish politics in Syria. In the belief that a solution to the Kurdish problems in Syria will only arrive after a solution is found in either the Iraqi or Turkish areas of Kurdistan, the Kurds of Syria, both as individuals and political organisations, have lent much support to these parties investing manpower, money and emotion in Kurdish strug-gles in these other areas of Kurdistan. As a consequence, their own political movement has suffered and has been stifled by the interference of external political parties in their affairs and by putting the interests of these parties above their own.

The first section of this chapter described the intervention of Barzani in Syrian Kurdish politics in 1970 in an attempt to reunify the left and the right wings of the movement. The result was the formation of a new party (*el-Partî*) loyal to Barzani and the KDP. That party, *el-Partî*, has split at least four times since its establishment and it appears that the majority, if not all of the divisions, were related to its lack of independence from the KDP. Sheikh Baqi described the involvement of the KDP in another party issue in 1973. As described in Chapter 1, the Ba'th Party had begun to build villages in the border regions of the Jazira to house Arabs moved into the region and to alter the demography of the Kurdish region. The leadership of *el-Partî* went to Iraq to ask advice on the appropriate course of action to prevent the arabisation of the areas. Baqi reported that Barzani's response was to say that Kirkuk had been subject to arabisation which, even with geographic and demographic conditions favourable to resistance, they had been unable to prevent. In Syria, without mountains and with divisions between the Kurdish areas, there were few options available. Barzani informed them that they should try to understand their government. The result was that Barzani wrote to Sheikh Musa Sadr in Lebanon who addressed the Syrian president on the matter. Sheikh Baqi explained this apparent dismissal of the issue and the fact that Barzani would not involve himself directly in the matter, as a result of the difficult situation that Barzani himself faced at that time which meant that he needed channels of communication through Syria to remain open.[87]

Parties such as *el-Partî* and *Pêşverû* of Abdul Hamid Darwish have been accused of relying heavily on the parties of Iraqi Kurdistan both for financial and political support and also for a solution to the Kurdish question in Syria. This reliance on external political parties renders the party more passive within the Syrian and Syrian Kurdish arenas. The parties seek out and rely on external advice on their policies and activities in Syria and wait for intervention from outside. The interests of the KDP and PUK have been prioritised over those of the Syrian Kurdish people and their concerns about preserving good relations with the Syrian authorities have been taken into consideration when defining policy or embarking on any political action against the state.

The issue of dependence on parties of Iraqi Kurdistan has been a reason given to explain many party divisions, including the division of *el-Surî* from *el-Partî* in 1975, of Sheikh Ali from *el-Partî* in 1981, of *Partîya Palên Kurdî li Sûriyê* from *Partîya Çep* in 1986. Tensions between the KDP and PUK of Iraqi Kurdistan have also been reflected within the ranks of the Syrian Kurdish parties. Alliance with one or other of the parties of Iraqi Kurdistan may also have played a part in the division of *Pêşverû* of Abdul Hamid Darwish in 1992. Abdul Hamid Darwish's party is firmly connected to the PUK of Talabani. Aziz Daoud who was in the Politburo of this party however, was closer to the KDP of Barzani. Parties that have become divided from their original party connections generally try to maintain good relations with all the Kurdish political forces outside Syria, while retaining independence from them and pursuing interests and demands defined by the Syrian state.[88] Obviously there are elements within the Kurdish nationalist movement in Syria that actively encourage relations with external Kurdish parties and believe that Kurdish political demands in Syria can be met through alliance with and even subordination to these parties. This is particularly true of *el-Partî* of Dr Hakim (formerly Nazir Mustafa). Indeed, it is reported that in Syria the popularity of *el-Partî* increased as a consequence of Kurdish political gains in Iraqi Kurdistan and that the strength of the party compared to many others is testimony that their position still has support in Syria.

The PKK also had an enormous impact on Kurdish politics in Syria which will be discussed further in later chapters. Their militant stance and the active engagement of the Syrian Kurds attracted thousands to its ranks in the 1980s and 1990s. The fact that the party overshadowed much of Syrian Kurdish politics weakened the Syrian Kurdish leadership. Although the PKK did not split the Syrian Kurdish political alliances as the KDP–PUK division did, the presence of the party in Syria and its activities there drew attention away from the existing Kurdish political parties. Attempts by members of the Syrian Kurdish leadership to emulate aspects of the PKK movement in order to attract Syrian Kurds to their indigenous parties and attract those drawn in large numbers to the PKK is arguably a factor involved in the establishment of new parties within the left. The Syrian Kurdish parties, however, remained subject to restrictions from the Syrian authorities, limiting the courses of action they could take and the difference they could make in Syrian Kurdish politics. In contrast, the PKK was permitted to operate freely in Syria providing that it helped to concentrate the political attention of the Syrian Kurds on Turkey. As a result, leftist elements within the existing parties attempted to assert a more militant line in the 1980s, by rejecting dependency on Iraqi Kurdish parties, asserting their independence and the need for dialogue with the Arab opposition and taking a slightly more aggressive stand against the policies of the Syrian government. Since the *Partîya Yekîtî ya Dêmokrat* (PYD, the PKK equivilant in Syria)[89] was formed in 2003 it has also attracted much support from among Syria's Kurds. Unlike the PKK, however, this party operated illegally in Syria and attracted the adverse attention from the Syrian authorities; many of its supporters were arrested and tortured or disappeared in the years preceding the Syrian uprising.

Significant changes in the international political climate were ultimately to have an effect on the Kurdish political parties in Syria. As shown in the section on ideology and method, the end of the Cold War led to a reorientation of Kurdish politics around the concept of democratic reform and human rights. The party that embodied these changes most clearly was the *Partîya*

Yekbûn Kurdi Sûriyê formed in 1990 from the amalgamation of three different political parties: *Partîya Kar a Kurd li Sûriyê* of Shiekh Ali, the faction of *el-Partî* led by Ismail Omar[90] and one faction of the *Partîya Çep a Kurdî li Sûriyê*. The party attempted to assert a more active political stance against the regime.[91] Although this party attempted to unite different political factions, in 1998 differences within the leadership caused a division between Ismail Omar and Sheikh Ali on the one side and Fuad Aliko and Hasan Salih, on the other. Thus, this retreat from ideological political orientations within the Kurdish movement in Syria did not witness a parallel decline in factionalism within the movement.

A further cause of dissent within parties is their relations with their branches in Europe and the USA. In the case of *Yekîtî*, part of the European branch broke off from the party as a result of disagreements over party policy. In 2009 Hasan Salih suggested that the party adopt a demand for autonomy of the Kurdish areas and change the party name to include the word 'Kurdistan'. Fuad Aliko opposed this idea and in a party meeting held in December 2009 it was decided that the party would not change the programme or the name. Despite the fact that the *Yekîtî* leadership were in agreement on the issue, the decision caused a fissure between the Syrian organisation and its European branch. Following Hasan Salih's stance, members of the European branch objected to the party's retreat from its more militant position. This group adopted the new name for the party, *Partîya Yekîtî ya Kurdistani li Sûriyê*, changed the party programme to include a demand for Kurdish autonomy within Syria, and formed a new leadership outside Syria.[92]

In the diaspora, numerous other attempts have been made to unite the Syrian Kurdish political movement and to establish new parties free from the restrictions imposed on those operating in Syria and offering a more effective leadership for the Syrian Kurdish political movement. The result, however, has been the further fragmentation of the political movement, with countless associations, political parties and umbrella organisations formed outside Syria attempting to provide better representation of the Syrian Kurds and unite the political movement.

Kurdish political activities in the diaspora as well as Syrian Kurdish internet sites, designed to provide up-to-date and impartial information on human rights and events in the Kurdish regions of Syria, have begun to have an important impact on the course of development of the political movement within Syria. Combined with transformations in socio-economic organisation within the Kurdish areas, simple access to unbiased and varied information, as well as the provision of a forum for discussion of the Kurdish question in Syria and for criticism of the political movement on the internet, has enabled the Kurdish youth to become actively involved in their politics without resort to the political parties themselves.

Attempts to Unite the Political Movement

Over the years there have been several mergers of parties or groups from within different parties. But the sheer number of parties existing in Syria means that these mergers have had little effect either on the overall political outlook or on the state of political fragmentation. Besides this, until 2008 there were three party coalitions. These broadly represented the three strands of the political spectrum. The first to be founded was *Hevbendi ya Dêmokrat a Kurdî li Sûriyê* (*Hevbendi*)[93] in 1992, which included *Pêşverû* of Abdul Hamid Darwish, *Yekîtî ya Dêmokrat* of Ismail Omar, *Partîya Çep* of Muhammad Musa and *Partîya Dêmokrat a Kurdî li Sûriyê* of Nusradin Ibrahim. The spokesperson of this organisation was Abdul Hamid Darwish. Following that, *Eniya Dêmokrat a Kurdî li Sûriyê* (*Eniya*)[94] was formed in 1996. This coalition included *el-Partî* of Dr Abdul Hakim Bashar, *Wekhevî* of Aziz Daoud and *Partîya Welatperêz a Dêmokrat a Kurdî li Sûriyê* of Tahir Safouk. Dr Abdul Hakim Bashar was the representative of this organisation. Both these coalitions signed the Damascus Declaration of 2005. In 2006 parties that did not sign the Damascus Declaration, and that did not join either *Hevbendi* or the *Eniya*, joined together to form the *Komîta Tensîqê ya Kurdî*, (*Komîta Tensîqê*)[95] consisting of three parties: *Yekîtî* of Ismail Hemi and Fuad Aliko, *Azadî* and *Şepêla Pêşerojê ya Kurdî li Sûriyê*. Following the Qamishli uprising of 2004, there were a number of additional attempts to unite the Kurdish political movement in Syria and establish a code of practice or 'authority' for all Syrian Kurdish political parties. This was a response to calls to address the continuing factionalism among the parties, to overcome differences between them and to agree on a general programme of demands with which to represent the needs of the Kurdish people. But even these attempts at unity were plagued by internal divisions, personal ambition, exploitation of differences and attempts to isolate more radical parties.

In 2005, when *Yekîtî* and *Azadî* held a demonstration to protest the assassination of Ma'shouq Khaznawi, in spite of warnings from the *mukhabarat* that any more protests would be met with counter-measures by the regime, Abdul Hamid Darwish attempted to create an alliance between *Hevbendi* and the *Eniya* against *Yekîtî* and *Azadî*. In efforts to establish a code of practice for the Kurdish political parties, involving meetings between all three alliances, Abdul Hamid Darwish attempted to isolate *Yekîtî* and recommended the expulsion of *Şepêla Pêşerojê ya Kurdî li Sûriyê* (which had a strong connection to *Yekîtî*) from the 'authority'. The request was rejected. When the three blocs were in a position to sign an agreement on a united political position and to put it into practice, Darwish, with the support of Ismail Omar, sought to reopen discussion on a fundamental issue: that of the definition of the Kurdish 'people' and 'land' in Syria.[96] At this point in Kurdish politics, this issue seemed to be impossible to resolve and remained at the heart of the divisions within the Kurdish political spectrum.

Only a year after its founding, differences arose within the *Komîta Tensîqê* between *Yekîtî* and *Azadî*. These problems had their roots in two issues. First, *Azadî* party did not consult *Yekîtî* when it boycotted the Syrian parliamentary elections held on 22 April 2007. Second, *Yekîtî* was seen to take into its ranks groups and individuals who defected from *Azadî*. Accusations from each side quickly developed into personal problems between Khayr al-Din Murad and Fuad Aliko pushing the two leaders to seek external support from the other's enemies.[97] Khayr al-Din developed relations with Abdul Hamid Darwish, a traditional rival of *Yekîtî* but politically on the opposite end of the political spectrum to *Azadî*, while Fuad Aliko became closer to Muhammad Musa of *Partîya Çep*, who had been in the leadership of this party with Khayr al-Din. The two had conflicted in the past over the leadership of the party, the result of which was the division of *Partîya Çep* in 1998 between the two leaders.

Darwish chose to exploit differences between *Yekîtî* and *Azadî* by proposing a plan for a new coalition of four parties, including *Azadî* as well as his own party, *Pêşverû*, and *Yekîtî ya Dêmokrat* from *Hevbendi* and *el-Partî* from *the Eniya* creating a new Kurdish 'authority' to replace the one devised between the three blocs in 2006.[98] In a bid to seize control and authority over the Kurdish political movement in Syria, break the existing alliances and isolate *Yekîtî*, the proposal would bring together some of the most important parties within one organisation led by Abdul Hamid Darwish himself. The proposal was rejected by *el-Partî* which presented a counter-project to establish a united Kurdish council.[99] On 30 December 2009 the Kurdish Political Council in Syria (*Encûmena Siyasî ya Kurdî li Sûriyê*) was formed. Its opening declaration claimed that the Council would work to build relations and understanding between the various parties and present a common vision and position and would also attempt to bring an end to the fragmentation of the Kurdish political movement.[100] It included eight of the then fifteen political parties.[101] The two main parties absent from this council were *Partîya Pêşverû* of Darwish and *Partîya Yekîtî ya Dêmokrat a Kurd li Sûriyê*, then led by Ismail Omar. Despite the fact that it included most of the political parties, the new council was unable to convert this framework into practical unity between the parties on general aims. The independence of the political parties continued to be prioritised above any unifying structure or framework.[102]

These examples of attempts at uniting the political movement show that previous allegiances between the different parties have been based only partly on political identity and position in the political spectrum. Alliances and enmities between political parties and their leaders have played an important part in determining the direction of political alliances. As a consequence, seemingly unusual alliances between parties that would otherwise be political foes have occurred in attempts to create blocs capable of diminishing the authority of other blocs. Some of these blocs have been, at the same time, fluid and fragile, lacking substantial political foundations and subject to further fragmentation and shifting allegiances.

The Consequences of Factionalism

This chapter has shown that the Kurdish political movement in Syria has suffered from fragmentation as a result of internal, Syrian and international causes. Yet, the description and analysis of the development of Kurdish political parties in Syria and of their divisions reveal that personal differences, ambition and the formation of blocs has been primary contributors to the fragmentation of the parties and that ideological and policy concerns commonly hide personal differences or develop into them.

The divisions and criticism within the political movement about the introduction of Marxism–Leninism to the movement illustrates that, at that time, the Kurdish political parties operated under an unwritten self-imposed understanding of the limits and demands of Kurdish political representation. The left broke this understanding with its adoption of Marxism–Leninism. Since the end of the Cold War, however, the Kurdish political movement has retreated from ideological commitments and returned to a more nationally defined political identity. Following the events of March 2004 further attempts to define and regulate the Kurdish political parties were made by the Kurdish leadership themselves. But attempts to establish a Kurdish code of practice and 'authority' led to the formation of new blocs and factions rather than to their unification.

The story of factionalism within the Kurdish party movement told here is not unfamiliar in the history of illegal leftist or resistance movements the world over, particularly before the end of the Cold War. Whereas many of these other movements have dissipated or developed into effective political parties as a result of some change in their legal status, the unique combination of factors that have contributed to the factionalism of the Kurdish party movement in Syria persists to the present day. The Syrian uprising and its aftermath may yet provide the circumstances necessary to transform the Kurdish political parties. But the particular circumstances of the Kurdish political parties have led them into a state of chronic factionalism and have weakened the parties ideologically and politically. The nature of the Syrian state and the relationship of the parties to it, as well as the absence of effective support for political action from Kurdish parties in other areas of Kurdistan, has thwarted attempts to steer the parties out of this situation. The simple fact that any effective political action or movement would have been met with debilitating and dangerous counter-measures from the regime has prevented the parties from crossing the boundaries of tacitly approved behaviours.

With the increase in the number of parties in the Kurdish political movement, the political parties became ever more absorbed in their own internal and inter-party politics rather than open to the demands of the Kurdish people to the state. This had important implications for the support that the parties received within the Kurdish communities in Syria, a question which is discussed in Chapter 7. Similarly, it restricted their ability to perform their roles in Kurdish society, to act on state policy towards the Kurds and Kurdish areas in Syria and to act with authority in the field of Kurdish national regeneration. It is to these social functions, examined in the following two chapters, that this book now turns.

CHAPTER 4

RELATIONS BETWEEN THE PARTIES AND THE STATE

Prior to the start of the Syrian uprising in March 2011, one of the most important functions of the Kurdish political parties, set at the centre of their *raison d'être*, was to address the Kurdish grievances against the state. In order to do this the parties had to enter into some form of relationship with the state, despite their illegality. The fact of their illegality affected and defined the essence of those relationships; it circumscribed the behaviour of the parties and limited their access to the state. As a result, various complex sets of relationships developed between the Kurdish parties and the state authorities. Some of them were contradictory to the essence of Kurdish politics in Syria, while others confirmed their commitment to challenging the state. Each party's position towards the state and its methods of engaging the government contributed to defining the identity and position of the party on the Syrian Kurdish political spectrum.

Parties employed, for the most part, three approaches towards relations with the Syrian state. One of these was to draw on Kurdish society itself by organising their own demonstrations and protests as a means of public expression of grievances. In addition, the majority of parties also developed and nurtured relations with the Arab opposition in Syria as a means of influencing the state at the Syrian national level (as opposed to acting as a regional or ethnic minority group). And lastly, party leaders occasionally entered into direct, but unofficial, negotiations with government representatives or even into secret relations with the security services. These, therefore, were each channels whereby the Kurdish parties engaged the Syrian state directly or indirectly. The structure of this chapter reflects these different channels, by discussing in turn the mobilisation and social action of the Kurdish population, the parties' relations with the Arab opposition and the parties' relations with the Syrian authorities and how these complex relations affected the parties' effectiveness with the Kurdish population.

Mobilisation and Social Action

Mobilisation or social action is a fundamental role of any political party or social movement, whether it is simply encouraging people to vote or driving them towards revolution. The Syrian Kurdish political parties have engaged in both conventionally political social actions such as demonstrations, protests and vigils, and more unconventional ones such as teaching Kurdish or organising Newroz celebrations. Here, mobilisation in the form of demonstration and more conventional party activities are examined, leaving cultural activities to the next chapter, which looks at the micro-level role of the parties in Kurdish society. This section examines the Kurdish political parties as potential conduits of social action and mobilisation. Party programmes express their desire to fulfil this role and, as nationalist parties that seek to challenge and change state policy towards the Kurds in Syria and to liberate the Kurds from their oppression, Kurdish political parties have attempted to rally society around the concept of the nation, around symbols of its culture and people's memories of its oppression.

As a consequence of the demographic and geographic division of the Kurds and of their oppression and history of resistance to domination by foreign governments, the Kurdish population in Syria is highly politicised and nationalistic, arguably more so than Arab society in Syria prior to the Syrian uprising. Kurdish society, with its politicisation and national sentiment for mass mobilisation is a resource for the parties, as yet not fully exploited. Of all the parties' roles in Kurdish society, that of being conduits of social action has possibly been the most important, but it has also been the most complex one to perform. Their ability, or willingness to mobilise Kurdish society, has been compromised by a number of factors, particularly by the state's imposition of 'red lines' around tolerated behaviour, the factionalism of the parties themselves and their relation to the Kurdish people's willingness to engage in public political actions. This willingness remains central to their relations with the Syrian Kurdish population and to popular perceptions of the parties. As actors positioned between the Syrian authorities and the Kurdish communities, their room for manoeuvre has been very limited. This position has produced a complex set of relations within which they have attempted to work towards finding a solution to the Kurdish problems in Syria, while maintaining their existence.

The authoritarian nature of the Syrian Ba'th Party government and the years of oppression of the Syrian people, particularly the Kurdish communities, have taken their toll on the ability and willingness of the people to organise, mobilise and address their claims against the state. Those traces of civil society that developed in Syria have been quickly suppressed or controlled by the regime.[1] Freedom of speech, opinion and assembly under the Ba'th Party have been severely restricted and, prior to the breaking of this silence in Syria in March 2011, the fear of the security services has prevented any social or political movement from developing to a point where it could challenge the regime. Apart from Kurdish reformism, no movement gained popular and mass support in Syria after the government's suppression of the Hama uprising in 1982. The regime's brutal response to this uprising pushed any opposition further underground and subjected it to additional surveillance and controls. As a consequence, opposition politics remained principally the domain of intellectuals and professionals, and became a field of private discussion and planning rather than of public action and mobilisation.

The Kurdish communities in Syria have behaved somewhat differently. Kurdish people, generally, have been more psychologically engaged with opposition politics due to the fact that the oppression they face is based on their ethnic and national identity. The political parties operate fairly openly within Kurdish society and call on the people for moral and financial support. Despite the politicised nature of the population, levels of participation in the parties and their activities prior to the 2011 uprising were not high. The consequences of involvement were and continue to be potentially devastating for the lives of individuals and also their families; the omnipresent nature of the Syrian security services creates a climate of fear, distrust and a sense of being under constant surveillance, which has prevented many otherwise politically motivated individuals from becoming involved. Consequently, while the necessary political consciousness has continuously existed within the Kurdish communities, the motivation to act politically under the rule of the Ba'th Party has been weak. Many factors have inhibited the ability of the parties to stimulate greater political action. The clearest is the fear of repercussions from the regime, but also, as discussed below, the parties themselves have been to blame for part of the failure to create an environment more favourable to active resistance. Indeed, in 2004 they even took steps themselves to prevent the continuation of popular mobilisation.

In a one-party authoritarian state such as Syria, demonstration or protest takes on a different meaning and significance from those they have in a democratic state. Public opinion on policy is not taken into consideration when formulating state policy; the only participation in politics required by the state consists of conforming to unspoken rules of behaviour and occasional expressions of support for the regime. The only demonstrations that are legal in Syria are those organised by the Ba'th Party. Rallies in support of the government or displays of protest connected with external issues, such as Palestine and Israel, but which also support the Syrian government's foreign policies, are still fairly common occurrences. State employees are given the day off work so that they can attend and they are obliged to do so. Consequently, any demonstration that does not include public displays of support for the regime, or that could be interpreted as a negative or critical reaction to the government or its policies, is illegal. Most organisations have not dared to attempt demonstrations against state policy and as a result oppositional demonstrations were extremely rare occurrences in pre-uprising Syria. When and if they happened, it was with the knowledge that to participate or to organise could result in arrest, torture and years of imprisonment for expressing opinions deemed threatening to the state.

Demonstrations organised by Kurdish political parties have been considered anti-regime by definition and threatening not only the security of the state but also its territorial integrity. Kurdish demonstrations in the Kurdish areas or in Syrian cities have been routinely met with arrests during the event and afterwards, and with police brutality against those taking part. On occasion, particularly when demonstrations have been spontaneous, the police have fired into crowds of unarmed demonstrators shooting and killing participants.[2] Those arrested for participating in or organising such events have faced charges stipulated in the Syrian Penal Code such as seeking to annex a part of Syrian territory and attach it to another state (Article 267), inciting racial or sectarian strife (Article 307), or seeking to weaken the Syrian national consciousness (Articles 285 and 286).

Demonstration and protest has not always been employed by the political parties in their attempts to address Kurdish issues in Syria. Indeed, it was only after the turn of the millennium that public demonstrations entered the political toolkit of the Kurdish political parties. Before then it would not have been possible to discuss the Kurdish parties as conduits of social action in Syria. The question of why parties only began to organise demonstrations at this time is returned to below after recounting briefly the history of demonstration amongst the Kurds of Syria.

The early Kurdish political parties did not engage in public demonstrations against the Syrian government and any social mobilisations seem to have been directed more in support of the Kurdish uprisings in Iraqi Kurdistan than against the government of Syria and its domestic policy towards the Kurds.[3] At this point, despite the establishment of *Partîya Dêmokrat a Kurd li Sûriyê*, the Kurdish national question remained primarily a pan-Kurdish issue. Understandings of Kurdish identity and any mobilisation and political action reflected this.[4] Efforts of the party were concentrated on the practicalities of political organisation within Syria, as well as on support for Barzani's 1961 revolution in Iraqi Kurdistan and establishment of communication channels between the Kurdish areas and the international community.[5] The struggle against the Syrian government had not materialised at this point.

Events in Iraq dominated Kurdish political thinking and it was not until the 1970s, when the Arab Belt project was implemented and when the results of the Hasaka Census became clear, that Kurdish politics in Syria began to tackle specifically Syrian Kurdish political issues.

Interviews suggest that during the 1970s restrictions on expressions of Kurdish identity and political nationalism were strict. Displays of Kurdish identity and culture were predominantly private, although imbued with political significance. For Newroz, families would generally celebrate as a group; placing lit candles in the window of the home was common practice, symbolic of the fire signalling revolution in traditional folklore.[6] In the Efrîn area interviewees have suggested that no demonstrations took place between the 1950s and 1970s. In the Jazira, however, there were protests against the implementation of land reforms in the 1970s and against the creation of the 'Arab Belt'. Kurdish villagers had reportedly blocked the paths of the Syrian authorities as they attempted to follow orders to forcibly remove the villagers from their homes in the Kurdish areas to the Syrian interior.[7] In the village of Ali Furo, the inhabitants and other protesters sat and lay in the path of vehicles and refused to leave. Approximately 90 residents of Ali Furo village were arrested and detained by the Syrian authorities.[8] In this case it appears that the protests were effective and the prospect of similar actions and arrests in all the designated villages prompted the authorities to alter their policy. Instead of removing all the Kurds from their homes, they began to move Arabs into specially constructed villages in the area, initiating artificial demographic change. It is not clear whether or not any Kurdish party was involved in or supportive of these protests but it seems that they were primarily local affairs organised by the inhabitants of the villages.

Other demonstrations that occurred were normally the result of the authorities' restrictions or attacks on Kurdish gatherings for Newroz or other such celebrations. For example, in 1986 a young boy, Sulaiman Hamad Amin, was killed in Damascus when police opened fire on the crowds protesting the authorities' attempts to prevent people from celebrating Newroz and, in Efrîn in north-west Syria, three more Kurds were killed.[9] In these cases the demonstrations were spontaneous and not organised by the Kurdish parties. The 1980s were generally dominated by the presence of the PKK in Syria and youths, hungry to engage in social action, were drawn to its ranks and were trained to fight in Turkey against the Turkish government. Support for the PKK within Kurdish communities, particularly in the Kurd Dagh and Kobanî regions, was very high. It is also true to say that much of the population felt duty bound to offer support, attend meetings and donate money, services or parts of their harvest to the party.[10] The ability of the PKK to monopolise popular mobilisation and public displays of Kurdish culture was a consequence of an implicit understanding between the Syrian government and the PKK that the organisation would not promote political activities against the Syrian government and that it would direct the attention of Syrian Kurds towards the Kurdish struggle in Turkey. As a consequence, political activities and consciousness were again directed away from the Syrian state and streets by the PKK and the Syrian Kurdish parties were unable or unwilling to attempt to compete with it.

Eventually, one party began to endeavour to draw the Syrian Kurdish political interest back to a focus on the Syrian state. Before the introduction of demonstrations to Kurdish politics, in 1993 *Partîya Yekîtî ya Dêmokrat a Kurd li Sûriyê*[11] adopted fly-posting in Syrian cities as a political weapon. This was a very significant move by the new party as it gave Kurdish demands public visibility and took Kurdish protest to the Syrian streets.[12] Posters denouncing state policy towards the stateless Kurds were placed on public buildings and walls in Syrian cities and towns.[13] Possessing or posting Kurdish party propaganda was, of course, illegal in Syria and remains so. One party leader estimated that more than 20 members were arrested for putting up party posters.[14]

Demonstrations entered the political vocabulary and toolkit of the Syrian Kurdish parties in 2001 or 2002. A demonstration appears to have taken place on 1 June 2001 in which 150 Kurds were arrested and many were injured when police attempted to disperse the crowds.[15] It is unclear as to whether or not this demonstration was organised by a political party; the date, having no particular significance to Kurdish politics, suggests that it was probably spontaneous. Then on 10 December 2002 *Yekîtî*[16] organised a demonstration marking International Human Rights Day. Protesters held placards reading: 'Citizenship for Kurds', 'Let Syria be a homeland for all its sons: Arabs, Kurds and [other] minorities', 'Down with the ban on Kurdish language and culture' and 'Respect human rights in Syria'.[17] Two members of the *Yekîtî* leadership, Marwan Othman and Hasan Salih, presented the Speaker of Parliament, Abd al-Qader Qadoura, with a communiqué demanding equal rights for the Kurds in Syria. It is reported that during the meeting Qadoura denied the presence of the Kurdish nation in Syria and said that there was no Kurdish question in Syria.[18] After two days, the two leaders were called back to Damascus from the Kurdish areas for what they thought to be further discussion of the Kurdish issue, but were arrested by the security services.[19]

The next demonstration was held on 25 June 2003, World Children's Day. The march on the UNICEF building in Damascus consisted of more than 200 children and accompanying adults holding placards and chanting slogans related to the difficulties in registering Kurdish children's names, of not being taught in their mother language and of discrimination in schools. In this demonstration *Yekîtî* was joined by *Partîya Hevgirtina Gelê Kurd li Sûriyê* and *Partîya Yekîtî ya Dêmokrat a Kurd li Sûriyê*. The *Hevbendi* (or *Tahaluf*) alliance of four Kurdish parties, headed by Abdul Hamid Darwish, rejected an invitation to participate on the grounds that the use of placards was a pretext for repression by the state authorities.[20] This demonstrates the link between the actual visual and verbal expression of political demands and subversion. As a consequence, the next demonstration held on 6 October 2003 in front of the Syrian parliament, marking the anniversary of the Hasaka census, was a silent protest in which no placards were used, but in which most Syrian Kurdish political parties participated, as did some of the Syrian Arab opposition and human rights groups.[21]

In the following year a number of demonstrations and protests in collaboration with the Arab opposition took place, particularly outside the courts in which trials of Kurdish and Arab opposition figures and of those arrested at previous demonstrations were being held. Kurdish students also began to organise themselves within the universities, holding rallies and assemblies to mark occasions such as the anniversary of the Halabja massacre. At the beginning of 2004 Kurdish students organised two further demonstrations in Aleppo.[22] This run of demonstrations, preceding the March 2004 Qamishli uprising, represented a new phenomenon. The use of public space and the diversity of actors involved were unheard of within the Kurdish movement in Syria, which had long been satisfied to work in the shadows.[23]

When spontaneous demonstrations erupted on 12 March 2004 and spread to all Kurdish areas in Syria as well as to Kurdish enclaves in Syria's cities, the solidarity of the Kurdish communities, their readiness for mobilisation and their years of pent-up frustration with state oppression were laid bare. The parties were moved into action and were heard to offer words of support to the Kurdish people. At the start of the uprising, the Kurdish parties effectively acted as representatives of the Kurdish people and sought to use the events as leverage against the Syrian authorities. They demanded the formation of a committee to investigate who was responsible for the events in the stadium on 12 March and to call for an end to arbitrary arrests and attacks on Kurdish residences, before they would agree to meet with any representatives of the security forces. Despite this, Abdul Hamid Darwish met with General Mansourah, head of the *mukhabarat* in Hasaka province, and consequently, on 13 March, meetings were held between the Kurdish parties and Ba'th Party leaders, including the Governor of Hasaka province.[24] With that, the parties became mediators for the Syrian authorities.

On 14 March the parties appealed for calm and an end to the protests. One member of the Kurdish party leadership suggested that the Syrian government's aim was to promote sectarian fighting between Kurds and Arabs and that all the parties, big and small, should work together in this instance in an attempt to avoid such a situation. He concluded that they had succeeded in averting such a crisis.[25] It is unclear whether the parties' call for calm was respected or whether calm was restored by the extent of the Syrian authorities' assaults on Kurdish areas. At least, the parties were in agreement in this instance and they chose not to exploit a situation which could have led the Kurdish political and national movement to a new level of engagement with the regime. As it was, the uprising lasted only ten days and the choice of the parties not to exploit the opportunity, nor to maintain that level of mobility and capture the interest of international observers meant that the parties maintained the status quo, failed to move Kurdish issues onto the discussion table and ended without concessions from the government.

In the years following the events of March 2004, the parties did, however, maintain certain levels of visibility in protest. After Sheikh Ma'shouq Khaznawi[26] disappeared in May 2005 the parties organised to demand his release from Syrian captivity. *Yekîtî ya Dêmokrat, Partîya Çep* (of Khayr al-Din Murad)[27] and *Yekîtî* led a demonstration of approximately 400 people in front of the Supreme State Security Court on 15 May 2005; on 21 May between 10–20,000 people took to the streets in a rally organised by *Yekîtî* in Qamishli. After his death was made public on 1 June 2005 and his tortured body had been returned to his family, spontaneous gatherings occurred and continued for the next two days with an estimated 10,000 people visiting the Khaznawi family's mourning tent. The political parties took part in these demonstrations and offered condolences to the family.[28] Other than the arrests of 15 Kurds on 2 June for insulting the Syrian government in their protests, the events were not suppressed by the authorities.

On 5 June, *Yekîtî, Azadî* and *Şepêla Pêşerojê* held a demonstration in Qamishli, despite warnings from the intelligence services that a continuation of protests would be met with repercussions. All other political parties refused to participate or support the move and advised the three parties not to demonstrate. The security services as well as members of the Teyy and Shammar Arab tribes, who had been called up and armed by the Syrian authorities, attacked Kurdish demonstrators with sticks and the police used live ammunition against the crowds. It was reported that groups of Arabs loyal to the regime, were organised and encouraged by the security services to loot Kurdish shops in Qamishli and Dêrîk and that looters were protected by Syrian soldiers. As a result, the ramifications and costs of demonstrating were felt not only by participants but also by shop-keepers far from the centre of the protests. The targeting of small businesses and non-participants by the authorities can be understood as a means of causing divisions within the Kurdish communities over Kurdish national politics and turning people against the parties and against the idea of popular mobilisation. The parties organising the demonstration were accused by other Kurdish parties of provoking the looting and bearing some of the responsibility for it.[29] The difference in how the parties dealt with the government's ban on demonstrations and the conflict between the parties that ensued made explicit the schism between those parties which were prepared to confront the government and those which were not.

After these events, protests and vigils which held symbolic significance became more popular with the majority of Kurdish political parties in the Kurdish areas and more frequent than demonstrations involving or attempting mass mobilisation or public expressions of dissent. The parties adopted acts of solidarity such as silent and candlelit vigils, the observation of minutes of silence and the wearing of black badges instead of marches and displays of public protest. In one way, these gatherings and symbols can be seen as attempts to connect to popular sentiment and the sense of injustice and to fulfil national obligations. This form of protest, however, can also be understood as a retreat, since the Qamishli uprising, from confrontation of the regime by the political parties. The majority of these protests were removed from the state capital and seat of Syrian politics, limiting any audience or media attention to the Kurdish areas. At the same time the political effect of the protest or demonstration was diminished by limiting political action to symbolic periods of silence or the wearing of black badges. Confrontation with the regime was avoided by remaining within the limits of the regime's 'red lines'. Despite this retreat, on 28 February 2009 several Kurds were arrested for taking part in a silent protest against Decree 49[30] indicating that the 'red lines' were subject to alteration at the whim of the state authorities and that, at this time, the regime's tolerance of Kurdish protest was wearing thin. Following this, in March 2010 some parties were heard to advise Kurds to avoid celebrating Newroz in public,[31] and, in June 2010, all Kurdish political parties refrained from gathering to remember Sheikh Khaznawi as they had done every year since his death. On this occasion approximately 20 people went to his grave.[32]

So why did Kurdish parties begin to organise demonstrations in the early 2000s? And what caused their apparent retreat after 2008? Several factors contributed to the development of visible Kurdish protest in Syria including internal aspects of the Kurdish party movement, the nature and policies of the Syrian state and changes in the international political arena and Syria's position within it.

An early example of the rise of Kurdish protest was the formation of *Partîya Yekîtî ya Dêmokrat a Kurd li Sûriyê* and its venture into public protest through posters, mentioned above. The party divided in 1998 producing a more radical break-off, *Partîya Yekîtî ya Kurd li Sûriyê*, which was formed from a faction of the *Yekîtî ya Dêmokrat* leadership. It was this party that was the first to organise a Kurdish demonstration in December 2002. *Yekîtî* emerged in the same year that the PKK was expelled from Syria. It is possible that the leadership sought to fill the vacuum left by the PKK and satisfy the need for a more militant organisation to attract the more radical sectors of Kurdish society. Since then, the *Yekîtî* party has been responsible for organising more demonstrations than most other parties and it seems that this party spearheaded the drive to publicly protest against the government and to move the Kurdish people on to the streets.[33] At the time of its formation, the programme and demands of this party were more radical than those of any other Syrian Kurdish party and it attempted to articulate the more militant currents of Kurdish society in the context of the new post-Cold War world order.[34]

Another radical action was prompted by the death of Hafiz al-Assad and the appointment of his son, Bashar al-Assad, in his place. This led to the brief opening up of civil and political space known as the Damascus Spring in the year 2000. The civil society organisations, associations and public debate that developed briefly brought the opposition out into the open and the possibility of democratic reform seemed less remote. Kurdish organisations and parties were involved in this; Arab–Kurdish dialogue was set in motion and the possibility of collaboration was tested.

A further political arousal followed, in the wake of the attacks on the World Trade Centre in New York on 11 September 2001 after which the United States labelled Syria as a rogue state. At the same time it accused Saddam Hussein of developing weapons of mass destruction, paving the way for the US invasion of Iraq in March 2003. The US stance towards these two Ba‘thist states, coupled with pre-invasion missions in Iraq and collaboration between the Kurdish peshmerga and US forces in combating the Islamic group *Ansar al-Islam* in northern Iraq, encouraged the Kurds to take more deliberate steps towards addressing their grievances. Events in Iraq renewed international interest in Kurdish issues and presented the Kurds with an opportunity to act more aggressively within Syria in the knowledge that the international climate was more favourable to them.[35]

The consequent retreat of the parties can be understood as a response to the counter-measures taken against Kurdish protest and mobilisation, particularly between 2008 and 2010. The number of fatal shootings by Syrian security personnel of Kurdish participants in demonstrations and Newroz celebrations held between November 2007 and June 2010 reached at least five.[36] This increase in the use of live ammunition against Kurdish gatherings was a reflection of a more general crack down by the security forces on Kurdish political and cultural expression in response to the increase in the frequency, visibility and size of Kurdish demonstrations. In April 2008 Kurdish sources reported that the the political security branch of the *mukhabarat* had issued an edict forbidding any gathering, protest or celebration without the approval of the Ministry of Interior, and prohibiting the raising of Kurdish flags. Any person violating this law would be referred to the Supreme State Security Court on charges of treason and seperatism.[37] Although the report was unconfirmed, Kurdish party leaders advised Human Rights Watch that, in a meeting with the Syrian security services in May 2008, they had been told that 'there are instructions from the leadership that gatherings are forbidden'. Despite the retreat of the majority of other Kurdish parties in Syria and the clear warnings from the regime, *Yekîtî* and the PYD chose to continue despite this ban on demonstrations.

In October 2009 *Yekîtî* announced that its annual demonstration, against the continued denial of citizenship to Kurds deprived of it through the Hasaka Census in 1962, as well as against Decree 49 of 2008, had been cancelled. According to a *Yekîtî* announcement, this was a response to requests from Syrian authorities in Hasaka province to cancel it with the promise that they would arrange a meeting between the party leaders and Syrian leaders in the near future.[38] The party justified its acceptance of this offer as a final attempt to seek a democratic solution to the Kurdish problem in Syria. The authorities failed to keep their promise of dialogue.[39] Following this, in December 2009 the party held its general assembly. A split within the party leadership arose, between Hasan Salih and Fuad Aliko, on the question of the proposed change of party name to *Partiya Yekîtî Kurdistani li Sûriyê* and the inclusion of a demand for autonomy of the Kurdish regions in Syria. Fuad Aliko opposed the proposed changes, and on 8 December 2009 the leadership held a meeting in which it was agreed that the changes would not be adopted. On 29 December Hasan Salih and two other members of the *Yekîtî* leadership were arrested.[40]

The retreat of the parties from public displays of dissent was triggered by the regime's retaliations against the Kurdish communities and the counter measures taken against the more militant sectors of the Kurdish party leadership. More than 243 cases of arbitrary arrest and detention of Kurds were reported in 2009, including many members of the political leadership.[41]

Relations with the Arab Opposition

As already mentioned the Kurdish movement used their relations with the Arab opposition in Syria as a political weapon to promote changes in state policy.[42] Even before the start of the Syrian uprising, relations between the Kurdish and Arab opposition were not as developed as one might have expected and had not developed beyond the limits set by the Arab nationalist agenda. This was a result partly of concentration on their respective agendas by both Kurdish and Arab groups, and partly of the constraints upon organised opposition in Syria. For Arab parties, association with Kurdish parties might have opened them to accusations by the authorities of 'threatening' the Arab identity and ideology of the regime and state. They may have been wary of relations with Kurdish parties because of the language used by some of them – for example, references to 'Arab settlements' in the Kurdish areas[43] which implies a similarity between Syrian policy in the Kurdish areas and Israeli policy in Palestine. Such language is somewhat provocative in a society where Arab nationalism is particularly popular[44] and it is reasonable to assume that some Arab apprehension remains concerning the Kurds in Syria. In the past, notably the 1960s, there were targeted propaganda campaigns against the Kurds which associated them with foreign interference, anti-Arab sentiment and separatism.[45] In a country where Arab nationalism is possibly stronger than in any other Arab country the association of the Kurds with forces inimical to national interests is bound to generate some apprehension towards political relations with a nationalist Kurdish population.[46]

Following the death of Hafiz al-Assad, Bashar al-Assad's inaugural speech signalled that he intended to reconcile the government with opposition forces[47] and unprecedented freedom of assembly was granted for Syrian activists and their supporters. An oppositionist civil society movement emerged in the year 2000, promoting democratic political reform. Meetings were hosted in the homes of people involved,[48] including party leaders and members of parliament, journalists, lawyers, academics, businessmen and philosophers who dared to speak out on behalf of human rights, economic and political reform and the need to develop an autonomous Syrian civil society.[49] In this climate, a Kurdish association called the Jaladat Bedirkhan Cultural Association was established in Qamishli; several opposition petitions were presented to the government;[50] two independent human rights groups were reopened and, up to May 2001, political prisoners were being released. The majority of those affected, including those in Kurdish political parties, were hopeful that the new leader would open up the political system, encouraging the development of democracy.[51] Kurdish–Arab dialogue began to develop as opposition groups attempted to develop connections between diverse organisations within Syria.

The so-called 'Damascus Spring' was brought to an end in August and September 2001 with a series of arrests of those pioneering the movement. Ten prominent personalities were arrested,[52] the Bedirkhan Association was closed and members and associates were arrested as early as March 2001.[53] In August 2001 many other democratic activists, including Kurds, some of whom had only recently been released from prison, were arrested.[54] Bashar al-Assad's speech opening the new parliament, following the elections of 2–3 March 2003, was used to convey a message to the opposition and to define the limits of reform referred to in his inaugural speech. He explained that the opposition, mainly opportunists and egoists, had 'misunderstood what he meant by democracy', interpreting it as freedom from controls and morality, and that they were damaging the national interest.[55] He verified what had already been made clear by the actions of the security services, that opposition of this sort would not be tolerated. The crack-down on the opposition that began in 2001 made it clear that reform would only take place according to the terms and timetable of the regime. New decrees placed even harsher restrictions, including executive regulations, on publishing, printing, distributing and selling any printed material from books to posters. As well as other strict and somewhat arbitrary restrictions, Article 16 of this decree (Number 50/2001) also limited ownership of periodical publications to Syrian Arabs suggesting that Kurds were ineligible.[56]

Both the Arab and Kurdish opposition continued to pursue democratic reform, and after the Qamishli uprising of 2004, the Arab opposition renewed its attempts to court the Kurdish political parties. The possibility of collaborating on a statement in favour of democratic reform brought the two groups together and on 16 October 2005 the majority of Kurdish parties in Syria, along with much of the Syrian Arab opposition became signatories of the Damascus Declaration for Democratic National Change.[57] The Declaration, compiled and published in a Lebanese newspaper, condemned the authoritarian politics of the state and set out demands for peaceful and far reaching reform of the state and government and the development of democracy in Syria. Included in the declaration was a paragraph on the Kurds in Syria:

> [We should] find a just democratic solution to the Kurdish issue in Syria, in a manner that guarantees the complete equality of Syrian Kurdish citizens with the other citizens, with regard to nationality rights, culture, learning the national language, and the other constitutional, political, social, and legal rights on the basis of the unity of the Syrian land and people. Nationality and citizenship rights must be restored to those who have been deprived of them, and the file must be completely settled.[58]

As mentioned in the previous chapter, the majority of Kurdish parties signed the Declaration in the name of the two Kurdish alliances, *Hevbendi* (*Tahaluf*) and *Eniya* (*al-Jabha*). Three of them, however, declined, rejecting it on the grounds that it did not address fundamental concerns of the Kurdish people and the Kurdish national question in Syria. The three were *Yekîtî*, *Azadî*, and *Şepêla Pêşerojê ya Kurdî li Sûriyê*.[59]

Since the efforts to collaborate with the Arab opposition began, many of the Syrian Kurdish parties have stressed the similarities between Kurdish and Arab cultures and the fact that in Syria interaction between the two groups is common and has forged a degree of cultural amalgamation on both sides.[60] The Kurdish regions in Syria do not form a contiguous geographical area today, as they do in Turkey, Iraq or Iran. Consequently, Kurdish party leaders have stressed the fact that their politics revolve around seeking a solution to the Kurdish question within the framework of the unity of the Syrian state and in alliance with the Arab opposition. For some, even before the start of the Syrian uprising, this did not rule out the possibility for the Kurdish areas of a special form of self-administration in which Kurds held administrative positions, had representatives in parliament and where education was in Kurdish as well as Arabic. Matters such as budgets and foreign policy, however, would remain the responsibility of the central government.[61]

Several authors and signatories of the Declaration itself were arrested after its publication and Kurdish leaders and activists attributed their own arrests and harassment by the Syrian authorities to their participation in the Arab–Kurdish dialogues.[62] It has been stressed by some interviewees involved in the Damascus Declaration that the development of good relations between the Kurdish and Arab opposition was seen to be particularly threatening to the Syrian government. The division between the two groups over the issue of the identity of the state and nation and the irreconcilable differences between Arab and Kurdish nationalists kept the Syrian opposition divided and weak. It was suggested by interviewees that understanding and unity between the two groups, then a long way off, would strengthen both sides of the opposition to the state. Before the start of the 2011 uprising, only one demonstration had been held in the name of the Declaration and its organisers failed to gain or actively seek popular support; indeed they did not require it. The supporters of the Declaration were mainly interested in internal organisational technicalities and in dialogue between intellectuals, professional and political activists, much like *Partîya Dêmokrat a Kurd li Sûriyê* in its early days. But the Damascus Declaration never attained the same level of wide support as this first Kurdish party.

The parties that did not sign the declaration claimed that its paragraph on the Kurds did not go far enough to address the Kurdish issue in Syria seriously. Parties such as *Yekîtî* and *Azadî* objected to the exclusion of any reference to constitutional recognition of the Kurds as a second nation in Syria, their right to live in their historic land and the administration of the Kurdish areas by Kurds. The Declaration was seen to reduce the Kurdish issue in Syria to one of minority and citizen rights rather than of national rights. For Sheikh Ali of *Yekîtî ya Dêmokrat*, the issue of national recognition of the Kurds in Syria was a matter that could be addressed in the future. Speaking candidly in 2007, he said that his party did not agree with the whole of the Declaration, but that neither did the Arab opposition parties.

The important thing about the Damascus Declaration was that the Arab opposition was willing to engage in dialogue with the Kurdish political parties and that they had begun to recognise, at least in theory, that the Kurdish nation was an integral part of the Syrian state. Through the continuation of dialogue, he believed that sectors of Arab society and parties which were influenced by Ba'thist propaganda against the Kurds and did not already accept the Kurdish right for national recognition could come to view the Kurdish issue in a more positive light.[63] He thought that through the development of democratic practices and institutions all Kurdish issues could be addressed and solutions found. In this way, the Damascus Declaration was seen, not as a solution to the Kurdish issue in Syria, but as a starting point for the development of democratic politics and understanding between Arabs and Kurds in Syria.

The Kurdish parties were said to be very active within the Declaration. Their experience and history of work in the opposition enabled them to take a leading role in the Syrian opposition movement and influence it on different levels. First, they were able to redress the misinformation spread about the Kurds in Syria through dialogue both with Arab nationalist parties and with individuals in the opposition and demonstrate the importance of the Kurds to the Syrian national question as well as to the development of democracy in Syria. Second, Kurds were able to act within it as equals with their Arab counterparts; hence they could assert their voice and participate in a political process at the pan-Syrian level. Third, the Declaration acted as a training ground for the practice of participatory politics, allowing each side to learn to accept the other and for both to work together in a future, democratic state.[64]

Supporting the Damascus Declaration and working with the Arab opposition came to dominate much of the Kurdish parties' immediate efforts to promote the Kurdish question in Syria. The belief that democratic reform of the state, beginning with the implementation of the terms of the Declaration, would allow the Kurds to occupy an equal position in the Syrian state, led many parties to invest much of their time and effort in developing relations and meeting with the Arab opposition. By many of its supporters, the Damascus Declaration was viewed as a long-term project, essential to the democratisation of the Syrian state and its politics and to the inclusion of the Kurds as equal partners within it.

It is possible to offer different interpretations of the motivations behind this shift in strategy for the parties. It could, for instance, be argued that state controls on and counter measures against Kurdish demonstrations (which commonly affect Kurdish civilians rather than party leaders) led the parties to seek out alternative resources for dealing with the questions of Kurdish rights in Syria. Against this, however, it should be noted that the parties only began to organise demonstrations after the year 2000, and not all party leaders have participated in them. The consequence of the parties' concentration on Arab–Kurdish dialogue seemed to be a clear increase in the distance between the political parties and the Syrian Kurdish population that they represent. The party work for the Damascus Declaration did not involve Kurdish society, or Arab society for that matter, and tended to by-pass the people, seeking a solution through intellectual discussion and faith building between the Arab and Kurdish parties to the Declaration. This concentration on dialogue with the Arab opposition not only did little to involve the Kurdish people, it also failed to produce tangible results on which decisions about support could be made. What is more it contributed to a neglect of the Kurdish communities' grievances and social needs, which led to the gradual withdrawal of Kurdish society's support for the political parties.

Relations with the Syrian Authorities

The issue of relations to the Syrian authorities has posed a 'catch twenty-two' situation for the Kurdish political parties. In order to address Kurdish grievances parties have been compelled to attempt to develop some form of direct relationship with the state, whether it is through confrontation, through seeking dialogue or through the moderation of Kurdish demands. Yet the political parties have often faced criticism when they have developed relations with the Syrian authorities, particularly with the *mukhabarat*. Consequently, to develop relations that would allow them to act as mediators between the Kurdish people and the state, has been something simultaneously desired, avoided or denied by Kurdish party leaders. The issue has been central to the Kurds' perception of their political parties and leaders and consequently is central also to the parties' ability to fulfil their social roles in the Kurdish communities or their political one in relation to the Syrian state. This section examines the forms of relationships that the Kurdish parties developed with state authorities prior to the Syrian uprising and the consequences of these on their relations with Kurdish society and their ability to address Kurdish issues in Syria.

It is clear from interviews with Syrian Kurds that, in order to address Kurdish issues in Syria, some party leaders fostered relations with the government and the security services.[65] The nature of these relations varied according to the political standpoint of the party, the personality of the leader and the sector of the Syrian authorities with which relations were made. While some would only engage the state in a public and official manner, others developed personal covert relations with members of the *mukhabarat* or with Ba'th Party officials in their regions. Since the Kurds have been denied official dialogue and are limited in their options and methods of negotiation, they have been forced to create opportunity where it might not have existed. The Kurdish leaders have faced much criticism from within the Kurdish communities because of what have been perceived of as underhand relations with the Syrian authorities.

The party leader most publicly criticised for his alleged relations with the Syrian *mukhabarat*, is the long standing leader of *Partîya Dêmokrat a Pêşverû a Kurdî li Sûriyê*, Abdul Hamid Haj Darwish. His relations with the head of the *mukhabarat* in Qamishli, General Muhammad Mansourah, have been widely discussed within Kurdish society. He is said to have believed that developing relations with the security services could promote understanding with them and even lighten the oppression of the Kurds.[66] His pre-uprising political stance accommodated the fears of the Syrian authorities more than any other Kurdish party in Syria. The party rejected the idea that the Kurds should be described as a second nation in Syria and sought only cultural rights for the Kurds and equality with Arab citizens. Some residents of Qamishli, familiar with Abdul Hamid Darwish, questioned his wealth, stating that he began his political career as a poor man who owned land but not enough to account for his present wealth.[67] Implicit in this questioning is the belief that much of his wealth was connected, directly or indirectly, to his relations with the Syrian authorities. Darwish, however, is clearly connected to the head of the Azizan clan which is part of the Kikan tribe and, according to some interviewees, much of his political and financial support is derived from the tribe.[68]

It has also been assumed by many Kurds that most, if not all party leaders developed personal relations with the authorities in order to facilitate their existence in Syria.[69] The arrest of a party leader and his release after only a few months or days, or his ability to travel without restrictions, were taken as confirmation of these relations. Because it is clear that all the leaders of the parties are known to the Syrian authorities, it is deduced that they have only been able to work as party leaders with the tacit approval of the *mukhabarat* and that were they true to the Kurdish people and the national struggle in Syria, they would not have been permitted to work in politics. If arrested they should not be released easily when thousands of prisoners of conscience suffer in Syrian prisons, are tortured or have disappeared. Leaders who were arrested and detained for longer periods, including Meshaal Temmo of *Şepêla Pêşerojê ya Kurdî li Sûriyê*, Mustafa Juma'a of *Azadî*, and Hasan Salih of *Yekîtî*, gained necessary national kudos but were, naturally, unable to assume their roles as leaders in the Kurdish national movement in Syria due to their imprisonment. In the case of *Azadî*, the party leadership was all but dissolved due to the arrest of leadership member Mustafa Juma'a, to the relocation of Khayr al-Din Murad to Norway, and to political differences within the leadership.[70]

So did party leaders gain anything from the state? Or did Kurdish leaders unwittingly pacify the Kurdish population and therefore gain tacit permission from the authorities to practice their politics among the Kurds? Or indeed, did the state deliberately seek to damage the power and reputation of party leaders by releasing them from prison or by not seeking to arrest them? These questions do not invite simple answers, even if it is possible to answer them at all. Indeed, the question of the parties' relations with the state is where Kurdish politics in Syria meets an impassable obstacle to its attempts to represent the Kurdish people and to reach a political solution to the Kurdish question in Syria. Prior to the Syrian uprising, the Kurdish public accepted that it was necessary and potentially beneficial to engage with state officials in order to negotiate a solution to one or all of the issues facing the Kurds in Syria. At the same time, the state was not trusted and, to this day, the only concession that the state has been willing to grant, even verbally, is a solution to the problem of the stateless Kurds. But, even then, the concessions offered by the state were minimal.[71] While this issue, discussed further in Chapter 6, is central to the Kurdish nationalist agenda, and has become a vivid symbol of national oppression by the state, the Kurdish parties and Kurdish population are adamant that its solution will not provide an answer to the Kurdish question in Syria. The government itself has used the issue to engage and placate the Kurdish parties on several occasions since Bashar al-Assad came to power, promising to address the situation of these Kurds. Until today, two alteration to the status of stateless Kurds have occurred: one enabling some of the *maktumiin* to apply to be registered as *ajanib*.[72] The other, a decree facilitating naturalisation, promulgated during the Syrian uprising, but which only benefits the *ajanib* Kurds.

The first request by Bashar al-Assad to meet officially with the Kurdish parties came in June 2011, during the Syrian uprising. Collectively the parties boycotted the meeting in condemnation of the brutal suppression of the protests. Prior to this there had been several direct yet unofficial meetings between party leaders and representatives of the state. These were generally arranged at the request of the state rather than in response to parties' calls for dialogue and have engaged party leaders as individuals rather than as representatives of Kurdish political organisations. Meetings with government officials have often come at times when tensions have risen and the Kurdish movement needed to be pacified. The promise of dialogue has been used as a means of preventing demonstrations and the further development of tensions, as was the case of the demonstration planned by *Yekîtî* for the 2009 anniversary of the Hasaka Census. The promise of dialogue made then was never fulfilled.

Unrest in the Kurdish regions in March 2004 demonstrated quite clearly the majority of the parties' position towards the regime. The parties called for an end to the protests on 14 March 2004 and acted to prevent further protests by cancelling the 2004 Newroz celebrations which were due to be held on the 20–21 March. Through their choice not to exploit the opportunity to mobilise the population further and to engage with much wider sectors of Kurdish society, they confirmed their commitment to the status quo – a fragile equilibrium based on non-confrontation between the Kurdish parties and the state. As mentioned above, from that point, commemorations of the events and solidarity with the martyrs were marked by wearing black badges and raising black flags. The parties promoted the observance of 'minutes of silence' and candle lit vigils to mark anniversaries of national importance and as a means of protest against current state policies and actions injurious to Kurdish national interests.[73] The impact of these forms of commemoration and protest was largely to increase solidarity within the Kurdish community. The combined effect of several commemorations and anniversaries and the growth in the numbers of participants caused ripples within the regime and after 2004 public gatherings, protests and demonstrations were subject to harsher repression by the state authorities, who on several occasions resorted to violence and the use of live ammunition to disperse crowds. This indicated clearly that the regime was not prepared to tolerate such levels of mobilisation or expressions of dissent and solidarity from among the Kurds.

The other forms of relations with the state developed by some party leaders are clandestine associations with members of the intelligence services. Interviews with Kurds who are not connected to any political party revealed that many Kurds in Syria believe that most party leaders developed such relations. On the one hand, one might explain these relations as having been necessary to prevent their arrest and enable them to protect members of their community from the state. On the other hand, and more importantly in relation to public opinion about the parties, these relations damaged the credentials of both the leader and the party. The leader is seen to compromise the position of the Kurdish nation in Syria, to damage the national cause and to betray the Kurdish people. This placed Kurdish party leaders and their parties in a precarious position between the state and the Kurdish people. Being true to the people and the Kurdish national cause placed them in extreme danger from the state and their arrest would remove them from their political work. Because membership of political parties has been low and the parties have been defined primarily by their leadership, the arrest of leaders has serious consequences for a party's ability to continue operating. To preserve the status quo and ensure their own and the party's safety, their ability to practice politics and their positions as self-appointed leaders of the Kurdish people in Syria exposes them to criticism from the people.

Consequently, what arose within the Kurdish party movement was the rough division of the Kurdish political parties into three groups broadly reflecting the right, left and centre of the Syrian Kurdish political spectrum. The right group fostered relations with the state and were able to engage in regular, unofficial dialogue with the Syrian authorities but had little or no support from the Kurdish masses (for example, *Pêşverû*). The left group expressed the national yearnings of the Kurdish people in terms which went beyond what is tacitly accepted by the regime; the leaders of these groups were removed from the political scene by the authorities and their parties suffered as a result (examples of these are *Şepêla Pêşerojê ya Kurdî li Sûriyê*, *Yekîtî* and recently *Hizb al-Ta'akhi*). Finally came those parties that occupied the centre ground. They sought dialogue with the state where possible, rejecting it when inappropriate and stayed within the 'red lines' of behaviour dictated by the state, but, when permitted by the regime, they remained active enough to maintain support from within the Kurdish communities (such as *Yekîtî ya Dêmokrat*). Within this middle ground we also find parties such as *el-Partî* which, although not very publicly active in the Syrian Kurdish political arena, rely on connections to Kurdish political parties in Iraqi Kurdistan for their support and connect the solution of the Kurdish question in Syria to the fate of their sister parties in other areas of Kurdistan. These parties have had the benefit of gaining legitimacy from leaders, activities and political circumstances outside the Syrian state. Although they are still defined as illegal and are constrained by the Syrian state, they attract members and supporters because of the common belief among the Syrian Kurds that a solution to the Kurdish question in Syria would come from one of the other areas of Kurdistan. The division between the right and left groups on the one hand, and the right and centre on the other, became more pronounced as a result of the parties' choices in the wake of the events of March 2004 and of the division of *Yekîtî* into two factions in December 2009.

Overall, the Kurdish peoples' criticisms of the political parties stemmed, at least in part, from the belief that the majority of, if not all, party leaders had formed relations with the Syrian *mukhabarat* or some other elements of the regime. The fact that it is normally low-level party members and political and cultural activists and not party leaders who are arrested has led to increasing questioning: first, of the depth of the leaders' commitment to the Kurdish nationalist agenda and, second, of the degree to which it is the leaders' complicity which explains why they remain relatively untouched by a brutal dictatorship.

Changing Political Rules

The Kurdish parties' relations with the state has depended largely on their political strategies, the extent to which they were prepared to confront the regime and the extent that the regime was prepared to tolerate their activities and political standpoint. In return for allowing the parties to exist, the Syrian government has required that they express reformist rather than revolutionary rhetoric and control popular mobilisation, preventing it when necessary. Direct and open relations with the regime and participation in the political processes of the state have been denied to the parties, and those meetings which have been held between the Kurdish parties and state officials have failed to yield any concessions. The closeness of the relationship between the party and the regime appeared to have been inversely related to the strength of the party's demands. The party suggested to have had the most contact with the government is the same that demands least from it. The parties that demand most from the government had senior members of their parties imprisoned.

The concentration of many of the parties on political work within the framework of the Damascus Declaration distanced them further from the Kurdish population. On the eve of the Syrian uprising, cooperation with the Arab opposition was still in its infancy and there was much ground to be covered in order to convince conservative Arab nationalist elements within it to accept the fact of Kurdish political organisation and to rethink their commitment to the Arab identity of the state and its people. The Kurdish experience of the uprising heightened the tensions between the two groups once more raising further obstacles to obtaining Kurdish rights in a post-Assad Syria.

Before the start of the uprising the Kurdish political parties were clearly characterised by their factionalism, their unwillingness to mobilise the Kurdish masses and their conformity to the regime's 'red lines'. Although their very identity continues to define the Kurds as threatening to the security of the state and the ruling party, in practice it seems apparent that the regime understood that party leaders would not go beyond the limits on behaviour which were normally tolerated. The regime's methods of ensuring that subversion further divided the population and its political organisations meant that, while notionally pursuing change, the parties worked to maintain the status quo rather than to challenge it. Although public protest was illegal, a certain amount of controlled protest was tolerated by the regime, providing the parties with opportunities to perform national duties and allowing them to legitimise their existence. At the same time, arrests of participants, party leaders and the encouragement of Arab retributions against Kurdish businesses worked to divide the parties, to prevent mass attendance at demonstrations and to limit their size and frequency. In effect, through controlled toleration of Kurdish political parties in Syria, the state provided an outlet for protest while containing its spread and expressions of dissent through the agents of Kurdish politics themselves, that is, the parties and their leaders.

While some parties appeared to welcome the chance to challenge the regime and make more radical and decisive moves in support of the Kurdish national struggle in Syria,[74] others were much more cautious about confronting the government and were careful not to cross the 'red lines'. The parties disagreed on tactics and objectives, much of party support and membership still coming from social networks rather than being tied to policy and party practice. Consequently, agreement among the political parties to take the Kurdish people to the streets was unimaginable prior to the Syrian uprising.

While demonstrations, vigils and protests occurred regularly, interviews with Kurds inside and outside Syria suggested that the adoption of minutes' silence and candlelit vigils represented an attempt to de-escalate and contain the surge in Kurdish nationalist sentiment after the Qamishli uprising of 2004. The majority of parties, rather than building on and harnessing this potential resource, opted to contain it in order to avoid confrontation with the regime and preserve the status quo. When they did push the boundaries of what was acceptable to the regime, the leadership itself faced arrest and imprisonment, crippling the parties' ability to continue such activities. In the end, both the passive and the more confrontational approaches of the different parties contributed to incapacitating the Kurdish national movement and prevented effective social mobilisation with political objectives.

CHAPTER 5

THE ROLE OF KURDISH PARTIES IN KURDISH SOCIETY

In the previous chapter, the addressing of Kurdish grievances against the state was defined as one of the roles of the Kurdish parties. In order to fulfil this role, the parties have reacted to the restrictions imposed on them by the regime and modified their behaviour to accommodate the fears and demands of the government. Another way in which the parties have dealt with these roles is to dedicate more of their activity to cultural and social issues within the Kurdish communities. This has been both a tactical decision and a consequence of illegality and state discrimination against the Kurdish people. The fact that the parties have been unable to engage the state in official and open dialogue or to take part as Kurdish parties in elections or parliament has led them to give more attention to their own people and to the social and cultural areas of life.

Further functions of the political parties have been derived from their attempts to protect the Kurdish people from the state and to preserve Kurdish identity from arabisation. One of these is the role parties have assumed in facilitating cultural expression and reproduction; and another is the part they have played in mediating in Kurdish social issues. These activities are accorded great importance within the Kurdish communities, although the ability to put them into practice has been complicated by the nature of Kurdish society itself. Traditional forms of social organisation remain important, while modern social relations are superimposed on the traditional and, as a result, deep generational divides have developed. The parties have adopted complex identities and duties which reflect the contrasts within Kurdish society, the strength of Kurdish national consciousness and the need for cultural expression and preservation. Consequently, the parties have taken on roles usually associated with traditional tribal leaders and the *aghawat*, such as mediation in social conflicts. At the same time, their practice in the cultural field has given them an opportunity to become agents of civil society among the Kurds in Syria.

This chapter examines the parties' relations to culture and social mediation. After a preliminary look at what is involved in these two functions, the chapter discusses those factors which have most influence on the parties' abilities to perform these roles. They have partly sprung from the illegality of the parties themselves and the general state of oppression of opposition politics and partly from the numerous opportunities to intervene in social practices, but also partly from the nature of Kurdish society itself. The chapter also shows how, prior to the Syrian uprising, the restrictions placed on the practice of Kurdish culture and on Kurdish gatherings at the same time defined and limited the parties' ability to play a prominent role in Kurdish society.

Facilitating Cultural Reproduction

In his book *Syria's Kurds: History, Politics and Society*, Jordi Tejel defines the most important role of the political parties as cultural framing[1] which is defined as 'conscious strategic efforts by groups of people to fashion shared understanding of the world and of themselves that legitimate and motivate collective action'.[2] Framing relates to the interpretation of events, objects, locations and other points of reference and how they are given meaning. Along with the organisational structure, it is said to be an essential ingredient of motivating individuals or collectives to participate in social movements.[3] As mentioned above, this chapter does not examine the parties as agents of cultural framing itself. Instead it defines the role of the party organisation as one of facilitating both cultural expression and reproduction.

The basis of this diversion from Tejel's analysis is based on the fact that although the parties have been involved in cultural framing, research suggests that this was a role more characteristic of the parties in the past. Cultural framing became associated with party organisations because of the involvement of Kurdish nationalist intellectuals within them. For example, Osman Sabri and others were heavily involved in the dissemination of Kurdish language publications and the promotion of literary and social development amongst the Syrian Kurds. While the early Kurdish parties were the home of the Kurdish intellectuals and hence, the home of nationalist articulation, political activists and intellectuals outside the ranks of the parties revealed in interviews that most intellectuals and cultural activists had, by the year 2000, left the parties.[4] Accordingly, the role of political parties in cultural activities, and particularly in cultural framing, has declined significantly. The current involvement of the parties in Kurdish culture, examined here, shows that the parties ought to be described less as agents of cultural reproduction and framing and more as facilitators of cultural expression and reproduction.

Culture, education and social activity have formed the central pillar of the Kurdish political movement ever since it began. As explained in Chapter 2, the development of Kurdish party politics occurred at a time of militant Arab nationalism, of the dramatic unification of Syria and Egypt into the UAR and of numerous land and economic reforms in the Kurdish regions that were interpreted as attempts to deprive Kurds of their territory and their education.[5] As one Kurdish analyst put it, the origins of the Kurdish movement in Syria were social because they attempted to defend the rights of farmers deprived of their land in the 1960s and 1970s.[6] The coupling of culture with politics, however, and the focus inward onto the Kurdish population had begun before then, with the Bedirkhan brothers and the failure of the Ararat Revolt in 1931. As described in Chapter 2, following the Ararat Revolt Kurdish intellectuals turned once more to cultural issues and a number of social, cultural and sports associations and clubs were established in the Kurdish areas and in Damascus which aimed at developing Kurdish national identity, psyche and consciousness and helping social integration within the Kurdish communities. When the Kurdish political party movement began in 1957, the main instigators of the movement were Kurdish intellectuals who attempted to combine political organisation and activities, intellectual and nationalist pursuits and leftist ideology with efforts to develop and protect the Kurdish culture and identity in Syria. They adopted nationalist doctrine and used heroes, martyrs and intellectual figures as nationalist symbols as well as promoting the use of the Kurdish language in the Latin script. Continuing the focus of the Bedirkhan brothers who pioneered the Kurdish cultural renaissance in Syria, the Kurdish political activists and Kurdish political parties in Syria initiated a non-violent, culturally focused political movement that attempted to develop and restore the Kurdish culture and tradition and to elevate the Kurdish community above its enemies through education, language and literature. The party organisations became vehicles used for cultural framing, to preserve and protect the Kurdish national identity from the state, to develop its differences from the officially defined Arab identity of the state and its citizens and to facilitate the expression of Kurdish culture and identity.

The early parties engaged in cultural framing and development largely through intellectual activities: publishing articles, poetry and prose in their papers and supporting intellectual activities which contributed to the shaping of Kurdish nationalism and national identity in Syria. In the 1980s, the parties became involved in the actual organisation of public cultural activities and events among the Syrian Kurds. This was an attempt to continue this cultural tradition and to further politicise Kurdish national identity amongst the Syrian Kurds as well as a response to changes in their local and national environments.[7] The organisation of such cultural events and activities helped the parties engage with the Kurdish masses. It facilitated the expression of Kurdish culture and its reproduction amongst the Kurds and complemented and supported the work done by the intellectuals. The fact that organising such activities was illegal lent extra importance to the act and set it firmly within the field of Kurdish politics. The actual adoption of such activities by the parties, however, and the fact that they placed them in the public rather than the private sphere, also imbued them with a political character that otherwise might not have been so prominent. As a result, the organisation of cultural events and groups, and participation in them, became something that involved risks of arrest for crimes associated with opposing the government.

Restrictions that the state placed on Kurdish cultural expression itself dictated what cultural activities the Kurdish political parties could involve themselves in. These restrictions were explained briefly in Chapter 1 and are given more detail in each of the following sections: language and folklore; music, dance and sport; and Newroz.

Language and folklore

In Syria, the Kurdish language, Kurmanji, has never been recognised as an official language. Moreover, the Kurds are forbidden from learning and/or teaching Kurdish in school or even privately. Such activities have been deemed criminal offences and are illegal. This is despite the fact that Kurdish is the mother tongue of the majority of Kurds in Syria who generally do not begin to learn Arabic until they start state education at the age of six. Kurdish continues to be used in 90 per cent of daily life in the Kurdish regions. The Ba'th Party's policy towards the Kurdish language stands in stark contrast to its policy towards other ethnic minority groups and foreign languages. Armenians, Assyrians and Jews are all permitted to teach their respective languages as well as cultural traditions and practices in private schools, cultural clubs and associations. Numerous private French, British and Russian schools and institutions still exist in Syria, and other European languages are freely taught.

The prohibition of teaching and learning Kurdish in each of the states which include Kurdish territory has meant that the grammar of the language has not been formally standardised and that many Kurds are illiterate in their mother tongue. Kurdish teaching still occurred in Syria but it was organised privately and conducted in secret.[8] Teaching Kurdish reading and writing is a task which has fallen on the Kurdish communities themselves, on the parties or on the individual and its solution has depended on the interests, initiative and efforts of the students. Lessons have generally taken place in private homes, but there are few people professionally qualified to teach Kurdish. Because of the illegality of the language in Syria, teaching and learning Kurdish became political offences associated with threats to state unity.

Restrictions on publishing under the Ba'th Party have also hindered the ability of Kurds to spread information about their language and folklore to the Kurdish communities in Syria. Kurdish publications were officially banned under the presidency of Adib al-Shishakli (1951–1954) and again during the years of the United Arab Republic from 1958 to 1961. Both regimes conducted campaigns against the Kurds in which Kurdish publications were seized and destroyed. The Ba'th Party has since enforced the ban on Kurdish language publications – books, newspapers, magazines and pamphlets. While some publications on general Kurdish issues have become available in bookshops in the last decade, most Syrian Kurdish authors and political parties have been forced to print and publish their books and material at much higher cost in neighbouring countries, normally Lebanon, and to smuggle them into Syria and distribute them themselves. Under the presidency of Bashar al-Assad, restrictions on publication and the press became even more draconian. In September 2001 the Syrian government replaced the 1949 General Law on Printed Matter.[9] The substitute Decree No. 50, which applied to publishers, printers, journalists, editors, authors, distributors and bookshop owners alike, consisted of more than 50 articles which restricted print media and expanded state control over it. Although heralded by the regime as opening up the media and allowing greater freedom of press, including the licensing of a number of independent newspapers and party organs of political parties within the Progressive National Front, it was condemned by human rights advocates as keeping the Syrian media in the Stone Age.[10] It provided for the imposition of harsh prison sentences and fines even for imprecisely defined offences.

As described in Chapter 2, the use of Latin script to write the Kurmanji Kurdish language was developed by Jeladet Bedirkhan and disseminated across the Kurdish regions through publications and political work by the Bedirkhan brothers in the 1930s. The journals published by the Bedirkhans introduced the use of the Latin script to the Kurmanji speaking areas, and Kurdish political and cultural activists and intellectuals developed and promoted its use.[11] Since their inception, the Kurdish parties have continued to use Kurmanji in their party papers and communications. *Denge Kurd*, the paper published by the first Kurdish party in Syria was printed in both Kurdish and Arabic.[12] Written Arabic, however, continues to be used more widely than Kurdish due to the fact that in Syria it is still more widely read than Kurdish.

Among the necessary credentials of a Kurdish political party leader is a sound knowledge of the Kurdish language and its written use.[13] This is a requirement that ensures that the language is used in political affairs; it sets an example and is a confirmation of the leader's national credentials and dedication to his cause. The majority of party leaders are university educated and were employed in professional positions before dedicating their time solely to party work.[14] Party leaders claim to have organised teaching of Kurdish in villages and in Kurdish cities or neighbourhoods.[15] Participation in such activities, however, like any other Kurdish political activity, has been illegal and so involved obvious risks. Indeed, people teaching Kurdish have been arrested on several occasions; for example, in August 2006, four Kurdish men were arrested in Aleppo for teaching the Kurdish language.[16]

Most Kurdish parties are not currently involved in supporting publication of literature and research on Kurdish history and language produced by Kurdish intellectuals. The larger and better financed parties have supported Kurdish journals such as *Hiwar* and *Pênûs*, both of which are defined as cultural journals. *Pênûs* focuses on Kurdish language and grammar and also publishes poetry, prose and Kurdish folklore. It is published primarily in Kurdish although it also includes articles in Arabic. The journal is printed in Osnabrück, Germany, and it appears that most of its contributors and staff live in Europe, whereas *Hiwar* is published in Arabic and is printed in Qamishli.[17] The journal *Hiwar* has concentrated on Kurdish folklore and on promoting Kurdish–Arab dialogue, with the aim of compensating for the damage done to Kurdish culture through misinformation and the restrictions on the use and publication of Kurdish language imposed by the Ba'th Party.[18] The journal has used language that is not antagonistic to the government and writes about Kurdish culture and language in a coded way. It has also published issues dealing with aspects of the Kurdish political movement and its history. Issue 60–61 of summer 2008 led with articles on the history of the Kurdish national movement in Syria and included articles by party leaders Ismail Omar and Abdul Hamid Darwish, an interview with Daham Miro and two articles on the Kurdish leader Nur al-Din Zaza. The issue also included interviews with and articles on Kurdish artists and on art and literature.[19] Issue 48–49 (Summer and Autumn 2005) published papers given at a conference on the Kurdish question in Syria held in Paris on 1 December 2005 in which academics, representatives of human rights groups as well as some party leaders and activists presented papers. In a bid to avoid the adverse attention of the regime, articles in the journal often discussed the Kurdish national movement historically rather than focusing on contemporary political parties and their activities or demands of the state. The journal is published illegally and has been periodically subject to attempts by the authorities to close it down.[20]

With the growth of national consciousness among the Syrian Kurds and the importance attached to the national language in addition to increasing movement between Iraqi Kurdistan and the Kurdish areas in Syria, it is likely that, as more and more Kurds learn to read and write in Kurdish, they will become better equipped to teach Kurdish reading and writing in the home and even in schools. Indeed, in Iraqi Kurdistan, since the establishment of Kurdish administration over the Kurdish areas of northern Iraq after 1991, education has been conducted in Kurdish and many Kurds are growing up unable to speak Arabic and unwilling to learn it, because it has been defined as the language of their oppressors.

Music, dance and sports

Music and dance are central elements of Kurdish culture and Kurdish music has been a target of the state since the 1950s. Kurdish gramophone recordings along with publications were seized and their owners imprisoned in a specific anti-Kurdish backlash following the overthrow of Adib al-Shishakli in 1954.[21] Similarly, from the 1990s until today, Kurds have been arrested for selling or distributing Kurdish music. The restrictions on the use of the Kurdish language have also had consequences for the legality of and ability to perform and sing Kurdish music and songs.

In 1987 the Culture Minister, Najar al-'Attar, issued an order which forbade the playing and circulation of Kurdish music cassettes and videos. Since its issue, this policy has been intermittently enforced and relaxed. Kurdish music had become fairly freely available in Syria prior to the uprising. Kurdish music shops in Kurdish towns and areas of Damascus were stocked with Kurdish music cassettes, and even some street stalls in Damascus played and sold Kurdish music publicly. At the same time, it was accepted by the vendors of Kurdish music and by professional singers that the public playing and singing of political or nationalist Kurdish songs would not be permitted.[22]

Most Kurdish party leaders claimed that their party had a dance and music group, a football team, a theatre group and that they taught Kurdish privately and secretly to Kurdish youths.[23] Although the parties do not publicise any relations to these groups, as Kurdish organisations, all would be classed as illegal by the Ba'th party. They have generally, however, operated without serious problems. All these groups have worked to maintain and support Kurdish culture and to promote community projects within Kurdish society. Dance and music groups perform traditional Kurdish music and dances and are commonly employed in Newroz festivals. Dancers don traditional Kurdish clothes and male groups normally perform marches to the Kurdish national anthem and mixed groups and children's groups dance to Kurdish music. Plays acted by theatre groups often contain representations of Kurds being oppressed and even beaten by members of the Syrian security services or tales from Kurdish national mythology, such as the story of Newroz. These have educated audiences about Kurdish national myths and about Kurdish experiences in Syria.

Although Kurdish music and dance has political significance and is associated with the quest for liberation and freedom, the actual practical involvement of the music, dance or theatre groups themselves in party politics is said to have been low. In many cases a group is adopted, or co-opted, by a party rather than established by it.[24] Young people, keen to involve themselves in Kurdish culture, have set up other groups, outside the parties. But the issue of funding has provided the parties with an opportunity both to encourage the expression of culture and to establish themselves as agents of civil society and to benefit from the use of culture as a propaganda tool.

Most parties also claimed to have their own football teams and also to sponsor others, providing them with funding, training and help with recruitment. Again the team's connection to the party is not public and, as with the music, dance and theatre groups, it is not common for teams to be made up exclusively of members of a party.[25] When asked about the reasons for organising football teams and other groups, party representatives commonly expressed a sense of social and national duty on the part of the party to ensure that the Kurdish youth have constructive activities in which they can become involved rather than get drawn into crime, drugs and other social misdemeanours.[26] High unemployment and the absence of opportunity and civil society in Syria mean that the youth in particular are vulnerable to such transgressions. The Kurdish political parties are the main organisations available and capable of organising the Kurdish youth in social groups with structured activities and party leaders maintain that there is no political content to their cultural or social activities.[27]

Between the 1970s and 1980s, the way that Kurdish culture was expressed and understood in Syria went from being primarily a private matter, that was not organised on a grand scale due to fear of repercussions from the Syrian authorities, to being controlled by political parties and involving more public events and activities: for example, the large scale Newroz celebrations, the wearing of Kurdish colours in clothes, and the use of music, dance and song in political organisations. Although Kurdish culture had been the subject of Kurdish political organisations and intellectual political activists before this point, the more public display of Kurdish culture adopted by the parties in the 1980s has been attributed to a number of factors. One is that, following the collapse of Barzani's September revolution in Iraqi Kurdistan in 1975, many of the Kurdish parties and Kurdish youth in Syria developed alternative ideas about how to approach the Kurdish question in Syria. Much like the renewal of cultural activities that was experienced in the wake of the Ararat Revolt, the shock of the collapse of the revolution reiterated the need of Kurds for local cultural activities. The parties themselves were forced to reorient their attention towards Syrian Kurdish issues and activities. Another suggestion is that the policy of Hafiz al-Assad, in the wake of the Hama uprising, was somewhat less aggressive towards the Kurds. Kurds began to celebrate Newroz without intervention by the Syrian authorities and the fact that the state made no attempt to stop them, encouraged the people to celebrate more publicly and the parties to give cultural activity a more prominent role in their organisations.[28] Beyond that, the PKK had a profound effect on Kurdish cultural expression and organisation in Syria, particularly in the regions of the Kurd Dagh and Kobanî. The PKK began armed attacks against Turkish military positions in the Kurdish areas in 1980, boosting Kurdish national consciousness and encouraging more public political action.

As mentioned in Chapter 1, the PKK arrived in Syria in 1980, and through its militancy, charismatic leadership and organisational capacity, attracted much popular interest and support. The PKK had begun armed operations in Turkey, its slogans were grand and simple in comparison to the Kurdish parties in Syria and it publicised symbols of Kurdish culture such as the colours of the flag and traditional Kurdish clothes. Its engagement of the Turkish army and government led many Kurds in Syria to question the ability of their own political movement to achieve any concessions from the government and turned their attention to supporting the armed struggle in Turkey. A prevailing idea was that, after a solution was reached in Turkey, the Kurds of Syria would be supported by the Kurds of Turkey and would be more strongly placed to make demands of the Syrian government. Following the example of the Syrian Kurdish political parties, the PKK also made culture an integral part of their politics, using it to spread party propaganda and attract people to the party. As a result, other Kurdish parties in Syria also sought to display Kurdish culture more publicly and develop their activities and political mandate.[29] In the 1980s Newroz celebrations were commonly dominated by those organised by the PKK, while smaller celebrations occurred on the fringes.[30]

The PKK faced fewer restrictions than other Kurdish political parties due to their relationship with the Syrian authorities. Consequently, they were able to express Kurdish identity, culture and politics in a manner that was out of bounds to Syrian Kurdish political parties. Their aggressive outreach tactics and what seems to be outright defiance of restrictions on Kurdish culture and national expression led thousands of Kurds in Syria to join their ranks and dedicate themselves to fighting against the Turkish state rather than to seeking a solution to problems within Syria. With hindsight, as already discussed, their effect on Kurdish politics in Syria has been described as damaging by many Kurds in Syria and by all leaders of Syrian Kurdish parties. Their impact on the practice of Kurdish culture, however, was invigorating and helped it to move out of the private into the public sphere.

Newroz

Probably the most important cultural event of the Kurdish calendar is Newroz. Occurring annually on the twentieth and twenty-first of March, Newroz is New Year, the first day of spring and it symbolises revolution, the end of tyranny and a new beginning. Legend has it that over 2,500 years ago the Kurdish people were ruled by King Zuhak. One day he fell ill and two serpents grew out of each of his shoulders. To prevent the serpents from eating his own brain, every day he would feed to the serpents the brains of two children. The brave blacksmith Kawa, who had lost a number of children to the King, led a rebellion against King Zuhak in which fires on the hill tops were used as a signal for the people to join together to defeat the despotic King. Kawa defeated the King and the people rejoiced in their new freedom. In accordance with this legend, Newroz is generally celebrated outdoors on hilltops. Large bonfires are lit and many people dress in the Kurdish national colours (red, green, yellow and white) and play music, sing and dance. The Kurds celebrate Newroz, both as a symbol of the passing of winter and the coming of the New Year and also as a symbol of freedom, life and revolution connected to the politics of the day. Newroz has become an annual time of tension in Syria.

Under Ba'th Party rule the celebration of Newroz has periodically been forbidden in Syria and has always been subject to restrictions.[31] Kurds claim that Syrian security personnel heavily policed the Kurdish areas at the time of Newroz and that Kurds were regularly prevented from travelling to celebrations and from wearing the Kurdish national colours.[32] Whether the celebrations were permitted, and their size if they were, was largely dependent on the political climate within Syria and the discretion of the provincial governors and local branches of the security services. It was reported that in 2009 Newroz celebrations were held in more than 18 different locations within the Kurdish regions of Syria and that 20,000–40,000 people participated in each.[33] In contrast, only a few Newroz celebrations were held in 2010, and the largest of them was that of the *Partîya Yekîtî ya Dêmokrat* (PYD) the party associated with the PKK, held in Raqqa. In 2010, many parties had advised against public celebration of Newroz, seemingly in response to measures taken by the regime against the Kurdish communities and political parties.[34]

The general formula for Newroz celebrations involves dance groups and singers performing, and speeches are often made. The organisation of the event itself has been illegal under the Ba'th Party. Consequently the logistics of organising Newroz celebrations are complicated and risky. The security services have routinely attempted to interrupt or prevent celebrations from taking place, often dealing with participants very harshly. Arrests are generally made arbitrarily, regardless of whether any Kurdish nationalist symbol was being displayed or whether resistance to the security forces was met with. The nature of the security services' reactions to the celebrations have varied from one place and from one year to another with no apparent pattern or reason, although their attitude towards Newroz celebrations has tended to parallel whether or not the regime has been prepared to tolerate public expressions of politics, such as demonstrations.

Newroz has been an event in which many of the Kurdish parties have traditionally been involved. Initially celebrations were held for party members in secret, away from the gaze of the Syrian authorities, interviews suggesting that the parties have been involved in facilitating public celebrations since the 1980s.[35] Before the intervention of the Kurdish political parties in organising cultural events and celebrations for the public, celebration was primarily family based and largely limited to symbolic acts such as lighting candles to represent the Newroz fire. Naturally, the ability of the parties to direct and maintain their role as organisers and facilitators of cultural expression and development within the Kurdish communities has been affected by state policy towards them. During the 1980s the use of the Kurdish colours was restricted and even the wearing a combination of red, yellow and green was a cause for arrest by the state authorities. Security forces would block the roads leading to places where Kurds intended to celebrate. Kurdish families were prevented from participating and members of the dance and music groups were arrested. It is reported by Kurds that during this period PKK-organised celebrations were held with little restriction, while those organised by other Kurdish parties met with obstacles.[36] In 1986, following demonstrations against the banning of Newroz, which involved the fatal shooting of a number of Kurds by the Syrian police and the security services, Hafiz al-Assad proclaimed that 21 March would be a national holiday in honour of motherhood, that is, Mothers' Day. While this proclamation did not grant official licence and freedom to celebrate Newroz, it has been interpreted as an attempt on the part of the government to diffuse tensions surrounding the celebration by making it a public holiday, not a day with unique cultural significance for the Kurdish population.

According to some informants, the political parties do not 'officially' organise Newroz celebrations. Rather those with adequate funds sponsor music and dance groups which perform during the celebrations. In some celebrations, platforms are provided for the party representatives to address the crowds. Despite its cultural identity, the fact that Newroz celebrations have a political meaning, and involve the support of the parties, means that they have also been subject to divisions in the party movement and to the parties' responsiveness to limits set by the Syrian regime. Consequently, separate celebrations occur for different parties and the extent to which they are openly nationalist has varied considerably. The possibility of Newroz being organised by a group of parties together, setting aside political differences, has been hampered not only by regional variations in the support for and presence of party representatives, but also by considerations given to policy of the regime and the consequences that uniting organisational capacities and celebrations would have for the Kurdish people and their political organisations. Parties such as *Peşveru* of Abdul Hamid Darwish opposed the idea of organising the celebrations together because of the belief that it would provoke an adverse reaction from the authorities against the Kurdish people that could cause a crisis for them.[37] Within the Kurdish communities, most celebrations are known to be connected to one party or another, and often the celebration which a family attends will depend on the political sympathies within the village or family. Relatives and communities sometimes gather in the place of celebration which has been organised by their party of choice. In some cases attendance depends on the region or town with most inhabitants attending a specific celebration for the local area, regardless of party sponsorship.[38]

In Syria it has been necessary to obtain permission from the *mukhabarat* for all social gatherings, celebrations and performances, including Newroz celebrations. Reports and interviews suggest that it was commonplace for the *mukhabarat* to refuse permission to hold any celebration unless certain conditions are met, such as signing agreements that no speeches or singing in 'foreign languages' would take place. Because Newroz is a Kurdish celebration, no official licences exist. Celebrations traditionally occur in the hills where stages are constructed. Mass attendance of public Newroz celebrations in the streets of Aleppo and Qamishli also became more common after the year 2000. The Syrian authorities have routinely blocked roads, destroyed stages, and made arrests before and during the celebrations.[39] The authorities have also marked the event with a number of fatal shootings, particularly in the few years before the start of the Syrian uprising, such as those which occurred in Qamishli in 2008[40] and during the PYD celebrations in Raqqa in 2010.[41]

After the Qamishli uprising of 2004, celebrations of Kurdish New Year became more daring: attendance was higher and participants publicly and openly flew the Kurdish flag and displayed other symbols of Kurdish identity and nationalism. Political speeches became more common and openly nationalistic. During celebrations organised by parties, party leaders, representatives and members have given speeches proclaiming their commitment to the Kurdish nation and its liberation. In the speeches, the celebration itself is connected to the Kurdish people and said to embody their aspirations for liberation. Some examples are: 'Newroz is the freedom of my country'... 'Newroz is a Kurdish day' and 'in the name of the Kurdish movement; viva Kurds, Newroz and Kurdistan'. Political goals are expressed as well as lamentations on the state of disunity among the Kurds: 'it is our right to live in our historic land without oppression'... 'We hope that we will celebrate Newroz all together; we should have one voice for our case, for our freedom, then we can ask for our right as one and we can struggle to obtain it.'[42] The Kurdish national anthem is played and traditionally a dancing group performs a march. Leaders of the march in the *el-Partî* celebrations of 2007 held aloft placards with the slogans: 'Martyrs of Qamishli – No to division of the movement – Yes to unity' and 'Give unity of the Kurds – get a free Kurdistan'. While this language was very daring and risky in the pre-uprising Syrian state, steps were taken to avoid specific reference to the Syrian state and, in the case of the *el-Partî* celebration in Kurd Dagh in 2007, the Syrian flag was displayed at the back of the stage, symbolising a commitment to the unity of the Syrian state, and repeated reference was made to Barzani rather than any Syrian Kurdish leader.

By 2011, the involvement of the Kurdish political parties in the organisation of Newroz had decreased and it was only those with political intent and sufficient funding and support that held celebrations. Moreover, tensions around the event itself were amplified following the events of March 2004, as the numbers of fatal shootings of Kurds by the security services and the intensity of campaigns of arrest increased.[43] This led some parties to distance themselves from the celebrations in attempts to appease the Syrian authorities. Two parties in particular were heard, in the lead-up to Newroz 2010, to advise their supporters to stay away from celebrations after warnings from the Syrian authorities.[44] As the involvement of the parties in Newroz waned, it appeared that other Kurdish individuals were beginning to attempt to use the Newroz celebrations for their own interests. It was reported that in 2009 and 2010 businessmen began to sponsor Newroz celebrations in the Jazira and used the events for promotion of their companies. The involvement of businessmen in the Newroz celebrations is an interesting and significant development that supports the assertion by some interviewees that the involvement of the parties in the celebrations and their monopoly on the organisation of Kurdish culture was declining.

While the preservation and development of Kurdish culture and national identity was a duty and an integral part of the Kurdish political party movement in Syria, it would be wrong to imply that Kurdish culture has been maintained and promoted solely on the initiative of the political parties. Since the year 2000 and the surfacing of the Syrian opposition in the Damascus Spring, and particularly following the Qamishli uprising of 2004, many Kurdish initiatives for addressing state discrimination and for facilitating and organising Kurdish cultural expression have been developed outside the parties' orbit. Kurdish groups independent of the political parties have set up Kurdish human rights organisations inside and outside Syria, seeking to address the Kurdish issue in Syria by connecting it to international human rights organisations and exposing human rights abuses by the state. A number of youth groups emerged after the Qamishli uprising with mandates similar to those of the political parties but which approached Kurdish cultural and political activities in a more grass-roots or populist manner.[45] These groups attempted to modernise and democratise Kurdish politics in Syria and provide an alternative forum for Kurdish nationalist activities. They came to play a leading part in directing the Kurdish response to the Syrian uprising in 2011.

The introduction of the internet to Syria in 2000, bringing expanded access to external organisations and information, encouraged initiatives and communication between Kurdish groups both inside Syria and outside it and it also encouraged more criticism of the political parties themselves. The internet provided access to numerous Kurdish educational sites, including some that help learning Kurmanji, some that provide information on human rights abuses against the Kurds in Syria and some that provide information on Kurdish history and culture. Indeed, during the Syrian uprising these communications technologies became invaluable, particularly in light of the media blackout that the Syrian government attempted to impose over Syria. The use of the internet has not been without its risks, even before the start of the uprising. It is monitored by government agencies and restrictions are placed upon its use; many sites are banned and arrests have occurred for posting information. During the uprising, groups connected to the regime even formed an electronic army designed to disrupt communications between protestors and to discover access codes, passwords and the identity of Syrian activists. Enterprising youths have been able to negotiate government controls and restrictions maintaining channels to the global information networks. The Kurdish younger generation in particular have been using easier access to gather information on the Kurds, download Kurdish music, communicate in chat rooms and through social networking with Kurds all over the world, share opinions and air criticisms of both the Syrian government and their own political movements. As a consequence individual initiatives have become somewhat less risky and in many respects easier and possibly more fulfilling and progressive than reliance on party publications and education for information on the Kurds. One interviewee commented, however, that the political parties maintained a monopoly over political organisation amongst the Kurds in Syria and that many new endeavours have failed to develop as a result.[46]

With the passing of time, the role of the parties in facilitating cultural expression and organising Kurdish cultural activities has declined.[47] While the political parties formerly engaged in cultural framing and other intellectual activities, in the past two decades this aspect of their political mandate has gradually weakened. This was primarily a consequence of the departure of many Kurdish intellectuals from the parties, the widening of the generation gap, a failure to exploit new communications technologies, and the growth of criticism of the parties, which is examined further in Chapter 7. On the eve of the Syrian uprising the parties continued attempts to organise cultural activities and facilitate the expression of Kurdish identity within the Kurdish communities but some cultural activists outside the party organisations have chastised the parties for not doing enough for Kurdish culture when it was in their ability to do more.[48]

Mediation and Power

As the previous chapter showed, on issues and cases that are national in character and involve the Syrian government, such as the Qamishli uprising of March 2004, the Kurdish political parties have attempted to act as mediators and a buffer between the state and the Kurdish people. And within Kurdish society, the parties have adopted the role of mediators in social problems, a role originally belonging to the traditional tribal leadership and notable families. The nationalist character of the Kurdish parties and the nature of the regime have meant that inside the Kurdish communities party leaders have been able to act with authority, influence their constituencies and intervene in social affairs. The perseverance of traditional customs and morals within the Kurdish communities has meant that the idea of leadership itself, even when self-appointed, still commands public respect and reverence. When coupled with their nationalist credentials and pre-existing authority connected to family lineage or wealth, party leaders have been able to intervene in Kurdish social affairs and to mediate in social problems. While party representatives deny that they get benefits from acts of mediation, it is arguable that the parties, and particularly their leaders, have been able to gain additional power, support and respect from this social aspect of their mandate.

Mediation has been described as one of the main roles of the Kurdish political party to which great importance has been attached.[49] But the ability of the parties to perform this role has also diminished, the reasons for which will be clarified below. Naturally, the role of mediator has been taken by members of the party leadership and, on the whole, it is local leaders known among the community, who are in a position to act in this way. Local authority and recognition is vital in this role and members of the leadership from outside the area of a dispute would not be able to intervene in the conflict unless it was also connected in some way to his area. Some parties are not represented in all Kurdish areas and therefore, their role in mediation would also be limited regionally.

The political parties are not the only forces in Kurdish society that are able to mediate in social problems. Small problems relating to a family or between two people in a village might only require the intervention of a family elder or someone neutral and respected within the village. Likewise, the specific nature of the problem might require the involvement of a mediator such as the local *mukhtar*, sheikh or even Ba'th Party official. Mediation, however, has become an area associated with the Kurdish political parties in Syria. Through looking at the questions of how this occurred and what explains the ability of the political parties to assume roles traditionally belonging to tribal leaders, the *aghawat*, sheikhs and village authorities, it is also possible to shed some light on the functions and position of Kurdish parties within Kurdish society in Syria. These questions are addressed by looking at three social dynamics: first, the breaking of traditional authority; second, the perseverance of links between the traditional Kurdish leadership and some of the political parties; and third, the public support for the political parties and respect for their endeavours in Syria.

The breakdown of traditional authority

For Kurdish party leaders to adopt mediation as one of their roles in society, the traditional leadership had to lose its grip on power over the Kurdish communities. The loosening of tribal relations among the Kurds in Syria is something that occurred over a long period of time and, by all accounts, it seems that different factors influenced the decline of the tribes in the different Kurdish areas.

The Kurd Dagh

As explained in Chapter 2, the power of the tribes and the *aghawat* had all but disappeared in the Kurd Dagh region by the 1950s. Pierre Rondot described the area's tribes in 1939 as being completely sedentary and, while preserving their culture and morals, their original social framework had broken up.[50] Similarly, Roger Lescot in 1940 commented on the 'extreme loosening of tribal connections in the society of the Kurd Dagh' due to the centralisation of Ottoman rule in the nineteenth century and the demise of local autonomy and the traditional tribal leadership. He described the power of the then notable families as being derived from material wealth rather than from more traditionally tribal power relations based on military conquests, force of numbers and loyal followers. He noted that individuals ceased to be members of tribes but became simple peasants, attached only to the land and its cultivation.[51]

This feature of socio-economic relations in the Kurd Dagh region gave it a political aspect different to that of other Kurdish societies.

The peasants' movements of the *Muroud* in the 1930s and 1940s and then the Syrian Communist Party in the 1950s had also encouraged peasants to assert their rights and to confront their landlords even before the implementation of land reforms in 1958. At this time, loyalty to the *agha* was a result of land rights rather than a commitment to any tribal relations or personal loyalty. The land reforms of 1958 destroyed any remaining power that large landowners had over the peasantry and over village life. The redistribution of land also contributed to freeing the peasantry from political and social obligations to their landlords and the traditional leadership as well as from economic ones. Due to the history of peasants' movements and the strength of the Communist Party in the Kurd Dagh, the effect of the reforms was almost immediate in this area.[52] With time, wealth based upon land ownership has been diminished further due to high fertility among the Kurds and the division of land through inheritance. After the land reforms, the sons of *aghawat* were left with smaller family estates to be divided between them. Today, the land of those sons is being divided between their sons and, in some cases, daughters. Generally large families among the Kurds mean that the new generation is not guaranteed any inheritance of land wealth associated with traditional Kurdish leadership, effectively ending any economic links to traditional leadership and power and loosening ties to the village. In this region the tribal system and notable families are present in name only. No power is derived from former nobility besides a formal reverence extended to elders whose reputation and standing in society stems from this tradition.[53]

After the establishment of the Syrian Kurdish political movement, the *Partîya Dêmokrat a Kurd li Sûriyê* and then *el-Partî* became the primary mediators in the region in the 60s and 70s. With their connections to Barzani's KDP, their representatives gained much respect and, for many, the party itself was known as 'Barzani's party' rather than as a Syrian Kurdish party with a corresponding agenda.[54] In the 1980s the PKK became very strong in the region due to its proximity to Kobanî, where Öcalan entered Syria, and to the Beqqa Valley in Lebanon where PKK training camps were concentrated. With the arrival of the PKK in the area, many of the functions of the Syrian Kurdish parties were co-opted by the PKK. Mediation became a means of spreading party propaganda and recruiting adherents and collecting donations for the party. The majority of Newroz celebrations were organised by the PKK and it is reported that their presence and position in the region was so great that they effectively controlled the area. They are said to have been involved in even the smallest of social conflicts.[55] This remained the situation until October 1998 when Abdullah Öcalan was expelled from Syria.

The loss of power and support for the PKK in the region was also immediate. In its place, however, the PYD which was established in 2003, operated illegally and as a Syrian Kurdish party. After the start of the Syrian uprising and the withdrawal of government forces the PYD gradually imposed Kurdish control over the area through erecting checkpoints and opening Kurdish schools, making it the main authority in the region. Possibly because of the absence of tribal relations or because of the distance from the centre of Kurdish politics in Syria (the Jazira region), other Kurdish parties have been less well represented in the Kurd Dagh. Parties that have been particularly strong in the region are the PYD because of its ideological connection to the PKK, *Yekîtî ya Dêmokrat* due to the presence of its leader, Sheikh Ali, in the region, and *el-Partî* because of its connections to the KDP, and *Azadî*, due to the presence of local leadership. Prior to the start of the Syrian uprising local residents suggested that mediation in the Kurd Dagh was primarily performed by respected individuals, local state officials and even by representatives of the Ba'th Party, and that the intervention of the political parties in social affairs was minimal.[56] The weakness of the state in the region during the uprising, however, enabled Kurdish parties to reassert authority in most Kurdish regions, the dynamics of which is examined in Chapter 8.

The Jazira

A similar process of socio-economic transformation has taken place in the Jazira, although tribal relations persisted for longer than in the Kurd Dagh. The Jazira was historically a seasonal grazing ground for Kurdish tribes from the mountains north of the area, yet habitation of the Jazira by Kurdish tribes goes back at least as far as the fifteenth century.[57] Most of the tribes of the Jazira originate from these same mountainous regions to the north or belong to tribes divided by the Syrian–Turkish and Syrian–Iraqi borders. Tribal relations in these areas were relatively stronger than those in the Kurd Dagh due to the remoteness of their territories, greater distance from major commercial centres and proximity to the border between the Ottoman and Safavid empires. Although settlement was encouraged by the French, tribal leaders continued to hold on to military power and retained armed retinues during the mandate years.[58] The acquisition of land by tribal chiefs and placing of family members in key positions in the local authorities worked to concentrate power in the hands of leaders such as Hasan Hajo Agha. Hajo Agha was the charismatic leader of the Haverkan tribal confederation and a Kurdish nationalist who was involved in Xoybûn, the Kurdish cultural revival and the Kurdish–Christian autonomy movement in the mid-1930s. For Hajo, and other tribal leaders, the tribe provided a source of political and economic power and social prestige. Besides this, nationalist political activities and leadership bolstered his reputation among the population of the Jazira.[59]

Land reforms in the Jazira region were begun in 1958, during the union between Syria and Egypt, and were revised in the 1960s and 1970s under the Ba'th Party government of Hafiz al-Assad.[60] The area already included a large number of tribal leaders owing to the migration of many from Turkey to the Jazira in the 1920s. During the mandate period, the French authorities had also rewarded tribal leaders loyal to the French with land and other privileges, and when land was redistributed during the reforms, the Arabs were disproportionately favoured over Kurdish inhabitants – a state policy that increased Kurdish poverty relative to Arab inhabitants in the region and which may have contributed to concentrating authority and power in the hands of the traditional Kurdish leadership rather than redistributing it, as was the case in the Kurd Dagh. Consequently, in the Jazira, the hold of the traditional families over power in the region was, and remains, greater than in the Kurd Dagh region.

What land was given to Kurdish peasants was often subject to rent agreements in which the farmer would pay a sum to the government for each dunem in his possession. But Kurdish farmers were not provided with legal documentation or proof of payment or occupation. Consequently, even when they had farmed the land for several years and had a legal right to claim ownership, they were not able to do so. Similarly, they were unable to sell their land and without documentation proving ownership or the right to it, the land was easily expropriated from them.[61] Kurdish inhabitants along the borders were particularly hard hit by the reforms in these areas. Arabs moved from Raqqa and Aleppo to the area by the government were the main recipients of land distributed by the state. It is claimed that they were given all necessary legal documentation and rights to the land[62] and that their villages were supplied with all utilities and services while Kurdish ones remained without running water or electricity.

It is believed by many Kurds that the land reforms and the Arab Belt were used as a means of breaking the power of nationalist leaders among the landowners, dividing the Kurdish communities from those across the border in Turkey and Iraq and of impoverishing the Kurdish population in the regions. At the time of the land reforms the Hajo family owned approximately 22 villages in the Tirbespî area, amounting to 180,000 dunums.[63] All the land belonging to the family was expropriated by the state and they were not compensated.[64] The land reforms struck the material foundations of the family's power in the region and broke their leadership. Divisions between the Kurds on either side of the border were achieved through the Arab Belt project in which Arabs were moved into the border areas and Kurds stripped of the land and forced out.

Compared to the Kurd Dagh, the workers' movement was not strong in the Jazira. The proximity of the Kurd Dagh to one of Syria's major and historic cities (Aleppo) and the movement of people between the areas contributed to the development of entrepreneurship and the independence of workers from the land. The Kurds of the Jazira region were cut off from their major commercial centres by the drawing of the border between Turkey and Syria. The majority of the regions towns were built during the mandate[65] and facilitated the settlement of tribes in the region by changing their habits and customs. The town of Qamishli was only built in 1926 on the land of one of the tribal leaders, Qaddur Beg.[66] But urban dwelling and commercial activity came to be dominated by Christian refugees who came into the region in the 1930s. Consequently, few Kurds lived in the region's towns;[67] opportunities for work outside agriculture and farming were limited and peasants remained tied to the land and landlords for longer than in the Kurd Dagh.

Several factors worked to preserve traditional socio-economic relations within the Kurdish communities in the Jazira, during and beyond the mandate period. The French encouraged the final settlement of any remaining semi-nomadic tribes through the provision of land and building towns in the region. In doing so they bolstered the authorities of tribal chiefs loyal to them with material possessions and positions of authority within the local mandate administration. Peasants did not assert their independence from semi-feudal relations with their landlords. The land reforms destroyed much of the remaining power of the tribes over Kurdish society and left behind it a system in which tribal relations are not strong but are respected and could be evoked when necessary and when the situation permitted. The dispossession of many Kurds from their land contributed to migration to the region's cities and also to the Syrian interior, to cities such as Damascus where they have sought menial work and congregated in the predominantly Kurdish area of Ruqqn al-Din and in suburbs such as Zor Ava, which is described in Chapter 6.

Kobanî

Whereas the primary cause of tribal decline in the Efrîn region was economic development and modernisation, in the Jazira it was the land reforms, and in Kobanî, one tribal leader argued the decline was the fault of education and modernisation. The tribal system represented traditional and conservative Kurdish society and attempts to maintain their power which was based on unquestioning loyalty and obedience to the tribal leaders. With the spread of education the tribe began to be seen as a hindrance to modernisation and also to Kurdish political aspirations. Tribal leaders had failed to encourage education among their people, even among their own children and had defended their own interests without involvement in the real political, social and economic problems within the Kurdish communities. The tribes began to be seen as representing and spying for Arab authorities in exchange for money. Consequently, without the support of the people the power of the tribal leaders was broken and in its place representatives of the political parties intervened in Kurdish social and economic problems as well as the obvious political issues, in some cases achieving rapid solutions to social problems that tribal leaders would never even address, including cases of revenge and feuds.[68] Kurdish political parties were viewed by groups of Kurds interviewed as a positive and progressive element and one that was crucial in bringing about social reform in the Kobanî region. The PKK in particular was described as having the greatest effect on Kurdish society, implying that in this region, tribal organisation persisted into the 1980s, which is when the PKK entered Syria.

In Kobanî the tribal system remains relatively strong in comparison to the Kurd Dagh and even to the Jazira. The levels of literacy and education are lower than the other Kurdish areas in Syria, particularly among women, with fewer people continuing education beyond the compulsory primary grades one to six.[69] Kurdish nationalism was not as strong in Kobanî as in the Jazira. Tribal leaders did not become involved in the Kurdish national movement as they did in the Jazira from the 1920s onwards and, as a consequence, the political parties did not gain such a prominent position within Kurdish society. The reformist ideas of the national movement did not alter society or tribal relations in the way that they did in the Jazira.[70] Tribal relations, however, have been weakened considerably in the region and much of this weakening is credited to the role of the PKK and the opening up of the region as a result of the state road linking Aleppo and Qamishli, which passes through the area. This has aided the development of closer relations between the three Kurdish areas and encouraged trade.

As far as it has been possible to ascertain, not all Kurdish political parties have been represented in the Kobanî region. The five larger parties (*el-Partî* of Abdul Hakim Bashar, *Yekîtî ya Dêmokrat*, *Yekîtî*, *Pêşverû*, and *Azadî*) had party organisations in the regions as well as the PYD. Other smaller parties may have had groups of supporters but they did not have organisational capacity.[71] In the region, people are said to have joined the parties in groups rather than as individuals as is the case in the Kurd Dagh.[72] Tribal chiefs are still called upon to mediate in social problems, particularly when the issues involve members of the tribe or of two or more tribes. Alongside this, party leaders have also been able to intervene in social affairs where the situation allows and the PYD in particular has been able to assert some authority in the regions. Prior to the Syrian uprising the parties were less well represented in the region.

From the above descriptions of the breakdown in tribal authority in the Kurd Dagh, the Jazira and Kobanî, it is clear that different rates of socio-economic change have existed in the three Kurdish areas of Syria. All of them, however, have led to an inevitable erosion of tribal relations. In the wake of the land reforms an opportunity opened for the new political party leadership to step in and adopt roles formerly filled by the traditional leadership. This task was facilitated by the fact that the political leadership in the Jazira included members of the traditional leadership as well as the new nationalist political activists and intellectuals. What remains of the tribal system in the Jazira and Kobanî, and to some extent in the Kurd Dagh region, is more of a sentimental attachment to the tribe and village than actual tribal socio-economic relations. In rural areas the tribes exist primarily in name and tribal leaders and elders are respected, but their actual power is limited. This overlap between traditionally tribal social roles and the modern institutional form of the political party prevented a vacuum opening up in the area of mediation and prevented the interference of the state in Kurdish affairs and the spread of civil conflict within the Kurdish communities that might have occurred in the absence of any regional and local leadership.

Attempts have been made by the state to bolster the power of the remaining tribes by inviting them to represent the Kurdish people by involving them in discussion of solutions to Kurdish issues. A delegation of approximately 30 Kurdish tribal leaders, nearly all of whom were from Dêrîk and Serê Kanîyê in the Jazira region, was invited to Damascus to discuss the issue of the stateless Kurds with a member of the Ba'th regional leadership, Muhammad Said Bikhaytan.[73] The tribal leaders, in support of the political parties and defining their position within Kurdish society, declined to act as Kurdish representatives in this instance. They informed the authorities that they were social leaders and that this was a political issue which they were not involved in, and that if they wanted a political solution, they should speak to the representatives of the political parties.[74] Similarly in April 2011 after the start of the Syrian uprising, Bashar al-Assad invited and met with tribal leaders from the Jazira. Eighteen Kurdish leaders and twelve Arab dignitaries and tribal leaders and three Christians gathered on the 5 April in a meeting that largely concentrated on the Kurds. Two party leaders asked to participate, Abdul Hamid Haj Darwish and Aziz Daoud, declined the invitation on the grounds that they were not invited as representatives of political parties and would not participate in meetings held as 'social gatherings'.[75] The tribal leaders present reiterated to Assad that they did not represent the Kurdish public and that he should meet with the political parties.

Links between the traditional and party leadership

The early Kurdish nationalist movement was dominated by the Kurdish nobility, intellectuals, tribal chiefs and some religious sheikhs. In the 1950s, with the formation of the KDP in Iraq, the development of the peasants' movements, the popularity of the Communist Party among Kurdish intellectuals and activists and the breaking of the power of semi-feudal landlords in Syria, the Syrian Kurdish political movement incorporated all sectors of society within one representative political party. Since then, the divisions within the party movement have reflected the broad social divisions within Kurdish society, forming a political spectrum and producing a right and left wing and a centre.

It is difficult to extract information about the connection of the existing political parties to their constituencies and to the traditional leadership. Party leaders interviewed repeatedly denied any connection between the parties and the traditional tribal system and power relations. One possible explanation of the adoption of mediation by party leaders is that the leaders themselves are directly connected to the traditional nobility. It is clear from looking at the personal profiles of party leaders and from interviews with non-party political activists and observers that many of them owe prestige and authority to their family background. One interviewee indicated that to know the parties, one must know the families.[76] Another suggested that most party leaders were related,[77] and yet another said that 90 per cent of the party leaders belong to the families of heads of tribes.[78] It has not been possible to examine the background and family of each party leader in detail or the relations between the leadership of each party, but what information has been accumulated indicates that most party leaders are from the Jazira and several of them belong to the Kikiyeh[79] and Kikan tribes[80] of Dirbasiye region.[81] For a number of party leaders these relations with the big Kurdish families facilitated the acquisition of additional power in Kurdish society. These included Abdul Hamid Darwish, Dr Abdul Hakim Bashar, Nazir Mustafa (d. 2008), Kamal Ahmed (d. 1998) Nusradin Ibrahim and Ismail Omar (d. 2010).[82] Families or tribes may also benefit from such relations. As mentioned in Chapter 3, tribal leaders competed to support and gain representation in the first Kurdish party in Syria as a means of gaining prestige in Kurdish society. At the time of writing, presenting their sons into the ranks of the Kurdish parties still offered a chance to further influence within Kurdish society and extend traditional forms of authority and influence through the modern medium of the political party. The deterioration of tribal power, however, and the division of Kurdish family networks as a result of the land reforms and the intervention of the *mukhabarat* in Kurdish society, has meant that the pursuit of power through the party for the realisation of tribal interests is limited in its effect.[83]

For leaders with a background of nobility or a relation to one of the large families, party leadership may act as a means of formalising pre-existing relations of power between the leader and the local community, which would have previously been based on semi-feudal relations of tribal leader or *agha* to his subjects. In such cases, mediation, a practice that was traditionally the ground of tribal, village leaders, sheikhs and *aghawat*, is arguably a means of validating authority within the local communities. As such, party leadership serves a personal interest in maintaining and reproducing local power relations in a different form. For example, Abdul Hamid Darwish, leader of the *Peşveru* is often involved in mediation in the Jazira region and it is said that he concentrates on mediation as a means of bolstering his position in society. His ability to mediate depends on the support of the Kikiye tribe.[84] Decisions and judgements made in finding solutions for social problems require an understanding in the community that judgement will be upheld and respected. For that, the tribal connections offer some guarantee of enforcement of decisions in the Jazira region. Interestingly, Abdul Hamid Darwish's position and ability to mediate is also accredited to his good relations with the Syrian authorities.[85] People choosing him to mediate in their conflicts believe that his decisions will have additional legitimacy because of these relations. Judgements are believed to have a quasi-legal status and will not be challenged by the state. Darwish is also commonly involved in mediating in any problems involving the state directly.[86] Similarly, apart from his position as a Doctor in Qamishli and his connection to the Gabarah tribe of the Amudê area, the Secretary General of *el-Partî*, Dr Abdul Hakim Basher, commands respect and authority in the region due to the party's relationship to the KDP in Iraq. Again, legitimacy is imparted on the judgements made by him on account of the party's alliance with the KDP and the strength of Barzani's leadership.[87] The former Secretary General of *el-Partî*, Nazir Mustafa, was also from a tribal family. His great grandfather was a leader in the Kurdish rebellion in Turkey and two grandfathers were leaders in the Sheikh Said Revolt and in Xoybûn. His father and uncles became members of the *Partîya Dêmokrat a Kurd li Sûriyê* in 1957 and Nazir Mustafa was raised as a loyal supporter of Barzani.[88]

Although it has not been possible to gather all necessary information to pronounce decisively on this subject or to provide specific data on tribal lineages and relations within the parties, research suggests that connections exist between elements of the traditional and modern party leadership, particularly in the Jazira region. As one might expect, these connections appear to be more common within the right and centre of the political spectrum of the Kurdish party movement. Other parties, particularly those to the left of the political spectrum, do not seem to depend so heavily on connections to the traditional families or nobility and such networks for political support.

Popular support

The ability of the Kurdish political parties to mediate also depends on popular support as well as on the belief that the leader's judgement will hold weight. If a party is able to win the support of large sectors of Kurdish society and is respected within it, the leadership gains authority and respect and, where personality permits, the ability to intervene in social affairs and pronounce judgement in conflicts. The first Kurdish political party in Syria established in June 1957 was successful in this. As described in Chapter 3, the party gained mass support among the Kurdish people in Syria. Even when the party divided in 1965 and when *el-Partî* was formed in 1970, the parties were trusted and respected. Mediation became an area associated with this new nationalist leadership and judgements of party leaders were treated as valid and just by the public, irrespective of whether they were. They were even considered to be better than the judgements of tribal leaders because they were seen to be acting in the interests of the Kurdish nation and to be neutral and devoid of personal interests. *El-Partî* in particular was known to resolve social conflicts and impose solutions without resort to the Syrian authorities.[89]

Estimates suggest that the first party, *Partîya Dêmokrat a Kurd li Sûriyê*, had more than 30,000 members in the early years of the political movement, showing that the people supported the party and its leadership. The leadership at that time consisted of a relatively small group of Kurdish intellectuals, professionals, religious and tribal leaders and renegades from the Communist Party with representatives in all of the Kurdish areas of Syria, including Damascus. As time passed and the political movement fragmented, particularly after 1980, the leadership of the parties weakened and became an area of confusion, even among Syrian Kurds. The political parties continued to practice mediation but their ability to mediate effectively weakened with the party divisions and the loss of support for the parties over time.

Before the start of the Syrian uprising, whether or not a party leader was invited to mediate or intervene in a social problem depended on the standing of the party and party leader in the particular area and on the availability of other forms of mediation and their suitability to the problem at hand. Because much of the prestige of the party leader has been derived from family connections and networks, it follows that those leaders who are well connected and belong to tribes which retain some authority, such as the Kikan or Azizan, have been better equipped to perform this role. Not all parties are represented in all Kurdish areas of Syria. Indeed, it appears that some of the smaller parties are constituted primarily of family members and that their influence extends only as far as their family relations permit. Consequently, it is likely that a leader of such a party would be able to intervene in matters relating to his immediate community and extended family. His authority, however, would be limited to those areas of support.

In the absence of civil society organisations and state institutions, not to mention an effective and just judicial system to deal with problems, the Kurdish people have sought internal solutions to social problems where possible and the parties have tried to prevent the intervention and involvement of the state by acting as mediators.[90] The Syrian legal system itself is corrupt and bureaucratic and decisions of the courts are often subject to delays. In contrast, the decisions of tribal leaders were implemented immediately and were binding, if not always just. In this manner the parties, if involved in mediation, have acted as a buffer between the Kurdish people and the state, pre-empting the involvement of state officials or, if they have connections to the state authorities, also acting as some unofficial form state representative. In the past, the parties' leaders commanded respect in Kurdish society because of their commitment and attention to the Kurdish nationalist cause and also simply because of their position as leaders, whether self-defined or elected. Judgements of the parties were considered just simply because the parties were respected and revered within Kurdish society. With the fragmentation of the political movement, social support for the parties has diminished and thus their role in mediation has decreased. Their ability to achieve legitimate solutions to problems was also impaired due to their division and illegality in Syria. Although the parties are still involved in mediation, before the start of the Syrian uprising it was reported that most problems were solved through the courts or increasingly, through the mediation of a local sheikh, landlord, notable family or even of representatives of the government.[91] One Kurdish source even suggested that the intervention of tribal leaders in social problems had increased in parallel to the decline of trust in the political parties.[92] The power vacuum opened during the Syrian uprising has left the field open for political parties to revive their social roles and once more assume positions of authorities in Kurdish society.

The Social and Cultural Role of the Parties

The role of the political parties in Kurdish society is threefold. First, the parties attempt to address Kurdish grievances. Second, they facilitate and maintain Kurdish culture and language. And third, they act as mediators in social problems within Kurdish communities and between the communities and other actors. Their capacity to perform all of these roles is both hindered and facilitated in different ways by the state and by the Kurdish communities themselves.

The ability of the political parties to adopt the roles of cultural framing and mediation in Kurdish society derives both from the cultural tradition within Kurdish nationalism in Syria and from the pre-existing social relations that are derived from tribal, or semi-feudal arrangements coupled with nationalist credentials. The absence of autonomous civil society organisations capable of promoting Kurdish culture, or of acting as intermediaries within Kurdish society, or between the Kurdish people and the state, required the assumption of these roles by some form of representative institution within Kurdish society. The final blows that fractured the tribal system among the Kurds in Syria were the land reforms that began in 1958. These coincided with the birth of the Kurdish political party movement in Syria, the leadership of which was able to fill the role of intermediary previously dominated by tribal chiefs. Meanwhile, state restrictions on Kurdish culture and expressions of Kurdish identity and politics began to be implemented, allowing the parties to pursue the cultural tradition of the Kurdish political and intellectual movement in Syria and adopt culture as a political tool.

The exact extent to which the political parties are connected to the former traditional tribal leadership, and the strength of those connections, is unclear. As has been shown, some party leaders, particularly within the right and centre, are known to be related to the leaders of tribes and supported by their tribes, and it is primarily these leaders who are able to intervene in social affairs. But, whatever the relationship, the parties are modern institutions with Kurdish nationalist agendas and, by all accounts, today the parties have more power than the tribes.[93] The political parties' leaders gained the respect of the Kurdish people through their endeavours on their behalf and from their family relations and historic position. But the strength of the party itself may be measured by the extent to which the leader is involved in mediation, by the scale of their support for cultural endeavours, by whether they are prepared to challenge the regime, by their popularity and by their scale of party organisation in Kurdish society. High levels of all these characteristics will not necessarily be found in one party, and so, for some parties, success in one area might undermine success in another.

In the presence of the authoritarian government and the absence of civil society in Syria, the Kurdish communities have allowed the political parties to act as facilitators of their culture and identity. The denial and suppression of Kurdish culture and identity by the regime has been one of the main issues that the Kurdish communities face. It has also been the basis for the arrests of Kurds, for statelessness, for expropriation of land and other policies aimed at arabising the Kurds and Kurdish areas. The politicisation and criminalisation of Kurdish culture has prevented the majority of Kurdish people from acting in ways that promote and publicise their identity. In the absence of any other traditional forms of nationalist leadership or organisation among the Kurds in Syria, it has been the Kurdish political party organisations that have stepped in to promote, maintain, reproduce and organise Kurdish cultural identity.

CHAPTER 6

THE STATELESS KURDS OF SYRIA

This chapter discusses a case within a case. It takes as its subject the approximately 300,000 Kurds in Syria who have been denied Syrian citizenship – the stateless Kurds.[1] Their statelessness was the result of a census that took place in Hasaka province of north-east Syria on 10 October 1962, the effects of which have had continuing and worsening repercussions for those affected. It has since evolved into one of the Kurds' most enduring grievances against the Syrian state and one of the central pillars of Kurdish political party demands. The issue has become an important nationalist symbol, because the existence of the stateless Kurds is a constant reminder of the discrimination that the Kurds as a national group have suffered at the hands of the Syrian government. Much attention in Kurdish political parties has been directed towards the issue of the stateless Kurds. Indeed, it is the one issue on which the Syrian government has displayed some willingness to engage the parties and to offer some concessions to them. For, in what is understood by Kurds to have been an effort to dissuade them from participation in the Syrian uprising, a presidential decree was passed in April 2011, granting *ajanib* Kurds the right to apply for citizenship.

At the time of writing, estimates of how many *ajanib* Kurds had actually benefited from the decree varied considerably and no official statistics were available. Some sources said that between 6,000 and 60,000 had received citizenship; others that nearly all had obtained it. Counting the *maktumiin*, however, the number who had received citizenship did not come close to the number who were stateless, and the majority of those excluded by the census of October 1962 continue to be denied citizenship. The decree only applied to *ajanib* Kurds, leaving, at the very least, 100,000 *maktumiin* Kurds[2] completely unregistered in Syria. These stateless Kurds form a particular group in whose interests the Kurdish parties claim to act. But apart from their political symbolism, they are also a group whose interests and capacity to mobilise politically have been defined and limited by a legal status imposed on them by the state. This has set them apart from the rest of Kurdish society in Syria both socially and economically. The questions of if and how this status affects their politics have not been answered.

This chapter looks at the situation and the politics of this specific group of Kurds and assesses their relation to the political parties until the start of the Syrian uprising. The first half of the chapter outlines how this group of Kurds became stateless in 1962 and how statelessness has affected their daily lives. The second half examines the economic, social and political consequences that this status has had for them and the forms of political organisation that have arisen among them. It seeks to determine whether they developed any particular forms of organisation among themselves and to assess the level of their political consciousness and their relation to the Kurdish political parties. It also incorporates an examination of the Kurdish migrant community of Zor Ava in the suburbs of Damascus, in which approximately 50 per cent of the inhabitants are stateless. Their experience highlights many issues common to all stateless Kurds including the effects of statelessness on the form of politics in which they have participated. The chapter ends by looking at the government's position on this issue.

This group has become an entirely new class formation, both in Syrian society and within the Kurdish communities; they are unrelated to the traditional social class and wealth structures connected to tribe and landholdings that have been described in the preceding chapters. Consequently, the stateless Kurds have developed socio-economic interests distinct from the majority of the Kurdish population of Syria. The consequences of statelessness, as well as nationalist sentiment, have had an important impact on the interests and form of politics that the stateless Kurds have engaged in or even created. But, while statelessness is a potent symbol of Kurdish national oppression in Syria, organised political activity by the stateless for the stateless does not appear to have been developed. While their sense of personal injustice has been lived daily and intensely, economic hardship, social exclusion and fear of repercussions from the state have negatively affected the capacity of this group to mobilise on their own behalf. Rather, the stateless Kurds, when politically active, have been motivated by their Kurdish national identity and have organised within the framework of the Kurdish political parties and national movement, or by economic interests which they share with other poor Kurdish migrants.

The 1962 Hasaka Census

The Hasaka Census took place at a time of heightened Arab nationalism in Syria and the rest of the Arab world. As described in Chapter 1, in the 1950s and 1960s the rhetoric and symbolism of Arab nationalism were used to define states and their leaders and to compete with rival states and keep them at bay. The Kurdish revolt in northern Iraq raised the Syrian government's fears about Kurdish separatism spreading to Syria's Kurdish population as a whole. Kurds had begun to organise politically within Syria in the late 1950s and were not accommodated within the state's legitimising rhetoric of Arab nationalism and Arab unity.

The Jazira region, which roughly comprises the province of Hasaka, in north-east Syria has always been the object of state attention and desire. The region is one of Syria's most fertile, producing most of Syria's wheat and cotton as well as being the source of its oil reserves. It borders both Iraq and Turkey, with which Syria has had tumultuous and troubled relations. Although the region is inhabited by several different ethnic and religious groups the Kurdish population is believed to form a majority in the area and is more concentrated in the border areas. All these factors combined to make the region a particularly sensitive one. The Kurdish population and its habitation of the northern border areas of Syria raised government concerns about several questions – the demographic character of the region, control over its economy, its security from Kurdish separatism and external intrigue and about the national identity of the region. The Hasaka census was part of a series of policies aimed at arabising the area in order to gain control over the region and its population and begin a process of artificial demographic change in the region in favour of the Arabs.[3] Kurdish sources estimated that, prior to the presidential decree of April 2011, approximately 20 per cent of the Kurdish population of Hasaka province were stateless.[4]

In what seems to have been an effort to concentrate landholdings in the hands of Arabs, and in order to justify both its policies in the area and its attempts to control the population, the Syrian authorities claimed that many Kurds had migrated to Syria for political and/or economic reasons after 1945 and had acquired Syrian identity documents illegally. While it is true that migration of Kurds from Turkey and Iraq into Syria did occur, research and evidence suggest that the scale of migration was not nearly as high as Syrian sources imply. The greatest numbers of Kurds crossed into Syria during the mandate period, when a number of revolts in the Kurdish areas of Turkey and were brutally suppressed by Atatürk's forces. Although the exact number of Kurds who came to Syria in this way, and who were accommodated by the French mandate authorities, is unknown, academic research suggests that it is around 25,000.[5] A number of Kurdish nationalist, tribal and religious leaders were among those who fled to Syria, bringing with them followers and family members and settling among the already existing Kurdish communities in Mandate Syria. As outlined in Chapter 2, several tribal and nationalist leaders who fled from Turkey were given land in the Jazira by the French mandate authorities for services rendered. This was not only a means of encouraging the nomadic Kurdish tribes to settle and release the agricultural potential of the fertile plains of the Jazira, but also a means of purchasing the good favour of the tribes, securing northern borders and developing new commercial centres such as Qamishli.[6] On the whole, the Kurdish tribes, if not settled already, began permanent settlement and restricted their seasonal migrations to within Syrian territory and particularly within the Jazira region.

The fertility of the Jazira region and the development of the area that had begun under the French attracted Kurds to the area. And Arab tribes were drawn there from Iraq and forced to establish permanent settlements by the state after international borders between Syria and Turkey and Iraq were established. As most of these were Bedouin tribes, settled agriculture was not a common form of subsistence for them, and the majority remained nomadic longer than the Kurdish tribes. Consequently, most land in the region was in Kurdish hands.[7] The land reforms and nationalisations during the UAR had been ill received by the Syrian middle classes and provided much of the rationale for the secessionist coup of 28 September 1961 which ended Syria's union with Egypt. In the year that followed attempts were made to reverse the effects of the reforms and re-establish the status quo prior to the union. Guarding against the redistribution of land into the hands of the Kurds, the government began discrediting beneficiaries of agricultural reform laws and Kurds began to be referred to as 'invaders' who were endangering the Arab character and the sovereignty of Syria. As mentioned in Chapter 1, local officials in Hasaka province began to pressure the government to take action, in the form of a census, against the 'illegal invasion of the Kurds into Syria' which 'represented a great danger to the security of Arab Syria'.[8] The driving force behind the census was Sa'id al-Sayyid, the governor of Hasaka province in 1962 and self proclaimed 'staunch Arab nationalist', whose ambition was the unity of the Arabs.[9]

A popular programme of anti-Kurdish propaganda demonstrated the anxiety that the Arab population and Syrian government felt about losing the region to a foreign state or losing control of it to a Kurdish majority. Under the pretext of securing the area from illegal immigrants and the potential threat that they posed to the security of the area, on the 23 August 1962, under President al-Qudsi, Prime Minister Bashir al-Azmeh published Legislative Decree 93, ordering an exceptional census to be conducted in the region in one day on an undetermined future date. The census aimed to differentiate between those who had a legal right to Syrian citizenship and those who did not, identifying in the process those who had acquired it illegally. The actual census took place on 5 October 1962 under the government of Khalid al-Azm. Accounts of participants and other stateless Kurds indicate that the inhabitants of Hasaka province were not given any warning that the census would take place or any indication of its potential consequences.[10] Moreover, the Kurdish population of this region were mostly rural and many were illiterate and had little contact with any state officials.[11] Consequently, their ability to understand the context of the census, to procure the necessary documentation or to complete census forms was limited.

There is some disagreement among Kurds about how the census actually took place. One stateless Kurdish source told how committees went to the *mukhtar* of each area taking a list of names of those eligible for citizenship from the *mukhtar* and registering only these people. He suggested that the members of the Census Committee did not even seek proof of residency until after the results were published and the Committee was inundated with appeal requests.[12] Another source suggested that on the day of the census, government representatives went from door to door through the towns and villages of Hasaka province demanding that the inhabitants provide documentary proof of their residency in Syria before 1940 and answer questions related to nationality.[13] A report by KurdWatch[14] suggests that both methods were used. Whether on the day of the census or after the publication of its results, the residents of Hasaka province were required to show copies of their individual or family extract from the civil registers or an identity card and a family register. Others attempted to prove their residency in Syria through providing documents of other kinds – service bills, proof of military service, proof of ownership of property, tax receipts, and land deeds that showed land ownership and residency prior to 1940.[15] Apart from the difficulty of obtaining extracts from the registers within such a short time period, in the 1960s numerous families had not been entered in the civil registers, whether or not they had migrated to Syria after 1940. Other documents that could prove residency had little or no importance for the Kurdish population of Hasaka province before the order for the census. Indeed, the majority of agreements between landlords and tenants were, and continue to be, verbal private agreements,[16] and economic and political activities were generally local tribal affairs. Even the concept of 'citizenship' had little real meaning to their lives. Consequently, many people were unable to provide the required documentation.[17]

The right of appeal was granted within three months of the publication of the results of the census[18] and the date before which inhabitants should prove residency in Syria was changed from 1940 to 1945. Many Kurds went to departments of the ministries of electricity or water, amongst others, in order to secure any documentation that would help their case.[19] But few villages were connected to national electricity, water or gas supplies before 1945, or even before 1962.[20] As a result, many did not possess or had not retained bills or receipts such as sheep tax payments dating back more than

17 years.[21] Some who had kept old documents were able to secure Syrian citizenship. Countless cases exist, however, in which proof of residency was supplied but citizenship was removed nonetheless. It is also reported by a Kurdish source that on discovering the extent of requests for these papers from state ministries the Syrian intelligence apparatus ordered the removal of the service records from the government offices in order to prevent people from using them to retain citizenship.[22] A Human Rights Watch report also states that archives holding relevant tax documents were sealed after a short time, preventing them being used as evidence against errors in the census.[23]

According to interviews conducted with Kurds in and outside Syria, apart from the difficulties of actually providing proof of residency in Syria prior to 1945, some Kurds deliberately avoided participation in the census because they were attempting to avoid conscription into the Syrian army.[24] The consequences of non-participation in the census were unknown to those who abstained or were not understood. The Syrian authorities never provided an explanation for the census to those whom it involved. Thus the urgency of registration was lost, especially since it was conducted on only one day.

The results of the census were studied after the Ba'th Party took power in 1963, by the specially formed Supreme Census Committee. It was given full authority over appeals against errors made in the conduct of the census, the right to correct errors, and the right to consider all of the following categories as Syrian citizens: those registered in the old civil registers prior to 1945 or who were members of the Christian denominations or the Assyrian minorities and who were registered in those registers as late as 1950;[25] those who could prove that they resided in Syria prior to 1945; and those who were civilian or military employees of the state and its public institutions at least ten years prior to the date of the census[26] (that is, before 1952).

In a letter to Human Rights Watch, the Syrian Embassy in Washington DC admitted that mistakes were made in the census. Syrian Arabs were registered as foreign while others without Syrian nationality were registered as Syrian citizens. These were corrected by the Committee and, consequently, there have not been any reported incidents of an Arab having been registered as foreign despite the migration of Arabs across the border between Iraq and Syria well into the 1960s. The Embassy's response implies that all 'Syrian Arabs' had an automatic right to Syrian citizenship, while Syrian Kurds did not.[27]

The results of the census

It is estimated that the census stripped between 120,000 and 150,000 Kurds of citizenship. Without citizenship of any other state, all became completely stateless. This number is far higher than that estimated for the number of

Kurds who fled to Syria from southeast Turkey escaping from attacks on the regions during the French mandate period. The official results of the census imply that the numbers of illegal Kurdish immigrants between 1945 and 1962, who came to Syria for primarily economic reasons, is five times higher than those who fled between 1920 and 1945 and that any migration of the Kurds to Syria has been motivated primarily by economic needs rather than by political ones.[28]

The final results of the census are said to have appeared in 1966, four years after the census and during the rule of the Ba'th Party.[29] Those who retained Syrian citizenship were registered in the normal civil registers, while those who were found to be illegal immigrants, or literally 'alien infiltrators', were registered in a special register of 'foreigners'. Henceforth, all within it were known as *ajanib al-Hasakah* – foreigners of Hasaka region (singular: *ajnabi*, plural: *ajanib*, feminine: *ajnabiyah*).[30] Lists of names were posted in the local registry offices for individuals to search for their names on the civil registers. Kurds whose names did not appear on the list of citizens or on the list of foreigners were left completely unregistered and are today those collectively known as the *maktumiin* (singular: *maktum*, feminine: *maktumah*) meaning 'unregistered' or literally 'concealed' or 'hidden'. Consequently, a large number of people did not find out that they had lost their Syrian citizenship because they were unable to attend the offices, or were unaware that their citizenship was at stake. All discovered at some point, however, that they no longer held citizenship, because Syrian identity cards have a limited validity and their form was changed, necessitating their renewal. Those affected found that they were unable to renew their documents, and with that, rights of citizenship were denied to them.[31]

The Kurds are believed to be the only ones affected by the census.[32] Thousands of Kurds who provided the required information, others who could not and some who deliberately avoided doing so, became foreigners in Syria whether or not they had migrated from Turkey or Iraq after 1945. Several Kurds born in Syria prior to 1945, including members of prestigious Syrian families and Syrian Kurdish officials, had their citizenship removed as a consequence of the census. Examples include: General Tawfiq Nizam al-Din (who became Chief of Staff of the Syrian army in 1956) and his brother 'Abd al-Baqi Nizam al-Din (who was a minister in the Syrian parliament), members of the family of Ibrahim Pasha Malli's, (who was one of the founding members of the Syrian parliament in 1928), Khalil Beg Ibrahim Pasha Malli and his sons, (Khalil Beg received a Syrian medal of honour in 1934 and was a member of the Syrian parliament in 1928, 1932, 1936 and 1943), the family of Ismail Ibrahim Pasha Malli (who was the leader of the campaign that freed Hasaka province from Ottoman control and was a member of the Syrian parliament from 1953 to 1954), and the family of Ma'mo Ibrahim Pasha

Malli (who was among the leaders of the campaign that liberated al-Raqqa and Dayr al-Zur from Turkish occupation).[33] These are just a few well-known examples. Furthermore, in many instances, members of the same family, even siblings, have been registered differently. For example, a man born in Syria in 1881 was classified as a Syrian citizen, while his son, also born in Syria in 1935, was registered as *ajnabi*, despite also having served in the Syrian military.[34] Mamo Alo's[35] parents, who had documents proving their family's residence in Syria dating back to 1860, were registered as foreign in the census of 1962. The sister of his father remained a Syrian citizen. Mamo and his three brothers were also registered as foreign. One of his brothers has four children. Three were registered as *ajanib*, one as *maktum*.[36] It has been common to find immediate family members composed of citizens, *ajanib* and *maktumiin* and cases such as these demonstrate the arbitrary nature of the denaturalisation of Syrian Kurds.

According to one source, almost all Kurds living along the borders with Turkey and Iraq had their citizenship removed so that they would not benefit from the land reforms in this area implemented in the 1970s.[37] Another source also confirmed that the majority of Kurds whose citizenship was taken were from the northern areas of Hasaka province. This also corresponds to the concentration of Kurds in the north of the region. This same source, who had personal contact with a government official in Amudê who was involved in the census, also suggested that the government's original plan was to remove the citizenship of 80 per cent of the Kurds and Christians of the region.[38]

All classes were affected by the census. It is thought, however, that the majority of Kurds who lost citizenship were from the countryside, especially from the areas around Dêrîk[39] and Serê Kaniyê. This was due, in part, to the fact that the cities were more developed and provided with more services than rural areas. Consequently, the circumstances in which documentation was required were greater and a culture of retaining documents and bills was more developed in the cities than in rural areas. It is also suggested that following the census a number of the Kurdish *aghawat* and other influential and wealthy Kurds were able to regain their citizenship either through appeal to the Syrian authorities, or by paying bribes.[40] As a consequence of this and because of the socio-economic structures of Kurdish society, it is thought that the majority of Kurds who were made stateless were peasants.[41]

Status

As mentioned above, there are two categories of stateless Kurd in Syria, which, despite the withdrawal of regime forces from Kurdish areas during the Syrian uprising, continue to define the official identity thousands of Kurds. The first is the *ajanib*; the second is the *maktumiin*. The *ajanib* are those registered as foreigners. They were not deported but denied normal civil rights associated with citizenship. Instead of standard citizenship identity documents, they carry a laminated paper on which their status is written. Originally white in colour, since the 1980s these papers are normally red or orange.[42] They cannot be issued passports. Although the presidential decree passed in April 2011 allowed *ajanib* Kurds to apply for citizenship, at the time of writing many had not been able to benefit from this decree and remained registered as foreign in Syria. The *ajanib* Kurds are denied the right to own property, land or businesses nor can they receive state subsidies; they may not own cars or any other vehicles; and they are excluded from many areas of employment in the public sector and from working in the legal sector. They may only work as doctors in the private sphere and face further restrictions working in other professions. They have no legal rights or representation. They are disenfranchised and are barred from running for public office and cannot leave the country. Marriages of male *ajanib* or *maktumiin* Kurds to Syrian citizens were illegal until 2005 when the Ministry of the Interior began to allow the registration of these marriages if special permission was obtained from the relevant state departments.[43] Children born of unregistered marriages were considered illegitimate, normally denied *ajnabi* status and, consequently, became *maktumiin*. The *maktumiin* are not registered at all and therefore do not officially exist. They are also subject to further discriminations. Kurds of Hasaka province who did not take part in the census of 1962 became *maktumiin*, even if they already held Syrian citizenship. Later, Kurdish children born of one of the following parentages were also given this status: both parents of *maktum* status; one parent of *maktum* status, no matter what the status of the other parent; and mother with Syrian citizenship and an *ajnabi* father.[44]

These Kurds, being completely unregistered, have even lower status than that of the *ajanib* and have no rights or opportunities in Syria. The *maktumiin* were not extended the same right to apply for nationality as the *ajanib* Kurds were in Decree 49 of April 2011. They are deprived of all the same rights as the *ajanib*, but, in addition, they face more difficulties accessing state education and they are barred from entering higher education.[45] Some carry a white piece of paper with their photo and family details recorded on it, issued by the local *mukhtar* (traditional village head or mayor) after checks on the family by the Political Security branch of Syria's intelligence services. Only with these documents can the *maktumiin* apply for a second paper granting them permission to enter state education. Not all, however, have been able to acquire these papers. They must be obtained in Hasaka province and the process of registering in school can be long and arduous; in many cases the process exposes family members to harassment, pressure from the security services and delays in starting school.[46] Provincial decrees made it even more difficult to obtain these documents. On 15 October 1999 the mayor of Hasaka province passed an internal memorandum, No. 7889-J, forbidding the *mukhtar* and the local administrations from issuing any documents to the *maktumiin*.[47] Although this decision was not fully implemented, it made the situation and daily life for the Kurds of this status considerably more difficult. One man interviewed in a suburb of Damascus had not been able to get his own paper. He carried only the paper of his *maktum* father, who was aged 70 and had been born in Syria.[48] On this paper issued by the *mukhtar* it stated that 'I the *mukhtar* know this man, and his family members are...' Here the man in question was named as his father's son. This piece of paper was his only form of identity document, his single form of official recognition and proof of his existence.

If they are able to acquire papers, and then obtain additional identification papers specifically for the purpose, Kurds with *maktum* status may be permitted to attend primary school up to year nine or in some cases up to age of 18.[49] Entry to secondary school, however, also requires security clearance and permission from the state security services. Those completing this level of education will not be awarded the normal qualifications.[50] Instead they receive a paper saying that they have completed the required exams but that their certificates are held by the Bureau of Examinations until the individual has been registered with the Bureau of Civil Affairs.[51] As a result, the *maktumiin* are barred from entering higher education.

After the Ministry of the Interior began giving permission to register marriages of stateless Kurds to Syrian citizens, it also became possible for a *maktum* individual whose parents were able to register their marriage to upgrade their status to *ajnabi*. But the process was reported to take one to three years of administering bribes, of lengthy and frustrating bureaucratic procedures and security checks in Hasaka province.[52] The problems and expenses involved in this procedure mean that many marriages of *ajanib* Kurds with women with citizenship remain unregistered and few *maktumiin* were able to follow this route for the sake of a red piece of paper and access to higher education. Indeed one stateless Kurd interviewed, who had followed this path, declared that it had made no real difference to his life.[53] It seems that this opportunity has only been available to those *maktumiin* born of the union between an *ajnabi* man and a woman with Syrian citizenship. There is no similar process available for the *maktumiin* of other marriages or for the *maktumiin* to acquire Syrian citizenship, even though many families have attempted to bribe officials to grant them citizenship.[54] More commonly, the *maktumiin* and *ajanib* use the names of people with citizenship, living or deceased, to enter higher education or employment.[55]

It is also reported that many children have gone unregistered and become *maktum* due to the political profile of the family, even if both parents are citizens. One Kurdish political activist spent four years in prison in Syria for activities on behalf of Kurdish rights. In what is believed to be a further punitive measure against him, his children were not registered in the civil registers, or the register of 'foreign' people, making them *maktumiin*.[56]

In 1996 Syrian official sources put the number of stateless Kurds at 67,465. They added that 84,000 people originally had their citizenship removed and claimed that following appeals the number was halved, decreasing to 40,587 in 1986, but then increased to 67,465 on 31 October 1995 as a result of marriages and births. These sources also add that a further 75,000 unregistered foreigners (*maktumiin*), who entered Syria illegally after the census, also resided in the area, but that no census of these people had been conducted.[57] Other official Syrian sources cited 120,000 as the number of stateless Kurds in Syria,[58] while one stateless informant suggested that the correct number is closer to 500,000 because of high fertility rates among the Kurds.[59] In 2010, KurdWatch acquired data from an official but unpublished census of the *ajanib* conducted in Hasaka province in 2008. This revealed the number of *ajanib* Kurds alone to be at least 154,000, double that given in 1995.[60]

Although Syrian law forbids it, it is reported that on several occasions, Kurds registered as *ajnabi* or *maktum* have received conscription orders for the Syrian military service and have been obliged to complete national service in the Syrian army. In Syrian nationality law, articles 43 and 44 stipulate that Syrian national service of two years is compulsory for anyone with Syrian nationality over the age of 19.[61] Therefore, the conscription of Kurds registered as 'foreign' violates even basic Syrian domestic law. It is not permitted for a person without Syrian citizenship to be employed within the armed forces, and, as a rule, Kurds (including those with Syrian citizenship) have been refused admittance to military and police academies. Despite their service to the state, these Kurds were denied even basic rights and standard Syrian military identity documents. One Kurd who attempted to re-acquire his Syrian citizenship on the basis of his national service met with rejection and the confiscation of his service documents which he had provided as proof of military service.[62] It is also reported that *ajanib* university students were required to participate in month-long, normally voluntary, military service sessions in the summer months, despite the fact that they were considered foreign and therefore ineligible to perform military service.[63]

The Syrian government's claim that the Kurds whose citizenship was removed were 'foreign infiltrators' is undermined further by the fact that it made no apparent attempt to repatriate any of these Kurds. Instead, they have been categorised as of 'unknown nationality' and constitute an economically, politically and socially marginalised section of the Syrian population, subject to daily discrimination and imposed hardship. The official purpose of the census was also undermined by the removal of citizenship from those who could and can prove their right to it and the return of citizenship to some

Kurds able to pay for it.[64] Similarly, it is reported that some of the *ajanib* in the late 1970s were given the option of signing a statement declaring that she or he was a 'Syrian Arab' in order to regain those rights associated with Syrian citizenship.[65]

Implications of Statelessness for Kurdish Politics in Syria

All the restrictions on the stateless Kurds described above contribute to defining them as a particular status group that does not have any equivalent in Syria. Their legal status, however, is not the only cause of their discrimination. This 'underclass' is defined by the economic, social and political consequences of statelessness and the younger generation especially suffers from additional forms of exclusion. In what follows it is shown that this group can be defined as an identifiable underclass located outside the formal wage-labour system and as a group they are silenced, marginalised and excluded. Nevertheless, they also depend on the formal system for day-to-day existence. It shows that while the economic and social consequences of statelessness produce interests specific to this group, their political organisation is defined primarily by their Kurdish identity.

Their class status derives not from class relations but from political discrimination against them as members of a Kurdish ethnic and national group and, consequently, the stateless Kurds include people of different levels of wealth and education. There is, for example, a division between the *ajanib* and *maktumiin*, the former having been more capable of escaping poverty and destitution due to their registration as foreigners and their better access to education and qualifications. Also, the group of Kurds who were originally stripped of Syrian citizenship came from differing parts of the class spectrum. Many were already married or educated and no stigma about statelessness had developed within the Kurdish community. It is true that the majority were peasants, but evidence suggests that this was not because peasants were deliberately singled out for this kind of oppression but rather was an accidental by-product of the census caused by the differences in services and culture between rural and urban areas and the fact that a number of *agha* and wealthy Kurds were able to bribe Syrian officials and retain their citizenship. In addition, with help from citizens, many *ajanib* Kurds were able to advance financially, indicating that there is some form of upward mobility among them. This is only rarely true for the *maktumiin*.

Economic consequences of statelessness
(property, finances and migration)

Economically, the stateless are set apart from the rest of Syrian society by a number of factors. Among those consequences of their statelessness which have an important causal influence on their economic marginalisation are property rights, access to employment and financial services and trends of urban migration, which are now examined in turn.

Neither the *ajanib* nor *maktumiin* Kurds have had any right to own or buy property, including land, vehicles and businesses. Although their properties were not taken from them as a direct result of the census, many stateless Kurds lost all their land to the state in the arabisation programme and land reforms of the 1970s, when they became ineligible for redistribution of land and when land was given to what are known among the Kurds as the '*maghmouriin*'.[66] For example, one family living in the area of Serê Kaniyê had all their land, amounting to 30 hectares, taken by the state.[67] Similarly a large number of Kurds worked as share croppers on the land of large landowners before the results of the census became known. During the land reform programmes, almost half the land in the Jazira region was transferred to state hands for redistribution.[68] With this, those without Syrian citizenship lost their rights to farm this land and lost their investments and what was, in most cases, their only source of subsistence. Without Syrian nationality, these Kurds did not benefit from the land reforms in the area, despite otherwise qualifying for land distribution.

Personal ownership of any houses and land remains unofficial and many Kurds were forced to sell their properties at greatly reduced prices.[69] The state still maintains the right to expropriate all land, houses, businesses, vehicles and any other property requiring a state licence and owned by the *ajanib* or *maktumiin*. It is reported that rumours often circulate that the government intends to remove these properties from the possession of the stateless Kurds.[70] Certainly, threats of eviction and expropriation of property are often used as a means of coercion and they live under the constant fear of being removed from their property. In some instances rent is extracted for properties by state officials in return for temporary and unofficial permission to remain in those properties.[71]

It is not possible for any stateless Kurds to rent property legally, even a hotel room. Consequently, with low incomes and high fertility rates among the Kurds and particularly within the poorer sectors of that society, living conditions commonly decline with the growth of the family. It is not uncommon to hear of a family of ten or more living in one room.[72] These conditions have led to a large number of houses being built on unused land, but without the obligatory state licences.

In attempts to gain more security in their lives, many stateless Kurds have chosen to register or buy properties in the names of family members or neighbours who hold Syrian citizenship. The security of their homes, however, is never guaranteed and it means that provincial and other services must also be registered in others' names.[73] Additionally, family disputes, inheritance and the law can have detrimental effects on the stateless Kurds. This system depends on trust and the good will of others and, although research has not yielded any cases of stateless Kurds having their properties taken by the legal owners, the fact remains that they are at the mercy of the owners. As 'foreigners' they cannot inherit property and, for any sense of personal security to be maintained, that relationship of trust and beneficence must continue for generations to come.[74]

Restrictions on employment opportunities have affected stateless Kurds considerably, in recent years even more so than in the past. The exclusion of stateless Kurds from public sector work was not an immediate effect of the census of 1962. Rather, it seems that decisions to exclude stateless Kurds have been issued at various times in different state sectors. For example, within the last 20 years the government stopped employing those without citizenship in the state Housing Association.[75] One *ajnabi* Kurd in state employment at the time of the decision was able to continue working in the state sector on daily contracts albeit with added job insecurity and less pay.[76] Citizenship came to be required for all public sector work and, even in the private sector, employers often required citizenship documents from employees. The *ajanib* and *maktumiin* were often rejected regardless of qualifications or suitability. Consequently, a large proportion of the *ajanib* and *maktumiin* were found in menial jobs and in the black or grey market trades. Before the start of the Syrian uprising it was common to find street traders, labourers in the building trade, cleaners, say, in Syria's major cities were *maktum* or *ajanib* from the Jazira province. In rural areas too, many worked as agricultural and seasonal labourers. Stateless Kurds commonly sought day labour, congregating in a particular place and competing with others for a day's work. Naturally, this type of work was insecure and income earned was low and irregular.[77] Other work that the stateless Kurds could often find was in the service industry, especially in restaurants and cafés. It was common to find that the dishwashing, cleaning and waiting staff in private restaurants are Kurdish and a portion of them stateless. The wages for this form of work were low, at approximately 200 Syrian Lira per day, the equivalent of £1.79 in 2012.

The opportunities for self-employment have also been extremely limited since registration and licences are required. Added to this, the ability of any stateless Kurd to raise capital is severely restricted and they are not permitted to rent any properties, including shops or other business premises. Depending on relations with relatives and neighbours, it may be possible to rent or buy a business property in someone else's name. The family of one informant owned three jewellery shops. Their capital for purchasing gold, however, was loaned by trusted acquaintances. Although Syrian citizenship is not required for the purchase and sale of gold, the possession of quantities of gold by a stateless Kurd would arouse the suspicion of the police.[78] They have no legal recourse if any attempt is made to confiscate their goods. The informant mentioned above recalled how problems with the police in coach stations were avoided by entering the station secretly or boarding the bus outside the station. Adding to their problems, the shops of the *ajanib* have been known to face regular closure, especially if the owners also have a political profile. Payments of bribes to security officials are usually required to reopen them.[79]

A large number of the stateless have been found making a living by selling goods on mobile street stalls (commonly drinks, cooked sweet corn, bric-a-brac, tapes and pirate CDs).[80] Even street trade, however, requires official licences and being without them has entailed regular payments of bribes to the local police, in order to continue their trade without fines or criminal prosecution.[81] In addition, many children work on these stalls, either for the family or often for others who exploit their labour. In Syria in 2002 the children of one stateless family, all of whom were *maktumiin*, would work selling pieces of watermelon from a small cart owned by someone else. It required the strength of three small children to push the cart around the worn out streets of Dêrîk. For their work they would receive just five Syrian liras[82] per day between them. Much of this work is seasonal and as a consequence insecure and irregular.

Although stateless Kurds have been discriminated against in employment, they have had little recourse to any other form of financial support. Commonly living on lower wages than marginalised Syrian citizens, the stateless Kurds have still had to pay government taxes and service bills in addition to bribes to the local *mukhabarat* and other Syrian officials. It goes without saying that there is no form of labour representation for stateless Kurds and that they cannot benefit from any that exist within their area or place of work. The stateless Kurds do not qualify for any financial services from any bank in Syria, including opening a bank account or basic borrowing. They are not entitled to normal state subsidies on prices of basic staples such as rice, flour and sugar, which are available to all Syrian citizens. Although already impoverished, they must pay many times the subsidised rates because they are considered to be foreigners.[83] For example, one kilo of sugar, normally costing 75 Qursh[84] in the 1960s, cost almost six times as much for the *ajanib* and *maktumiin*.[85] This situation continues. Before the uprising began, sugar, at the subsidised rate, was only one Syrian lira.[86] The *ajanib* and *maktummin* had to pay the free market price of approximately 30 Syrian liras.

The Hasaka Census and the resulting creation of the stateless underclass altered the demography of the province in a number of ways. On one count, the ratio of Kurds to Arabs was officially lessened by removing from the Kurds an historic claim to land and their majority status in the region. Secondly, the poverty that came hand in hand with statelessness, and the lack of available employment in Hasaka province, caused mass urban migration of stateless Kurds to Syria's large cities, both in the region and in the Syrian interior. And thirdly, many stateless Kurds found ways to leave Syria illegally and have sought refuge in other countries. Organised people-trafficking enterprises developed in Hasaka province, helping hundreds of Kurds leave the country.

After the effects of the census results began to take their toll on the people, especially the loss of land rights of Kurds in rural areas, a wave of migration to the cities within or bordering the Kurdish-inhabited regions took place. Landless peasants were left with little or no means of subsistence; rural labour requirements, generally tending to be seasonal and often dominated by family members, were further reduced by the state's land redistribution programmes. In addition, the lack of private investment in the region meant that most other work opportunities were within the state sector, out of bounds to the stateless Kurds. The scarcity and insecurity of the regional labour market led people to search for work opportunities in Syria's cities.[87]

The first wave of urban migration occurred within Hasaka province, many individuals (commonly young males) and whole families moving to the cities in search of work. But without property or basic rights, the cost of living in the cities was higher than in the rural areas and, with no access to social security, subsidies, pensions, health services or banking services, living conditions for the majority of the stateless Kurds were harsh. Later on, underdevelopment in the province led many more to move further afield to larger cities in the Syrian interior, especially to Aleppo and Damascus, where they congregated in urban slums. Wages earned by migrants were often shared with the family remaining in the Jazira. It also became common, however, to find the rest of the family following the relative to the city so that incomes and expenses were combined, resulting in new generations of Kurds being born and growing up in the city.[88]

As a result of good harvests, some lessening of the flow of Kurds from Hasaka province to the cities occurred in the decade between 1980 and 1990. The cotton, wheat and vegetable harvests and state encouragement of vertical drilling for wells stimulated demand for manual labour in rural areas. While many families had already left their villages owing to loss of land, some seasonal migration back to the villages occurred during this period.[89] After 1990, natural droughts, worsened by the Turkish dam projects which restricted the flow of water through the Syrian Jazira, affected harvests and, consequently, reduced the demand for labour. During this time corruption in the government administration also forced many producers to share their profits with security officials in exchange for services.[90] It is also reported that regular changes in government regulations on agricultural irrigation has left many farmers burdened with debt.[91] Corruption and debt negatively affected profits and the capacity of farmers to hire extra labour. In turn, the flow of urban migration increased again. Decree 49 of 2008, which made official permission a requirement for the development of any inner-city land in the region, appeared to have significant economic effects. The negative impact on the construction industry, which in Qamishli alone was reported to have resulted in a two-thirds reduction in building activity,[92] caused further migration of stateless Kurds and other unskilled labourers from the region.

Although thousands of Kurds have since returned to the relative safety of Syria's Kurdish regions since the militarisation of the uprising, the urban migration of thousands of *ajanib* and *maktumiin* Kurds from Hasaka province to Damascus led to the development of entirely new areas of the city. Prohibited from purchasing or renting any properties, the stateless Kurds were forced to make alternative living arrangements. Thousands built or bought illegal homes both in the outskirts of Damascus and on available land inside Damascus without licences from the Syrian authorities. The population of one particular area in the suburbs of Damascus, Zor Ava, was almost 50 per cent stateless Kurds from the Jazira region. Literally meaning 'forced to build', the name itself stems from the reality of the situation for these migrant Kurds.

At the time of writing, the fate of the inhabitants and properties of this area was unknown. Return migration had occurred, but many others had remained in the area. Others had been arrested and detained or killed by regime forces and buildings had been destroyed. What follows is a description of pre-uprising Zor Ava. Whether the course of the Syrian uprising and its future resolution will alter the demography and the economic, social and political conditions in this area irreversibly can not be foreseen. For now, however, the area continues to be characterised as Kurdish and its history illustrative of the conditions of statelessness.

Zor Ava

At the beginning of the Syrian uprising, the Zor Ava district in the suburbs of Damascus accommodated approximately 5,000 Kurdish families,[93] about 2,000 of which were stateless,[94] and a minority of poor Arab families.[95] The area has been inhabited since the early 1980s when Kurdish migrants came to work in the construction of a large housing project, known as *Mashrou'a al-Dumer*,[96] (now officially called *al-Sham al-Jadid*).[97] The construction workers built simple homes in the narrow valley that lies in the shadows of the housing project on one side, and the Presidential Palace on the other. The police frequented the area and the houses were destroyed several times but were always rebuilt. Gradually the settlement spread and became permanent, although no building in the areas was licensed.[98]

Most inhabitants still worked in construction. But, unemployment and crime in the area were increasing because of poor education, isolation and depression among the Kurdish youth.[99] The illegality of the buildings in this neighbourhood and its occupation by migrant Kurds from the Jazira meant that the government was unwilling to invest in the area, leaving the people suffering from the consequences of poor sanitation and lack of electricity, clean water and surfaced roads.[100] Residents recalled at least four deaths of inhabitants resulting from electrocution as locals tapped into state power lines; they also claimed that one girl had been shot by police in 1987 as residents demonstrated in an attempt to get state water supplies.[101] The houses were connected to the state electricity supply in 1990 and only in 2003 were water supplies extended to the area. Most of the streets in the neighbourhood were surfaced in 2003 or 2004. The extension of these services to the neighbourhood was also accompanied by the registration of all houses. But the homes of the stateless are registered in the name of the government not the residents. They have no documents proving ownership and, while they are not required to pay rent to the government, they must pay taxes.[102]

The stateless residents of one home expressed their concern about government plans to widen the main road in Zor Ava, on which they lived. The widening of the road would require the demolition of their property and their *ajnabi* status meant that they were unlikely to receive any compensation.[103] The insecurity of this form of housing is demonstrated by the destruction of a large residential area in the Duwayla'ah area of Damascus, to the east of the old city. Hundreds of houses were built without state permission in a stretch of unused land approximately 50m deep either side of a main road. In January 2006, all these buildings were demolished in order to widen the road. The inhabitants of this area were left homeless and during the destruction of the buildings; one Kurdish woman was beaten to death by police as she attempted to prevent the demolition of her home.[104]

The building of these areas lead to the creation of new communities primarily consisting of poor migrant and stateless Kurds, with common interests and common problems. In such communities new forms of cooperation and collaboration developed in order to serve these interests. In Zor Ava, a local committee was established to lobby the government for electricity and water supplies. The committee included stateless Kurds, Kurdish party members and leaders, and other residents.[105] It took six years of campaigning and demonstrations to get electricity and ten years to get water. Even then, all drains in the area were built by committee members and local inhabitants, not contracted by the government.[106] The representation of all sectors of the Zor Ava community on the Committee demonstrates that this form of political action was conducted on a local level, based on social and economic interests common to both citizens and the stateless.

The suburb of Zor Ava also became a place of Kurdish political party activity. Kurdish parties held regular meetings in the area in attempts to recruit members, to politicise the Kurds there and to gain support for their activities. Compared to the Damascene Kurds who have lived in the capital for generations, Zor Ava Kurds' connections to the Kurdish regions remained strong and active. Their physical distance and social, political and economic alienation from mainstream society meant that the possibilities of integration into a Syrian Damascene society were severely limited. As a result, for Kurdish politics in Damascus, the migrant Kurds of this region became a potential source of numerical support for parties and their local activities. Indeed, more than one Kurdish source suggested that more poor stateless Kurds were members of Kurdish political parties than wealthy Kurds.[107] This claim is implicitly supported by the Syrian security services' attitude towards the area. The neighbourhood of Zor Ava was raided by the police at three in the morning during the Qamishli uprising of 2004 and a number of Kurdish residents were arrested. It is also well known among Kurds in Damascus that the neighbourhood has been kept under heavy surveillance by the *mukhabarat*.[108] This suggests that the security services themselves have considered the area and its inhabitants to be a potential political threat and to contain subversive and destabilising elements of society.

Social consequences of statelessness

The economic implications of *ajanib* and *maktumiin* status described above have also had a number of social consequences. Within Kurdish society everyone is aware that the condition of statelessness is a consequence of the Hasaka Census, that this status is unjust and that it does not have the same foundations as class differences or differences related to tribe–non-tribe and the *agha*–peasant divisions that formerly divided Kurdish society. Among the wider Syrian society the situation is very different. Their statelessness automatically identifies them as Kurdish and labels them as alien and potentially disloyal and subversive elements in society. The stateless Kurds are regularly treated with contempt by state security personnel and when dealing with state bureaucracy. Also, as we have seen, there is real discrimination against the stateless in employment.

The social consequences of statelessness for the *maktumiin* Kurds have been more acute than for the *ajanib*. Although the *ajanib* have faced discrimination in education and are limited in the type of work they can obtain, they have been able to enter higher education and obtain work in the private sector in some specialist areas and some have even retained jobs in the public sphere. For the *maktumiin* limitations on education have meant that they commonly have only a very basic education, are unable to secure regular employment and are impoverished. Few *maktumiin* have attempted to pursue education – because of the difficulties and costs involved, because the basic needs of the family often require even young children to find work and because, even with an education, the form of employment available to these Kurds is very limited and qualifications do not open up opportunities for them. Yet, all stateless Kurds have reported discrimination in school and university, inability to join university clubs and associations and difficulties and delays in obtaining the necessary security clearance and permission.[109] Likewise, even with an education, the opportunities of employment are very poor. Consequently, the majority of stateless Kurds, and particularly the *maktumiin*, have fallen into the underclass category. Uneducated, impoverished and drawn to urban slums, the stateless Kurds became a population of declassed and underprivileged elements of urban industrial centres. Their unique status distinguished them from and relegated them beneath the working class in Syria.

The Kurdish population, generally, is sympathetic to the cause of the stateless Kurds and, within Kurdish society, the issue is understood as an injustice by the regime against the Kurdish nation. It is a central political issue for the Kurds and integeral to the Syrian Kurdish national agenda. This means that, at least in theory, the idea of a Kurd with citizenship marrying one without is not considered strange or in any way negative. In fact it may be seen as a positive patriotic action in the sense that it would potentially help the stateless individual to escape some of the restrictions arbitrarily imposed upon him or her. Despite this, the real consequences of being stateless in Syria has meant that, with time, educational and economic fissures have developed between Kurds with citizenship and those denied it, and prejudice related to statelessness has arisen, especially concerning marriage.

While many of the elder generation of stateless Kurds were married and already had work when the results of the census were published, with time it became more difficult for the stateless to find employment, even within Kurdish society, and a stigma around statelessness developed.[110] Many Kurds reported that in recent years the issue of citizenship had become a serious concern of the families or individuals with citizenship looking to marry. Kurds with Syrian citizenship would ask if an individual has citizenship before agreeing to a marriage. Generally, these families would refuse marriages to the *ajanib* or *maktumiin* Kurds.[111] The stateless Kurd came to be seen as undesirable, not because of the statelessness itself, but because of the economic and social conditions that accompany it; the illegality of marriage and the subsequent status that any children born of the marriage will inherit. One *ajnabi* informant recalled how his engagement was broken off because the family of his fiancé, who held Syrian citizenship, would not allow the marriage to take place. The primary reason was that any children would become *maktumiin*.[112]

Also, when it comes to politics, it has been suggested that many Kurds have considered the stateless Kurds to be untrustworthy. Their poverty and destitution has left them open to threats, coercion or cooption by the *mukhabarat*. As a consequence some individuals believed them to be easy targets for the state authorities and more likely to inform on others within their national group in order to maintain their standard of living or improve it.[113] This adds another more political dimension to the social stratification that has more recently affected the stateless Kurds. One might expect that as a consequence of this the *ajanib* and *maktumiin* would be more inclined to live, socialise and work together. With common problems and circumstances there is commonly greater affinity between stateless Kurds than between a stateless Kurd and one with citizenship.[114] Interviews with stateless Kurds in Syria, however, suggest that this was not the case. While they may have relied on others from this group for moral support, they connected their living arrangements and social life to family connections and their politics to their Kurdish identity.[115]

Political consequences of statelessness

The issue of the stateless Kurds and the return of citizenship to them has been at the top of the agenda of all Kurdish political parties in Syria and, for the stateless Kurds, the Kurdish parties are their only form of social, economic or political representation in Syria. The parties have organised demonstrations marking the anniversary of the census, calling for the return of citizenship and all rights associated with it to all those affected by the census. The issue has been brought forward by the parties whenever representatives have met with government officials and attempts have been made to bring the issue to the attention of international governmental and non-governmental organisations by Kurds in exile. It was suggested by a number of *ajnabi* informants, however, that their membership of Kurdish political parties was not based on the desire for citizenship.[116] The issue of the stateless Kurds is just one issue in a long line of demands that the Kurdish parties have made on the regime, and the return of citizenship to the *ajanib* and *maktumiin* alone does not solve the Kurdish problem in Syria and make the parties redundant.[117] One interviewee described his interest in politics as being based on the injustices he faces as a stateless Kurd in Syria, as a member of the Yezidi community, as a party member and first and foremost, as a Kurd. It was not a personal interest related to status but a communal interest connected to national identity. When asked if he thought that a solution to the problems of the stateless Kurds could be achieved through the Kurdish parties, his answer was:

> There will be no solution – Kurds in Syria will never be granted citizenship – Kurdish parties cannot achieve that aim – that aim is not in their hands. They want to achieve it but that needs a decree by the

president himself and those who are supporting him, and that will not be achieved, in my opinion. Why? Because they think that granting citizenship will not solve the Kurdish problem in Syria; because they know that Kurds do not want citizenship – they want a country. . . they want schools; they want federalism; they want to determine themselves, to rule themselves by themselves.[118]

Although some Kurds have obtained citizenship since April 2011, this move came as the regime faced the biggest ever challenge to its rule and as part of an attempt to prevent Kurdish involvement in the Syrian uprising. Kurdish parties as well as popular protests of stateless Kurds at the time made it clear that move would not satisfy Kurdish political demands in Syria. This suggests that for stateless Kurds, party membership was not motivated by the desire for personal justice. The same source quoted above suggested that stateless Kurds, fuelled by their sense of injustice, would become members of Kurdish parties if only they also had money. He thought that, due to their circumstances, stateless Kurds were, on the whole, inclined to be supporters of Kurdish parties and that the conditions of poverty and their immediate concerns prevented many from becoming full members.

The number of stateless Kurds in the party ranks is not clear. The secrecy of party membership and limitations on how much the party leadership is willing to admit mean that it is not possible to give any estimates of the proportions of stateless Kurds in the party membership in comparison to those with Syrian citizenship. What is clear is that to date there are no stateless Kurds in any of the party leaderships in Syria. This may be explained in part by the fact that few stateless Kurds are educated to a high level and it is only relatively recently that stateless Kurds have been graduating from university in Syria. Consequently, these Kurds are still considered to be too young and inexperienced for positions in party leadership.[119] But it is also plausible that the circumstances of the stateless Kurds have been a disincentive to climb the ranks of the parties. The exposure of the members of the party leaderships to the *mukhabarat* and police causes a significant increase to their exposure to risk and harm. Consequently, the impact on a stateless Kurd and his or her family could be greater than on someone with citizenship.

The discrimination against stateless Kurds has actually worked to strengthen Kurdish communal bonds and to fuel Kurdish nationalist sentiments. Kurdish nationalism among the stateless Kurds is high and it is suggested that most stateless Kurds support the Kurdish political parties, even if they are not members.[120] While bearing the weight of the state's discrimination against the Kurds and embodying a major part of the Kurdish struggle in Syria, many stateless Kurds have struggled with the weight of their status itself and not with the state. Consciousness has easily been dominated by economic issues such as employment, daily income and food rather than the struggle for citizenship or national rights. Indeed, the culture of social or political organisation among the stateless Kurds in Syria has been weak, in Hasaka province or among the migrant communities in Syria's cities.[121] The development of this culture has of course been impeded by rule by emergency law in Syria, the illegality of such organisations and the negative consequences of involvement in them.

Possible networks of social and financial support for stateless Kurds suffering poverty and hardship could have been provided by the tribe and by the Kurdish political party. Stateless interviewees denied, however, that they or their families received any form of support from the tribes, in the past or in more recent years. As has been shown in Chapters 2 and 5, before the 1960s the Kurdish tribes played an important social and political role in Kurdish society but that the role of the tribes in Kurdish politics and Kurdish society generally has diminished dramatically. Tribal organisation, although retaining social meaning in the community, has had little consequence for political or economic problems within Kurdish society.[122] As such the ability of tribal leaders to address the issue of statelessness, socially or through dialogue with the government, has also been very limited. Indeed, amongst the Kurds statelessness has been defined as a political issue, and accordingly, tribal leaders have ceded authority for dealing with it to the political parties. As was suggested in Chapter 5, the Kurdish political party elite filled the vacuum left by the tribes, serving as social and political mediators in Kurdish society and providing some economic support to those in need, as well as attempting to represent Kurdish political interests. In comparison to the tribes, the parties acquired some ability to address statelessness and party leaders have claimed to help stateless Kurds in dire need of financial assistance; they provided individuals with financial support, or money to fund university students or to receive medical treatment. When asked if they received any support from the parties, however, stateless Kurds raised the point that the parties do not have the facilities to give this.[123] Most Kurdish parties are not supported financially by any outside organisations. The funds they raise are mostly donated by their members in and outside Syria, and from sales of party papers. It appears that the support that they are able to provide to the 300,000 plus stateless Kurds has been limited.

Despite the moral and symbolic support of Kurdish parties and their attempts to pressure the regime to return Syrian citizenship to those Kurds from whom it was taken in 1962, the parties have been unable to release these Kurds from the bonds of their circumstances. They have been unable to mitigate the effects of statelessness or protect them from persecution by the state. It is arguable, however, that, Kurdish identity and Kurdish politics has been one way in which stateless Kurds have remained integrated into

Kurdish society. Without Kurdish nationalism and the sense of national solidarity the circumstances of these Kurds could have been much worse. The solidarity and sense of community within Kurdish society has facilitated mechanisms of support for this group that are otherwise absent in Syrian society. As a consequence of nationalist politics and aspirations, this group maintained great potential to mobilise politically – not simply in order to effect a change in their circumstances, but as part of the wider Kurdish community and identity. This mobilisation was practically demonstrated after the beginning of the Syrian uprising when stateless Kurds played an important part in protests.

The State and the Stateless

Until after Bashar al-Assad came to power in the year 2000, the Syrian state had continuously denied and ignored the plight of the stateless Kurds. The concluding observations of the United Nations Human Rights Committee on Syria's second periodic report to the International Covenant on Civil and Political Rights, included a clause stating that '[t]he State party should take urgent steps to find a solution to the statelessness of numerous Kurds in Syria and to allow Kurdish children born in Syria to acquire Syrian nationality'. In response, the Syrian Arab Republic stated that:

> With regard to paragraph 27, the Kurds who enter Syria from neighbouring countries are shown special concern by the Syrian authorities, who endeavour to solve their humanitarian, administrative and practical problems. Special concern is also shown for Kurdish children born in Syria, who are treated in the same way as Syrian citizens, without any discrimination or preference. The Syrian authorities are making a very careful study of the situation of these Kurds, taking into account all the circumstances that induce them to enter and live in Syria.[124]

As this chapter has shown, Kurds without citizenship, including children, have been unjustly discriminated against by the Syrian authorities and the state system. Yet, the year 2002 was the first time since the census took place, that the issue of the stateless Kurds was addressed publicly by a Syrian government official. The president, Basher al-Assad, while conducting the first presidential visit to Hasaka province since 1949, talked of finding a solution to the plight of the stateless Kurds in Syria. Then, in 2004, after the Qamishli uprising shook the Kurdish regions of Syria, further promises were made by state officials to deal with the situation. In April, Mustafa Tlas agreed to return citizenship to a mere 30,000 Kurds.[125] On 1 May, in an al-Jazeera TV interview, Bashar al-Assad spoke of returning citizenship to those who had a right to it. Then in the summer of 2005 Information Minister, Mehdi Daklallah cited 120,000 as the number of Kurds without citizenship in Syria, still less than half the number estimated by Kurdish sources. Again, on 10 November 2005, in an address to Damascus University, Assad, reiterated his intention to resolve the issue.[126]

Addressing the delay in dealing with the stateless Kurds in his inaugural speech of 17 July 2007, President Assad blamed political circumstances such as the US invasion of Iraq in 2003 and the riots in Qamishli in 2004.[127] But by 2010 still no solution to the problem had been found and not a single Kurd had had her or his citizenship returned. Indeed, underlying this inaction on the subject was a distinction between the *ajanib* and the *maktumiin* made by the President in his speech. It seems that his intention was not to address the issue of the *maktumiin* at all and that his understanding of the *ajanib* issue was as a technical problem rather than a political matter. Indeed, in an interview Assad reduced the whole Kurdish question in Syria to one of technical errors that occurred in the conduct of the census in 1962.[128] State officials continued to claim that the majority of stateless Kurds did not have a right to citizenship; Mustafa Tlas stated that 'tens of thousands of Kurds have come to Syria from Iraq and Turkey. We have told them [Kurdish leaders] frankly that those who are Syrian will have that nationality recognised, but not the others'.[129] And in its third periodic report to the United Nations International Covenant on Civil and Political Rights in 2004, the Syrian government stated that:

> Directives have been issued recently to resolve the situation of those who do not carry Syrian nationality; however, this situation cannot be resolved under a single decree but requires specific decrees for each case, which needs time. Once again we affirm that there is no discrimination or discriminatory measures against them.[130]

There is evidence that state officials made attempts to begin this process of examination of each case, conducting some form of census of stateless people in Hasaka province. In 2005 Kurds of the region stated that officials had interviewed them, asking about the status of family members and their numbers.[131] Others, however suggested that this 'census' was far from comprehensive. Then, in 2008 a more thorough census of *ajanib* Kurds was conducted. There was no attempt or pretence of addressing the issue of the *maktumiin* and the president made it clear that the regime would not be doing so.[132]

Although Bashar al-Assad conveyed his intent to naturalise the *ajanib* there was opposition to this move, and the President's denial that the issue was even remotely political denied the Kurdish parties any political capital that could be gained from its solution. Kurdish sources generally believed government statements to be false promises; they considered the new 'census' to be a cynical attempt both to weaken the momentum that the Kurdish political movement had achieved after the events of 2004 and to appease the concerns of western governments and human rights groups.[133] With the arabisation programme in mind and the knowledge that regime legitimacy was founded on the ideology and rhetoric of Arab nationalism, it seemed clear that for the Syrian state the return of citizenship to the stateless Kurds would cause a number of problems for the government. The return of citizenship to more than a quarter of a million Kurds would require that the state distribute a large portion of the land in state possession to these Kurds, both as compensation and in accordance with the principles of the socialist-style land reforms of the 1960s and 1970s.[134] It is likely that this would have the effect of increasing the Kurdish presence in the region, both officially in the Syrian civil registers, and through the reversal of the trend to migrate out of the region. It appeared that the bishops of Christian churches in Hasaka province also opposed the naturalisation of stateless Kurds in the belief that those denied citizenship were indeed illegal immigrants and on the grounds that return of citizenship would upset the balance between Kurdish and Arab citizens in the region, to the advantage of the former. Finally, they alleged that the Kurdish population was not loyal to the state.[135]

Within a month of the start of the Syrian uprising, Bashar al-Assad published Decree 49 on 7 April 2011 granting the right for *ajanib* Kurds to apply for citizenship. As foretold in Bashar al-Assad's references to the stateless issue in previous years, the attempt to deal with the stateless issue was not comprehensive. It did not include the *maktumiin* Kurds, nor did it broach the issue of compensation. Generations of *maktumiin* Kurds, estimated by some sources to number between 140,000 and 160,000, continue to be dismissed as illegal immigrants and denied any form of recognition. The promulgation of the decree was regarded with suspicion amongst Kurds and as an attempt to persuade them to stay out of the protests. As an artificially created underclass, bearing the oppressive policies of the state towards the Kurds as well as the burdens of economic and social marginalisation in Syria, stateless Kurds were driven to stand in protest against the regime, not only by inequality and hardship, but also by Kurdish nationalism.

The process of obtaining Syrian citizenship following Decree 49 of April 2011 was not straightforward and Kurds reported a number of obstacles to actually receiving Syrian citizenship. Initially *ajanib* Kurds were wary of applying for citizenship fearing that the process would be used against them and that citizenship would obligate them to perform military service. Even when applications had been processed and accepted, the identity documents issued to the Kurds had to be 'activated'. This involved an interview with the state security. Whether or not the names of these people would be entered onto the lists of citizens, allowing them to apply for a passport, was unclear. This was controlled by a different department from the one which processed the applications.[136]

Although the Syrian authorities denied that the *ajanib* and *maktumiin* Kurds in Syria have been subject to undue discrimination and that they have faced persecution, the reality of the situation on the ground in Syria testified to the opposite. Stateless Kurds in Syria and in exile reported daily abuses of their human rights, degradation by Syrian officials and police and the *mukhabarat*, denial of basic state services, hardship and humiliation. In many cases, the state's contention that these Kurds were alien infiltrators is disproved by documents possessed by many Kurdish families in the Jazira region, and the general attitude of the Syrian authorities towards the Kurds in Syria suggests that this has been a population that they would rather were demobilised and destitute. Oral and written testimonies about how the census took place – the mistakes that occurred, the discrimination of the Syrian officials, the consequences of their registration as foreigners and of non-registration – leave little doubt that the census was part of a wider programme of arabisation in the region. Begun during the height of Arab nationalism in the Middle East and continued under the Ba'th Party, Arab nationalism and fear of Kurdish nationalism have led to the social exclusion of approximately one-quarter of a million Kurds under the pretext of state security.

It has been argued that the stateless Kurds in Syria formed an under-class and that this status was a result of economic, social and political consequences of statelessness. These specific consequences gave rise to forms of politics available to this group which they utilised in accordance with their respective interests. Economically these interests have been best served through cooperation with others affected by similar issues, such as access to state services, the occupation of unlicensed housing and engaging in forms of quiet encroachment[137] upon the state common to the underclasses and marginalised groups. This has been a method of coping with the economic consequences of their status.

Their legal status has been regarded as part of the wider discrimination against the Kurds of Syria, not simply as a technical error as Bashar al-Assad implied. Their interests in justice and the return of citizenship is an issue on which they are unable to face the state alone. Instead, the framework of the Kurdish political parties and the wider Kurdish issue in Syria is used to campaign for these rights. A solution to it has been sought, not through organisation as stateless people, but as Kurds within Kurdish political parties or in spontaneous reactions to government actions perceived to be directed against the Kurds, such as in the Qamishli uprising of March 2004 or the additional state restrictions imposed on land ownership and its use in 2008. Socially, also, their primary identification as Kurds rather than as stateless has helped to limit the social exclusion that they face in Syrian society and, more recently, within the Kurdish community also. Consequently, for these Kurds, Kurdish nationalist politics has served the dual purpose of limiting the social damage caused to them by their legal status and provided their only available channel for political representation and potential change.

Yet, under the rule of the Ba'th Party regime, the two identities, that of being an underclass and that of being Kurdish, have had a negative effect on one another. Preoccupation with daily survival has meant that political activism has been quite removed from the reality of their daily lives. Also, the nature of the regime and the consequences of political action construed as opposing the government added to the quietude of this group of Kurds. Consequently, whereas this group might otherwise have rallied to the Kurdish parties prior to the outbreak of the Syrian uprising, if their political activities had been directed more towards political and social action, their economic status restricted their ability to do so. Since March 2011, it has been the circumstances in Syria, rather than Decree 49 itself, which have removed this economic obstacle to participation. The majority of Syrians have had their lives transformed by the uprising and the normal economic infrastructure of the state, working conditions and services have been disrupted or destroyed. In the Kurdish areas under the control of the Supreme Kurdish Council, the legal status of the *ajanib* and *maktumiin* has no bearing on the distribution of services, aid or food. As a consequence, statelessness, while remaining a legal status under the ruling regime, has lost some of its negative consequences due to the retreat of the state from Kurdish areas in Syria.

CHAPTER 7

THE EVE OF THE SYRIAN UPRISING: CRISIS AND CONSCIOUSNESS

The picture that has been painted of the Kurdish political movement has so far not placed great emphasis on the relations between the parties and popular opinion. The book has provided a view of the realities of the Kurdish political party movement in Syria under Ba'th Party rule, their role in Kurdish society and their position within the Syrian state. Popular opinion about the parties and their roles, however, and more generally popular national consciousness, are crucial to understanding contemporary Kurdish party politics in Syria. The opinion of the Kurdish public about the parties is a critical factor in their ability to mobilise the Kurdish population and it sheds light on inherent problems of the party system. By all accounts the Kurdish parties' movement was in the midst of a crisis on the eve of the Syrian uprising and the parties had lost much of their former support among the Kurdish population in Syria. Yet, at the same time, Syrian Kurdish national consciousness was said to be at its highest ever level.[1] While, on the face of it, the simultaneous appearance of these two trends is puzzling, further analysis suggests a strong connection between the two.

The crisis in Kurdish party politics grew from two main factors. The first was the withdrawal of support by the Kurdish population. Party members, particularly intellectuals, withdrew from party work in large numbers and the parties did not enjoy the respect and popularity that they once did. Second, the parties disengaged from the Kurdish population. The result, whether intentional or not, was that the parties became increasingly distant from the Kurdish people in both their method and their politics. Public criticism of the parties became louder and the parties failed to react positively.

In effect, the Kurdish party movement had hit a wall and had only limited means of surmounting it.

Criticism of the parties concentrated on a number of factors: factionalism, general weakness of policy and ideology, excessive focus by the parties on external organisations and issues, the domination of personal problems within the leadership, alleged relations with the state and inability to achieve any concessions from the state on Syrian Kurdish questions.[2] All these issues have been introduced in the preceding chapters, particularly in Chapters 3 and 4 which dealt with the development of Kurdish party politics after 1957 and relations between the parties and the state. It is clear from the examination of the history of the Kurdish party movement in Syria and of their policies and methods, that all these factors have been features of the Kurdish political party movement since soon after its inception in 1957. Two questions arise from this: why is it that these features seem to be inherent in the Kurdish political party movement and why is it only in recent years that the party system has been described as being in crisis? This chapter tries to answer these two questions in turn. It also explains how and why this crisis of the parties has arisen and accounts for the apparent contradiction between the growth of both crisis and consciousness within the Kurdish political movement in Syria and explains the connections between them.

The Inherent Deficiencies in the Kurdish Party Movement

It is clearly not one single factor which has led to the factionalism of Kurdish political parties in Syria or to the fact that the parties are so influenced by internal and personal differences. Nor is it a single factor which led party leaders to develop relations with members of the Syrian security services in spite of its repression of the Kurds and their own illegality. A number of explanatory theories present themselves, all of which have contributed in combination to producing the form of party politics that exists among the Kurds of Syria.

We can start with the fact that the parties have shown a chronic inability and unwillingness to mobilise the population and organise effective social or political action. Their failure partly follows from the illegality imposed on them by the Ba'th regime and from the interference of the state authorities in the parties' internal affairs. Illegality might also account for their tendency to seek protection among their political opponents – in this case the agents of oppression of the Kurds themselves. The illegality of the parties and of the political and social actions organised by them, coupled with its potentially severe consequences, limited the parties' willingness and ability to confront the regime. The political parties have been tolerated by the regime so long as they remain within its 'red lines' and did not form a united political body or mobilise the Kurdish population *en masse*. These unwritten 'red lines' were in constant flux and the development of sustained or regular popular mobilisation, like those which occurred after March 2004, was followed by crack-downs on party leaders, members and other political and cultural activists, redefining what the parties were able to do or achieve without confrontation or arrest. The rise in public expression of dissent from the Kurdish population and from within the party movement in the decade following the end of the Cold War demonstrated clearly that, in order to exist in their illegal state, the parties had to avoid the very things that Kurdish society expected of them.

Additionally, members of Kurdish society themselves became unwilling to engage in endeavours such as demonstrations when they considered them to be ineffective and dangerous. Besides potential concessions from the state there has been little reward for participation in Kurdish political parties or political actions in Syria, whereas, in Iraqi Kurdistan or Turkey, the political parties rewarded *peshmerga* with a salary, and the PKK guerrillas entered a close social network, gaining respect and honour within a well-funded political party. In Syria, party members have been required to donate a portion of their salaries to the party,[3] and party leaders generally finance their own full-time work in the party through monies accruing from land ownership and family wealth.[4] The only obvious benefits of involvement in politics to the individual have been confined to the leadership which gained prestige within the Kurdish communities. The potential repercussions of involvement in illegal party activities, particularly when the parties are factionalised and unable to command mass support, have been very serious. Added to this, the effectiveness of political action by parties with such a limited capacity for participation is questionable and has provided another reason for parties and individuals to avoid it, creating a downward spiral in both political action and participation.

Illegality can also be used to explain factionalism within the party system and the focus of many parties on external political organisations and issues, such as relations with the Kurdish parties of Iraqi Kurdistan or the courting of the Arab opposition in Syria. The lack of avenues for advancement of the party within the state political system or even direct engagement with the state, has led to an inversion of political focus upon internal issues and on the Kurdish community itself and also to externalising solutions to Syrian Kurdish issues. As a consequence, organisational issues and personal differences within the parties have taken on greater significance than they might otherwise have done and caused factions and blocs to form within and between parties. Lack of incentive to stay within a particular party when problems arise has made the formation of an alternative party an attractive option and factionalism of the party system the result. The Kurdish political parties in other states, the Arab opposition and even international organisations have acted as networks through which the parties have negotiated their illegality and sought solutions to Kurdish issues in Syria while by-passing the state. The domination of the political parties of other areas of Kurdistan over those of Syria, however, has been tacitly encouraged by the government. Despite the state position towards its own Kurdish population, it allowed the PKK, the KDP and the PUK to operate freely from within Syria.[5] This is said to have facilitated the involvement of the Kurds of Syria in the affairs of Kurdistan of Iraq and Turkey to the neglect of their own political issues and movement.

The continuation of factionalism over the history of the party movement as well as other internal problems can also be explained by the interference of the Syrian security apparatus in the internal affairs of the parties, not simply by the imposition of restrictions upon them. Although there is little actual proof of state intrigue, the belief is widespread that the *mukhabarat* have infiltrated the party ranks, incited dissent within them, and supported the establishment of new parties or factions.[6] While this may be a valid cause of factionalism, it has not been possible to prove or disprove it, and even if access to *mukhabarat* personnel in Syria had been possible, considering the nature of the state, it is highly unlikely that this sort of information would be disclosed to foreign researchers.

Illegality and state intrigue do not provide sufficient explanation in themselves for the parties' deficiencies. While providing an explanation for most problems within the party movement, these two factors are external to the Kurdish political parties and imposed on them by the state. Illegality has not prevented political organisations in other states from gaining mass support and leading groups of followers in effective social action, resisting factionalism or concentrating on issues important to their constituencies. Even within the Kurdish political sphere, the examples of the KDP or the PUK in Iraqi Kurdistan or the PKK in Turkey are testimony that illegality does not actually prevent banned political organisation from mobilising wide sectors of the population or confronting oppressors. These parties have prioritised their own struggles above those of other areas of Kurdistan and have strong charismatic nationalist leaders with secure support bases, who have prevented the fragmentation of the political movement. But there are important differences between the Kurdish areas in Syria and those in Iraq or Turkey. This leads to the analysis of the second factor, specific to the Syrian Kurdish environment and society, that helps explain why factionalism, in particular, seems to be inherent within the Kurdish party movement in Syria.

So the second set of factors explaining the parties' deficiencies is the geographic and demographic conditions in Syria. These have had an important impact on the development of Kurdish politics in Syria, particularly with regard to mobilisation and the failure to develop a united Kurdish movement. Although their tactics differed considerably, both the PKK and the KDP developed disciplined and well trained military wings which used the mountain terrain in the Kurdish regions to their advantage. Acts of revolution, uprising and resistance have been identified with particular leaders and have added to the credentials of those leaders. In comparison, conditions in Syria were not favourable for the pursuit of armed struggle against the state. Indeed, over the years, a few small groups advocating the use of arms in Syria were established by Kurds. But the terrain is unfavourable for such tactics and they did not gain the necessary support to sustain such a movement; those involved were arrested soon after launching their activities and with the leaders' arrests, the organisations ceased to operate.[7] The Kurdish regions in Syria are smaller and are not as mountainous as those in Iraq, Turkey or Iran and do not form a contiguous geographical area. Consequently, in comparison to Iraq or Turkey, mobilisation of the Kurds in Syria has been more exposed to surveillance by and counter measures from the regime. On the whole, Kurds from Syria joined the KDP *peshmerga* or the PKK rather than develop indigenous armed movements.

Geography, demography and history have also led to differences developing between the Kurdish areas in Syria, and these have had a significant effect on politics. Migration into the Jazira from Turkey in the 1920s concentrated Kurdish political and national activists in this region. Its strategic importance to the Syrian economy and state security made the Jazira the focus of state policies aimed at containing the Kurdish 'threat' and, consequently, the centre of Kurdish political organisation in Syria. Before the beginning of the Kurdish party movement, in all Kurdish areas, both political and cultural groups remained largely local and connected to local individuals, groups or social networks. The organisation of the Kurds in a political party in 1957 was intended to bridge social and physical divides between the areas and to represent and attract members and supporters from all Kurdish areas and all social spheres. While it was successful for some time, expanding the influence of Kurdish political organisation across the Kurdish regions has been problematic. Successive divisions within the party ranks have been influenced by regional and social divisions as well as personal alliances and networks. Loyalties and factions within parties commonly follow existing local social and personal networks, so when a faction breaks away from a party forming its own organisation, the party encounters geographic and demographic obstacles.[8] Without representatives in other areas and as a result of state controls over telephones, transport networks, printing, publication and distribution of printed matter, many parties have faced problems extending their influence across these regional divisions.

Local relations and minor cultural differences, such as differences in dance and traditional clothes, or in local dialect and accent between the Kurdish areas as well as differences in the strength of tribal relations and levels of development have also led to the appearance of social barriers between the areas. This has presented a further obstacle to the effective political organisation of Kurdish society as people generally congregate around political leaders familiar to their local communities. The parties are strongest in the Jazira region where most party leaders come from, and where tribal relations still have some bearing on social and political networks and relations.

A third explanation for the factionalism of the party system arises from the make-up of the leadership and the nature of Syrian Kurdish society. For the duration of the Kurdish political party movement in Syria, Kurdish society in Syria has involved a complex combination of traditional and modern socio-economic relations, networks, and mores. The Kurdish political movement in Syria began with a leadership consisting of an arrangement of representatives of various social groups with different interests and agendas. Between 1957 and 1958 the leadership of *Partiya Demokrat a Kurd li Sûriye* expanded to include intellectuals, Communist Party renegades, teachers, religious leaders and tribal chieftains. In comparison, the two main Kurdish parties of Iraq, the KDP and the PUK, were based on traditional tribal groupings and religious orders connected to specific geographical areas. The PKK in Turkey began life as an explicitly Marxist guerrilla organisation whose leader, Abdullah Öcalan, gained his authority through charisma and personal identification of the party with his character, ideology and the Kurdish identity itself, as well as the effective use of the Marxist–Leninist concept of the 'new man' through which he appealed to the Kurdish masses.[9] Consequently, all these parties gained popular support, whereas the majority of the leadership of *Partiya Demokrat a Kurd li Sûriye* were arrested only three years after it was established and, under pressure from the Syrian authorities, quickly succumbed to internal differences within the leadership dividing the party and with it the support base. Its president Dr Nur al-Din Zaza resigned from the party in 1962 after his release from prison in 1961[10] and its secretary, Osman Sabri, left Syria in 1970 to pursue political work in Turkey.[11] As a result, no one leader gained the support necessary to drive the political movement in Syria and party leadership became an area of competition between suitors for power within the Kurdish communities and a means of extending the life of traditional power relations.

The persistence of semi-tribal social and power relations, particularly within the Jazira region where the majority of party leaders are from, facilitated the formation of blocs based on familial and local networks of supporters within the parties. Consequently, a number of smaller parties exist which are limited in constituency and support and, as a consequence, lacking in ability to perform social functions or political actions.[12] Nonetheless, they operate as any other larger party does and, the regular creation of blocs of parties, described in Chapter 3, suggests that they are liable to become pawns in power politics between other larger parties. The reformist tendencies of the intellectuals have often come into conflict with the interests of more conservative sectors of Kurdish society and its political leadership. The effect of this is discussed further below and it is enough to say here that the persistence of traditional tribal relations and interests, alongside more modern, nationalist trends embodied by the Kurdish intellectuals, created a tension within the parties and between the parties and the younger generations within Kurdish society.

Thus, illegality, the interference of the state in the internal affairs of the parties, geographic and demographic conditions in Syria and the persistence of semi-tribal relations in Kurdish society, all offer some explanation as to why the Kurdish political party system seems to be inherently fragile, partial to factionalism and unable to obtain any concessions from the state. Yet, these are all factors that have affected Kurdish politics in Syria since the inception of the Kurdish party movement and none of these explanations account for why it is that Kurdish society only began to characterise the party movement as being in crisis in the few years preceding the start of the Syrian uprising.

The Party System in Crisis?

The question of why, at this point, the parties began to be described as being in crisis can only be answered through examining what changed in Kurdish society in Syria, what brought about that change, and what led members and supporters to increase their criticisms of the parties and even disassociate themselves from party activities. Interviews suggest that the seeds of crisis were sown in the late 1980s as a result of increasing internal power struggles and fracturing of the parties.[13] Since these effects were felt from 1990 onwards, this section uses evidence from the period 1990 until the eve of the Syrian uprising in 2011 to explain the supposed onset of crisis.

One obvious explanation for the withdrawal of support from the parties by both members and non-members is the continued factionalism of the political party movement uncompensated by any major political gains in more than 50 years of activity. The growth of criticism was natural in these circumstances as was a general mood of disenchantment with the system. Other developments have occurred, however, alongside the successive division of the parties. Interviews and academic literature suggest four primary factors have been involved in precipitating the crisis in Kurdish politics in Syria: the withdrawal of intellectuals from the party ranks, the development and availability of information technologies, the growth of generational differences within Kurdish society and, finally, the rise in popular consciousness amongst the Syrian Kurds.

The withdrawal of Kurdish intellectuals

One of the most important aspects of the party crisis is that the majority of Kurdish intellectuals left the ranks of the parties in favour of pursuing their nationalist and cultural activities independently. This led to a further divide within the Kurdish political and national movement, between the politicians and political parties on the one hand and the intellectuals and independent cultural and nationalist activists and organisations on the other.

Kurdish intellectuals began to leave the party ranks at the beginning of the 1990s, opting to work independently outside the party framework. The majority left party work due to the great number of what they considered to be unjustified divisions within the party ranks. A further reason for their withdrawal was what has been described as the appearance of an incapable or unqualified leadership whose interests departed from their own.[14] Problems began to arise between the intellectuals and the political leadership of the parties when the former found themselves subject to accusations of being unrealistic, unprincipled and of meddling in internal party affairs. It appears that, on the one hand, the critical stance of the intellectuals towards the leadership and the numerous divisions within party ranks threatened the party leadership, and on the other hand, the intellectuals found that they were restricted in their ability to achieve their aims, particularly the nationalistic ones, within the ranks of the political parties.[15]

The withdrawal of the intellectuals had a decisive impact on the parties and was one of the factors that pushed them into a crisis. Kurdish intellectuals played an important part in the cultural and social role of the parties and in the processes of defining and developing national identity, aiding its expression and keeping the parties connected to the Kurdish people through cultural and social activities. Since their withdrawal, the parties' abilities to perform social roles, particularly that of cultural framing, has diminished to the extent that it is no longer appropriate to characterise it as a party function. Even the parties' role in facilitating cultural expression and reproduction through social organisations and cultural events, described in Chapter 5, has declined. The importance of the intellectuals to the identity of the parties and of the Kurdish national movement in Syria could hardly be greater. As shown in Chapters 2, 3 and 5, nationalist cultural organisation preceded political organisation in Syria and it was Kurdish intellectuals who were the primary pioneers of the Kurdish nationalist movement and who initiated the first Kurdish party in Syria. With the formation of the party in 1957, culture and the development of Kurdish national identity became central pillars of

Kurdish party politics. The involvement of intellectuals in the rank and file of the parties connected more traditional social elements of Kurdish society with the more nationalist, progressive and modernising ones.[16] Progressive conceptions of nationalism, developed initially by the Bedirkhan brothers and their associates, connected Kurdish nationalism with modernisation and social development and included emancipatory elements such as equal rights for women.[17] Culture and the development of language were key components of the Kurdish nationalist movement in Syria which the political parties inherited when Kurdish intellectuals co-founded the first Kurdish political party in Syria.

More than 50 years after the establishment of the first Kurdish political party in Syria in 1957, cultural activities and projects to develop Kurdish national identity and promote Kurdish rights in Syria are increasingly pursued outside party ranks and without the parties' direct involvement. Many independent intellectuals criticise the parties for not pursuing cultural and educational activities, such as opening publishing houses to promote Kurdish literature and publication, which one interviewee suggested that they could do by naming the publishing house with an Arab name, as he himself had done.[18] The work of the intellectuals in developing Kurdish nationalism outside the political parties is an area that deserves further attention. The scope of this book has not allowed for in-depth research into the latest endeavours of Kurdish intellectuals to promote the Kurdish issue, to influence the politics of the state and to develop the Kurdish national identity. Many Kurdish intellectuals, however, as well as artists inside and outside Syria, continue to seek to publicise the Kurdish issue in Syria through their work. Through poetry, prose, music, art and photography as well as through the publication of articles, memoirs and histories of the Kurdish national movement and of the Kurdish areas in Syria they seek to preserve their identity and history and to develop their culture.

In the context of the repression of the Kurds and the government's association of Kurdish identity with threats to the security of the state, the work of the Kurdish intellectuals has clear nationalist and political content. State restrictions on expressions of Kurdish culture and language help to identify cultural activities and publications as explicitly political. Consequently, much artistic work remains illegal and criminal despite the artists' disassociation from the political parties; if arrested, they face the same treatment as those directly involved in political parties.[19]

Based on the central importance of the intellectuals to the Kurdish political movement from 1957 until today, it is possible to argue that the withdrawal of the intellectuals from Kurdish political parties in Syria has caused a fundamental change in the substance of Kurdish party politics in Syria. Numerous interviews testify that since intellectuals began to withdraw from the Kurdish political parties, the involvement of the parties in cultural affairs has weakened.[20] This has compromised one of the most important purposes of the parties.

Communication technologies

The development of information technologies and their introduction to the Syrian public has had a far-reaching impact on the Kurdish political movement. Information technologies, particularly the internet and mobile phones, have had profound implications for the importance of generational differences to the make-up of Kurdish society. They have widened the gap between traditional Kurdish society and the younger generations who have grown up with the internet and mobile technology and are further removed from traditional socio-economic relations. This has had further consequences for the political parties, examined in this section.

The internet was introduced to the Syrian public in the year 2000 and mobile phone operators in 2001. Until 2010, only two mobile phone operators had been granted contracts in Syria,[21] although in August 2010 the government agreed to issue one further contract.[22] According to figures from Mobile World, mobile phone penetration in Syria was said to be at 44 per cent in March 2010,[23] among the lowest in the region.[24] The dissemination of the internet has been limited by the low number of personal computers in Syria, estimated at 800,000 at the end of 2005,[25] a penetration of just 4.2 per cent.[26] In the same year, internet users were estimated at only 875,000 and subscribers at 233,000.[27] In 2008, however, the International Telecommunications Union estimated actual internet use in Syria to be 17 per cent,[28] and by June 2011 it was reported to be 19.8 per cent. The Syrian Public Telecommunications Establishment (or Syrian Telecom), which was a public corporation affiliated to the Ministry of Communications and Technology with a monopoly over telecommunications and their governance,[29] imposed heavy restrictions on the use of the internet. Consequently, the full potential and impact of the information technologies on the Kurdish political movement in Syria has not yet been felt. But, despite limited access, the younger generation, urban youth and students who study IT in school and university, or frequent internet cafés and computer labs, as well as those able to finance a home connection, received a significantly different education after the year 2000 to that of earlier generations.

The availability of internet and mobile phone technology has been a double-edged sword for the Kurdish parties. On the one hand, mobile phones enabled freer communications within the parties, between members and within the leadership as, with the right know-how, a user is able to avoid phone taps. Also, the option to disseminate information by email and on the internet has helped some parties to extend their areas of influence, whereas geographic and demographic divisions between the Kurdish regions previously hindered the spread of some parties beyond their local areas. On the other hand, public access to the internet has allowed Kurdish individuals and groups to publish, access and compare information with much greater ease. While the internet is monitored in Syria and many sites are banned, many of the younger generation are technically skilled and are often able to circumvent state restrictions on access. Consequently, Kurds in Syria are able to bypass political parties for information on Kurdish issues within Syria and outside it and to access alternative, neutral or less partisan information than they might have access to within their local communities.

Increasing numbers of Kurdish journalists, activists and intellectuals, both inside Syria and in the diaspora, use the internet to publish articles about the political movement and its internal affairs. Often using pseudonyms to avoid identification, not only by the Syrian authorities but also by the political parties, Kurdish activists have increasingly criticised the parties. This has exposed to the general Kurdish public, the internal workings of the parties and their domination by personal issues. Kurdish intellectuals, disenchanted with the parties, have also been provided with an alternative forum for publishing their research and articles, which had previously been limited to party papers and journals. Independent Kurdish organisations in the diaspora have developed websites dedicated to conveying impartial news coverage of Syrian Kurdish issues and of human rights abuses against the Kurds.[30] The internet also became a place of discussion, criticism and responses, particularly among Kurdish intellectuals and independent writers, but also involving members of the party leadership. This growing criticism of the parties has not always been well received. The publication of an article by the independent Kurdish writer Muhammad Juma'a on many Kurdish websites[31] prompted a harsh response from Abdul Hamid Darwish against him and other writers, calling the political parties to work together against 'malicious misinformation' and untrustworthy writers who were seeking to undermine the leaders of the Kurdish movement.[32]

Independent activists and intellectuals have made increased use of the internet to inform the Kurds and international observers of the situation inside Syria, to expose the human rights abuses suffered by Kurds and to promote Kurdish culture and unity. The same cannot be said of the political parties. A brief survey of party websites reveals that they change name and domain frequently, that they cease to operate without warning, that many parties do not have websites at all, that some that do exist are not up to date and that pages are often missing and links broken. It is also difficult to find information about parties since most of them publish their party paper, various articles about Kurdish issues and little else. Most do not even include their political programmes on their websites, and consequently, copies of them are obtainable only through direct contact with the parties themselves.[33] Most websites are produced and maintained in the diaspora, primarily in Germany, due to the controls on the use of the internet that exist in Syria. The party branches in the diaspora, however, remain subordinate to the party leadership in Syria.

Another important effect on Kurdish national consciousness came from the development of Kurdish satellite television. The introduction of mobile phones and the internet to the Syrian public had an important effect both on national consciousness and on generational differences in Kurdish society, although their dissemination has been limited by financial constraints and state controls over information. In contrast, the development of Kurdish satellite television had a wide impact on all sectors of the Kurdish communities in Syria, not just in terms of knowledge, but also in terms of pride in their nation and its achievements. The Kurdish population was exposed to a constant stream of news about the Kurdish regions, educational films on Kurdish issues, documentaries, chat shows, Kurdish language programmes, political propaganda and music, all of which stimulated the interest of Syrian Kurds in their heritage and history and culture as well as their desire for political results inside Syria.

Unlike internet and mobile phone technology, satellite dishes are prolific and installed in most Kurdish homes. The skylines of Kurdish areas, such as Ashrafiyah in Aleppo, are dominated by the hundreds of circular satellite dishes on apartment buildings. The first Kurdish satellite channels were founded in 1995. Since the year 2000, after Iraqi Kurdistan became self-administering, channels based in Europe and in Iraqi Kurdistan have been broadcasting around the clock. Many channels are connected to Kurdish political parties; Med TV was the first channel, founded in 1995 and connected to the PKK. It was broadcast from England until April 1999, when it had its licence revoked by the ITC. It then began broadcasting from Belgium under the name Medya TV. After its licence was again revoked in February 2004, the channel announced that a new channel, Roj TV,[34] would begin transmission on 1 March 2004, authorised by the Danish government. The channel in all its manifestations has faced charges of supporting terrorism because of its coverage of PKK festivals and broadcasts 'likely to encourage or incite crime or lead to disorder'.[35] Since its founding, Roj TV has faced pressure from the Turkish government to stop broadcasting on the grounds that it supports a terrorist organisation, the PKK, and in 2010 it was facing charges from the Danish government of encouraging the activities of the PKK.[36] Channels emanating from Iraqi Kurdistan include KurdSat, which was founded in 2000 and belongs to the PUK and Kurdistan TV which belongs to the KDP. The number of Kurdish satellite channels reached 20 in 2009,[37] including many independent channels such as Kurd 1, which was authorised by the French Higher Audiovisual Council, is owned by the Kurdish singer Shivan Perwer and began broadcasting in April 2009.

Satellite television brought the Kurdish struggle in Turkey and the political, cultural and infrastructural development of Iraqi Kurdistan into the Syrian Kurdish home. Images of toppling of statues of Saddam Hussein, of the Kurdish flag flying in the streets of Iraqi Kurdistan and the election of Jalal Talabani as president of Iraq on 6 April 2005 and that of Masoud Barzani as President of the Kurdistan Region in June 2005 were watched by millions and celebrated as a victory for the Kurdish people. In Syria, the nation ceased to be merely imagined. Rather, Kurdish satellite channels became windows into the other areas of Kurdistan. Iraqi Kurdistan became both a vision of the present and an aspiration for the future.

Generational differences

Although not all Kurdish communities or individuals have access to the internet or an interest in reading about such issues, the fact that it is available, and that the interest of Kurdish youth in Kurdish national politics has heightened considerably in the last decade, means that through personal interest or by word of mouth, new information about the internal dynamic of the political parties in Syria spread and produced further criticism of them. On the eve of the Syrian uprising, this criticism of the parties was heard increasingly from the younger generations within Kurdish society, particularly those aged between 18 and 35 who were thirsty for change and eager to become involved in Kurdish nationalist activities. This gave rise to a new generational divide between the traditional leadership, the existing party leadership and Kurdish youth.

The majority of the Kurdish party leadership are aged from 60 upwards. When they entered into politics many of them were as young as 15 years old.[38] When Kurdish party politics began in 1957, the Kurdish political parties were seen as a modernising, progressive element in society, a contrast to the traditional tribal system. The parties prohibited honour killings, sought to resolve land disputes, to end the discriminatory practices against women, such as restrictions on clothing, which were enforced by some of the tribal leaders, and generally to adopt a positive attitude on involving women in the national struggle.[39] There was some conflict of interest between the tribes and the parties, and the division of the first party in 1965 and the establishment of *el-Partî* in 1970 reflected these social divisions within Kurdish society.

Many of the existing party leaders are attached to the traditional nobility and former tribal leadership of the Jazira region and grew up experiencing the final demise of semi-feudal tribal relations, with parents and elders retaining traditional mentalities and understandings of social and political organisation. Through the land reforms of 1958 and the arabisation projects carried out in the Jazira in the 1970s, notable families lost most of their power and land. While some of the sons of tribal leaders and the landed aristocracy came to lead political parties[40] the distribution of land and wealth through inheritance means that generation after generation are growing more and more detached from traditional social and economic relations and family wealth. The younger generations have developed in a different social, economic and political context from that of the party leaders, and, while they remain highly nationalistic and committed to preserving traditional Kurdish cultural practices and customs, their exposure to and involvement with modern information technologies has had a considerable impact on their mentalities, and their capacity for critical thinking and understanding of the Kurdish issue in Syria.

State, university and even private education in Syria has been controlled by the government and its content dictated by them. Exposure to information technologies and the benefit of years of cultural activity among the Kurds, promoted national identity and the values of freedom, democracy, human rights and justice. The younger generations have thereby been equipped with a new confidence in their national identity and the ability to express it. They have developed new political ideas and an antipathy to the connection of many parties and their leaders to the traditional families and Kurdish nobility in Syria. They have been critical of their preoccupation with internal party politics, the weakness of their ideology and policy and their failure to gain any concessions from the state. These young people are also the future leaders of the Kurdish political movement, and their experience of it is likely to be considerably different from that of the present party leaders. They are unlikely to have the same financial capacity that enables the majority of the current leadership to work full time in the party without a popular support base.

Prior to the start of the Syrian uprising, intellectuals, independent activists and the Kurdish youth had increasingly been seeing the parties as undemocratic institutions that reflected the interests of an elite group detached from Kurdish society and that had not achieved anything for the Kurdish people in Syria in more than 50 years of party work.[41] The younger generation, having witnessed the successes of the Kurds in Iraqi Kurdistan and equipped with information available from multiple sources, were eager for change and eager to seize opportunities to further their political demands on the Syrian government. No alternative Syrian political organisation, however, had succeeded in challenging the domination of Kurdish politics by the existing political parties. Only two parties, the PYD and *Şepêla Pêşerojê* of Meshaal

Temmo, both independent of the other parties, were considered capable of gaining support among and mobilising sectors of the Syrian Kurdish population. Yet, for many, the association of the PYD with the PKK tarnished its reputation, and the assassination of the charismatic Temmo in October 2011 damaged the party.

The consequences of the spread of information technology among the Kurds was to increase open criticism of the political parties in Syria and the internet more than anything else exposed the internal party problems to the Kurdish public. This resource has highlighted generational differences within Kurdish society and provided intellectuals and independent Kurdish activists with an alternative forum for publishing their work. The majority of parties have, so far, failed to exploit information technologies, particularly the internet, to their advantage. This has accentuated the shift in popular opinion about the parties, converting their original image as modernising, progressive, nationalist organisation, to a new image as elitist organisations, detached from the Kurdish population and from changes in the international, regional and local environments.

The rise of national consciousness

Prior to the start of the Syrian uprising all interviewees agreed that, in general, the Kurdish population in Syria was more nationalistic, more prone to political action and thirsty for change than ever before.[42] This heightened national consciousness had developed over the preceding decade, and culminated in the spontaneous 'uprising' of the Kurds in Syria in March 2004. After that, levels of awareness, mobilisation and commitment were maintained among the Kurdish population. But at this point in time, these new attitudes had not been exploited by the political parties.

Arguably, the progressive rise in political and national consciousness amongst the Kurds in Syria began after the end of the Cold War, when a series of events and processes would gradually increase Kurdish hopes of finding a solution to their oppression in Syria. This is not to say that national consciousness was not widespread or strong before these events. On the contrary, it is arguable that the Kurds in Syria have been more politically conscious than Arab society in Syria. This is simply due to the Kurds' historical circumstances: their need to create a Kurdish nation-state, the division of Kurdistan, the repression of Kurdish political and cultural activities in Syria and other areas of Kurdistan and the politicisation of ethnic identity, not to mention the various revolutions and uprisings across the Kurdish regions. The political conditions within the Syrian state have stifled the free expression of Kurdish identity and political demands and relegated them to the private sphere and to underground political and cultural activity. But as a result of developments since the end of the Cold War, and especially since the year 2000, confidence in the expression of national identity and political demands gradually expanded and became more public, external and defiant. Kurdish youth in Syria began actively seeking out information about their nation in a manner that former generations were not able to do.

The events and processes that encouraged the Kurds to increase their visibility in Syria and stimulated national consciousness originated from both outside and inside Syrian territory. The rise of the human rights discourse and examples of international intervention, such as the US Operation Provide Comfort which imposed a no-fly zone over the Kurdish areas of northern Iraq from 1991 to 1996, and in the Kosovo war in 1999, encouraged the belief that international organisations and governments would intervene to protect the rights of minority groups such as the Kurds. The no-fly zone in Iraq effectively allowed Kurdish self-administration and autonomy to develop and this protected status was extended by Operation Northern Watch which ran until May 2003. Further intervention by the USA in Iraq in March 2003, the toppling of the Ba'thist regime in Iraq and the capture and execution of Saddam Hussein allowed Kurds in Syria to believe that, although deeply embedded in the Syrian state, the Assad regime was not immune to aggressive intervention and that the Kurds had found support in Western countries. The subsequent recognition of the Kurdish government as legitimate in the Transitional Administrative Law of 8 March 2004 and the recognition that the Kurdish areas constituted a federal unit in the constitution of 2005 were interpreted as victories for the Kurdish nation.

Within Syria a number of other factors worked to encourage the Kurds to increase the visibility of their cultural and political identities and demands. Responding to changes in the international order, the *Yekbûn* Party was formed in 1990, and in 1993[43] it embarked on the first acts of organised Kurdish street protest – a poster campaign condemning the state's policy towards the stateless Kurds. As described in Chapter 4, after its division in 1998 and in the wake of the Damascus Spring, the new *Yekîtî* party stepped up the visibility of Kurdish protest by organising a demonstration in Damascus marking International Human Rights day, on 10 December 2002. Demonstrations became regular but infrequent events involving not more than a few hundred participants, but their significance for the visibility of Kurdish protest and the effect on Kurdish national consciousness was significant. The new methods and more daring demands of *Yekîtî* attracted the more radical among the Kurdish youth, in particular those who sought change and believed the party to be significantly different to other Kurdish parties in Syria.

Between the *Yekîtî* demonstration of 10 December 2002 and the Qamishli uprising of 12 March 2004, several demonstrations were held which increased the visibility of Kurdish protest and national identity in Syria. Kurdish–Arab cooperation was stepped up and in early 2004 Kurdish student groups began to organise protests within the universities.[44] In March 2004 a series of events culminating in the Qamishli uprising demonstrated to the world that the Kurds in Syria were not disunited, as the state of their political movement suggested. On 8 March, Kurds in Syria took to the streets to celebrate the re-emergence of federalism in Iraqi Kurdistan. On the 10 March, in Damascus, a joint Arab–Kurdish demonstration was held marking the anniversary of the 1963 Ba'th Party coup, while in Qamishli large crowds of Kurds gathered to mark International Women's Day with folklore groups and poetry readings. The peaceful and culturally oriented gathering in Qamishli ended in the arrest of many participants[45] thus fuelling anger and frustration with the state authorities.

On March 12 the fatal shooting of ten Kurds in the football stadium in Qamishli rapidly led to the eruption of protest across the Kurdish regions and within Kurdish enclaves in Syria's cities. This was the first time in the history of the Kurdish political movement in Syria that mass mobilisation around Kurdish identity and encompassing all Kurdish areas had been directed against state power. Although the 'uprising' was crushed by the Syrian authorities and restrictions on Kurdish activities and controls in the Kurdish areas were increased in its wake, the uprising and its martyrs became important Kurdish national symbols and the scale of the protests added to the confidence of the Kurds in their ability to defend their rights. Mass demonstrations in Qamishli the following year reflected the continued levels of mobilisation among the Syrian Kurds.

The events of March 2004 marked a peak in Kurdish national consciousness and mobilisation. Opportunities to propel the Kurdish political movement into greater engagement with the state in the wake of the Qamishli uprising were, however, rejected by the parties in favour of maintaining the status quo. The Qamishli uprising was an expression of the new degree of national consciousness among the Syrian Kurds, but it is arguable that the Kurdish parties were not prepared for the levels of mobilisation of the Kurdish population demonstrated in March 2004. The events were unprecedented in the history of the Kurdish party movement in Syria and the parties had no plan of how to exploit such an occurrence to their advantage and to that of the Kurdish people in Syria. The state of factionalism and disunity among the parties prevented any agreement among them about how to respond both to the state authorities and to the Kurdish people. The recourse to negotiation with the *mukhabarat* undermined any attempts to exploit the situation early on and the parties appealed for calm in order to avoid further bloodshed.

In the wake of these events, the parties attempted to establish a Kurdish 'authority' that represented the Kurdish movement in Syria. But, as a result of this project, competition between the parties for leadership of the Kurdish political movement intensified, causing new fissures and blocs to emerge within the movement.[46]

As the Kurdish people witnessed these changes in international and regional relations, in Iraqi Kurdistan and in their own national movement, their belief that it was possible to change the situation for the Kurds in Syria grew. The rise of popular national consciousness among the Syrian Kurds led to greater criticism of the political parties, and here we return to the idea put forward at the beginning of this chapter, that the political parties' descent into crisis and the rise in national consciousness are connected. The desire for change among the Kurdish population, particularly the youth, was not met or accommodated by the political parties and their failure to positively respond to the rise in Kurdish national consciousness, particularly during and after the events of March 2004, led to fierce criticism of the parties from various sectors of Kurdish society. Instead of harnessing the rise in national consciousness, exploiting the opportunities presented by the introduction of the internet to Syria or seeking reform in response to criticisms from Kurdish intellectuals within party ranks, the parties opted to maintain the status quo in Syria. As a consequence, their role in Kurdish society weakened and involvement in inter- and intra-party politics deepened. Many parties decided to rally around the Damascus Declaration rather than court their own communities and make the reforms necessary to develop into a progressive political movement capable of re-engaging the Kurdish youth and intellectuals.

The Parties on the Eve of the Uprising

At the beginning of this chapter, two questions were posed: first, why was it that factionalism and other deficiencies of the parties seemed to be inherent to them? And, second, why it was only in recent years that the party system was described as being in crisis? Illegality and state intrigue, Kurdish geographic and demographic conditions in Syria and the duality of traditional and modern socio-economic relations in Kurdish society have all posed seemingly insoluble obstacles to Kurdish political unity and to effective mobilisation of the Kurdish population in Syria. Added to this, political and social developments, which affected Kurdish national consciousness and contributed to increasing criticisms of the parties over the past two decades, pushed the parties into what has been described as a crisis. The withdrawal of Kurdish intellectuals from party ranks, the introduction of the internet to the Syrian public and the rise in national consciousness among the Kurds all contributed to widening the gap between the population and the parties. These technologies increased the visibility of the parties' internal problems and exposed them to increasing criticism. The parties were castigated for their inability to exploit opportunities for mobilisation due to the factionalism within the movement, the often shifting political alliances and enmities between and within them and their attempts to preserve their existence by observing state limits to political activities and demands.

When drawing conclusions about the parties it is important to remember the particularly difficult circumstances under which the Kurdish parties have operated in Syria and the seemingly insoluble conundrum that they have faced, between existence and resistance. Without the support of the Kurdish public and the primary intellectual agents of Kurdish nationalism in Syria, the character of the parties and their mandate was compromised. The political parties were unable to accommodate criticisms emanating from the Kurdish intellectuals, to employ information technologies to their advantage, to engage the Kurdish youth or to react positively to the rise in Kurdish popular consciousness. These factors pushed the Kurdish political party system into the crisis which characterised Syrian Kurdish politics on the eve of the Syrian uprising. This crisis of confidence in the parties influenced the dynamics of the Syrian uprising in the Kurdish regions and amongst the Kurdish people.

CHAPTER 8

THE KURDISH RESPONSE TO THE SYRIAN UPRISING

The Kurdish political party movement entered the Syrian uprising stricken with internal problems and focused on maintaining a precarious balance of relationships – with the Kurdish population, the Arab opposition and the ruling regime – none of which were bearing fruit. The uprising itself provided the context necessary for instituting profound changes within the Kurdish political movement. It destroyed the regime's control over public expression of dissent and its 'red lines' were irreversibly contravened. At the time of writing the uprising is still continuing and the question of whether the parties can overcome their fragmentation, bridge their differences with the youth and intellectuals and re-orientate their politics towards the direct needs of the Kurdish people in Syria still cannot be definitively answered. This chapter offers an analysis of the political manoeuvring of the Kurdish parties during the first 18 months of the uprising, explaining the considerations behind party decisions in positioning the Kurdish population within the Syrian uprising. It examines the national and internal political dynamics that resulted in a large part of the Kurdish areas falling under Kurdish control in June 2012 and provides a tentative analysis of the experience of 'Kurdish self-rule' in Syria and reactions to it beyond the Kurdish regions. The chapter summarises the changes that the uprising has induced in the Kurdish political movement, asking whether the political parties have been able to overcome the crisis that characterised them at the beginning of the uprising.

Political Manoeuvring and Alliance Formation

Initial reactions

The start of the Syrian uprising and the political quagmire that it became led observers and analysts to delve deeper into the Kurdish issue in Syria.

For the first year of the uprising, much of the media and the Arab opposition portrayed the Kurds as holding back from participation in the revolution; in some sense they blamed them for the continuing deterioration of the situation in Syria. Concessions made to the Kurds by Assad early on prompted the idea that Kurdish parties would continue to work to maintain the status quo. The Kurds, known for their history of resistance to oppressors and persistent in their struggle for rights in Syria and beyond, were looked upon negatively because of the relative calm in the Kurdish areas of Syria. Thinly veiled threats emanated from members of the Arab opposition, suggesting that if the Kurds continued this stance, they would not be guaranteed rights in a post-Assad Syria. In August 2011 Samir Nashar, who became a member of the Executive Committee of the Syrian National Council (SNC), was even more explicit, saying 'we accuse the Kurdish parties of not effectively participating in the Syrian revolution... It seems that these parties continue to bet on a dialogue with the regime. This stance will certainly have consequences after the fall of the regime.'[1]

The situation on the ground was different. Concentration of the limited field coverage by the media on hotspots such as Hama, Homs and Deraa and on the Sunni Arab opposition, as well as the historic neglect of Kurdish issues in Syria, left the Kurdish areas and the Kurdish political actors on the sidelines of media attention. At the same time, the concentration of international and regional powers on the Syrian Arab opposition, left the Kurds out of the spotlight and unsure of what support they could muster at this historic moment. In most Kurdish areas organised groups of Kurdish youths held regular demonstrations, reclaiming public space from the regime, protesting alongside Syrian Arabs and establishing themselves as the primary actors on the streets. They adopted the slogans of the unified Friday protests, and repeated the chant, 'the Syrian people are one...one, one, one', and called for the overthrow of the regime. Friday 20 May 2011 was dubbed 'Azadî Friday', meaning 'Freedom' in Kurdish and reflected the growth of coordination between the organisers of Arab and Kurdish protests. In this period it was youth organisations that came to the fore.[2] Youth groups spearheaded the protests of the Kurdish street, rallied support and articulated Kurdish demands including support for the uprising and for the fall of the regime. Participation in the protests was continuous and increased over the first year of the uprising.

As well as biased media coverage and misinformation, the idea that the Kurds did not participate also arose from the more calculated reaction of the political parties to events in Syria. For the first five months of the uprising, the majority of Kurdish political parties did not officially call their members, supporters and the Kurdish people to the streets and did not explicitly call for the fall of the regime. This said, the majority of the parties called for change in the system and refused dialogue with the regime, insisting on the need for fundamental changes to the organisation of Syrian politics and to authoritarian rule. They prioritised removing systemic factors involved in the oppression of the Kurds in Syria recognising that Kurdish problems in Syria were not simply a matter of leadership. The reactions of the Kurdish parties were not uniform and some of them, such as the more radical parties, *Şepêla Pêşerojê*, *Azadî* and *Yekîtî*, supported the protests more actively from the early days of the uprising. Members of their leadership participated in demonstrations and actively supported youth organisations.[3] On Azadî Friday (20 May 2011) leaders of *Azadî* and *Yekîtî* gave speeches at demonstrations in Serê Kanîyê declaring support for the Kurdish youth and demanding a halt to the violent response of the government, the lifting of the siege on Syrian cities and the release of all political prisoners.[4] *Şepêla Pêşerojê* also explicitly called for the fall of the regime. Yet it was the youth that led and maintained the protests.

The apparent restraint of the majority of the parties must be understood in the context of their political history. At the beginning of the revolution the political parties, like all other opposition groups in Syria, were not adapted to revolutionary struggle. They had always worked against the regime, at least in a coded manner, and sought to maintain their political agenda within the context of the uprising, but they were divided amongst themselves and constrained by their efforts to exist and to dispel accusations of separatism. Dominated by the older generations and their political experience in Syria, the Kurdish parties feared that if they rushed to the streets or called for the fall of the regime the implicit understanding with the regime forces that allowed them to exist would be broken, setting in motion a protracted government campaign against the Kurdish political parties and Kurdish regions. The Kurdish uprising of March 2004 involved the largest and most protracted acts of public and mass dissent that Syria had experienced since the state crackdown on the Muslim Brotherhood in Hama in 1982. The regime's suppression of the Kurdish uprising by force and the lack of support or reaction from the Arab opposition in Syria led to fears that if the regime turned again against the Kurdish areas, support from the Arab opposition might once again be absent.[5]

The Kurdish parties, meanwhile, had been negotiating to obtain Kurdish rights from the regime for more than 50 years and the eruption of demonstrations in Arab cities, far from the Kurdish hinterland, was viewed with caution. The initial protests began in response to a local event in Deraa, spreading to other Syrian cities which came out in support. The spread of the demonstrations took place in the context of the wider 'Arab spring'. The example of the protest movements in Tunisia, Egypt and Libya and the possibility of change encouraged an attempt to reclaim the Syrian streets. Amongst the Kurdish parties and much of the Kurdish people, there was a sense that this movement had to begin from the Arab streets and had to be sustained by the Syrian Arab opposition and youth groups. Kurdish parties had, for more than a decade, been taking their protests and politics to the street, and now it was time for the Arab opposition and public to make their mark. Additionally, the fragility of Syria's social make-up has always been used as a justification by the regime to rule with a heavy hand. The full involvement of Kurdish political parties early on could have facilitated the regime's attempts to label the uprising as sectarian and divisive and contributed to its failure.

Since 2005 the Kurdish parties had been negotiating with the Arab opposition very seriously within the framework of the Damascus Declaration. The Declaration, however, did not go far enough towards satisfying Kurdish demands in the event of potential regime change in Syria. The domination by Islamists and Arab nationalists in the opposition groupings emerging at the start of the uprising raised fears of what alternative to the Assad regime might materialise and generated a wariness of cooperation without its basis being made explicit.

Turkey's hosting of Syrian Muslim Brotherhood meetings and its support of the establishment of the Syrian National Council increased these new fears about their political agenda in relation to the Kurds and about what would follow the fall of Assad's regime. Turkey's continued attempts to control its own Kurdish issue and population meant that the Turkish government would be unlikely to support Kurdish demands in Syria. It was feared that any funding to and hosting of opposition meetings and activities would have Turkey's political agenda behind it.

For the Kurds and the Kurdish political parties these apprehensions about the Arab opposition proved to be realistic early on in the uprising. Fears of the domination of the Muslim Brotherhood and Arab nationalists over the Turkish backed Syrian National Council were given additional potency by comments, derogatory to the Kurds, made by leading SNC figures. As with previous attempts to unite Kurdish and Arab opposition groups, Kurdish demands for constitutional national recognition in Syria, decentralisation of political power and for the name of the state to be non-discriminatory in terms of national identity were met with repeated opposition by Arabists and Islamists within the organisation.

Instead of falling in behind the emerging opposition alliances, the reaction of the Kurdish political parties was to form a political union to represent the Kurds to the rest of the Syrian opposition and on 16 May 2011, in Qamishli, the parties formed a new alliance under the name of the Syrian Kurdish National Movement. The alliance united the then 12 parties within the Kurdish Political Council (formed in December 2009) with those of the Kurdish Democratic Alliance (the four parties of *al-Tahaluf*) and the PYD. The position of the alliance leant towards the right wing of the Kurdish party movement, calling for the recognition of Kurds as a 'significant component of the Syrian people' and for 'cultural rights of ethnic and religious minorities in Syria' to be protected and guaranteed.[6] Despite this clear retreat of many of the parties from Kurdish demands for 'self-administration' and constitutional recognition of the Kurds as a nation in Syria, only two parties were not included within the alliance and their exclusion was due to rifts between them and the parties of which they were splinter groups.[7] This position was explained by party representatives as a tactical move to enable the organisations to engage with the Syrian opposition, and dispel stereotypes of the Kurds as separatist.

This initial alliance did not last. According to Dr Alan Semo, foreign affairs representative of the PYD, disagreements arose about the methods of electing a congress.[8] The PYD suggested elections should be by the Kurdish people, whereas the rest of the political parties favoured elections from within the political party membership. The collapse of the union, however, brought with it new efforts to bring the various parties together on a common platform.

Meanwhile, the government itself had taken a number of steps to woo the Kurds in efforts to prevent their entering into the uprising *en masse*. The stateless Kurds, Kurdish Newroz celebrations, the repeal of Decree 49 of 2008 were all questions on which the government attempted to appease the Kurds. In this context, in June, several leaders of Kurdish political parties were invited to meet with members of the government. This was the first time in the history of the Kurdish political party movement that its members had been invited to meet Syrian officials as representatives of Kurdish political parties. The move was viewed as a further effort to neutralise the Kurdish opposition and prevent this group from further involvement in anti-regime protests. The Kurdish parties, however, as a united group, refused this invitation, stating that they would not enter into any dialogue with the regime while it continued to use force against protestors.[9]

The Kurds continued to negotiate with other opposition groups and numerous attempts were made by Kurdish political parties, individually and in alliance with others, to form part of the groups that emerged in the first few months of the uprising, notably the Syrian National Council and the National Coordination Body for Democratic Change (NCB). The Kurdish political organisations sought both participation and representation in the uprising and its representative bodies as Syrian citizens and as Kurds struggling for a new Syria. Successive meetings of the Syrian opposition and SNC, however, resulted in Kurdish walk-outs and boycotts as the leadership insisted that Syria was an Arab state and part of the Arab nation. The PYD, *Yekîtî*, *Partiya Çep* (of Muhammad Musa), Nusradin Ibrahim's *Partîya Dêmokrat a Kurdî li Sûriyê*, and *el-Sûrî* were amongst the founders of the NCB but all the Kurdish parties except the PYD were to leave the organisation due to its limited commitment to Kurdish rights. Due to the inclusion in its ranks of a number of ex-regime officials and Syrian opposition figures believed to be tolerated by the regime, other opposition groups accused the NCB of being an extension of the regime or infiltrated by it.[10]

In July 2011, the National Salvation Conference was held in Istanbul. Kurdish representatives attended the conference only to walk out in protest against the absence of any seats for Kurdish representatives in the Preparatory Committee of the Conference and against the use of the name Syrian Arab Republic which denied the existence of other national groups in Syria. Successive meetings leading to the announcement of the formation of the Syrian National Council on 23 August 2011 met with similar reactions from Kurdish parties and activists. The sole Kurdish party to remain a member of the SNC and its executive committee was *Şepêla Pêşerojê* of Meshaal Temmo.[11] Temmo was assassinated by masked gunmen on 7 October 2011, not long after his declaration of support for the SNC. His murder was seen as a consequence of his outspoken support for the fall of the regime, for the Kurdish youth movements and the SNC and even for his criticism of other Kurdish political parties.

Attempts by the SNC to establish itself as the representative opposition body of the Syrian uprising were thwarted in the months that followed by successive comments by leading members of the Syrian opposition that had the effect of alienating the Kurds. Refusals to consider relinquishing the inclusion of the word 'Arab' in the name and identity of the state left Kurdish political organisations frustrated and excluded, as Kurds, from participation in efforts to form a united representative opposition body. On 26 October Burhan Ghalioun, a leader of the SNC, said in an interview that:

> Of course, Syria is an Arab state...there is no discussion about this...there is no debate that Syria is an Arab country because the majority of the population are Arabs... The discussion is not about the identity for Syria. Kurds...you cannot tell the Syrian Arabs that you are not Arabs...is that OK? Here is the wall.[12]

Pre-existing tensions and fault-lines affecting relations and cooperation between the Kurdish and Arab opposition in Syria were renewed and reaffirmed, adding to Kurdish fears about the future of Syria. The SNC was viewed as being opposed to Kurdish demands for national recognition and decentralisation in Syria and potentially even worse than the Ba'th Party.[13] Some went as far as saying that the SNC and the Ba'th Party were two sides of the same coin and that any Kurd remaining within the SNC would be considered a traitor. Abdulbaset Sieda, who in June 2012 became president of the SNC, rejected these claims. He noted that the Muslim Brotherhood had changed significantly and accepted civil and democratic rights in Syria. Of course there were Arab nationalists who found it difficult to accept the SNC national project aimed at pluralism and tolerance but they were committed to work with the SNC.[14] Despite protracted discussions between Kurdish politicians and the SNC, they failed to reach a common ground acceptable to the Kurdish bloc. The decision of the Kurdish parties not to join either of the two main opposition groups of that time led to questions and speculations about Kurdish political affiliations in the new environment ushered in by the start of the Syrian uprising.

The KNC

In an unprecedented move, on 26 October in Qamishli, the majority of Kurdish political parties put aside internal differences in a conference including ten Kurdish parties,[15] independents, Kurdish youth organisations, Kurdish women's organisations, human rights activists and professionals. The outcome of the conference was the establishment of the Kurdish National Council (KNC). The aim was to unite the Kurdish opposition in one bloc and establish a united and representative Kurdish voice in Syria, particularly in the context of Kurdish concerns about the agenda of several actors within the SNC, especially the Muslim Brotherhood. The rationale behind the move was to position the Kurds as a bloc which would be able to represent Kurdish interests and enter relations with other Syrian opposition groupings. The Council replaced all former Kurdish party blocs such as *Hevbendi* (*al-Tahaluf*) or the *Eniya* (*al-Jabha*), which were dissolved, and membership of all Kurds involved in the SNC and the NCB was withdrawn. Initially seven, of what were then seventeen Kurdish political parties, remained outside the KNC.

Against the background of the historically fractured Kurdish political movement in Syria, the establishment of the KNC was momentous. The conference unified the Kurdish voice on a number of issues. It held the Syrian regime wholly responsible for the crisis in Syria and recognised it as a revolution. It called for complete change of the infrastructures of government and for the building of a secular, democratic, parliamentary, pluralist and decentralised country, free of racism. It described the Kurdish people as indigenous to their historic land and demanded their constitutional recognition as a nation and a key component of the Syrian population. It called for a just and democratic solution to the Kurdish issue in Syria and for the right to self-determination of the Kurds. It extended its support to the Kurdish youth organisations and rejected dialogue with the regime.

Four main assertions can be made on the significance of the establishment of the KNC to the Kurdish movement in general and its place within the ever intensifying tensions within the opposition movement in Syria. The first is that amongst the political parties a fundamental shift of the Kurdish political spectrum occurred in the new approach to the Kurdish issue and Kurdish rights in Syria. The shift occurred in particular in the right wing of the Kurdish parties, which altered their agendas to become closer to the aims of the more radical parties. The parties moved away from minimal demands for minority and cultural rights in Syria and from limiting political activity to the private sphere that had enabled right wing parties to engage with the regime. Parties such as that of Abdul Hamid Darwish's began to talk of regime change and even of Kurdish self-determination in Syria.

The second significant result of the establishment of the KNC was that it marked a very decisive step towards uniting the Kurdish political movement and Kurdish political demands in Syria. It brought the parties together with independents and youth organisations which had been spearheading Kurdish demonstrations during the revolution, thus going some way towards unifying the Kurdish voice in Syria. The shift in political agenda of many parties was an attempt to reflect the voice of the Kurdish street in Syria. The political parties also displayed a willingness to concede a degree of political power and responsibility for the Kurdish political position in Syria to the youth organisations. This attempt to work together began to address the widening generation gap in Kurdish political representation and the division that had developed between Kurdish intellectuals, activists and politicians.

A further advance was that it confirmed explicitly the Kurdish interest in and commitment to the uprising, and to working alongside the rest of the Syrian opposition, but in distinction from it, with a particular agenda defined by Kurdish political demands (for a secular, democratic, pluralistic state in which the Kurds are granted the right of self-determination). This shift in favour of change, rather than management of the status quo, necessitated the coordination of the parties' demands that have taken place.

In sum, the establishment of the KNC marked a new era in Kurdish politics in Syria. Whether the motive for its formation was a response to the need to unify the Kurdish voice in the face of the regime and the Syrian Arab opposition, an attempt to counter the steadily increasing political power of the PYD in the Kurdish regions in Syria, or a combination of these factors, is secondary to its effect. The establishment of the KNC in October 2011 was a decisive move by the political parties towards addressing the fractures within the political arena as well as the alienation of the Kurdish youth and Kurdish intellectuals. Within the KNC, Kurdish political parties had an opportunity to begin a new period in Kurdish politics in Syria appropriate to the new circumstances. Additional Kurdish parties joined the protests under the banner of the KNC, echoing the pan-Syrian slogans and the call for the fall of the regime, as well as adopting their own slogans, reflecting specifically Kurdish demands.

Of the 257 participants in the founding meeting of the KNC, 100 were political party members, 25 representatives of youth groups and 132 were prominent independents chosen by the political parties. The KNC is led by an executive committee in which each constituent political party holds two seats, and a further 25 seats are allocated to independent activists, NGOs, youth and women's organisations. In the initial meeting of 26–27 October a 45-person executive committee was elected including 20 party representatives and six representatives of Kurdish youth organisations. The second meeting of the KNC, held in Erbil on 28–29 January 2012, brought Kurdish intellectuals and activists in exile together with the political parties to establish a common agenda. The executive committee was expanded to 47 to include representatives of an additional Kurdish party. Then, in February the committee was expanded again to accommodate two further political parties. In July 2012 there were said to be 16 Kurdish political parties within the KNC, bringing the number of party representatives in the executive committee to 32.

In many ways the establishment of the KNC addressed several features of the crisis of legitimacy that the parties were facing on the eve of the Syrian uprising. As well as uniting the majority of the parties within a single organisation and coordinating their political objectives, it incorporated youth movements, intellectuals and independent activists. It signalled that the parties were attempting to pool resources from within the Kurdish communities and to reform the political movement in response to the Kurdish street and their new political environment. Pre-existing fault lines, however, were not addressed adequately and continued to negatively affect the overall representativeness of the KNC.

Within the KNC, each political party was given equal representation, and decision-making capacity. The division of power within the KNC did not reflect the strength of particular parties in comparison to smaller ones. This was an obvious area of contention within the KNC. The question of the extent to which the KNC should develop relations with the Syrian opposition, and the continuation of unilateral actions of parties bound by it, were further sources of tension between the parties involved. The representation and decision making power of the independent activists and youth organisations was relatively minor compared with that of the political parties. Realising the importance of the youth groups, as the voice of the Syrian Kurdish street, the parties took steps to harness them within the KNC. In doing so, many of the youth groups became associated with particular political parties, forfeiting their independence, and limiting their activities. Those that remained independent of the parties but which joined the KNC, likewise became subject to the domination of the KNC by the parties. As a consequence of the political partisanship that developed within the youth movement, a fragmentation of this movement occurred, reflecting the parties' factionalism and the divisions between the parties and Kurdish society. The involvement of the parties in the youth movement contributed to rendering the youth groups less effective and less active as the uprising has progressed.[16]

Alternatives and opposition to the KNC

Although most of the Kurdish political parties were included under the umbrella of the KNC, some opposition to this organisation remained within the Kurdish political arena. The seven parties that remained outside the KNC were *Azadî, Yekîtî Kurdistani, Şepêla Pêşerojê, Rêkeftin, Partîya Dêmokrat a Kurdî li Sûriyê* of Abdul Rahman Aluji,[17] *Partîya Hevgirtina Gelê Kurd li Sûriyê* and the PYD; their decision not to join the KNC reflecting pre-existing divisions within the Kurdish political movement. Members of the more radical left (represented by *Şepêla Pêşerojê* and *Yekîtî Kurdistani*) had previously formed an alternative alliance called the Union of Kurdish Democratic Forces in Syria along with *Partîya Dêmokrat a Kurdî li Sûriyê, Partîya Hevgirtina Gelê Kurd li Sûriyê* and *Rêkeftin*. Although they participated in the initial meetings on setting up the KNC, for a number of reasons they abstained from joining the new alliance. The Chairman of the *Şepêla Pêşerojê*'s office of general communications raised four points of objection to the KNC: i) the failure of the KNC to commit to the overthrow of the regime, ii) that it should adopt a stronger position of support for the youth, iii) demands for the Kurds should be more concrete and not influenced by external interests, and iv) that independent activists should have a stronger representation in the council.[18] *Şepêla Pêşerojê*'s position on the Kurdish issue differed in a number of ways, including its demand that the Kurds be recognised as a 'main' nation in Syria rather than a 'second' nation, and that the Kurdish issue was not a regional one, thus emphasising the idea of the Kurds as equal partners in the Syrian state with a stake and representation in the political organisation and processes of all other areas of Syria.[19] With the inclusion of *Yekîtî Kurdistani, Partîya Dêmokrat a Kurdî li Sûriyê* and *Rêkeftin* into the KNC early in 2012, the Union of Kurdish Democratic Forces in Syria came to be almost reduced to a single party (*Şepêla Pêşerojê*) rather than remaining an umbrella organisation.

As for the PYD, according to parties within the KNC the party was invited to the meetings forming the KNC. It opted out of the organisation, however, preferring to work alone on its own agenda. Soon after the establishment of the KNC, reports began to emerge about the growth of tensions between the PYD and the KNC. In November 2011 the party began erecting checkpoints in the Kurdish area of Efrîn, and reports surfaced accusing the PYD of kidnapping political activists, imposing its authority over Kurdish areas and of fights between PYD and KNC supporters.[20] Accusations against the PYD connected them to the regime and their actions were seen as an attempt to curb Kurdish political activity and create divisions within the Kurdish population. The probability that Assad was using the Kurdish card against Turkey by supporting the PKK reflected on the PYD, which had itself been associated with the PKK. Also, the PYD's inclusion in the NCB, an opposition group that was accused of being close to the regime, and which until September 2012 supported dialogue with the regime, seemed to add weight to these claims. The PYD's gradual assertion of control over Kurdish areas from November 2011 was viewed as an aggressive move by many supporters of the KNC as well as by independent activists and youth organisations.

On 16 December 2011 the PYD formed a coalition named the Peoples Council of Western Kurdistan (PCWK). As well as the PYD, the PCWK included five organisations: *Tevgera Civaka Demokratik a Rojava* (*Tev-Dem*, the Western Kurdistan Democratic Society Movement), *Yekitiya Star* women's organisation, the Union of Families of Martyrs, the Education and Language Institution and the Revolutionary Youth Movement of Western Kurdistan.[21] All organisations within the PCWK were connected to the PYD, making the PCWK an umbrella organisation for PYD affiliated groups rather than one consisting of different political parties and agendas bound together. The resolution of the founding conference of the PCWK included the following resolution: to support the peaceful, democratic popular movement aimed at making a radical change in the infrastructure and institutions of the political system, to reject foreign intervention, to unify the position of the Kurdish political parties, as well as the youth organisations and to establish local councils through free elections. The document did not call for the fall of the regime nor specifically for Kurdish rights, other than the renaming of Kurdish towns, villages with their Kurdish names, the right of self-defence of the Kurdish people and a commitment to building democratic social institutions, including those for 'disseminating the mother tongue, namely, Kurdish'.[22] Other than these, most points in the declaration were general to Syria, and reflect a commitment to the development of a democratic and pluralistic tolerant state and society and support of the peaceful popular movement. While the organisation's armed units allowed the PCWK and, through it the PYD to assert power and authority over Kurdish areas, the political manifesto of the PCWK neglected many of the Syrian Kurdish political aspirations.

One Year In

A year into the uprising, the Kurdish position in Syria began to shift in response to the increasing militarisation of the conflict and to the Arab opposition's rejection of Kurdish calls for self-determination and political decentralisation. Further comments about the Kurds by SNC leader Barhan Ghalioun,[23] NCB leader Hassan Abdul Aziz, and the Muslim Brotherhood were taken as confirmation that the Kurdish demands would again be sacrificed to Arab nationalist and Islamist political programmes. The Kurds retreated further into a Kurd-specific political agenda and concentrated on the protection of Kurdish people from the worst effects of the uprising. In the Kurdish regions, alongside the pan-Syrian slogans, placards displaying uniquely Kurdish messages appeared. The 30 March became the Friday of Kurdish Rights. In response to Ghalioun's denial of a Kurdistan in Syria, on 20 April youth groups and parties alike held banners reading 'Here is Kurdistan'.[24] Friday 6 April became the 'Friday of putting Kurdish rights above any council'. The 11 May was dubbed 'Victory from God' in the national protests. In most Kurdish areas, however, it was referred to as the 'Friday of celebrating Kurds in Aleppo', in response to regime attacks on the majority Kurdish area of Sheikh Maqsoud in Aleppo a few days before.

Although not adopted by all groups, this public focus on Kurdish issues was a significant separation of Kurdish interests and symbols of the uprising from the rest of the Syrian opposition and from protests in other areas of Syria. At the same time, Kurdish groups, especially the PYD were entrenching themselves in the Kurdish regions of Efrîn and Kobanî particularly, establishing checkpoints and local councils, which they claimed were to support the local Kurdish communities, maintain order and protect civilians. The moves were also described as preparation for the fall of the regime, when Kurdish groups would need to be ready to take control and govern Kurdish areas effectively.[25] In the absence of any such preparation by the parties of the KNC, the PYD actions were looked upon with concern but also as a necessary development in the Kurdish regions given the increasing militarisation of the Syrian uprising.

The regimes increasingly violent responses to the Syrian opposition and the taking up of arms by rebel groups had a very significant effect on the Kurdish position in Syria. Syrian troops were concentrated in cities bearing the brunt of Assad's repression of the uprising and re-deployed away from Kurdish areas, where clashes with regime authorities were limited and more isolated occurrences. In the power vacuum that was left and in an attempt to shield the Kurdish areas from the increasingly brutal retaliations of the regime, armed Kurdish groups belonging to the PYD, secured borders around Kurdish towns and regions and moved into government buildings establishing a Kurdish administration.

Amid the militarisation of the conflict in Syria, the SNC made an attempt to reach out to the Kurdish communities through its National Charter on the Kurdish issue. At the same time tensions between the PYD and the KNC intensified. Alongside these alterations in the Kurdish position within the uprising, on 21 April 2012, the KNC drafted a new interim political agenda. This programme omitted the call for self-determination included in earlier political programmes. This decision reflected divisions within the organisation over joining the SNC, and was interpreted by many as a significant political move away from specifically Kurdish political demands towards an accommodation of the SNC interests. Critics of the parties considered it a retreat, or at least a more accurate reflection of party demands. They argued that the earlier championing of self-determination reflected a calculated desire on the part of the Kurdish leaders to gain popularity and legitimacy in the context of the Syrian uprising.[26] The change in the KNC agenda was interpreted by many as a submission to pressures from the Arab opposition and a compromise of Kurdish demands in Syria. Even if understood, however, as an attempt to build relations with the wider Syrian opposition, which the Kurdish parties had initially prioritised, KNC–PYD relations arguably had an important effect on the decision. The decision of the KNC to alter its manifesto took place as PYD–KNC relations deteriorated. The PYD's moves to assert control over the Kurdish areas and politics threatened the KNC. In this context the development of relations with the SNC, and even with the Free Syrian Army (FSA), took on a new meaning: it held out the possibility of countering the advancement of the PYD politically and militarily. Despite having adopted a new National Charter on the Kurdish issue in Syria, public opinion about the SNC continued to nurture fears of its domination by Arab nationalists and the Muslim Brotherhood.

Representatives of the KNC explained this change in its programme as a step towards uniting the Syrian opposition on a Syrian national agenda and removing obstacles to achieving the hopes of the Syrian people.[27] It was described as a tactical move that would allow them to engage with the Syrian opposition and help to refute claims that the Kurds were separatist. Reportedly, the foreign affairs committee of the KNC had encountered problems in dealing with the SNC because the right of self-determination was interpreted by many within it as a sign of Kurdish separatism.[28] The term itself was replaced with the demand for recognition of the national rights of the Kurdish people in Syria in accordance with international conventions and agreements.[29] The new phrase was said to imply the right to self-determination, through recourse to international laws such as the International Covenant on Civil and Political Rights, the International Covenant on Economic, Social and Cultural Rights and the UN Charter. Party leaders continued to talk openly of self-determination for the Kurds of Syria and, in particular, of federalism for Kurdish areas in Syria. Nevertheless, the unity and outreach into the Kurdish community that the KNC provided through its more radical and rigid political agenda appeared to be weakened after this. Again, the

KNC was criticised for compromising Kurdish demands, not responding to the Kurdish street and failing to take practical measures to support Kurdish protestors and youth movements.

The PYD's Power Play

The power vacuum in the Kurdish regions of Syria provided the PYD with an opportunity to put into practice Öcalan's theories of democratic autonomy and confederation and to apply a form of bottom-up self-management, distinct from that of state systems. Beginning with social organisation within Kurdish areas establishing institutions (from schools to prisons) to address social problems, the PYD and the PCWK moved their focus to protection of the regions through 'civil defence'.[30] PYD co-chair, Asya Abdullah, described the democratic autonomy project as both a new form of self-government and a philosophy of life, transferred to the population through educational academies.[31]

With increased control by the PYD in Kurdish areas of Syria and its emergence as the most powerful Kurdish party outside the KNC, questions about the party's connections to the PKK and the Syrian government resurfaced. As described in Chapter 1, the PYD had acted illegally in Syria and had been targeted by the regime prior to the uprising as part of the agreement between Turkey and Syria in 1998 to combat PKK activity. Many PYD members had been arrested since its establishment in 2003, but the Syrian uprising altered political agendas and allegiances in Syria as well as beyond it. Cooperative relations between Turkey and Syria unravelled in the face of Assad's violent crackdown against protestors. Independent reports and Turkish intelligence suggested that Assad was again supporting PKK activities in Turkey and allowing the PYD to operate freely in Syria.[32] These allegations also came from the Arab opposition as well as from within the Kurdish communities in Syria themselves. The evidence to support such accusations included the following: the PYD party leader, Salih Muslim, exiled from Syria in 2010 and then encamped with the PKK in the Kurdistan region of Iraq, returned to Syria in 2011, reportedly with as many as 2,000 PKK guerrilla fighters, without intervention by the regime; initially the PYD did not explicitly call for the fall of the regime and remained open to dialogue with it; it openly established a number of Kurdish language schools without interference from Syrian authorities; it was accused of preventing and disrupting protests against the regime in Efrîn; it erected checkpoints and began policing Kurdish areas in the presence of regime security services and its takeover of Kurdish towns and regions was peaceful and swift, raising suspicions that they had an agreement with the Syrian authorities to secure the areas from the FSA and to incite sectarian divisions within Syria.

Each point here was refuted by the PYD. The party categorically denied any connections to the Assad regime or to the PKK, aside from an ideological affinity with Öcalan's theory of democratic confederation.[33] In response to questions about the parties' policies regarding the regime and how the PYD could set up language and cultural centres without authorisation from the government, Salih Muslim responded with the following:

> We demand a fundamental change to the oppressive system. There are some who hold up the slogan: the fall of the regime. In contrast we demand the fall of the oppressive authoritarian system. Our problems are not problems of powers. The ruling powers in Damascus come and go. For us Kurds, this isn't so important. What is important is that we Kurds assert our existence. The current regime does not accept us, nor do those who will potentially come into power. Our politics differ from a politics that seeks power. That needs to be clear.
>
> [S]ince the beginning of the unrest, the regime has had no possibility to attack us. If it does attack us, it will see what happens. We are profiting from the unrest. It is a historical chance for us. We have a right and are making use of it. We do not kill anyone and we also do not fight against anyone. We are preparing our people and ourselves for the period after the fall of the regime. [34]

As a political party the PYD has a more aggressive political strategy than the other parties and, although it has never taken up arms in Syria before June 2012,[35] its strategy bears some similarities to that of the PKK. A cadre party, involving strict organisation, training and regular political, cultural and social activities, the party promotes the use of practical steps towards political goals and the exploitation of opportunities in order to further party objectives. Organisationally it claims to be independent, but it shares an ideology with the PKK and a loyalty to Abdullah Öcalan. It is also one of the parties within the *Koma Civakên Kurdistan* (KCK or Union of Communities in Kurdistan) which is led by Öcalan and *Kongra-Gel*, and which also includes the PKK, PJAK (*Partiya Jiyana Azad a Kurdistanê* in Iran) as well as the armed wings of the PKK and the PYD. The PYD defines itself in relation to the Syrian state rather than to the Kurdish issue in Turkey. Nonetheless, Öcalan's ideology, Turkish policy and Kurdish activities and activists in Turkey feature heavily in party statements, symbolism and rhetoric. The PYD has taken advantage of the power vacuum in Kurdish regions and has resisted FSA entry into Kurdish areas. Their actions, however, cannot be understood as proof of collusion with the Syrian regime and the party has repeatedly rejected such accusations, Salih Muslim stating that the PYD had 'no relations with the regime at all', but that it would not fight someone else's battle.[36] Yet, alongside its practical steps on the ground in Syria, the PYD has demonstrated repeatedly a commitment to supporting the Kurdish struggle in Turkey, and resisting the encroachment of Arab and Islamist opposition groups, which it claims are supported by Turkey, into Kurdish regions in Syria.

Amongst the Kurds in Syria the PYD provokes strong opinions, either in favour of it or against. This is due to their tactics, their focus on Turkey, their association with the PKK, and, consequently, presumed PKK relations with the Assad regime. As soon as it began, the push by the PYD to gain control of Kurdish areas in Syria met with opposition from amongst the Kurds. Although the Efrîn region already had a strong PYD presence, pockets of resistance to their domination emerged. For example, in the village of Gazwiyeh, a local group was formed in 2011 when the PYD attempted to establish a checkpoint in the borders of the village. The group did not allow the PYD to do this, instead establishing their own checkpoint.[37] Evidence of further attempts to curb the control of the PYD over Kurdish areas emerged alongside additional reports of PYD attacks on Kurdish activists. KurdWatch reported that on 15 May 2012, a group of Kurds, calling themselves the 'Liberation of Efrîn' and claiming to be part of the Free Syrian Army, fired shots into the air in an attempt to intimidate a PYD guard in the town of Kafr Jenna. The previous day the group had attacked a Syrian Army guard near Kafr Jenna seizing weapons and ammunition.[38] Other battalions of Kurdish army defectors have since been formed seeking to fight the regime and to counter the force of the PYD.[39] Clashes between PYD and KNC supporters at protests began to occur regularly, and there were frequent reports of aggressive attempts to disrupt the political activities of other parties and groups, including arresting and detaining Kurdish political activists, and even of their torture.

Although it has been very hard to judge the popularity of the KNC or the PYD, it is fair to say that some of the PYD tactics in Syria had negative effects on the KNC. On 8 June 2012 the first PYD checkpoints were erected in Qamishli where support for the KNC was stronger than for the PYD.[40] The spread of PYD checkpoints brought it into further conflict with the KNC. At the same time, the PYD's strategy exposed the weakness of the KNC on the ground in the Kurdish regions. Criticism of the KNC grew on account of its apparent unwillingness to take decisive steps to protect the Kurdish regions, to give practical support the Kurdish youth or to confront the PYD. According to Azad Muhiyuddin, a number of Kurdish independent activists had left the Council, critical of its lack of activity on the ground and of its decision-making processes which were dominated by the political parties.[41] Others spoke of a sense of resignation in the face of the prominence and domination of the PYD over social and political affairs in the Kurdish areas and referred to it as a necessary evil.[42] Azad Muhiyuddin stated that:

> Whether we want it or not, the PYD is currently the strongest force in al-Qamishli. Without the PYD nothing works. What the PYD has accomplished in fifteen days, the Kurdish [National Council] could not achieve in five months.[43]

Demonstrations in the Kurdish regions became more and more divided. In Qamishli as many as four or five separate demonstrations were held every Friday, most of them starting from the Qasimo Mosque in the western district of Qamishli. Protests were organised by the PYD, the Kurdish National Council, as well as *Şepêla Pêşerojê ya Kurdî li Sûriyê* and various youth groups. In comparison, demonstrations became less frequent in the Efrîn region where the PYD's power was greatest, and where organisation of protests by groups unaffiliated with the PYD was restricted.

The threat of civil war

The threat of civil war loomed over Syria as the uprising came to be militarised. There were reports of increased activity of militias, massacres by groups connected to the regime and revenge attacks which sent death tolls soaring. The semi-tribal nature of Syrian society and the location of different ethnic groups and sects meant that the main effects of a civil war situation would likely be confined to specific geographical fault lines within the country and specific cities. The Kurdish regions had thus far avoided a regime campaign against the Kurdish political movement and, in the absence of an influx of the FSA, the almost entirely Kurdish region of Efrîn could remain free of conflict based on Sunni, Alawite and Shi'a divisions. The Jazira was more likely to feel the affects of civil war with its mixed population, including Arab tribes, and various Christian denominations as well as Kurds.

A more immediate threat to Kurdish interests came from within the Kurdish regions themselves. The eruption of isolated but regular clashes between PYD and KNC supporters in Qamishli in May raised the possibility of conflict amongst Kurds. Kurds of different political orientations had been set on a collision course, on the one side the political parties that originate from 1957, represented primarily by the KNC, and on the other the PYD and its armed units. Conflict escalated at the beginning of June 2012. On 3 June inhabitants of Basute village in the Efrîn region opposed the PYD when its People's Defence Units (YPG's)[44] attempted to establish a checkpoint in the village. It was reported that the PYD consequently kidnapped seven activists from the local coordinating committees and released them only when the villagers agreed to the erection of the checkpoint.[45] Then on 7 June, 12 Kurdish activists, who had taken part in a KNC meeting the previous night, were taken by the PYD and held in custody awaiting trial in special courts established by the PYD.[46] The PYD claimed that these were acts of self-defence against people who had attacked their checkpoints and that their security measures were intended to protect the Kurdish people, neighbourhoods, villages and towns in the face of escalating violence and civil war in Syria.[47] These few events are examples and only a fraction of those reported over the following months. The PYD denied many of these accusations but also accused other Kurdish activists of colluding with the Turkish government on several occasions, a charge it also levied against the SNC and the FSA.

The imbalances between the PYD and the KNC were clear, the latter opting to pursue peaceful struggle while the former armed its YPG's as a defensive strategy. In late July 2012, however, Masoud Barzani confirmed that a 'good number' of young Kurds who had fled from Syria were being trained under the guidance of KDP *peshmerga*.[48] According to Hêmin Hawrami, the head of the external relations department in the KDP, a 'very small' number of Syrian Kurds 'were trained in basic training in camps in the region in order to fill any security gap after the fall of the Syrian regime'.[49] Estimates put this number at anywhere between 600 and 3,000. This was in addition to Syrian Kurdish army defectors who had fled to the Kurdistan Region of Iraq.[50] These armed forces were primed to become part of a national force, controlled jointly by the KNC and PCWK, for the defence of Kurdish areas in the wake of the fall of the regime. Although the support of the KDP of *el-Partî* in Syria and for the formation of the KNC suggested that these units would fall under the control of the KNC in the event of any PYD–KNC conflict. Nevertheless, the KNC's commitment to peaceful struggle and its refusal to take up arms against other Kurds meant that the KNC continued to combat the influence of the PYD verbally, by trying to gain support on the ground for its political policies and by attempts at cooperation with the PYD itself.

The Erbil Agreement and the 'liberation' of Kurdish areas

Prompted by the prospect of an escalation of PYD–KNC tensions and Kurd-on-Kurd conflict in Syria, Masoud Barzani decided to intervene in Syrian Kurdish affairs once again. Under pressure from him, on 11 June 2012 representatives of the KNC and the PYD, mediated by the KDP Iraq, met in Erbil (Hawlêr) to reach a solution to the problems that had developed between the two groups and to agree on some power sharing and division of labour in the Kurdish political and social arenas. Dubbed the Erbil Agreement, the resulting minutes of the meeting set out a plan with the following proposals:

1. Establish a joint Supreme Committee of both councils to coordinate political and diplomatic work as well as to develop a unified political

objective. This objective will be based on the immutable values of the Kurdish people as a nation and ethnicity in Syria and should work towards the overthrow of the dictatorship in Damascus, the construction of a democratic, pluralistic state and the creation of a new Syria with many ethnicities. This new Syria will satisfy the aspirations of our people by recognizing its existence as an original people in the constitution. The Kurdish question must be solved democratically.

2. Establish a Supreme Organizational Committee of both councils to coordinate practical work in the field in all regions.
3. Establish subcommittees to coordinate practical work in the field in the individual regions.
4. Cease all propaganda activities.
5. Abolish all forms of armed presence in the Kurdish regions and communities.
6. Establish joint, unarmed protection committees.[51]

A supplementary agreement on the functions of the resulting Supreme Kurdish Committee (SKC) was signed on 1 July before the committee of five representatives of the KNC and five of the PCWK was formed on 9–10 July in Qamishli. Within days, the PYD had stepped into the power vacuum left by the redeployment of the Syrian military away from the Kurdish regions as rebels moved into the key cities of Damascus and Aleppo. First taking control of Kobanî, by 29 July 2012 all of the following towns were declared 'liberated' and under Kurdish control: Efrîn, al-Darbasiyah (Dirbasiye), al-Ma'bada (Girkê Legê), Malikiyah (Dêrîk), Qahtaniya (Tirbespî), al-Qos (Ala Qews), Amuda (Amûdê), Ayn al-Arab (Kobanî), Jindires (Cindirês), and Ra's al-'Ayn (Serê Kaniyê), as well as the Ashrafiyah and Sheikh Maqsoud districts of Aleppo.

The Erbil Agreement itself was very significant. The parties jointly asserted their commitment to Kurdish unity and to achieving their aims of self-rule and protecting Kurdish areas. The agreement involved compromise on both sides, but for the parties within the KNC it allowed them to reassert their position as representatives of Syrian Kurds and to check the PYD's unilateral seizure of control over both the Kurdish areas and Kurdish political and civil organisation. Dr Abdul Hakim Bashar described KNC interests as avoiding civil war, distancing the PYD from the regime and encouraging the PYD to serve Kurdish interests.[52] For its part, involvement in the SKC imparted legitimacy to the PYD and its actions. The experience of SKC control, however, was somewhat mixed. The differences in the tactics of the two sides naturally led to the continuation of tensions between them. The dynamics of power within the organisation suggested that the lion's share was held by the PCWK despite the 50-50 division of authority and responsibility. The PYD continued to act unilaterally without consultation of the KNC, for example, occupying government offices in Dêrîk and establishing governing councils. Security in the Kurdish areas and borders was dominated by the People's Defence Units (YPG's), an organisation created by the PYD which broke relations with the SKC in September 2012, declaring itself independent of any political organisation. In reality the YPG's retained their connection to the PYD and facilitated PYD activities and policies. The KNC was unable to secure the return of Kurdish army defectors who received training in the Kurdistan Region of Iraq, the PYD blocking their return under the premise that they would only be permitted to return 'when they are ready to join the ranks of the People's Defence Units',[53] implying that the PYD expected security to be solely their area of responsibility. The PYD referred to the SKC as the chief decision making body on security matters. Reports indicated, however, that the SKC did not even recognise the People's Defence Units which operated outside the ambit of the Committee and which had declared on 18 September 2012 that they would not abide by decisions of the SKC.[54]

In late September 2012, the two sides were brought together once again in an attempt to salvage the Erbil Agreement. Agreement was reached on a number of issues: that Qamishli would be the headquarters of the SKC, with branches in Efrîn, Kobanî, Amûdê and Dêrîk; that borders would be jointly administered and orders would come solely and directly from the SKC; a humanitarian aid committee would be formed; a justice committee would be formed with the task of managing the legal system in Kurdish areas; that a reconciliation meeting between the PYD and the KNC would be held.[55] The conciliatory tone of the agreement testified to the concerted attempt on both sides to prevent a civil war between Kurds in Syria that could have serious regional ramifications for the wider Kurdish issue. But, at the time of writing, tensions between the two sides remain, particularly on the issue of security.

The Experience of Kurdish Control

The experience of Kurdish experiments in self-rule was successful in many ways. The agenda of the political parties and the reality on the ground had begun to reflect popular calls from the street for Kurdish self-rule, self-determination and the establishment of a federal Kurdish region in Syria. The experiment was one step towards achieving that aim. The parties' commitment to unity had been severely tested by its internal political dynamic as well as external interference, but had, at the time of writing, withstood attempts to undermine the credibility of the PYD and to break the nascent Kurdish autonomy that had developed after June 2012. The PYD had been able to secure Kurdish areas, providing necessary protection from the worst effects of the Syrian uprising. In spite of the obvious detrimental consequences of unemployment, inflation, shortages of basic goods and services that go hand in hand with protracted conflict, some semblance of normal daily life in Kurdish areas was maintained. Schools managed by Kurdish parties provided education to children and adults alike and even taught the Kurdish language freely. Many businesses continued to trade, and bakeries and factories managed by the PYD maintained supplies of basic goods, and in comparison to FSA-held areas, many of which were in ruins, Kurdish areas remained relatively peaceful. Were it not for the PYD's armed groups and its practical management of Kurdish areas there is little doubt that the Efrîn region would have been used by the FSA, or Salafist groups, as bases for rebel actions in and around Aleppo, and that it would have become a target of regime attacks. At the time of writing, aside from the regime's attacks on the Kurdish areas of Aleppo and on Serê Kaniyê, the Kurdish regions had been spared the brutality demonstrated by the regime in other areas of Syria.

Opinions of and practical experience of Kurdish rule in Syria was mixed. The PYD claimed to be governing approximately 60 per cent of Kurdish areas in 2012, and by February 2013 as much as 80 per cent.[56] While Dr Abdul Hakim Bashar (who was at the time the leader of the KNC) said that 'no Kurdish cities have been liberated. Syrian security forces have a presence in every Kurdish city.'[57] Questions were also raised about the extent of the SKC's control. Reports from inside Syria showed that regime forces, including *mukhabarat* and even the military, were still present in areas claimed to be under the control of the SKC. Other reports suggested that the Efrîn region was free of any government representation and completely under the control of the PYD, while in 'liberated' cities and areas in the Jazira region, plain clothed security services could still be seen monitoring developments while Kurdish parties controlled and administered local affairs without interference from the regime. Some critics of the parties accused the PYD of being aided by the security services in Qamishli.[58] At the same time, others questioned the representativeness of Dr Bashar and his commitment to Kurdish unity.

Although the PYD had acted decisively and swiftly when divisions within the KNC had prevented other parties from doing so, and although it had made concerted efforts to dispel external criticism, the PYD had been unable to convince the majority that it was free of ties to the PKK. The PYD continued to face accusations of collusion with the regime and there was even talk of a dictatorship of the PYD.[59] It was accused of extorting taxes and levies on goods brought over the borders under their control. Control of public facilities such as petrol stations and factories were said to have been handed to the PYD by the regime. In late October 2012, when PYD representatives in Kobanî ordered nine Kurdish parties to lower the Syrian independence flag after clashes between the PYD and the FSA in Ashrafiyah district of Aleppo[60] further tensions developed between the KNC and the PYD. The events led local representatives of the KNC in Efrîn and Aleppo to temporarily suspend their membership of the SKC. *El-Partî* of Dr Abdul Hakim Bashar withdrew from the SKC and stationed armed men outside party offices to protect the building and party members from possible PYD retaliations.[61] The KNC parties placed the blame for threatening the unity of the Kurdish political movement on the PYD actions and, for their part, announced a cooperation agreement between *el-Partî*, *Yekîtî* and *Azadî* (of Mustafa Juma'a) in Kobanî.[62]

Reports from within the Kurdish regions suggested that a sense of acquiecense to their situation had arisen.[63] The unity of the political movement was being maintained and Kurdish areas were being protected and managed by Kurdish forces and had, thus far, been spared the worst effects of the uprising. Although criticisms of the political system that had emerged in the Kurdish regions abounded, the fear of the regime and concerns about what might follow its overthrow produced a resignation to managing the existing balances of power within the Kurdish regions.

National responses to Kurdish 'self-rule' (Syria, Turkey and the KRG)

During the Syrian uprising the Kurdish regions and political parties have proved to be much less prone to external interference and to falling prey to the interest and agendas of external political powers than Arab opposition groups. This was due primarily to the fact that, historically, the Kurdish issue has not been adopted as a cause by competing state powers in the Middle East, which have seen the Kurds and Kurdish nationalism as a threat to their interests rather than a way of meeting them. International powers have also regarded the pursuit of Kurdish interests as an obstacle to preserving the status quo in the Middle East. While this left Kurdish political parties in want of significant political or financial support for the pursuit of Kurdish national rights, they have not been entirely immune to the effects of external power plays. Certainly the Kurds have been used as pawns in inter-state rivalries and, as detailed in Chapters 1 and 3, ties between Kurdish political parties in neighbouring states and those in Syria have complicated Kurdish politics there. These same relationships and their regional and international implications have had significant bearing on the attempts of Kurds to muster support from Western governments during the uprising.

The assertion of control over Kurdish areas took the Syrian opposition as well as Turkey and international observers by surprise. The Kurdish issue sprang into the international media and became the subject of several reports by think tanks.[64] Commentators began to talk of a Kurdish spring emerging from the fallout of the Arab spring. Suddenly the consequences of Kurdish self-rule in Syria for the wider Kurdish question and regional politics became a pressing issue. The spectre of Sykes–Picot re-emerged and the idea of a domino effect through the different Kurdish regions made redrawing the map of the Middle East a real possibility. An existing federal entity in Iraq, nascent self-rule in Syria, renewal of activity by the PKK in Turkey and by Kurdish political groups in Iran were all signs that the Kurds were moving towards achieving additional rights from their respective governments.

The reaction of the Syrian government to the Kurdish takeover was muted, to say the least. With attention focused on Syria's major cities and its campaign against the Sunni Arab rebel opposition forces in these areas, the regime did little to prevent the Kurdish takeover of areas and towns in the Kurdish regions. Remaining elements of the *mukhabarat* continued to monitor developments in the regions but did little to interfere. Some Kurds claimed that Syrian authorities had attempted to instigate inter-Kurdish conflict and provoke sectarian tensions in Syria through their hands-off approach to developments in the Kurdish regions. This back seat taken by the regime, as the PYD moved into government offices, erected checkpoints and took control of border crossings, fuelled fears of Kurdish separatism amongst the Sunni Arab opposition and was taken as evidence of PYD connivance with the regime by Syrian opposition figures and by Kurdish opponents of the PYD. By allowing Kurds to control Kurdish regions the regime was understood to be deliberately fomenting sectarian differences that would damage the momentum of the uprising.

The view of the Syrian Arab opposition was generally negative. The idea of political decentralisation was not popular within other political opposition groups in Syria. Historically, the spectre of sectarianism and the break-up of the Syrian state has been a fear played upon by the regime since its rise to power and has been ingrained in the Syrian psyche. The experience of federalism in Iraq, for most Sunni Arab Syrians, has not been viewed as a success story, as it is by the Kurds. Its application in Syria is viewed as a precursor to national secessionism and religious conflict at the expense of the majority.

The Syrian National Council viewed the assertion of Kurdish control over Kurdish areas as not in the interests of the Kurds, their regions or the wider Syrian situation and urged the SKC to cede control of these areas to the FSA. The prospect of Kurd-on-Kurd conflict within the Kurdish regions was a real possibility, as was conflict between Kurds and Arabs or Assyrians, particularly in the Jazira region. Abdulbaset Sieda, a Kurd himself, saw the Kurdish issue as a Syrian issue best dealt with in cooperation with other peoples in the Kurdish areas and in Syria as a whole.[65] The fulfilment of this vision of the SNC national project was prevented by outspoken members of the opposition, who continued to accuse the Kurds of separatism and categorically rejected any form of decentralisation.

The FSA as a whole did not have a public or official position on the Kurds and their assertion of control in Kurdish regions. The FSA was composed of various groups and battalions which remained predominantly local, and amongst whom cooperation was not coordinated centrally. Several FSA groups publically spoke out against Kurdish separatism in reaction to the Kurdish moves. Colonel Riad al-Asaad, FSA leader, stated that they would not allow any territory to be separated from Syria and that 'we will never leave Qamishli for the agenda of any Kurdish faction, and we are willing to fight for each inch of Syrian land'. He added that the FSA were not ready to open up a second front with the Kurds at this time, implying that, after the fall of the regime, FSA forces could be redeployed.

A few Kurdish battalions are to be found affiliated with the FSA, but the Kurdish opposition is concerned about the predominance of brigades with Islamic and jihadist names. One rebel group named itself the 'Martyr Saddam Hussein' raising obvious outrage amongst Kurds. Many FSA groups accused the PYD of working with the regime, and for its part, the PYD accused the FSA of working for Turkish interests and of being under Turkish control.[66] In late October 2012, PYD and FSA forces clashed in the Ashrafiyah district of Aleppo. At the time of writing, some tensions remained between the PYD and the FSA but evidence of cooperation and alliance building between the Kurds and the FSA also existed.[67] Kurdish parties, in particular the PYD in the Aleppo region, had provided shelter for FSA fighters escaping regime attacks and had even helped to transport arms to the FSA.[68] While the Kurdish parties were intent on preventing FSA entrenchment in Kurdish areas, preferring Arab rebels to 'liberate' Arab areas, they worked to facilitate their struggle against the regime by providing refuge and coordinating efforts in areas where their interests coincided. Given the fears of what may follow the fall of the regime, caution remains in Kurdish relations with the FSA. Dr Abdul Hakim Bashar feared that the aggressive PYD tactics in the Kurdish regions would push Kurdish youth towards the FSA in attempts to protect themselves and their communities from the PYD.[69] Indeed, evidence of this existed in the Kurdish regions and Abdulbaset Sieda implied that the experience of what Kurds on the ground were referring to as a 'PYD dictatorship' was encouraging Kurdish youth groups and some parties to develop relations with the SNC.[70]

The Syrian crisis and the Kurdish seizure of control over northern Syria presented Turkey with immediate problems. Its own Kurdish issue and the upsurge in violence on the part of the PKK in Turkey and the PYD–PKK connection all complicated the Turkish position on Syria's Kurds. Declarations from Ankara suggested that Turkey would intervene against any attempt of the PKK to establish bases in northern Syria. Turkey feared that an autonomous Kurdish area in Syria with a strong PYD presence would provide a haven for the PKK to launch cross-border attacks. As Turkish relations with the Kurdistan Regional Government improved and the PKK bases in the Qandil Mountains of the Kurdistan region became less secure, northern Syria, and in particular a Kurdish entity, was viewed by Turkey as an area in which the PKK could seek to establish bases.

While PYD officials categorically denied that they are connected to the PKK, admitting only an ideological affinity with it, Turkish intelligence agencies claimed to have evidence to the contrary. Turkey's position on any form of Kurdish self-rule in northern Syria was guided by its desire to to contain its own Kurdish 'problem' and prevent any haven for the PKK, seen as synonymous with the PYD, from developing there. These interests, and the presently entrenched PYD presence in the Kurdish areas set a pretext for Turkish involvement in Syria and support for a future Sunni Arab domi-nated central government intent on claiming back territory controlled by the Kurds. Meanwhile, the situation in Syria and the parallel increase in PKK activity in Turkey pressed the importance of finding a just and democratic solution to the Kurdish issue in Turkey. In the absence of such a solution, the PKK remained a thorn in Turkey's side and a complication in Ankara's relations in Syria.

The Iraqi KDP has played a particularly influential and instrumental role in Kurdish politics in Syria during the uprising. Masoud Barzani was influential in forming the KNC in October 2011, and in brokering a peace-ful agreement between the PYD and the KNC in Erbil in June 2012. The KDP has sought to overcome inherent divisions and weaknesses within the Kurdish political parties' movement by encouraging and facilitating unity between them. Yet, this decisive intervention in Syrian Kurdish affairs has raised questions about Masoud Barzani and the KDP's interests in the region and highlighted the political manoeuvrings and power plays involving the KDP, Turkey and the PKK.

The idea that the KDP was seeking influence amongst the Syrian Kurds and in a post-Assad 'Kurdistan Region of Syria' was raised in several reports. Analysts explained the part played by Barzani in terms of an attempt to make a bid for leadership of the pan-Kurdish nation.[71] This prompted some to suggest that Syrian Kurdistan had become an arena for PKK–KDP cooperation.[72] Any power struggle between the two parties could result in the split of the region between the two spheres of influence, increasing inter-Kurdish conflict and limiting the influence of the KDP to Syria's eastern Kurdish regions. Consequently, the KDP's involvement in the PYD–KNC relations was viewed as an attempt by the KDP to extend its influence amongst Syrian Kurds.

An alternative scenario was that Turkish interests played a more impor-tant part than those of the PKK. Relations between the KRG and Turkey, and the development of a strategic oil pipeline between the two countries, in spite of the PKK, led observers to point to cooperation between Ankara and the KRG in curbing the influence of the PKK on Syrian Kurdish affairs.

Strengthening the KNC and countering the force of the PYD was in Turkey's interests, although Ankara itself was unable to directly intervene with support for the KNC because of its own Kurdish issue and its support for the SNC and the FSA. The poor representation of KNC parties in the western Kurdish regions and the concentration of party leaders in the Jazira has prevented the KNC from gaining enough influence in the western Kurdish regions in Syria (Efrîn and Kobanî) to balance that of the PYD. Moreover, its position in the Jazira has been threatened by unilateral PYD actions and control over security. Consequently, KNC cooperation with the PYD became essential for the KDP to maintain balance between the two forces and for the KRG, and Turkey, to acquire an influence in any Syrian Kurdish region that develops.

Indeed, Barzani's intervention in Syrian Kurdish affairs has positioned him as a mediator between Turkey and both the PYD and the PKK. For Turkey, Barzani's support of the SKC facilitates the containment of the PYD, places pressure on it to distance itself from the PKK and establish itself as a definitively Syrian Kurdish political party. This also allows Turkey some indirect influence on developments within the Kurdish areas of Syria. For the PYD, involvement in the SKC indirectly imparts that legitimacy, which the PYD lacks due to its association with the PKK, and opens a door for dialogue with the Turkish government. For Syrian Kurds, Barzani's intervention has relieved tensions between the various political groups and provided a tentative balance to the PYD power play.

International responses

This indeterminate position between opposition to a decentralised Syrian Kurdish entity by the non-Kurdish opposition on the one side, and limited support from the Kurdistan Region of Iraq on the other, is maintained by the absence of any international declaration of support for Kurdish demands. Despite attempts of Kurdish party leaders and political activists in the diaspora to win support from western governments for Kurdish demands in Syria, these governments, as well as Middle Eastern ones have focused political and financial support on the main Syrian (Arab) opposition groups, particularly the Syrian National Council, the FSA and the Syrian National Coalition. The sensitivity of the Kurdish issue to political relations inside Syria and its regional relations, to Turkey, a potential EU member, and indeed to the geopolitics of the region, has prevented Western governments from backing Kurdish demands or even from pressuring the Arab opposition to concede to political decentralisation of the state. In the event that this stance continues and the Kurds are left with little external support aside from that within the KRG, they are likely to continue their strategy of defence against both the regime and the Syrian opposition.

Governmental and non-governmental institutions have shown serious interest in the Kurdish issue in Syria, collating information from various experts and organisations. This interest picked up considerably when the Kurds began to assert control over Kurdish regions and the implications of the Kurdish issue in Syria to the geopolitics of the region became a pressing matter. There have been, however, no decisive steps towards practical or moral support for Kurdish demands in Syria and the Kurds and the Kurdish regions remain caught between the various local, regional and international actors and political agendas involved in the Syrian uprising. Once again the Kurdish political parties have become resigned to maintaining a status quo established to facilitate their existence.

The first year of the Syrian uprising proved decisive in positioning the Kurdish political parties in relation to the regime and the Syrian Arab opposition. Tentative steps were made by both sides to engage the Kurds and influence their position. But neither side committed itself to guarantee Kurdish rights or to provide the recognition and the political decentralisation that the Kurds required in this historic moment. Consequently, the Kurds have found themselves caught between the regime and the Arab opposition with little option but to entrench in the Kurdish regions, protect themselves from the worst effects of the Syrian uprising and take whatever steps are possible to establish a reality on the ground that would ensure Kurdish rights are recognised and demands fulfilled. The power vacuum left by the regime was filled by the Kurdish political parties, in particular the PYD, who adapted to the requirements of Kurdish self-rule, establishing local councils, distributing foods, water and fuel. The practical experience of Kurdish self-rule encouraged changes within the character of the Kurdish parties turning them into organisations engaging in the politics of power and governance. The commitment of the parties to unarmed struggle meant that the PYD obtained a monopoly over security and even over local councils and the distribution of goods and services.

Amid the political manoeuvring and coalition building of the political parties, a parallel dynamic saw Kurdish youth groups and intellectuals organising with much greater force and establishing themselves as the grass roots voices of the Kurdish street. The youth became the primary agents of the uprising in the Kurdish areas leaving the parties to follow their lead. They adopted manifestos indistinguishable from the majority of those of the political parties, a fact which blurred distinctions between the political parties and the youth organisations. Yet while criticism of the parties was heard from within them, the youth organisations did not develop into political parties or challenge their claim to representation of the Kurdish political movement. Instead the monopoly over Kurdish politics of the parties that traced their origins to 1957 was challenged by the rise of the PYD. This forced the parties to redress their focus on internal disputes and on relations with the Arab opposition and turn their attention to the practicalities of shielding Kurdish regions from the conflict in Syria, preparing for the fall of the regime and for self-rule.

Although the removal of the regimes 'red lines' allowed the parties to decisively address their internal factionalism and detachment from Kurdish society, the parties which trace their genealogy to 1957 remain constrained by their external environment, internal divisions and their unwillingness to relinquish personal power to those outside the party remit. Instead of pooling valuable resources and opening up the party movement to reform, the incorporation of the youth groups, independent activists and intellectuals within the KNC rendered these other groups less effective on the ground and subjected them to the domination by party interests. The PYD became a further constraint on the parties' ability to negotiate their new political environment. It acted decisively when the KNC was consumed with internal factionalism. It armed groups for the defence of the Kurdish people and regions when the KNC remained constrained by its past and committed to non-violent struggle. It has led the management the Kurdish regions when the KNC was rendered ineffective by its concerns that challenging the PYD would lead to inter-Kurdish conflict. While through its establishment and its call for a federal Kurdish entity in Syria the KNC has risen to the challenge posed to the achievement of Kurdish rights by the non-Kurdish opposition, it has surrendered to an unfavourable and unqual balance of power with the PYD within the Kurdish regions.

Despite imbalances in power relations between the Kurdish parties and although problems remain, all parties have displayed a strong commitment to the unity of the Kurdish political movement embodied in the KNC, the PCWK and the SKC. The establishment of the SKC and its management of the Kurdish areas laid the institutional foundations for the achievement of the Kurdish vision of what would follow the end of the uprising. Through this early experience of Kurdish 'self-rule' the Kurds have attempted to position and ready themselves for the power vacuum and potential conflict that would develop in the wake of the overthrow of the regime. Neither the regime, nor the Syrian Arab opposition have accepted Kurdish demands in Syria and worrying questions remain as to the opposition's commitment to even basic rights to freedom of culture, expression and identity.

While most parties of the KNC committed to federalism as the only viable solution to the Kurdish issue in Syria and as the best protection from the prophesied descent into civil and sectarian war after the fall of the regime, questions remain about the exact form of a Kurdish federal entity or autonomous region that might emerge from the crisis. External support for such an entity is, so far, also limited. The Kurds, however, having achieved such significant political advances, albeit without the resources of the state and in an uncertain position, will not easily relinquish the degree of control that they have obtained during the Syrian uprising.

EPILOGUE

THE NEW WORLD OF SYRIAN AND KURDISH POLITICS

In March 2011 the Kurdish political parties entered into the Syrian uprising, their historic chance to attain Kurdish demands. At the time, they were burdened with a crisis of legitimacy caused by internal factionalism, disengagement with the Kurdish youth and intellectuals and a focus on external political avenues. The new circumstances in Syria and the power vacuum left by the regime in the Kurdish areas ushered in a fundamental shift in Kurdish politics in Syria, opening opportunities for the parties to develop into organisations with a stake in the politics of state, as entities that practice the politics of governance. Yet, the parties' crisis of legitimacy continued to affect their decision-making processes and their ability to negotiate the challenges that the uprising brought with it.

In the wake of the 2004 Qamishli uprising protest became more common and visible, but did not add any new dimension to organised protests in Syria. Rather, the parties restricted protest to symbolic acts of solidarity. There were no verbal or visual references to those held responsible for the deaths of those now revered as martyrs, and no references to the political identity of the victims of state repression. The warnings from the regime and the counter-measures taken against participants in these events and the political parties' leaders from 2008 triggered an additional retreat of the parties and distanced them further from their stated aims and from Kurdish society. The research conducted for this book showed that the events of March 2004 were significant, more in terms of confirming popular nationalist consciousness and the unity of the Kurdish people, than in terms of any particular watershed in the actual politics of the parties. Consequently, when the parties failed to exploit the opportunities presented to them and criticism of them became more widespread, March 2004 became an important milestone in the party movement's descent into crisis. The contradiction between this heightened national consciousness and the crisis in the party movement exposed the parties' disengagement from Kurdish society.

By contrast, although the Syrian uprising of 2011 brought to the fore these inherent problems within the political party movement and their relation to Kurdish society, the retreat of the regime from Kurdish areas also allowed the parties room to manoeuvre politically within the emerging dynamics of the uprising. The emergence of the Syrian opposition from underground, as well as the virtual withdrawal of the regime from Kurdish areas provided the historic and unprecedented opportunity for the parties to make decisive moves towards obtaining Kurdish rights in Syria. But at the same time, it exposed the parties to new challenges in relation both to the Kurds' position within the Syrian state and to internal Kurdish political dynamics.

The parties not only needed to commit themselves to a path that could bring the full wrath of the regime against them, but they have also had to confront the possible complications of future relations with the Syrian Arab opposition and with the Kurdish PYD. Negotiating this political minefield, while maintaining their nationalist principles and commitment to peaceful methods, has brought further criticism upon the parties from within the Kurdish population as well as from the wider Syrian Arab opposition. Hailed as the 'decisive minority' in Syria with the ability to turn the situation in Syria from an uprising into revolution and topple the regime, the Kurdish parties have been accused by the Syrian opposition of thwarting the efforts of the rebels and prolonging the conflict in Syria. At the same time the parties are constrained by the Arab opposition and by the PYD. The failure of the Arab opposition to concede to or to adequately consider Kurdish demands for a decentralised political system in Syria has left the Kurdish parties alienated from the main opposition groups and unable to engage meaningfully with the movement of the majority. The PYD seizure of control over Kurdish territory has also led to an intensification of tensions between the Arab opposition and the Kurds as FSA spokesmen accuse the Kurds of separatism. For its part, the PYD's unilateral implementation of its democratic autonomy project brough with it the threat of inter-Kurdish conflict and has left the Kurdish parties of the KNC somewhat sidelined in the management of the Kurdish regions.

Pressure from the Kurdish street forced the parties to face issues such as the alienation of Kurdish youth and intellectuals from the party system, its fragmentation and failure to present a united Kurdish voice in Syria and the urgent need to clarify its position towards the regime. Two years into the Syrian uprising, issues that had characterised the party crisis continued to affect Kurdish efforts to position themselves as part of the main Syrian opposition movement and to make a decisive claim to national rights in Syria. Meanwhile, they have also had to manage the insecurity and damage generated by the regime's attempts to retain control in Syria.

The early parts of this book contain a historical description of the rise of Kurdish nationalism in Syria, the foundation of the first Kurdish political party in Syria and its fragmentation, and the analysis of the parties' roles and functions in Kurdish society. The object of that description was to reveal the aspects of Kurdish nationalism, political organisation and society in Syria that contributed to the crisis of legitimacy which threatened the parties on the eve of the uprising. This crisis proclaimed itself through a number of conflicts of interest — between traditional and modern forms of leadership, intellectuals and politicians, the older and younger generations, radical and conservative political leaders and the right and left wings of the Kurdish political parties. These contradictions, present to some degree throughout the period that has been described, have prevented the adaption and development of political organisations in response to changes in their environment and have caused much of the Syrian Kurdish population to feel alienated from parties altogether.

Yet, the parties have not merely been the victims of their circumstances under Ba'th party rule. The analysis of the Kurdish political party movement in Syria revealed the extent of the complicity of the parties and their leaders in their own oppression. The range of choices about how to pursue their aims and confront the regime has, of course, been limited. In some cases it may be true to say that they had no choice. But the illusion of choice can also lead to discord between the parties and their constituencies when they are seen to make the 'wrong' decisions. The submergence of the parties into inter-party, intra-party and personal rivalries, and the absence of democratic processes in most of them, are factors that the party leadership do have the capacity to alter. The decisions not to exploit new resources, such as the internet, or political developments, such as those in Iraqi Kurdistan, are perceived by some in Kurdish society to have reflected a lack of commitment to the Kurdish national cause. Besides this, the parties' failure to elicit any concessions from the state after more than 50 years of operation, along with their factionalism, elitism and internal politics, were found in one interview after another to be the main points of criticism of the parties from Kurdish people in Syria.

In some ways the story presented in these pages stands in contrast to romantic visions of dissident political organisations, inhibited in their political and national goals only by their external circumstances — the victims of more powerful and oppressive rulers. In other ways, however, this book confirms these visions in relation to the Kurdish political parties in Syria. Throughout the book I have tried to show how the Kurdish party movement has been trapped by the circumstances resulting from Ba'th Party rule in Syria. The attempts to negotiate their illegality in Syria through networks of external relations have often proved inimical to the parties' interests in obtaining concessions from the state and maintaining relations with their constituencies. Added to this, adherence to the regime's 'red lines' and its interference in the internal affairs of the parties created a constant internal conflict within and between parties as they attempted to challenge state policies or to protect the Kurdish population from the inevitable counter measures of political action. In a similar way, the reaction of the Arab opposition to Kurdish demands has steered their policies away from active participation in the main opposition groups that emerged in the first year of the uprising and towards establishing a Kurdish bloc representing uniquely Kurdish interests, intent on protecting the Kurds from both the Assad regime and its possible Arabist or Islamic successor.

This has been a story not just of crisis and detachment from Kurdish society. The party movement has also been successful in many ways. Not least, their survival in the hostile political environment of Ba'thist Syria, which can be seen as testimony that they have operated effectively as political institutions, reacting both to the political realities of life under authoritarianism and Arab nationalism in Syria and to the division of Kurdistan. The parties have existed and developed in a state where political opposition is not tolerated and, as Kurdish parties, their very identity is treated as threatening to the security and territorial integrity of the state and the legitimacy of the ruling regime. The parties retain a monopoly over political organisation amongst the Kurds in Syria and even the government's attempts to restore the political power of tribal leaders failed, as the tribes conceded authority to the parties themselves. Until the 1990s the parties had strong connections with Kurdish society and actively worked to facilitate the expression of Kurdish culture and identity and involve the Kurdish communities in the reproduction of it. They acted as vehicles for disseminating the nationalism developed by Kurdish intellectuals within their ranks and thus became identified with a Syrian Kurdish polity and its representation. The task of representing Kurdish political demands in Syria is not an easy one to fulfil and, as this book has shown, the consequences of involvement in Kurdish politics in Syria are particularly severe. Party leaders continue to earn respect and prestige from this position despite the criticisms which they arouse. This implies that the party institutions themselves are still considered to be legitimately if imperfectly representative of the Kurdish people.

The nature of Syrian Kurdish society, and the parties' attempts to exploit it in order to ensure survival in Syria, eventually led to the development of fault lines within party movement. The illegality of the parties, and the limits set by the government on expression of Kurdish culture and politics, gave rise to the pursuit of power through other means. Drawing upon traditional social networks connected to tribal relations enabled the parties to maintain power in Kurdish society despite restrictions on political organisation, canvassing and communications between and within Kurdish areas. This interaction of traditional forms of authority and power with modern institutions and progressive notions of national identity is what has given Kurdish politics in Syria its distinct character. It also embedded in it the seed of the crisis that developed within the party movement and contributed to the transformation of the fundamental mandate and role of the parties in Kurdish society. By the start of the Syrian uprising, the inherent contradictions within this 'traditional–modern' formula had come to the fore and could no longer be sustained. The nature of the crisis and the divisions between Kurdish politicians and intellectuals demonstrated that this formula had become untenable. The consequence of this crisis was a further fragmentation of Kurdish politics between the intellectuals and the leaders of the political parties.

The analysis of historical evidence together with many interviews with Kurdish intellectuals and cultural activists seem to suggested that, although the institution of the parties initially allowed the intellectuals to widen their area of influence inside the Kurdish communities, the divisions between intellectuals and politicians which the intellectuls encountered in the parties has led to their isolation, and marginalisation and eventual withdrawal of membership and support for the party organisations. The contribution of the intellectuals to the core of the identity of the parties is revealed by examining both the historical role of the intellectuals in cultural and nationalist framing and then the effects of their subsequent withdrawal from the party ranks. This book has argued that, as a result of the intellectuals' withdrawal, the nature of the parties has been transformed from nationalist, leftist reformist and culturally oriented parties driven by Kurdish intellectuals, to parties dominated by an elite group, many of whom are connected to the traditional Kurdish leadership and are detached from the Kurdish masses and seemed to work to manage the status quo. The implications of this, particularly in light of the developments since the start of the Syrian uprising, are highly significant. The division between politicians and intellectuals could feasibly result in a complete separation of culture and politics among the Kurds of Syria as intellectuals now continue framing outside the ranks of the parties whose mandate has shifted to accommodate the new political dynamics in Syria and the prospects of Kurdish self-rule. Yet, as long as the regime or the Arab opposition define Kurdish identity as threatening to the state and its territorial integrity and national unity, Kurdish culture and expression of Kurdish identity will remain politicised.

The complexity and detail of the various political relations involved in the Kurdish political parties in Syria testify that this story has not been simply a case of nationalist politics, authoritarianism and its effects on sub-state, ethnically defined political organisation. It has been about the interaction and conflict between loyalties to multiple levels of identity and political representation. Approaching the subject from the sub-state level allowed me to provide an overview of all these levels of relations and identity. Throughout this book, the sub-state, class, underclass, local and regional loyalties and relations, as well as those to the state, the nation, the sub-nation and the international, have featured as a sub-text, essential to the understanding and explaining of Kurdish politics in Syria. The Kurds in Syria are a sub-state ethnic and national group, concentrated in particular geographical areas of Syria which have a demographic and national extension into and connection with fellow nationals in neighbouring states and in the diaspora. Yet this book demonstrated how the Kurds in Syria also came to be defined and to define and distinguish themselves as Syrian Kurds, with loyalties to the Syrian state itself. As nationalist political parties defined by the Syrian state the Kurdish parties could, and did, provide a channel for the development and expression of this Syrian Kurdish national identity and the management of this polity. For more than 50 years the parties' loyalty to the Syrian state has been demonstrated by countless reiterations that the Kurds are not separatist and that they are committed to the unity of the state. Yet, during the Syrian uprising Kurdish attempts to secure their rights have again been interpreted as separatist by the non-Kurdish opposition. In the absence of any free, unrestricted avenues for the expression, formalisation and legitimatisation of Kurdish identity under the Ba'th Party, and in the absence of guarantees from the Syrian Arab opposition, it appears that the Kurds in Syria and their political parties have given renewed attention to non-state identities and networks of support. The pan-national identity and the other areas of Kurdistan, the sub-state, local level social networks, such as the family and in some cases tribal relations, have gained in importance. On the state level, the more general pursuit of human rights, pluralism and democracy within the Syrian state remains a priority, but one which the majority of Kurds believe cannot be achieved through the existing opposition alliances or through a centralised political unit.

The Kurdish political parties in Syria began life in 1957 with a wide and representative support base and a nationalist political agenda that envisaged a shift in the balance of powers in Syria and recognition of and representation in government of the Kurdish national group. They boasted a social mandate that connected them to Kurdish society and which promoted civil and cultural development. They combined features of political parties with traditional social networks, activities and aims commonly associated with interest or pressure groups and social movements, pushing the boundaries of the political party and the 'political' further downwards into the private or social sphere. Despite their unusual 'political' character the Kurdish parties in

Syria have maintained a mandate through which they intend to influence the state on behalf of the Kurdish communities in Syria. Yet, for many of them, fractures between the politicians and intellectuals inside the party movement, generational differences and inaction all exposed a significant retreat from the nationalist agenda that initially defined them, and an accommodation to the regime's interests in controlling the Kurdish communities. The degree to which this reflected political realism and pragmatism in the face of continued state repression of the Kurdish communities, or was more an effort to secure the interests of individuals involved in the parties' leaderships, varied from party to party.

To some extent the Syrian uprising is facilitating the dissolution of the party crisis. The opportunity it provided for youth movements to express their voice, politics and criticisms led to attempts to bridge the generational divide in the political movement. Relations between the youth and the parties remain fraught. It is likely, however, that in any self-governed Kurdish entity that emerges from the fall of the regime and the fallout of the uprising, the Kurdish youth organisations will politicise explicitly and challenge the parties' monopoly over political organisation. Already Kurdish intellectuals have formed organisations to monitor the parties and advise them. After the eventual stabilisation of the situation, these organisations will become more effective and less constrained by efforts to promote unity and a single Kurdish voice. As for the parties of the 1957 genealogy, they will adapt further to their changing circumstances and to challenges posed by the PYD, either by embracing the youth and intellectuals or by further entrenching their politics in existing tribal and familial networks.

At the time of writing the uprising is still in progress. Kurdish political relations in Syria and beyond have certainly entered into a new phase but, with it, the mystery about the internal dynamics of Kurdish political parties and their relations to each other, to Kurdish society and to the parties of other areas of Kurdistan was renewed. Propaganda describing the successes of the Kurdish political movement in Syria in governing the Kurdish areas, protecting the Kurdish people and preventing the worst of the negative effects of the uprising from impacting too heavily on the Kurdish areas is more readily available. More profound information including details about what has occurred in the Kurdish areas is limited. Reports continue to appear accusing the PYD of acting unilaterally and of its authoritarian practices; divisions between political parties within the KNC continue to affect their ability to operate effectively; Kurdish parties in other areas of Kurdistan continue to have a significant impact on Kurdish politics in Syria; parties continue to act independently of the unions formed to synchronise the voices within the Kurdish opposition, and reports from inside Syria suggest that Kurdish control might not be as secure as it appears to be. All Kurdish parties and organisations are intent on maintaining unity and securing the Kurdish areas and the political demands for which they have been fighting for more than 50 years, and the PYD, despite criticisms of its unilateral actions, methods and political agenda, is a Kurdish party, is armed and securing Kurdish areas from external interference.

Continued claims from within the main Syrian opposition bodies that Syria is an Arab state and that Kurdish demands for decentalisation represent separatism, have forced Kurdish political parties to abandon, at least temporarily, their focus on developing relations with the Arab opposition and to refocus on maintaining security within the Kurdish regions and protecting the Kurdish populations from both the regime and from Arabist and Islamist rebel organisations. Whether the Kurds will be able to withstand challenges to the autonomy they have developed in Syria is, for now, unclear. Questions certainly remain about how political organisations such as these might cope with the experience of self-rule and civil war following the fall of the regime and about what opposition to them will emerge from the Kurdish street in the aftermath. For now, while the uprising continues and the Syrian opposition remains divided, the concentration on unity and on securing and managing Kurdish regions by all parties and organisations within the Kurdish bloc, leaves unresolved fault lines within the Kurdish political movement and between Kurdish and Arab opposition groupings.

APPENDIX

DIAGRAM OF PARTY
DIVISIONS 1957–2012

Key

Kurdish Party Names

PDKS (M) – *Partîya Dêmokrat a Kurdî li Sûriyê* (Provisional Leadership)

PDKS el-Parti – *Partîya Dêmokrat a Kurdî li Sûriyê (el-Partî)*

PDKS – *Partîya Dêmokrat a Kurdî li Sûriyê*

PDKÇS – *Partîya Dêmokratî Kurdî Çep li Sûriyê*

PKDKS – *Partîya Kar Dêmokratî Kurd li Sûriyê*

PDK (el-Suri) – *Partîya Dêmokrat a Kurdî ya Sûrî (el-Sûrî)*

HGKS – *Partîya Hevgirtina Gelê Kurd li Sûriyê*

PÇKS – *Partîya Çep a Kurdî li Sûriyê*

PÇKS – Komîta - *Partîya Çep a Kurdî li Sûriyê- Komîta Navendî*

PÇKS – Kongra - *Partîya Çep a Kurdî li Sûriyê- Kongra*

PKKS – *Partîya Kar a Kurd li Sûriyê*

PYDKS – *Partîya Yekîtî ya Dêmokrat a Kurd li Sûriyê*

PYKS – *Partîya Yekîtî ya Kurd li Sûriyê*

PDPKS – *Partîya Dêmokrata Pêşverû a Kurdî li Sûriyê*

Wekhevî – *Partîya Wekhevî ya Dêmokrat a Kurdî li Sûriyê* (formerly *Pêşverû*)

PSKS – *Partîya Sosyalist a Kurd li Sûriyê*

PWDKS – *Partîya Welatperêz a Dêmokrat a Kurdî li Sûriyê*

ŞPKS – *Şepêla Pêşerojê ya Kurdî li Sûriyê*

PAKS – Partîya Azadî ya Kurdi li Suryê

PYD – Partîya Yekîtî ya Dêmokrat (PYD)

PRDK – Partîya Rêkeftina Dêmokrat a Kurdistani – Sûriyê

PYKS-Kurdistani – Partîya Yekîtî ya Kurdistani li Sûriyê

PDPKS-Reform – Partîya Dêmokrata Pêşverû a Kurdî li Sûriyê – reform movement

Names of Party Leaders

SB – Salah Bedr al-Din
FA – Fuad Aliko
SU – Sabghut Ullah Fath Ullah
MM – Muhammad Musa
KM – Khayr al-Din Murad
DM – Daham Miro
JM – Jamal Mulla Mahmoud
SA – Sheikh Ali
KA – Kamal Ahmed
NI – Nusradin Ibrahim
NM – Nazir Mustafa
IA – Ismail Omar
HD – Abdul Hamid Darwish
TS – Tahir Sadun Safouk
AD – Aziz Daoud
AY – Abdul-Baqi Yousef
AHB – Dr Abdul Hakim Bashar
ARA – Abdul Rahman Aluji
LMF – Dr Lezgin Muhammad Fakhri
AKS – Abdul Karim Sako
MT – Meshaal Temmo
RBS – Rezan Bahri Shaykhmus
JM – Jangidar Muhammad
MO – Mustafa Oso
MJ – Mustafa Juma'a
SM/AM – Saleh Muslim and Asya Muhammad
NM – Nash'at Muhammad
OD – Omar Daoud
FY – Faisal Yusef

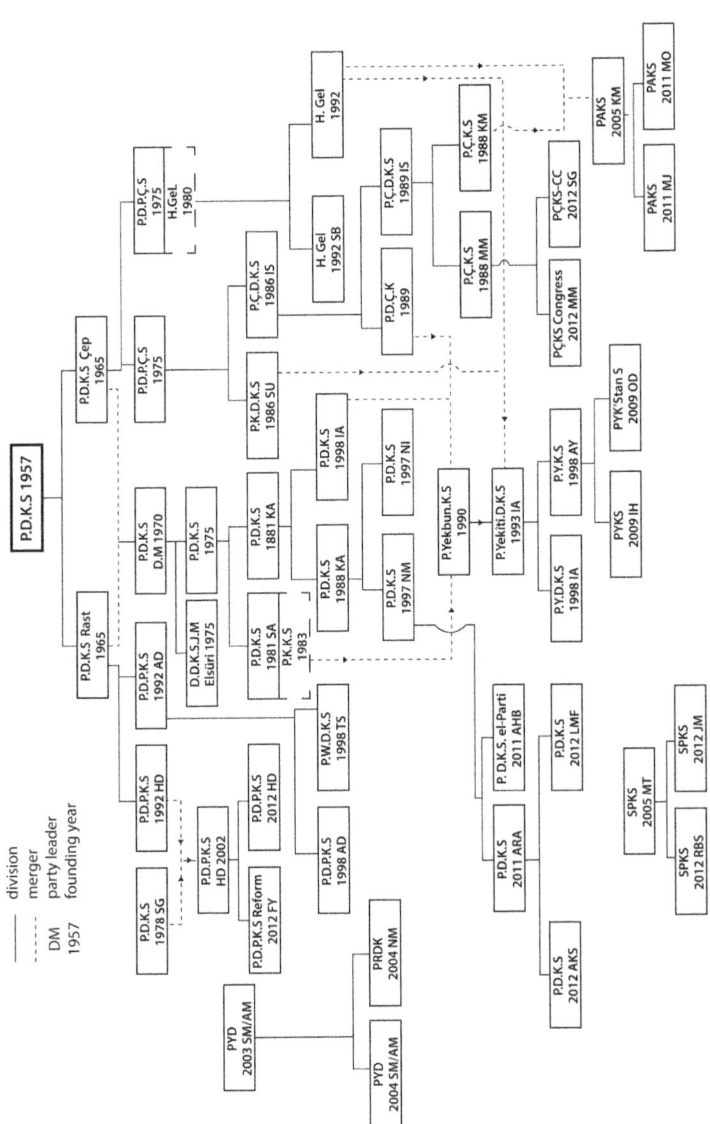

division
merger
DM party leader
1957 founding year
P.D.K.S 1957
P.D.K.S Çep 1965
P.D.K.S Rast 1965
P.D.P.Ç.S 1975 H.GeL 1980
P.D.P.Ç.S 1975
P.D.K.S D.M 1970
P.D.P.K.S 1992 AD
P.D.P.K.S 1992 HD
P.D.K.S 1978 SG
H. Gel 1992
H. Gel 1992 SB
P.Ç.D.K.S 1986 IS
P.Ç.D.K.S 1989 IS
P.Ç.K.S 1988 KM
P.Ç.K.S 1988 MM
P.D.Ç.K 1989
PÇKS-CC 2012 SG
PÇKS Congress 2012 MM
PAKS 2005 KM
PAKS 2011 MO
PAKS 2011 MJ
P.D.K.S 1975
P.D.K.S 1881 KA
D.D.K.S.J.M Elsüri 1975
P.D.K.S 1981 SA
P.K.K.S 1983
P.D.K.S 1988 KA
P.K.D.K.S 1986 SU
P.D.K.S 1998 IA
P.D.K.S 1997 NI
P.D.K.S 1997 NM
P.Yekbun.K.S 1990
P.Yekiti.D.K.S 1993 IA
P.Y.D.K.S 1998 IA
P.Y.K.S 1998 AY
PYKS 2009 IH
PYK'Stan S 2009 OD
P.W.D.K.S 1998 TS
P.D.P.K.S 1998 AD
P.D.P.K.S 2012 HD
P.D.P.K.S HD 2002
P.D.P.K.S Reform 2012 FY
P.D.K.S. el-Parti 2011 AHB
P.D.K.S 2012 LMF
P.D.K.S 2011 ARA
P.D.K.S 2012 AKS
PYD 2003 SM/AM
PRDK 2004 NM
PYD 2004 SM/AM
SPKS 2005 MT
SPKS 2012 JM
SPKS 2012 RBS

NOTES

Introduction

1. Estimates of the number of Kurds in Syria vary considerably and all are subject to political considerations. Due to the fact that the Kurds are not a recognised minority in Syria there are no official or unofficial statistics. The estimate of 3 million is given as a average number between conservative estimates of 8 per cent of the Syrian population, and estimates which put the number near to 5 million favoured by nationalist Kurds.
2. The name Kurdistan is used to denote the areas of Syria, Turkey, Iraq, Iran and the former Soviet Union in which the Kurds form a majority. Its use in this book is not meant to have any political connotations. It is merely a means of simplifying discussion of a complex political and geographical entity.
3. Arabisation refers to state policy in the Kurdish areas believed to seek to change the demography of the Kurdish regions in favour of Arabs, to remove historical reference to the historical Kurdish presence in these areas and to force assimilation of the Kurds to the Arab culture and language.
4. By referring to the 'party movement' or the 'Kurdish party movement' in Syria I mean the totality of organisational structures and activities of the group of Kurdish political parties that trace their origins to first Syrian Kurdish political party, formed in 1957. These parties are interconnected and share a common history. Parties such as the *Partîya Yekîtî ya Dêmokrat* (PYD), (see glossary of parties) being formed in 2003 and, at least ideologically, connected to Abdullah Öcalan rather than to other Syrian Kurdish political parties, are not included within this working definition of 'party movement'.
5. Jwaideh 2006: 3–4.
6. Heywood 2002: 247.
7. Ayubi 1995: 165.
8. Carothes 2006: 41.
9. Lust-Okar 2008: 3.
10. Posusney 2005: 10.
11. Alhamad 2008: 37.

12. Leverett 2005: 1. For example George 2003: 4–5; van Dam 1996: 1–2; Hinnebusch 2001: 20; Zisser 2001: 5.
13. For example, Nikolas van Dam (1996) refers to the Kurds primarily in describing the ethnic diversity of the state (pp.1–2), the Arab identity of the state (p.18) and the exploitation of ethnic minorities to further the interests of the French mandate authorities and post-independence leaders (pp.26, 28, 29). In his book on the Ba'th Party and Syria, Robert Olsen (1982), also mentions the Party's discrimination against the Kurds in Syria briefly, in a more general, but equally brief, discussion of the party's position on the Kurdish question (pp.14–16). Hinnebusch discusses the Kurds only in the context of the Syrian Communist Party and Syria's support of the PKK. In Hourani's *Syria and the French Mandate: The Politics of Arab Nationalism, 1920–1945* (1987) the Kurds in the Syrian Jazira region are given a little more detailed examination. Here he describes the Christian–Kurdish autonomist movement in the Jazira in some detail but the other Kurdish areas are neglected and it is limited in its historical scope to the mandate period.
14. *Assad* by Patrick Seale, mentions only the Iraqi Kurds (1988: 90–91, 242–243, 355, 360). Likewise, while providing an invaluable examination of the social, political and economic structures of authoritarianism in Syria, Volker Perthes's *The Political Economy of Syria under Assad* (1995) gives the Kurds no attention at all.
15. My first book, *The Kurds of Syria: An Existence Denied*, was published in 2005 under the pseudonym Harriet Montgomery, in order to avoid such problems.
16. For example Lesch 2005: Chapter 5, 'Seasons in Damascus' pp.81–97; Leverett 2005: 91–94; Pace and Landis 'The Syrian opposition: the struggle for unity and relevance, 2003–2008' in Lawson (ed.) 2009: 120–143.
17. Jabar and Dawoud's (2006) edited volume entitled *The Kurds* does not include any chapter on the Kurds of Syria. Nor does that of Shahrzad Mojab on *Women of a Non-State Nation; the Kurds*.
18. For example Wadie Jwaideh (2006). Xoybûn was a Kurdish political organisation which was based in Syria but which involved primarily Kurds who were in exile from Turkey (see Chapter 2 of this book). Jordi Tejel (2006, 2007) and Vahé Tachjian (2004) have both published in French on Xoybûn, the Kurdish–Christian and Kurdish-Armenian alliances and Kurdish nationalism during the French mandate. Both works have provided important historical detail and analysis making significant contributions to Kurdish studies generally and to historical literature on the Syrian Kurds. However, of the works mentioned here, neither dealt with the Kurds of Syria as a distinct polity, as Tejel's later publication did (2009).
19. McDowall was an early example of this, including a short essay on the Kurds of Syria in an appendix in *A Modern History of the Kurds* (first published in 1996) outlining the historical development of Kurdish nationalism in Syria and the repression of the Kurds. At the time of its publication, this was an important introduction to the Kurdish issue in Syria. However, it discussed the history of the political parties from 1957 until his time of writing, as well as the role of the PKK in Syria, over just two pages. Other

examples of such works are two edited volumes on Kurdish nationalism: Robert Lowe's chapter entitled 'Kurdish nationalism in Syria' is the final chapter in Ahmed and Gunter (eds.) (2007). Nelida Fuccaro's chapter 'Kurds and Kurdish nationalism in mandatory Syria: politics, culture and identity' in Vali (ed.) (2003). Both chapters are the only ones on the Kurds in Syria and both are the final chapters of the books.

20. There are, of course, exceptions to this general formula, and the articles of Nelida Fuccaro, on 'The Kurds of Damascus,' (in Vali (ed.) 2003: 191–217), and Fuccaro (2003) 'Ethnicity and the city: the Kurdish quarter of Damascus between Ottoman and French rule, c. 1724–1946.' In *Urban History*, 30 (2): 206–224) and of Julie Gauthier, on the Kurdish politics around the Qamishli 'uprising' of 2004, (in Lawson (ed.) 2009: 105–119) as well as Tejel and Tachjian's works. In addition, the efforts of the European Centre for Kurdish Studies in Berlin, publishing a number of articles and reports on the Syrian Kurds, is widening the scope of attention on the subject.

21. Montgomery 2005.

22. Visas have not been not issued to those declaring an interest in conducting research on the Kurds in Syria. The last human rights organisation to gain permission to conduct research inside Syria was Human Rights Watch in 1995. Published authors such as Alan George have been banned from entering Syria due to the content of books or articles critical of the regime and dealing with opposition politics.

23. Doctoral studies included those of Jordi Tejel, Eva Savelsberg, Vahé Tachjian and Harriet Allsopp. The books, articles and reports produced in this period included Jordi Tejel 2009; Harriet Montgomery 2005; Robert Lowe 2006; Gambill 2004; Gauthier 2009; and several reports by KurdWatch published between 2009 and 2010 as well as those by Human Rights Watch and Amnesty International.

24. Examples include those of Muhammad Mulla Ahmed, Abdulbasset Sieda, Khalil 'Issa and Salah Bedr al-Din.

25. Kurdish websites include: www.amude.net, www.knntv.net, www.efrin.net. Publications by KAWA, the Kurdish Institute in Paris, the European Centre for Kurdish Studies in Berlin, amongst others. Some Kurdish websites also have sections where electronic books are available. The majority deal with cultural issues.

Chapter 1. The Kurdish Political Parties in Syria

1. The number of political parties in Syria is often changing with new divisions and alliances or factions forming new parties. While research has shown that at the time of writing the number of Kurdish political parties in Syria was 20, the number is given with caution and an understanding that by the time that this book is published, the number of parties may have changed. For example, it is unclear as to whether or not a few parties formed in 2009 and during the Syrian uprising continue to operate and whether some parties now exist only in exile without representation in Syria. During the

Syrian uprising, the change of conditions in the Kurdish areas and attempts to capitalise on this new political environment caused a number of divisions of parties and new parties were established. At the time of writing details of all these reported divisions were not available. Likewise, the incorporation of these new factions in this discussion of Kurdish politics in Syria would add further confusion to an already complicated subject without adding to the analysis. Consequently, the number of parties sited here is said to be approximate and to represent the main parties of the Kurdish party movement to date.

2. The Kurdish Democratic Party in Syria. As shown in Chapter 3 the name of the party when it was founded is subject to dispute. Some say it was *Partîya Dêmokrat a Kurdîstan li Sûriyê*. It is not doubted that the party carried this name at some point, however, there is disagreement as to when it had this name. I have chosen to use the name *Partîya Dêmokrat a Kurd li Sûriyê* here, for the simple reason that it was used by the party longer than the other name.

3. McDowall 1998.

4. The area is known locally as Kurd Dagh or Ciya Kurmanc, both meaning 'Kurdish Mountains'. The first was the Ottoman name for the area. The second is the literal Kurdish translation, Kurds speaking the Kurmanji dialect being known as Kurmanj.

5. Spelt Kurmanci in the Kurdish script this is the Kurdish dialect of Syrian Kurds, also spoken by Kurds in Turkey and the northern Barzani regions of the Kurdistan Region of Iraq.

6. Fuccaro 2003: 193.

7. IMF March 2010.

8. Energy Information Administration, August 2011.

9. Aykan June 1999.

10. Vanly 1992: 144.

11. Ahmed 2001: 32.

12. Lescot 1988/1940; Hamo 2001. Interview with Khalil Rashid Ibrahim, 31 July 2006.

13. Muhammad Talab Hilal makes this connection in his study of the Jazira, and it arose again during the propaganda campaign against the Kurds in the 1960s, see also McDowall 2000: 483 n.24, PRO FO371/164413.

14. Syria was divided into six semi-autonomous states: Damascus, Aleppo, Jebal Druze, Latakia, the Sanjak of Alexandretta and Greater Lebanon. The latter was granted its own mandate in September 1926.

15. Hinnebusch 1990: 71–72.

16. Ibid., 72

17. It is said that his mother was Kurdish and father Arab.

18. McDowall 2000: 471.

19. Lawson 1994: 503.

20. Heydemann 1999: 30.

21. Lawson 1994: 504.

22. Hinnebusch 2001: 4.

23. See Barnett 1988.

24. McDowall 1998: 16–17.
25. Ahmed 2001: 68.
26. *Muharibah al-isti'mar* (could alternatively be translated as 'fight against imperialistic exploitation').
27. Ahmed 1988: 30.
28. Seale 1988: 54.
29. Ibid., 67.
30. Hinnebusch 2001: 2–4.
31. Perthes 1995: 36–37; Zisser 2001: 7.
32. van Dam 1996: 68.
33. Seale 1988.
34. Emergency Law was declared in Syria in 1962. The Ba'th re-issued emergency law after taking power in 1963. It remained in place until April 2011 and was the *de facto* legal framework of the state. After the outbreak of the Syrian uprising in March 2011 Emergency Law was abolished in an attempt to demonstrate that the regime was reforming. However, the extraordinary powers that the law had granted the President and Syrian security services were renewed through new 'anti-terrorism' laws.
35. Constitution of the Syrian Arab Republic: Preamble, Article 1, pt 2 and 3, Article 8 and Article 43.
36. Before the year 2000 the minimum age of a Syrian President was 40. Article 83 of the Constitution of the Syrian Arab Republic.
37. Hilal n.d. (dated by Ismet Cheriff Vanly as November 1962).
38. Ibid., (1962). The report is said to have been circulated inside the government. A copy was acquired by *el-Partî* and has been reproduced secretly, circulated among Kurdish politicians and others. The government insisted that this was an independent work and that it did not reflect official government opinion or policy.
39. In short the plan proposed i) the displacement of the Kurds from their land; ii) denial of education to them; iii) the extradition of 'wanted' Kurds to Turkey; iv) denial of opportunities for employment; v) an anti-Kurdish propaganda campaign; vi) replacing local Kurdish religious clerics with Arab ones; vii) the implementation of a divide and rule policy in the Kurdish areas; viii) the settlement of Arabs in the region; ix) the establishment of a *cordon sanitaire* along the border with Turkey; x) the establishment of collective farms for Arab settlers; xi) the denial of the right to vote or hold office to anyone lacking Arabic; and xii) the denial of Syrian citizenship to non-Arabs wishing to live in the area. Hilal n.d. (1962): 49.
40. Although Bashar al-Assad issued a decree in April 2011 allowing stateless Kurds to apply for naturalisation, at the time of writing it was still unclear how many had been able to benefit from this decree. Some sources claimed that only 50,000 had been issued with Syrian citizenship documents, while others suggested that the majority of *ajanib* Kurds had received them.
41. Interviews with Kurdish lawyer, 05 September 2002; Kurdish author, 04 September 2002; representative of *Partîya Yekîtî ya Dêmokrat a Kurd li Sûriyê*, 21 December 2002. HRAS November 2003.

42. Bedr al-Din 2003: 25.
43. This party merged with the *Partîya Çep a Kurdî li Sûriyê* in May 2005 forming *Partiya Azadî ya Kurd li Sûriyê*.
44. Bedr al-Din 2003: 25.
45. Interview with Kurdish family from Kobanî, 31 August 2002.
46. Ibid.
47. Ibid. Kobanî area itself remains predominantly Kurdish. Observations by author.
48. Interview with Kurdish family from Kobanî, 31 August 2002.
49. KurdWatch July 2010: 9.
50. Ibid., 4–5.
51. Following this, on 19 November 2009 the President issued Decree 432 defining all border regions. Included were all regions with an international border, ie. all Syrian regions except for Hama. On the sparsely settled border with Jordan, a five kilometre strip of land was defined as the border region. On the Turkish and Lebanese borders, cities were listed separately. The exceptions were the provinces of Hasaka and Qunaitirah where the provinces in their entireties were defined as border areas. KurdWatch July 2010: 8.
52. Under the previous statute, the Ministry of Agriculture and Land Reform held responsibility for the approval process. KurdWatch July 2010: 7.
53. See, for example, Kurdish Aspect 01 June 2010.
54. KurdWatch July 2010: 9.
55. Amnesty International 10 March 2005.
56. In early 2004, it was reported that the organisers of a private New Year's Eve party in Kobanî were required to sign a declaration that no singing in a non-Arab language would occur at the gathering in order to obtain permission from the political security branch in Aleppo to hold the party. It was also required that the Kurdish singer, Rashid Sofi, who would be present at the celebration, should sign a declaration that he would not sing. He did not sign. When during the party he was passed the microphone so that he might sing, undercover security personnel in the audience prevented him from singing by force. Fighting among the security personnel and members of the audience ensued. Reported on the Kurdish website Serhildanaqamislo.com, 8 January 2004.
57. For example, Salah al-Din Ayubi was Kurdish, as was Ibrahim Hananu, leader of the Syrian independence movement in Idlib. Husni Za'im who led the coup of 1949 was Kurdish. Many Kurds were involved in the founding of the Syrian parliament in 1928, e.g. Ibrahim Pasha al-Mali, and have held important positions in the Syrian parliament and within the ruling parties before the Ba'thist take-over.
58. Copies of decrees and lists of name changes occur in several books on the Kurdish question in Syria, for example: Bedr al-Din 2000: 216–232; and Sieda 2003: 172–194.
59. For example one photography studio in Efrîn had to change its name from Efrîn 21 to Efrîn 23. The number 21 making reference to the date of Newroz, Kurdish New Year, celebrated on 21 March.

60. For example, a girl, named Kurdistan, was expelled.

61. Interviews with many Kurds from all regions, all names withheld by author.

62. Since the start of the Syrian uprising Kurdish parties have voiced additional aims and agendas, including calls for a federal Kurdish entity in Syria. At the time of writing, however, many parties had not yet made corresponding changes to their party programmes.

63. Interviews; seven parties in Germany, party internal organisation documents of *Yekîtî, Hevgertin* and written responses from both *Partiya Çep* and, *el-Partî* (Yasîn Dêrkî) and the above parties.

64. Interview with Kamiran Bêkes, 21 December 2002.

65. Interviews with party leaders, 2006. For example: Nazir Mustafa, 12 August 2006; Ismael Omar, 12 August 2006; Sheikh Ali, 30 July 2006.

66. Written response to questions Haji Sulaiman, January 2003.

67. Interview with Yasîn Dêrkî, 17 December 2002.

68. Interview with Kamiran Bêkes, 21 December 2002.

69. For example see the party programmes of *Partiya Azadî ya Kurd li Sûriyê, Partiya Yekîtî ya Kurd li Sûriyê, Partiya Çep a Kurdî li Sûriyê, Partiya Dêmokrat a Kurdî li Sûriyê (el-Partî), Partiya Dêmokrata Pêşverû a Kurdî li Sûriyê,* or *Partiya Çep a Kurdî li Sûriyê.*

70. For example *Partiya Dêmokrata Pêşverû a Kurdî li Sûriyê* of Hamid Haj Darwish.

71. For example *Partiya Yekîtî ya Kurd li Sûriyê.*

72. See party programme of *Partiya Yekîtî ya Kurd li Sûriya,* Article 6.

73. Party programme of *Partiya Azadî ya Kurd li Suryê.*

74. For example, compare the party programmes of *Partiya Azadî ya Kurd li Sûriyê* and *Partiya Yekîtî ya Kurd li Sûriya* with *Partiya Dêmokrata Pêşverû a Kurdî li Sûriyê.*

75. Interviews with Nazir Mustafa, 12 August 2006; Mamo Alo, 28 November 2006; Khalil Daoud, 06 August 2006 and 10 June 2007; Mustafa Juma'a, 09 July 2007; Sheikh Ali, 22 June 2007; and others.

76. Interviews with Kurdish party representatives of *Partiya Yekîtî ya Dêmokrat a Kurd li Sûriyê, Partiya Dêmokrat a Kurdî li Sûriyê (al-Partî), Partiya Hevgirtina Gelê Kurd li Sûriyê,* December 2002.

77. Restrictions on printing, publishing and distributing printed material are set out in Decree 50 of 2001. For more information on this decree see HRW 31 January 2002.

78. Interview with Abdul Basset Hamo, representative of *Partiya Yekîtî ya Kurd li Sûriyê,* Germany, and written account of the dialogue between the two *Yekîtî* leaders, Hasan Salih and Marwan Othman, and the Speaker of Parliament, Qader Qadourah, that took place two hours before the start of the demonstration outside the Syrian parliament in Damascus, 10 December 2002.

79. Another common charge against Kurdish political activists is attempting to sever part of the Syrian state and attach it to a foreign state.

80. A further example of the police aggression with which Kurdish demonstrations have been met is the World Children's Day demonstration in Damascus in 2003. On 25 June 2003, approximately 380 children held a peaceful march on the UNICEF building in Damascus.

The march was descended upon by more than 400 security personnel and the crowd was forcibly dispersed. Seven male adults were arrested and it was reported that children were beaten by the police and a number of them were injured. The seven men arrested at the demonstration were tried in the Supreme State Security Court on 27 June 2004 and charged with 'belonging to a secret organisation' and 'attempting to sever part of the Syrian territory and annex it to a foreign state'. The trial was condemned as unfair by Amnesty International. Although rarely imposed, the death penalty is the maximum sentence for conviction of any of these 'crimes'. Amnesty International, MDE 24/048/2004, 29 June 2004.

81. *Serhildan* in Kurdish, or *intifada* in Arabic. The term 'Qamishli uprising' is used in this book to refer to the events of March 2004. Obviously the word 'uprising' is contentious and its use here is not meant to imply any political bias. Rather it is employed instrumentally to refer to the series of events that took place in the Kurdish areas of Syria.

82. Reported on www.qamishlo.com (site now unavailable) and www.amude. com. Through the organisers of these sites video footage of the clashes in the stadium was sent out in a number of small files and aired on Channel Four News.

83. HRAS April 2004: 3.

84. KurdWatch December 2009: 4. The report was instrumental in fuelling anger amongst the Kurds and escalating the violence.

85. HRAS April 2004: 3.

86. Interviews with participants.

87. Reported on www.qamishlo.com (site now unavailable) and www.amude. com. Confirmed by KurdWatch December 2009: 9.

88. KurdWatch December 2009: 9. According to reports gathered by KurdWatch, groups from the Tayy and Shammar tribes were armed and escorted by Syrian security forces to confront protesters in demonstrations following the death of Sheikh Ma'shouq Khaznawi in June 2005. KurdWatch December 2009: 16.

89. HRAS 16 March 2004: 1–2.

90. HRAS April 2004: 7.

91. Ibid., 2.

92. Ibid., 3.

93. Ibid., 2.

94. Bashar al-Assad interview on al-Jazeera satellite television station 01 June 2004.

95. KurdWatch December 2009: 16.

96. Gambill April 2004.

97. Gauthier 2009; Tejel 2009.

98. For example Robert Lowe of Chatham House.

99. Interview with Central Committee members of *Hevgertin*, 22 December 2002.

100. Such as: *Hizb al-Ishtiraki al-Dimoqrati al-Arabi*; *Hizb al-Sa'b al-Dimoqrati al-Suri* of Riad Turk; *Hizb al-'Amal al-Shiu'i al-Suri* of Safwan Akash and Fatha Jamous; the lawyer Hasan Abdul Azim, former MP Abdul Majid

Manjourah, independent Islamic activists such as Dr Abdul Razaq al-Eid (head of a centre for Islamic studies) to name but a few.

101. For example, the goals of the Damascus Declaration include the following: to 'emphasize Syria's affiliation to the Arab Order, establish the widest relations of cooperation with the Arab Order, and strengthen strategic, political, and economic ties that lead the [Arab] nation to the path of unity'. The Damascus Declaration of 16 October 2005.

102. *Partîya Yekîtî ya Kurd li Sûriyê*; *Şepêla Pêşerojê*; and *Partiya Azadî ya Kurd li Sûriyê*.

103. Interview with Kurdish family from Kobanî, 31 August 2002; leader of tribe from Kobanî, 05 July 2007.

104. Interview with representative of *Partîya Dêmokrat a Kurdî li Sûriyê (al-Partî)*, 17 December 2002; representative of the Western Kurdistan Association, 12 February 2003. McDowall cites 7,000 unaccounted for. McDowall December 1998: 65.

105. Confirmed by various interviews with Syrian Kurds in Syria, Germany, Britain and France conducted between August 2002 and May 2004.

106. Al-Mulhim 1999: 167–170.

107. The parties in Syria adopting the ideology and structure of the PKK are *Partîya Yekîtî ya Dêmokrat* (PYD) led by Salih Muslim and *Partîya Rêkeftina Dêmokrat a Kurdistani – Sûriyê* led by Nash'at Muhammad (formerly Fawzi Shengal) which split from the former. Interviews with Syrian Kurdish party representatives, Germany 2002 and in Syria 2007.

108. Interview with Dr. Latif Rashid (PUK), 27 March 2003.

109. Interview with Dalshad Miran (KDP), 27 January 2004.

110. Interview with Nazir Mustafa, 12 August 2006.

111. In 2007, physician and signatory of the Damascus Declaration, Kamal Labwani, was sentenced to 12 years hard labour on charges of 'communicating with a foreign country and inciting aggression against Syria' after visiting the USA and meeting with US officials, journalists and human rights organisations there. HRW 10 May 2007.

Chapter 2. The Birth of a Syrian Kurdish Polity, 1920–1957

1. While other organisations did exist, many of them cultural, the lack of information available rules out meaningful discussion of them. The four organisations examined in this chapter played important roles in determining the course of political, social and economic development of the Kurdish areas.

2. Author of Mem u Zîn.

3. At the time of Sharaf Khan's writing there were 40 such principalities.

4. McDowall 2000: 41–47.

5. Zurcher 2001: 52–54.

6. Olsen 1989: 5–7.

7. Ibid., 7–15.

8. Ibid., 153.

9. Lescot 1988/1940: 103.

10. Turkey feared a French–Kurdish alliance. Velud 1991: 334.
11. Velud 1991: 334–336 and n.214, p.398.
12. The Sheikh Ismail Zade family owned approximately 20 villages in the Efrîn region (Lescot 1988/1940: 105), as did Hajo Agha in the Jazira.
13. Those that lived and worked on land owned by the *agha* or those seeking protection of the *agha*.
14. Lescot 1940 (arabic translation): 54.
15. Interviews Syria 2007.
16. Particularly the al-Yousef and Shamdin families of Hayy al-Akrad in Damascus. McDowall 2000: 467–468.
17. Ahmad 2001: 54. Ibrahim Hanunu, leader of the uprising in Idlib and Kurd Dagh area, was Kurdish.
18. Velud 1991: 334.
19. van Dam 1996: 4; Bou-Nacklie 1993: 647.
20. Torrey 1964: 10.
21. van Dam 1996: 4; McDowall 1998: 16.
22. Torrey 1964: 10.
23. See for example Tejel 2006.
24. Jaladat Ali (1893–1951), Kamuran (1895–1978), Sureya (1883–1938).
25. Emin Ali was one of the sons of Bedirkhan Beg and had been one of the leaders of the Erzincan revolt of 1889. Bedirkhan Beg was reported to have fathered as many as 99 children, several of whom played important roles in the Kurdish nationalist movement.
26. In the course of the rebellion, Bedirkhan declared his territory independent and began minting his own coins. Faced with the strength of the Ottoman state, which was backed by Britain and France, Bedirkhan surrendered in 1846. Most of the Kurdish nobility were exiled or resituated in Istanbul where they could be observed and controlled more easily. Bedirkhan himself was moved first to Istanbul in 1847 and then exiled to Crete.
27. The journal 'Kurdistan' established by Mîr Bedirkhan Begs' son Medhat Bey Bedirkhan in Cairo in 1887 and published in Geneva and Folkstone in 1892 by his brother Abdul Rahman Bedirkhan, criticised Turkish policy in Kurdistan.
28. Özoğlu 2004: 80; Olsen 1989: 15.
29. For example, *Kürdistan Neşri Cemiyeti* (the Society for the Propagation of Kurdish Education) 1910, *Kürdistan Muhibban Cemiyeti* (the Society for the Friends of Kurdistan) 1912, and *Kürt Hevi Talebe Cemiyeti* (the Kurdish Hope Student Organisation) 27 July 1912. Özoğlu 2004: 80.
30. Özoğlu 2004: 79.
31. Olsen 1989: 15.
32. Ibid., 18, 21.
33. For example the Paris Peace Conference 22 March 1919, where Sherif Pasha presented a map of Kurdistan. Özoğlu 2004: 39.
34. Articles 62–64 of the Treaty of Sèvres dealt specifically with the Kurds and Kurdistan, where it was stipulated that the Kurdish region would have local autonomy and the right to independence to be granted by the League of Nations following a referendum after one year of the signing of the treaty.

35. See for example Jwaideh 2006; Tejel 2007; McDowall 2000.
36. Olsen 1989: 126.
37. Meaning 'independence' in Kurmanji Kurdish.
38. The distinction between Turkey and Syria in this period is somewhat misleading as both were newly created states which had little meaning to the Kurdish population aside from the obvious oppression experienced within the boundaries of the Turkish state. Even when the borders were drawn, Kurds continued to adhere to and act upon tribal and kinship networks that spanned these new divisions (Jwaideh 2006: 144). When Kurds fled to Syria, they remained within Kurdish areas. There is also little research which examines the involvement of Kurds from Kurdish areas included in Syria in Kurdish nationalist organisations that developed towards the end of the Ottoman Empire and whether they continued these efforts after the division of Kurdistan. Jwaideh mentions that Kurdish intellectuals and nationalists were also present in Damascus and Aleppo. In 1919 the Damascus based newspaper, *al-Mufid*, which was owned by Yusef Haydar and Khayr al-Din al-Zerguli printed a long article on Kurdish independence encouraging the Kurds to claim a free Kurdistan. Copies of this paper were distributed in Aleppo and copies of the article disseminated in many Kurdish towns (Jwaideh 2006: 144).
39. (Independence League/Association.) Kurdish spelling. Also spelt Khoybun, Khoyboun and Hoybun.
40. There is some dispute about the date of the founding conference. See Ahmed 2000: 37–38.
41. Among the participants in the founding congress were: Jaladat Bedir Khan; Dr Nouri Dersimli; Dr Shukri Muhammad Sakfan; Hajo Agha, head of the Haverkan tribe; Bozan Shahin Beg, head of the Barazan tribe; Mustafa Shahin Beg, brother of the former; Amin Ahmed Berikhan, head of the Raman tribe; Bedir al-Din Agha Habsbani; Mamduh Salim, from the Kurdish party leadership in Turkey; Fahmi Laji, clerk of Sheikh Sa'id; Mulla Ahmed Shawzi; Faqh Abdullah al-Jazari (Ahmed, 2000: 44; Jwaideh 2006: 211).
42. Ahmed 2000: 37–38.
43. Ibid., 45–46.
44. AIR 23/416. Special Service Officer Mosul to Air Staff Intelligence. 'Form of Oath. Khoybun Society.' Baghdad, February 26, 1930, cited by Tejel 2009: 18. Also quoted in Arabic by Ahmed 2000: 46.
45. Ahmed 2000: 46.
46. Ahmed 2000 *Jama'iyat Khoybun wa al-'alaqat al-kurdiyah-armaniyah.* (KAWA, Bonn Germany), p.47.
47. Also known as the Ararat Revolt. Agri is the Kurdish name for the region and mountain.
48. Jwaideh 2006: 211.
49. McDowall 2000: 468.
50. Tachjian 2004: 24–25.
51. Ibid., 26–28.
52. Hamo n.d.: 25; Tejel 2009: 21–22.

53. Hamo n.d.: 25.
54. Tejel 2009: 21–22.
55. Hamo n.d.: 17.
56. This is more common in the Kurd Dagh and Kobanî where the population is less mixed with Arabic speaking communities.
57. Hamo n.d.: 28–29.
58. Izady 1992: 180.
59. Interviews with Kurdish nationalists in Syria.
60. Tejel 2009: 27–28.
61. Ibid., 27–28.
62. Ibid., 27–28.
63. Ibid., 29.
64. Jwaideh 2006: 146.
65. Some Kurdish groups allied themselves with this counter movement.
66. Savelsberg et al 2003: 14–15.
67. Ibid., 15–16.
68. Ahmed 2001: 54. According to Ahmed, Turkish authorities protested the establishment of these Kurdish clubs near to the Turkish border and the French called for their closure in 1939. Ahmed 2001: 54–55.
69. Tachjian 2004: 14.
70. Velud 1991: 333.
71. Ibid., 291, 300, 301, n.167, p.392; Tejel 2009: 30.
72. Tejel 2004: 30.
73. Tejel 2009: 29–32.
74. The report of Msgr. Hebbé cited by Tejel 2009: 36.
75. Tejel 2009: 13.
76. Literally meaning 'the adherents' or 'followers'.
77. Lescot 1988/1940: 104.
78. Ibid.
79. Eli n.d.: 501.
80. Such as Rashid Hamo and Dr Mihemed Eli, both from the Kurd Dagh region.
81. Interview with Kurd from Kurd Dagh.
82. Poem quoted by Eli n.d.: 502.
83. Nebi Houri, also known by the name Cyrrhus, the remains of a byzantine city, the tower of which has become a shrine for a local Muslim saint, Nebi Houri. Situated approximately 70km north of Aleppo in the vicinity of Azaz the site dates back to 230 BC–thirteenth century AD.
84. Interview with Khalil Rashid Ibrahim, Grandson of Rashid Ibo (*Muroud* leader), Syria 31 July 2006.
85. Lescot 1988/1940: 109.
86. Ibid., 108, 110; Eli n.d.: 502–503.
87. Ibid., 110 and n.13.
88. Eli n.d.: 505–506. The family of Rashid Ibo only returned to Syria after Syrian independence. Interview with Khalil Rashid Ibrahim, 31 July 2006.
89. Eli n.d.: 506. Sheikh Ibrahim Khalil died under mysterious circumstances.
90. Interview with Khalil Rashid Ibrahim, 31 July 2006.

91. It is arguable that most would have been aware of the dissemination of the new Kurdish journals and possibly of some of their content even if they were not able to read them themselves.
92. See for example Perthes 1995; van Dam 1996; Steale 1998.
93. Ahmed 1988: 21.
94. Cigerxwin joined the Syrian Communist Party in 1948.
95. Members included Rashid Hamo, Shawkat Na'san, Muhammad Ali Khoja, Qadir Ibrahim. The organisation was discovered in 1952 and those involved were arrested and imprisoned in Meze prison, Damascus. Ahmed 1988: 23.
96. Eli n.d.: 516–517, 526.
97. Ahmed 2001: 58. Another incentive for joining the party was the provision of scholarships to study in the Soviet Union. A large number of Kurds left Syria in this manner.
98. Ahmed 1988: 21.
99. Hamo n.d.: 41.
100. Ahmed 1988: 21; Hamo n.d.: 41.
101. Ahmed 1988: 21.
102. Hamo n.d.: 41–42.
103. Ahmed 1988: 23. Ahmed recounts that Rashid Hamo and Muhammad Ali Khoja visited the Jazira in 1949 in an attempt to join the ranks of Xoybûn, only to be informed of its closure by Abdul Rahman Ali Younis Agha. While in the Jazira, they made contact with other political figures such as Dr Ahmed Nafiz and Hajo Agha.
104. Ahmed 1988: 21.
105. Hopwood 1988: 37. Torrey cites 17 seats. Torrey 1964: 262.

Chapter 3. Kurdish Political Parties, 1957–2011

1. See Appendix for diagram of party divisions.
2. On 18 October 2010, Ismail Omar passed away unexpectedly.
3. Azadî split in October 2011, between Mustafa Juma'a and Mustafa Oso, leaving two parties of the same name. Before this, Khayr al-Din Murad led the party.
4. See Appendix.
5. Democratic Party of Iranian Kurdistan (KDP-I) formed on August 16, 1945 and led by Qazi Muhammad. Currently led by Mustafa Hijri. The KDP of Iraq held its first congress on August 16, 1946.
6. Now officially called Ruqqn al-Din. Many Kurds who had been involved in Xoybûn were exiled to Damascus by the French.
7. Ahmed 1988: 24. This club, like many others, was closed down by the French after the outbreak of World War II.
8. Fucarro 2003: 220. Rashid n.d.: 38.
9. The society for the revival of Kurdish culture. Also said to have been called *Anjaman*. Ahmed 1988: 25.
10. Ahmed 1988: 25.

11. Ahmed 1988: 26. Dr Zaza was a doctor of social studies who lived in Switzerland until 1956 when he returned to Syria.
12. Hamza Nouiran was a Kurdish intellectual and former member of the Syrian Communist Party.
13. Interview with Jamal Sheikh Baqi, leader of the *Partîya Dêmokrat a Kurdî ya Sûrî (el-Sûrî)*, 26 June 2007.
14. Interview with Jamal Sheikh Baqi, 26 June 2007.
15. Ahmed 1988: 27. Ahmed goes on to question their recollection of the Sheikhs involvement, implying that he had an important role at least as early as 1957, that him and Osman Sabri had been in contact from the 1940s and that his home in Qamishli had been used to discuss political activities and to accommodate other members of the committee.
16. All members of the leadership agreed that 14 June would be considered the founding date of the party.
17. Although no documentary evidence remains, the leaders recount that the organisation's central aims and objectives included the following: i) the freedom and unity of Kurdistan, ii) the ending of colonial domination, iii) the development of democracy as a means of achieving the national rights of Kurds in Syria, iv) the Kurdish language to be taught in schools in Kurdish areas, and v) equal rights for women. Ahmed 2001: 20; Darwish 2000: 21.
18. Ahmed 1988: 22.
19. Ahmed was a Kurdish teacher, politician, author and one of the founders of *Jam'aiya Wahidat al-Shabab al-Dimoqratiyin al-Akrad* (the Organisation of United Democratic Kurdish Youth).
20. Ahmed 1988: 26.
21. Darwish 2000: 18, 73.
22. Interview with Jamal Sheikh Baqi, 26 June 2007. Baqi stated that he had interviewed Osman Sabri and discussed this point with him.
23. Tejel (2009: 49) cites the source for this information as M. Jemo 1990: *Osman Sebri, Apo: Analyse bio-Bibliographique*, University of Sorbonne Nouvelle, pp.33–4.
24. Rashid n.d.: 33.
25. Many members of Xoybûn were exiled to Damascus by the French authorities.
26. For example, Muhammad 'Issa Mulla Mahmoud who was liberal in his religious philosophy did not see any contradiction between the political ideology espoused by the party and his religious beliefs.
27. The committee included Dr Zaza, Rashid Hamo and (possibly) Khalil Muhammad from the party leadership and Jamil Hajo and Arif Abass from the beys. Ahmed 1988: 30.
28. In particular Dr Zaza, Rashid Hamo and Hamza Nouiran are said to have developed strong relations with tribal leaders.
29. Ahmed 1988: 34, 35, 38.
30. For example in Dêrîk. Ahmed 1988: 41.
31. Ahmed 1988: 41.
32. Including Muhammad Ali Khoja, Khalil Muhammad, and Cigerxwin. Ahmed 1988. However, it is also said that these members of the leadership

were sent to Iraq to represent the organisation and support the Kurdish revolution in 1961. Interview with Kamal Saydo, 20 December 2002.

33. Ahmed 1988: 42.

34. Ibid., 43, 46. Interview with Kamal Saydo, 20 December 2002. Others went into hiding, from were they continued to operate the party organisation, e.g. Hamid Darwish.

35. Interview with Kamal Saydo, 20 December 2002 (Saydo was among those interned in Meze in 1960). Interview with Muhammad Mulla Ahmed, 20 December 2002. Ahmed was also among those arrested. Ahmed 1988: 46, 50.

36. Dr Zaza's side included Hamid Darwish. Osman Sabri's side included Sheikh Muhammad 'Issa Mulla Mahmoud.

37. Muhammad Mulla Ahmed claimed that Dr Zaza was expelled from the party. Interview, 20 December 2002.

38. Qassim seized power in Iraq in 1958. His government initially extended all rights to the Kurds and they were declared one of the two nations in Iraq. Barzani, however, sought to negotiate autonomy for the Kurdish regions and when promises were unfulfilled and the government displayed authoritarian tendencies, Barzani presented Qassim with an ultimatum. Qassim's response was to launch a military campaign against the Kurds in September 1961.

39. Interview with Kamal Sydo, 20 October 2002.

40. Kurdish Democratic Party in Syria (Left).

41. Osman Sabri had close personal relations with Mustafa Barzani. He left the party in 1969 and moved secretly to Turkey.

42. Kurdish Democratic Party in Syria (Right).

43. Darwish still leads the same party although its name changed to *Partiya Dêmokrata Pêşverû Kurd li Sûriyê*.

44. Interviews with Kamiran Hajo, 10 April 2003; Dr Latif Rashid, 27 March 2003; Sanko Mahmoud, 27 March 2003. KNK Bulletin: Kongra 2001: 42–43.

45. Tejel 2009: 87.

46. Interview with Dr Latif Rashid and Sanko Mahmoud of the PUK, 27 March 2003.

47. Daham Miro was a tribal leader. He was arrested in 1973 with other members of the leadership. The party was led by Hamid Sino while he was in prison.

48. Haji Sulaiman, written response, January 2003.

49. Sieda, written response to questions: 26 March 2010.

50. The leadership of the SCP had been arrested at the same time as the leadership of *Partî Dêmokrat a Kurdî li Sûriye* in 1960. It appears that during the 1960s the two parties enjoyed more cooperative relations as a result of this shared experience.

51. Sieda written response to questions, 26 March 2010.

52. Ibid., 31 July 2010.

53. Secretary General of *Yekîtî ya Dêmokrat* and party representative in the Kurd Dagh region.

54. *Hizb al-Amal al-Kurdi fi Suriya*/The Kurdish Labour Party in Syria.

55. Interview with Sheikh Ali, 22 June 2007.

56. For example, *Partiya Palên Kurd li Sûrî*/*Hizb al-Shaghilah* (the Kurdish Labour Party in Syria); *Partiya Kar a Kurd Sûriyê* (The Kurdish Workers

Party of Syria formed in 1981 by Sheikh Ali); *Partiya Sosyalist a Kurd li Sûriyê* (the Kurdish Socialist Party in Syria formed in 1978 by Salah Gido).

57. Interview with Dalshad Miran, 27 January 2004.

58. *Hizb al-Shaghilah al-Kurdi fi Suriya* or Kurdish Labour Party in Syria.

59. Interviews with Jamal Sheikh Baqi, 26 June 2007 and Sheikh Ali, 22 June 2007.

60. Soft policy refers to a party position that is flexible and acquiescent to the Syrian authorities demands of the parties and limits on them; which accommodates their interests in controlling political mobilisation and expressions of politics and ideas considered to be threatening to the state and its security; and that allows for the development of relations with the authorities, including the *mukhabarat*.

61. Sieda written response to questions, 26 March 2010.

62. Ibid.

63. Ibid.

64. For example *el-Sûrî* of Sheikh Baqi and *Partîya Kar* of Sheikh Ali.

65. *Partîya Çep* of Khayr al-Din Murad joined with other factions forming *Azadî* in 2005.

66. Dalshad Miran 22 January 2010: *Azadî* was formed in 2005; *Hizb al-Taakhi* in 2009; *Harakat al-Badil* in 2009; *al-Mubadirah al-Wataniyah* in 2009; *Itihad al-Watani al-Hurr* in 2008; *Harakat Huriyah Kurdistan* 2008; *Harakat al-Muthaqafiin*.

67. HRW 15 April 2009.

68. Its name in Arabic is *Harakat Itihad Hurriyah Qamishlo,* Unity and Freedom Movement of Qamishli.

69. *Harakat Itihad Hurriyah Qamishlo* 20 March 2008.

70. Interview with Kamiran Hajo, 31 May 2010; Sieda written response to questions, 26 March 2010.

71. Sieda written response to questions, 26 March 2010.

72. Ibid.

73. For example Kamal Ahmed. Interview with Sheikh Ali, 22 June 2007.

74. Interview with Sheikh Ali, 22 June 2007.

75. As occurred with Dr Hakim Bashar who took over the leadership of *el-Partî* in 2008.

76. Interview with Sheikh Ali, 22 June 2007.

77. Interviews with Sheikh Ali, 22 June 2007 and Khalil Daoud, 10 June 2007.

78. Sieda written response to questions, 08 August 2010.

79. As happened with the Syrian Communist Party in the early 1970s. See Ismael 1998: 155–191.

80. Sieda written response to questions 08 August 2010; interviews with Kurdish journalist 21 June 2007; Kurdish Lawyer 20 June 2007.

81. The details of the disagreement are not known. Sieda written response to questions 26 March 2010.

82. Interview with Jamal Sheikh Baqi, 26 June 2007.

83. Sieda written response to questions, 26 March 2010.

84. Interviews with Kurdish family in Efrîn, 25 June 2007; Kurdish journalist, 21 June 2007; Kobanî tribal leader, 10 July 2007.

85. Interview with Sheikh Ali, 30 July 2006.

86. Within the Kurdish political movement in Syria there were three coalitions of parties. The *Eniya, Hevbendi*, and the non-aligned parties in the *Komita*. In December 2009 a Kurdish Political Council was formed including eight of the parties. These coalitions were then replace during the Syrian uprising with the Kurdish National Council. See the glossary of parties.

87. Interview with Jamal Sheikh Baqi, 26 June 2007.

88. Interviews with Kurdish party leaders; Sieda written response to questions, 26 March 2010.

89. Sharing an ideology with the PKK and adopting flags picturing Öcalan, this party has been assumed to have a connection to the PKK or Kongra-Gel.

90. Formed in 1988.

91. Interviews with Sheikh Ali, 30 July 2006; Ismail Omar, 12 August 2006 and others.

92. Interview with Aziz Othman, 16 March 2010.

93. *al-Tahaluf al-Kurdi fi Suriya* or the Kurdish Democratic Alliance in Syria.

94. *al-Jabha al-Dimuqratiyah al-Kurdiyah fi Suriya* or the Kurdish National Front in Syria.

95. *Lajnat al-Tansiq al-Kurdiyah* or the Committee of Kurdish Coordination.

96. Miran 16 February 2009.

97. Ibid.

98. Ibid.

99. Ibid.

100. Announcement of the establishment of the Kurdish Political Council, Rojava News 30 December 2009.

101. The parties were: 1. *Partîya Dêmokrat a Kurdî li Sûriyê (el-Partî)*; 2. *Şepêla Pêşerojê ya Kurdî li Sûriyê*; 3. *Partîya Welatperêz a Dêmokrat a Kurdî li Sûriyê*; 4. *Partîya Yekîtî ya Kurd li Sûriyê*; 5. *Partîya Azadî ya Kurd li Suryê*; 6. *Partîya Çep a Kurdî li Sûriyê*; 7. *Partîya Dêmokrat a Kurdî ya Sûrî (el-Sûrî)*; and 8. *Partîya Wekhevî Dêmokrat a Kurdî li Sûriyê*.

102. Sieda written response to questions, 08 August 2010.

Chapter 4. Relations between the Parties and the State

1. For example the Damascus Spring civil society movement which arose after the death of Hafiz al-Assad in 2000. Most of the leaders of the movement were arrested in 2001 effectively destroying the movement. See Alan George 2002.

2. Examples of the Syrian authorities use of lethal force against Kurdish protests and gatherings include: Qamishli 12 March 2004 and following days; Newroz in Raqqa 2010; Newroz, Damascus and Aleppo 1986.

3. Interviews with Khalil Daoud, 06 August 2006; Kamal Saydo, 16 December 2002.

4. Interviews with Sheikh 22 April 2010; Kamal Saydo 16 December 2002 Interview with Khalil Daoud, 06 August 2006.

5. Interviews with Kamal Saydo, 16 December 2002; Dalshad Miran of the KDP, 08 November 2002 and 27 January 2004.

6. The myth of Newroz involves a blacksmith revolting against a despotic king. He lit fires on the mountains to inform his supporters of victory and to summon them.

7. The families of approximately 340 Kurdish villages in the Syrian–Turkish–Iraqi border area were ordered to leave their homes and were told to resettle in the non-Kurdish interior of Syria in areas such as Dayr al-Zur.

8. Interview with Jawad Mella, 12 February 2003; Ahmed 2001: 78.

9. Vanly 1992: 163.

10. Interviews with Kurds from Kurd Dagh region.

11. Previously known as *Partîya Yekbun a Kurd li Sûriyê*, it was formed from the merging of three parties including *Partîya Kar* of Sheikh Ali, a faction of *el-Partî* led by Ismail Omar and one of the Left parties. It later changed its name to *Partîya Yekîtî ya Dêmokrat a Kurd li Sûriyê* and a further faction from *Hevgirtin*, led by Fuad Aliko joined the party. In 1998 the party split forming *Yekîtî* and *Yekîtî ya Dêmokrat*. See Appendix.

12. Gauthier 2009: 106–107.

13. Interview with Sheikh Ali, 30 July 2006, Ismail Omar, 12 August 2006; Aziz Othman, 11 May 2010; Marwan Osman, 10 May 2003.

14. Interview with Sheikh Ali, 30 July 2006.

15. Kurds Information, 20 June 2001–20; July 2001.

16. Which had spilt from *Partîya Yekîtî ya Dêmokrat a Kurd li Sûriyê*.

17. Middle East Media Research Institute 16 December 2002.

18. Written account of the dialogue between Hasan Salih and Marwan Osman and the Speaker of Parliament, Qader Qadourah, two hours before the start of the demonstration outside the Syrian parliament in Damascus. 10 December 2002, by Abdul Basset Hamou 23 December 2002.

19. Syrian Human Rights Committee, 17 December 2002. Interview; Abdul Basset Hamou. 19 December 2002; written account by Hamou, 23 December 2002.

20. Gauthier 2009: 107.

21. Gauthier 2009: 107.

22. The first demonstration was held on 20 December 2004 in front of the Military tribunal. The second, on 22 February outside the Military Court where seven Kurds arrested while participating in the UNICEF demonstration were being tried. Kurdish students in Aleppo began demonstrating to protest issues such as the connection of the Students Union to the Ba'th Party and the governments abolishment of its obligation to employ graduating engineers and architects, on 27 January 2004 and 26 February 2004 respectively. Gauthier 2009: 109.

23. Gauthier 2009.

24. Ibid., 115.

25. Interview with Abdul Karim, 29 June 2007.

26. Ma'shouq Khaznawi was a liberal Kurdish cleric from the Jazira, who, after the events of Qamishli 2004, began preaching publically about Kurdish rights. He is believed to have been assassinated by the Syrian authorities, on

account of this outspoken support for Kurdish rights and/or for his development of relations with the Muslim Brotherhood.

27. This party merged with others forming *Azadî* later in 2005.

28. KurdWatch December 2009: 17

29. Ibid., 18–19.

30. Decree 49 of 10 September 2008 restricted rights of ownership and the use of land in the border areas of Syria and disproportionately effected Kurds. More than 580 Kurdish peasants had their rights to use land in the Dêrîk area removed from them in March 2010. Support Kurds In Syria news report 01 June 2010.

31. Particularly *Yekîtî ya Dêmokrat* and *Pêşverû*.

32. Information from Khaznawi's son.

33. According to party representatives other political parties were always invited to join the organisation of the demonstration, however, it was reported that they routinely refused, or if agreeing, that they would change their position near to the event. Interviews with Abdul Basset Hamou, 19 December 2002; Aziz Othman, 11 May 2010.

34. Interviews with Abdul Baset Hamou, 19 December 2002.

35. Interviews with Muhammad Daoud, 20 December 2002; Abdul Basset Hamou, 19 December 2002.

36. HRW 2009; ACCORD May 2010: 34–35.

37. HRW 2009; See also Miran, 16 February 2009.

38. KNNTV 12 October 2009.

39. Interview with Aziz Othman, 11 May 2010.

40. The other members of the leadership arrested were Muhammad Ahmad Mustafa and Ma'ruf Mulla Ahmad. On 16 February 2010 Hasan Salih was sentenced to one year imprisonment, reduced to eight months.

41. ACCORD 2010: 86. For example: Mustafa Juma'a Bakr, Sa'doun Mahmoud Sheikho, and Muhammad Sa'id Hussein al-'Amr, leading members of *Azadî* were sentenced to three years in prison. Hasan Salih, Muhammad Ahmed Mustafa and Ma'ruf Mulla Ahmed of the *Yekîtî* leadership were arrested in December 2009.

42. The Arab opposition refers to Arab political parties, organisations and human rights and civil society organisations that are illegal in Syria and stand in opposition to the current regime. The ones that have developed relations with the Kurdish political parties are generally those which seek the democratic reform of the Syrian state and which have grouped together within the Damascus Spring of 2000 and the Damascus Declaration of 2005.

43. This language has been used in relation to the 'Arab Belt' policy and general arabisation of Kurdish land.

44. Interview with Obeida Nahas, 27 March 2003.

45. McDowall 1991: 1 of 2.

46. Interviews with Obeida Nahas, 27 March 2003; Sanko Mahmoud, 27 March 2003.

47. Inaugural speech of Bashar al-Assad 2000: 27–30.

48. Such as that in the home of Riyadh Sayf, who established an informal group called 'Friends of Civil Society' in August 2000, which by November 2000

were open to anyone interested. The forums changed to 'Forums for National Dialogue'. Sayf established his own political party in January 2000 called The Movement for Social Peace. Al-Kharrat 2001.

49. Conversations with academic involved in the Damascus Spring and Damascus Declaration, 25 July 2006. Al-Kharrat 2001; and many other reports and articles of HRW and AI, 2000–2003.

50. The Statement of 99, the Statement of 1000, and 'Towards a national social contract in Syria'. For text see George 2003: 178–193.

51. Pers. Com with academic involved in the Damascus Spring and the Damascus Declaration, 25 July 2006.

52. Those arrested were: Ma'mun al-Homsi, Riyadh Sayf, Riad Turk, Aref Dalilah, Walid al-Bunni, Kamal al-Lubwani, Habib Salih, Hasan Sa'dun, Habib 'Issa, Fawwaz Tello. Charges against them related to crimes against the state, for example, Riyadh Sayf, arrested on 06 September 2001 was charged with 'violating the constitution' and Ma'mun al-Homsi, arrested 09 August 2001, with 'insulting the constitution', 'opposing the government' and informing to foreign elements. A.I. 03 March 2003, HRW 07 September 2001 and 2002 World Report.

53. Alan Kader 2001: 26. Interviews with Kamiran Hajo, 10 April 2003; 'Izz al-Din Mella 12 August 2002.

54. For example Riyadh Sayf, Walid al-Bunni and Ma'mun al-Homsi were released in 2006, Aref Dalilah in August 2008, Kamal al-Lubwani was released in September 2004 only to be arrested again on 8 November 2005, and in May 2007 he was sentenced to 12 years in prison. HRW World Report 2002 and 2003. On 23 December 2002 journalist Ibrahim Hamidi who had also recently written on the Kurds of Syria, was detained on charges of 'publishing false information'. MEIB, January 2003. And two outspoken Kurdish politicians were arrested on 12 December 2002 following their demonstration outside parliament.

55. *Akhbar al-Sharq* 11 March 2003.

56. HRW World Report 2001: 3 of 8.

57. The parties signed the declaration in the names of their alliances, as *Tahaluf (Hevbendi)* and *Jabha (Eniya)*.

58. Translated text taken from SyriaComment.com.

59. *Tiyar al-Mustaqbal al-Kurdi fi Suriya* (Kurdish Future Movement in Syria) of Meshaal Temmo.

60. Interview with Sheikh Ali, 05 July 2007.

61. Ibid.; Khalil Daoud, 06 August 2006.

62. For example, Sheikh Ali believed that his arrest in January 2007 was connected to his relation with the Damascus Declaration (Interview 05 July 2007). Likewise, another interviewee and his family were harassed by the authorities. He believed that this was connected to his work promoting Kurdish–Arab dialogue for *Yekîtî ya Dêmokrat* and hosting and participating in meetings of the Damascus Declaration.

63. Interview with Sheikh Ali, 05 July 2007; interview with Kamiran Hajo, 31 May 2010.

64. Interview with Kamiran Hajo, 31 May 2010.

65. Interview with party leaders, political activists and non-party Kurds in Syria and in Europe between 2002 and 2007.

66. Interview with Kurdish publisher, 30 June 2007.

67. Interview with Kurdish lawyer, 20 June 2007.

68. Ibid.; Sieda written response 08 August 2010.

69. Interview with non-party Kurds in Syria and Europe 2002–2007.

70. Miran 22 January 2010.

71. In a meeting with Kurdish party leader Hamid Darwish, Mustafa Tlas (the former Minister of Defence, until 2004) suggested that 30,000 stateless Kurds would have their citizenship rights reviewed.

72. Interviews with *ajanib* Kurds, Syria 2007.

73. KurdWatch December 2009: 15, 21.

74. *Yekîtî* was one such party which pushed the regimes 'red lines'. However, the division in the party between the Syrian organisation and that in Europe over the inclusion of a demand for autonomy for the Kurdish regions in Syria shows that, in Syria, the party remained vulnerable to pressures from the regime to conform to its red lines.

Chapter 5. The Role of Kurdish Parties in Kurdish Society

1. Tejel describes the Kurdish parties in Syria as having three functions: first, as guides and unwitting guinea pigs to test the limits of the Syrian regime *vis á vis* the Kurdish movement in Syria. Second, they have become a replacement or alternative to local authorities, particularly in the rural areas, through their involvement in mediation in local problems such as land disputes and honour crises. Third, and most important, is their role in cultural framing among the Syrian Kurds.

2. Tejel cites Snow et al 1986: 464 as the source of this definition. This extract does not however appear in the cited article.

3. Snow et al 1986: 464.

4. Sieda written responses to questions, 20 September 2010; interviews with Kurdish publisher, 30 June 2007; Haval Yousef, 20 August 2006.

5. Interview with Azad Ali, 11 June 2007. Hilal's study on the Jazira (Hilal 1962/3) and the memoirs of Sa'id al-Sayyid (see KurdWatch March 2010) demonstrate that this line of thinking was present among top ranking state officials in this region.

6. Interview with Azad Ali, 11 June 2007.

7. Interview with Sieda and his written response to questions, 04 July 2010.

8. Interviews with Sheikh Ali, 30 July 2006; Mustafa Juma'a, 09 July 2007; Kurdish publisher, 30 June 2007; Kurd from Efrîn, 20 June 2007, amongst others.

9. See for example HRW 31 January 2002.

10. HRW 31 January 2002.

11. Osman Sabri himself wrote and published a book on writing in the Kurdish language entitled 'Alif Baa Kurdi' in 1954 which promoted the Latin-based writing system.
12. Interview with Kamiran Hajo, 31 May 2010.
13. Interviews with party leaders, Khalil Daoud, 10 June 2007; Sheikh Ali, 22 June 2007; Dr Abdul Hakim Bashar, 12 August 2006; Marwan Osman, 10 June 2003.
14. For example Isamil Omar was a teacher of Geography, Nazir Mustafa a lawyer, Dr Abdul Hakim Bashar was a practicing children's doctor, Fuad Aliko was a math teacher, Nusradin Ibrahim has a Masters in Mathematics, Muhammad Musa and Aziz Daoud both have degrees in Philosophy.
15. Interviews with party leaders, Syria, 2006, 2007. Khalil Daoud, 10 June 2007; Sheikh Ali, 22 June 2007; Dr Abdul Hakim Bashar, 12 August 2006; Jamal Sheikh Baqi, 26 June 2007.
16. See Amnesty International 2007.
17. See for example *Hiwar* 58–59, Winter and *Pênûs* No 17, Spring 2005.
18. Interview with Azad Ali, 11 June 2007.
19. Issue 60–61, Summer/Autumn 2008.
20. Interview with Azad Ali, 11 June 2007.
21. McDowall 1998: 17.
22. Pers com. with Kurdish music vendors in Damascus, August 2002.
23. Interviews with Kurdish party leaders, Syria 2002, 2006, 2007.
24. Interview with Aziz Othman, 11 May 2010.
25. Interview with Khalil Daoud, 10 June 2007.
26. Interviews with Abdul Karim, 29 June 2007; Kihalil Daoud, 10 June 2007.
27. Interviews with Kurdish party leaders, Syria 2002, 2006, 2007.
28. Interview with Kamiran Hajo, 31 May 2010.
29. Tejel 2009: 105.
30. Interviews with Kurds from Efrîn, Syria June 2007.
31. The first time that Syrian officials encouraged Newroz celebrations, even sending officials to participate in them and to cover it on Syrian television, was in March 2011. This change of policy took place amid attempts by the government to appease the Kurds and prevent their involvement in the nascent Syrian uprising. Bashar al-Assad even commented that he had not known that Kurdish Newroz celebrations were so festive and that had he known he would have joined in. Bassam Mustafa 21 April 2011.
32. McDowall 1998: 50–51.
33. ACCORD & DIS 2010: 33.
34. By the end of 2009 a number of political party leaders from *Yekîtî*, *Azadî* and *el-Partî* had been arrested. Several Kurds had been arrested in a silent protest against Decree 49 in February 2009, marking the anniversary of the Qamishli uprising of 2004, and of Halabja on 16 March as well as during Newroz celebrations (when more than 50 Kurds had been arrested).
35. Sieda written response to questions, 04 July 2010.
36. Interviews with Kurds from Syria (2002–2009) confirmed this.

37. Interview with Kurdish publisher, 30 June 2007.
38. See for example KNNTV 21 February 2010. Kurds of the region of the Aliyan tribe celebrated in Hilaq village, while those of Terbispi and surrounding areas went to Dêrîk.
39. See *Yekîtî* party statement 23 March 2009. In 2009 in Efrîn a Kurdish man was arrested simply for lighting a fire, traditional in the Newroz festival.
40. Three Kurds were shot dead and five others injured when police opened fire on Kurds after an argument broke out between Kurdish youths and a police officer. Source AFP 21 March 2008; HRW 23 March 2008 and 26 March 2010.
41. In 1986 a young boy, Sulaiman Hamad Amin was killed when police opened fire on crowds celebrating in Damascus and three Kurds were killed in Efrîn. Montgomery 2005: 105. In 2008 three Kurds were shot dead and five others injured when police opened fire on Kurds after an argument broke out between Kurdish youths and a police officer. (Source AFP 21 March 2008; HRW 23 March 2008 and 26 March 2010.) In Qamishli three were killed when plain-clothed intelligence officials fired on the crowds when they failed to disperse after police had used tear gas and fired live ammunition in the air. HRW November 2009: 3, 23–24.
42. Speeches given at *el-Partî* Newroz celebration in the Kurd Dagh, March 2007.
43. See for example HRW 2009: 18, 22–25.
44. See *Yekîtî* Party statement 23 March 2009.
45. For example, *Tevgera Cewanen Kurd* (the Kurdish Youth Movement) was established in 2005.
46. Interview with Kurdish journalist, 21 June 2007.
47. Interviews with Kurdish publisher, 30 June 2007; Kurdish lawyer, 20 June 2007; Farzan Domar, 04 July 2007; Sieda written response, 26 March 2010.
48. Interview with Kurdish publisher, 30 June 2007.
49. Interview with Abdul Karim, 29 June 2007.
50. Rondot 1939: 95.
51. Lescot: 1988/1940: 104.
52. Interview with Sheikh, 22 April 2010; Kurdish family in Efrîn, 25 June 2007.
53. Interviews with Kurds from Kurd Dagh region, Syria and Europe; Kurdish family in Efrîn, 25 June 2007.
54. Interview with Kurds from Kurd Dagh; Sheikh, 22 April 2010.
55. Interviews in Syria and Europe; Kurdish family in Efrîn, 25 June 2007.
56. Interview with Sheikh, 22 April 2010.
57. See Rondot 1939 and Velud 1991.
58. For example Hajo Agha of the Haverkan and Qaddur Beg. See for example Fuccaro 2003: 215; and Velud 1991.
59. Fuccaro 2003: 215–216.
60. Sieda written response to questions, 24 April 2010; KurdWatch March 2010.
61. Interview with Haval Yousef, 20 August 2006. Sieda 2003: 72.
62. Sieda 2003: 72.

63. A dunum is an Ottoman unit of area still commonly used in former Ottoman territories. Its value varies from place to place. In Syria it is equivalent to 1000m^2.

64. Interview with Kamiran Hajo, 31 May 2010.

65. Including Hasaka, Qamishli, Amûdê, Dêrîk (Malkiyah), Ras al-'Ayn (Serê Kaniyê).

66. Qaddur Beg was the former Qaimmaqam of Nesibin and proprietor of the land on which Qamishli was built. The first house in Qamishli was built in 1926. Velud 1991: 301.

67. For example, a survey by the French High Commission in 1941 puts the number of rural and urban Kurds in the *qada* of Qamishli at 38,470 to 1200, respectively, in the *qada* of Hasaka, 5720 and 59; in the *qada* of Tigre, 12,150 and 400. Velud 2000: 73.

68. Interview with Kobanî lawyer and tribal leader, 05 July 2007.

69. State education from grades 1–6 was made compulsory in 1981.

70. Sieda written response to questions, 04 July 2010.

71. Ibid.

72. Interview with Kobanî resident, 21 June 2007.

73. Interview with Khalil Doud, 10 June 2007.

74. Interviews with Haval Yousef, 20 August 2006; Khalil Daoud, 06 August 2006 and 10 June 2007.

75. Bassam Mustafa 21 April 2011.

76. Interview with Kurdish Lawyer, 20 June 2007.

77. Interview, London, Anon.

78. Interview Haval Yousef, 20 August 2006.

79. For example, Ismail Omar and Fuad Aliko. Sieda, written response to questions, 26 March 2010.

80. For example, Hamid Darwish and Meshaal Temmo. Sieda, written response to questions, 26 March 2010.

81. Sieda written response to questions, 26 March 2010.

82. Interviews with Sieda written response to questions, 26 March 2010; Haval Yousef, 20 August 2006.

83. Sieda written response to questions, 26 March 2010.

84. Ibid., 24 April 2010.

85. Ibid.; Interview Haval Yousef, 20 August 2006.

86. Interview with Haval Yousef, 20 August 2006.

87. Sieda written response to questions 24 April 2010; Haval Yousef, 20 August 2006.

88. Interview with Nazir Mustafa, 12 August 2006.

89. Sieda written response to questions, 26 March 2010.

90. Interview with Abdul Karim, 29 June 2007.

91. Sieda written response to questions, 26 March 2010; interview with Sheikh, 22 April 2010.

92. Interview with Haval Yousef, 20 August 2006.

93. Interviews with Haval Yousef, 20 August 2006; Gelo, 10 July 2007; Farzan Domar, 04 July 2007; Kobanî lawyer and tribal leader, 05 July 2007; Sieda written response to questions, 26 March 2010.

Chapter 6. The Stateless Kurds of Syria

1. It is not possible to give any accurate numbers of stateless Kurds in Syria because no public census of Kurds or stateless Kurds has yet been conducted. Even the results of the 1962 census are not available to the public.
2. There is no census data available to base estimates on other then the government estimate of 1995 that 75,000 Kurds were unregistered, which, based on the government's policy towards the Kurds, can be assumed to be an underestimation.
3. Refugees International 2006: 1.
4. Sieda written response to questions, 05 December 2006; interview with Haval Yousef, 20 August 2006.
5. Savelsberg at al 2003: 10. Haval Yusef (n.d.) cites 22,000.
6. Velud 1991: 301, 333, 433–434.
7. Christians of the areas generally favoured the cities, being engaged primarily in merchant trades.
8. KurdWatch March 2010: 6.
9. Ibid.
10. Interview with *ajanib* Kurds group, 11 June 2007.
11. KurdWatch March 2010: 9.
12. Interview with *ajanib* Kurds group, 11 June 2007.
13. Sieda written response to questions, 17 November 2006.
14. An independent internet portal that reports on human rights abuses against the Kurdish population in Syria. KurdWatch March 2010: 10.
15. Sieda written response to questions, 17 November 2006.
16. Sieda: 2003: 102.
17. Interview with *ajanib* Kurds group, 11 June 2007; KurdWatch March 2010: 9.
18. Article 20 of Decree 93. KurdWatch March 2010: 8–9.
19. Sieda: 2003: 102.
20. Many villages are still not connected to state mains supplies.
21. Interview with Kurdish lawyer, 05 September 2002.
22. Sieda written response to questions, 17 November 2006. Sieda 2003: 102.
23. HRW 1996: 14–15.
24. HRAS, November 2003; Interviews with Kurdish lawyer, 05 September 2002; Kurdish author, 04 September 2002; Kamiran Bekes, 21 December 2002; A*janib* Kurds group, 11 June 2007.
25. According to Abdalbaset Sieda, the committee included one Christian from Damascus who supported the rights of Armenians and Assyrians to retain citizenship. As a result of his lobbying through the church, the date before which Christians were required to prove residency in Syria was changed to 1950 instead of 1945 and the majority of Christians retained Syrian citizenship.
26. HRW 1996, Appendix A.

27. Ibid.
28. Between 1945 and 1962 in Turkey, the Kurds were not politically organised and consequently faced no major conflicts with the state authorities. In Iraq, one of Barzani's rebellions ended in 1945 and after that a further rebellion began in 1961 against Qassim's government. The period in question (1945–1962) was relatively quiet in the Kurdish areas of Syria's neighbour states, Iraq and Turkey. While economic migration could account for some migration of Kurds to Syria, taking into account the underdevelopment of the Jazira region, it is extremely unlikely that 120,000 Kurds could have entered the Jazira illegally, for economic reasons, and would have also then been able to illegally aquire Syrian citizenship.
29. Sieda 2003: 101.
30. In Hasaka province and to the Kurds, this word refers to one category of stateless Kurd, and not to other foreigners.
31. Sieda written response to questions, 05 December 2006.
32. Sieda: 2003: 101.
33. Haval Yusef n.d.; Yekîtî, September 2003: 6.
34. HRAS, November 2003: 6.
35. Mamo Alo is an interviewee classified as *ajanib* in Syria.
36. Interview with Mamo Alo, 28 November 2006.
37. Interview with Jawad Mella, 27 October 2003.
38. Sieda written response to questions, 17 November 2006.
39. For example, a government census of *ajanib* Kurds conducted in 2008 put the number of *ajanib* in the small town of Dêrîk at 48,200. In Amudê there were 28,000, Qamishli 12,500. KurdWatch March 2010: 13.
40. Sieda written response to questions, 17 November 2006; KurdWatch March 2010: 13.
41. Sieda written response to questions, 17 November 2006.
42. It has been reported that yellow cards have also been issued. Interview with Mamo Alo, 24 January 2007.
43. It is unclear whether this was extended to all *ajnabi*–citizen marriages.
44. If a Syrian citizen marries an *ajnabi* or *maktum* it may be possible to get special permission to have the marriages registered, in which case the children may be able to retain citizenship or take *ajnabi* status. However the procedure is very complicated and requires investigation by the Political Security Directorate. KurdWatch March 2010: 15–17.
45. I am aware of only one, exceptional case in which a *maktumah* female was given her high school diploma and leave to take a BA in the University of Aleppo by the Minister of Higher Education in Damascus. Interview with Mamo Alo, 02 February 2007.
46. HRW 1996.
47. *Itihad al-Sha'ab*, November 2001: 6–7. Confirmed by KurdWatch March 2010. HRAS, November 2003: 8.
48. The interview took place in 2007, indicating that his father had been born in 1937, well before the cut-off point (of 1945) for retaining Syrian citizenship in the 1962 census. Interview with *maktum* Kurd, 28 June 2007.

49. Mamo Alo (02 February 2007) claimed that the *maktumiin* could attend school until age 18, which is also confirmed by KurdWatch March 2010: 19. An interview with a group of four *ajanib* Kurds, two of whom had *maktumiin* children suggested that in Hasaka province itself, children were normally permitted to attend secondary school, but that outside this region the normal rule of only allowing primary education applied. Interviewees suggested that often whether or not a child would be granted permission to study beyond primary level depended on the mood of the officials dealing with the case. (11 June 2007). Human Rights Watch also states that the *maktumin* may only attend school up to year nine (normally age 12). HRW 1996.

50. Equivalent to A'levels. Interviews with stateless family in Dêrîk (names withheld). Interview with Mamo Alo, 24 January 2007. HRW 1996.

51. HRW 1996, copy of 'Special Notice of Successful Completion by Unregistered Persons'. Appendix D.

52. Interview with Mamo Alo, 02 February 2007; stateless Kurdish family 2, 28 June 2007.

53. Conversation with stateless Kurd, Damascus, 14 July 2007.

54. I was informed that one wealthy Kurdish man had paid for Syrian citizenship as recently as 2005, demonstrating further the arbitrary nature of denial of citizenship to Kurds. Interview with Stateless Kurdish family 1, 28 June 2007.

55. Lynch and Ali January 2006; Interview with stateless Kurdish family 2, 28 June 2007.

56. Interview with Mamo Alo, 02 February 2007. This denial of citizenship as a punative measure has also happened to the children of Arabs with political profiles.

57. HRW 1996: Appendix A.

58. Information Minister, Mehdi Daklallah cited 120,000 as the number of Kurds without citizenship in Syria. See IRIN 20 November 2005.

59. Interview with Mamo Alo 02 February 2007. Most other Kurds from Syria questioned about the number of stateless Kurds estimated 500,000.

60. KurdWatch March 2010: 13.

61. National service was reduced from two and a half years in 2005.

62. McDowall 1998: 53.

63. Interview with Mamo Alo, 28 November 2006; Kurdish Lawyer, 05 September 2002.

64. Interview with Kurdish lawyer, 05 September 2002. HRAS, November 2003.

65. Lynch and Ali 2006.

66. Meaning 'people of the flood' and referring to Arabs moved from Raqqa district to specially built state villages on the border areas of the Jazira when the al-Assad Dam was built in the 1970s.

67. Interview with Mamo Alo, 24 January 2007.

68. Bedr al-Din 2003.

69. Interview with *ajanib* Kurds group, 11 June 2007.

70. Sieda written response to questions, 17 November 2006.

71. Ibid.

72. Observations of homes of stateless Kurds in Dêrîk 2002 and in Zor Ava 2007. Interview with Mamo Alo, 24 January 2007.
73. Sieda written response to questions. 05 December 2006; Interview with Mamo Alo 02 February 2007.
74. Interview with Mamo Alo, 24 January 2007.
75. Interview with stateless Kurdish family 2, 28 June 2007.
76. Interview with stateless Kurdish family 2, 28 June 2007. This qualified man, with years of experience in his job, earned 400 Syrian Lira per day, the equivalent of £4.00.
77. Interview with *maktum* Kurd, 28 June 2007; *ajanib* Kurds group, 11 June 2007; stateless Kurdish family 2 and 1, 28 June 2007.
78. Interview with Mamo Alo, 24 January 2007.
79. Ibid.; *ajanib* Kurds group, 11 June 2007.
80. Selling goods on a mobile street stall requires permission from the local council. Interview with *ajanib* Kurds group, 11 June 2007; stateless Kurdish family 2 and 1, 28 June 2007.
81. Interviews with *ajanib* Kurds group, 11 June 2007; stateless Kurdish family 2 and 1, 28 June 2007; Interview with and observations of street trader, Damascus August 2002.
82. In 2002, five Syrian lira was equivalent to ten pence.
83. Yousef, 04 October 2004.
84. There are 100 Qursh to one lira.
85. Sieda written response to questions, 05 December 2006.
86. Interview with Mamo Alo, 24 January 2007. One Syrian lira at the time of writing in 2013 was approximately one penny.
87. Sieda written response to questions, 29 November 2006; interviews with *ajanib* Kurds group, 11 June 2007; stateless Kurdish family 2 and 1, 28 June 2007.
88. Sieda written response to questions, 29 November 2006. Interview with *ajanib* Kurds group, 11 June 2007; stateless Kurdish family 2 and 1, 28 June 2007.
89. Interview with Mamo Alo, 02 February 2007.
90. Sieda written response to questions, 05 December 2006.
91. Interview with Haval Yousef, 20 August 2006.
92. KurdWatch July 2010: 11.
93. Interview with Jamal Sheikh Baqi, 28 June 2007.
94. Lynch and Ali 2006.
95. Interviews with Jamal Sheikh Baqi, 28 June 2007; Mamo Alo, 24 January 2007.
96. 'The Dumer project'. Dumer is the name of the town next to which the project was built.
97. 'The New Damascus' (or Syria).
98. Interview with Jamal Sheikh Baqi, 28 June 2007; stateless Kurdish family 1, 28 June 2007; stateless Kurdish family 2, 28 June 2007.
99. Lynch and Ali 2006.
100. Sieda written response to questions, 05 December 2006.
101. Interviews with stateless Kurdish family 1, 28 June 2007; stateless Kurdish family 2, 28 June 2007.

102. Interview with stateless Kurdish family 1, 28 June 2007.

103. Ibid.

104. Reported on Amude.com. While in Syria I saw the site of the demolitions. Local residents said that many other homes in the area were built without licence.

105. Interviews with stateless Kurdish family 1, 28 June 2007; stateless Kurdish family 2, 28 June 2007.

106. Interview with stateless Kurdish family 2, 28 June 2007.

107. Interviews with Jamal Sheikh Baqi, 28 June 2007 and 26 June 2007; stateless Kurdish family 2, 28 June 2007.

108. In attempting to visit the area in July 2007 many of my informants refused to take me there because of the presence of the *mukhabarat*. They compared the area to Qamishli where state policing and surveillance are very high. Eventually, I was taken to observe the area and to meet and interview some local families after dark, in order to avoid attention.

109. Lynch and Ali 2006: 3.

110. Interview with *ajanib* Kurds group, 11 June 2007; stateless Kurdish family 2 and 1, 28 June 2007.

111. Interview with *ajanib* Kurds group, 11 June 2007; Mamo Alo, 24 January 2007.

112. Interview with Mamo Alo, 24 January 2007.

113. Conversations with Kurds, Damascus 2002. Names withheld.

114. Interview with Mamo Alo, 24 January 2007.

115. Interview with *ajanib* Kurds group: 11 June 2007; stateless Kurdish family 2 and 1, 28 June 2007.

116. Interview with Mamo Alo, 24 January 2007; *ajanib* Kurds group: 11 June 2007; stateless Kurdish family 2 and 1, 28 June 2007.

117. Interview with Mamo Alo, 24 January 2007; *ajanib* Kurds group, 11 June 2007.

118. Interview with Mamo Alo, 24 January 2007.

119. Ibid.

120. Interviews with Jamal Sheikh Baqi, 2806/07; *ajanib* Kurds group, 11 June 2007; Mamo Alo, 24 January 2007; stateless Kurdish family 2, 28 June 2007.

121. Sieda written response to questions, 05 December 2006.

122. Interviews with party leaders, Sheikh Ali, 06 August 2006; Nazir Mustafa, 12 August 2006; Ismail Omar, 12 August 2006.

123. Interviews with Stateless Kurdish family 1 and 2, 28 June 2007; Mamo Alo, 02 February 2007, 24 January 2007; *ajanib* Kurds group, 11 June 2007; *maktum* Kurd, 28 June 2007.

124. UN CCPR 08 May 2001.

125. See Kurdistan Observer, 28 April 2004. It is also reported that this initiative had been proposed before the Qamishli uprising and then was frozen because of it. See Lynch and Ali January 2006.

126. IRIN News 12 August 2006; Aslam 15 February 2006.

127. Amude.com 18 July 2007; KurdWatch March 2010.

128. Interview with Turkish television station Sky News in December 2005, cited by KurdWatch March 2010: 23–24.
129. Institut Kurde de Paris May 2004.
130. UN CCPR 19 October 2004.
131. Zoepf, 28 April 2005. Interview with Mamo Alo, 02 February 2007.
132. KurdWatch March 2010: 22–23.
133. Interviews with Mamo Alo, 02 February 2007, 24 January 2007.
134. Interview with Haval Yousef, 20 August 2006.
135. KurdWatch March 2010: 24.
136. Thomas McGee, written response, 01 October 2012.
137. Bayat 1997.

Chapter 7. The Eve of the Syrian Uprising: Crisis and Consciousness

1. Here national consciousness is associated with identification with Kurdish culture, actively seeking to increase public expression of pride in national identity and awareness of and interest in Kurdish issues and seeking an end to their suppression in Syria.
2. Interviews with independent Kurdish activists in Syria, 2006, 2007.
3. Interview with party leaders, Syria 2002–2007.
4. There are of course exceptions, for example Aziz Daoud is said to be of a poor family and supported by serious intellectuals within the political leadership in Syria. Sieda written response to questions, 26 March 2010.
5. The PUK was founded in Damascus and retains offices in Syria. The KDP has offices in Syria, in Damascus and Qamishli. The PKK was based in Syria from 1980 until 1998 when Öcalan was expelled.
6. Interviews with Jamal Sheikh Baqi, 26 June 2007; Sieda written response, 26 March 2010; Kurdish Lawyer, 20 June 2007 amongst others.
7. For example, *Harakat Hurriyah Kurdistan* established in 2008 and was crushed by the Syrian authorities in 2009. Its leaders were arrested and sentenced with eight to ten years imprisonment.
8. This is true for both the new party and the old party. The old party may lose a faction based in one area, thus diminishing its power in that area.
9. White 2000: 139.
10. Dr Zaza left Syria for Lebanon in 1963 where he stayed until the government returned him to Syria, where he was arrested. After his release he fled to Turkey in 1967, and then in 1970 he moved back to Switzerland where he remained until his death in 1988.
11. According to Muhammad Rashid, author of a biography of Osman Sabri, in 1969 Sabri resigned from the party after the party leader Salah Bedr al-Din and other members of the leadership began developing relations with other parties and members of the security services without consulting Sabri. He went secretly to Turkey in 1970, but after witnessing his

son's death there, he returned to Syria where he was imprisoned. Rashid 1994: 35.

12. Such as *Partîya Dêmokrat a Kurdî ya Sûrî (el-Sûrî)* of Jamal Sheikh Baqi and *Partîya Dêmokrat a Kurdî li Sûriyê* of Nusradin Ibrahim.

13. Sieda written response to questions, 20 September 2010.

14. Sieda written response to questions, 04 July 2010. Interview with Kurdish publisher, 30 June 2007.

15. Interview with Kurdish Publisher, 30 June 2007.

16. As it was developed by the Bedirkhan brothers, Kurdish nationalism was a modernising and progressive force that aimed to 'civilise' the Kurdish people and westernise them.

17. The 'women question' first entered Kurdish press in 1913 in the publication *Roji Kurd*. Klein 2001: 26, 28, 42 n.2.

18. Interview with Kurdish publisher, 30 June 2007.

19. For example, charges of attempting to separate part of Syrian territory and attach it to a foreign state, belonging to a proscribed organisation, inciting sectarian strife, spreading false information about the state, weakening the national sentiment, all stipulated in the Syrian Penal Code.

20. Sieda written response to questions, 26 March 2010; interviews with Kurdish publisher, 30 June 2007; Kurdish lawyer, 20 June 2007; Kurdish journalist, 21 June 2007.

21. Syriatel, owned by Rami Makhlouf, first cousin of Bashar al-Assad, and MTN Syria.

22. At the time of publication in 2013, there were still only two operators.

23. Cellular-News 25 August 2010.

24. ITP.net, 02 June 2009.

25. The Syrian population in 2005 was approximately 18.5 million. In 2010 the population was estimated to be more than 22 million.

26. UN ESCWA 0309/07: 6.

27. Ibid., 8.

28. US State Department 11 March 2010.

29. UN ESCWA 0309/07: 5.

30. For example www.amude.net and www.kurdwatch.org which are both run from Germany.

31. The article published on 7 May 2009 was entitled 'The reality of the conciliation in Tahaluf'/'*Haqiqat ra'ab al-sad'a fi al-tahaluf*'.

32. Miran 22 January 2010.

33. An exception is *Yekîtî*, (http://yekitimedia.org/) which includes much party documents and up to date news in Arabic, Kurdish, German and English.

34. Founded on 1 March 2004.

35. ICT 1999.

36. See for example DPA 25 February 2010; Rojhelat 31 August 2010.

37. 1. Kurdistan TV, 2. ROJ TV, 3. KurdSat, 4. Zagros TV, 5. Newroz TV, 6. MMC, 7. Newroz Channel, 8. Geli Kurdistan, 9. Vin TV, 10. Kurd 1, 11.

TISHK TV, 12. Rojhelat TV, 13. ASO SAT, 14. Kurd Channel, 15. Rojawa TV, 16. Partow TV, 17. Komala TV, 18. Payam TV, 19. KNN, 20. KMC.

38. For example Ismail Omar became a member of *el-Partî* when he was 15 as did Nazir Mustafa former leader of *el-Partî*. Interviews 12 August 2006.

39. Interview with tribe leader and lawyer from Kobanî.

40. For example Nazir Mustafa, Abdul Hamid Darwish and Ismail Omar.

41. Interviews with Kurdish journalist, 21 June 2007; Kurdish lawyer, 20 June 2007; Kurdish publisher, 30 June 2007.

42. Interviews with Syrian Kurds 2002–2010, Syria and Europe.

43. Having changed its name to *Partîya Yekîtî ya Dêmokrat a Kurd li Sûriyê*.

44. Kurdish students in Aleppo began demonstrating to protest issues such as the connection of the Students Union to the Ba'th Party and the states abolishment of their obligation to employ graduating engineers and architects, on 27 January 2004 and 26 February 2004 respectively. Gauthier 2009: 109.

45. Gauthier 2009: 110.

46. Sieda written response to questions, 20 September 2010.

Chapter 8. The Kurdish Response to the Syrian Uprising

1. KurdWatch 08 August 2011.

2. Youth organisations such as Union of Young Kurdish Coordinating Committees, Kurdish Sawa Youth Coalition (part of the Local Coordinating Committees), the General Commission of Kurdish Youth Mobility in Syria, Tevgera Ciwanen Kurd, Avahi Coalition for the Syrian Revolution, Coordinating Committee for Brotherhood, Aleppo, Efrîn Youth Coordination, and the Alind Kûbanî Coordination played a leading role in the first year of the uprising. Many of these organisations existed before the start of the uprising. *Tevgera Cewanen Kurd* was established following the Qamishli Uprising.

3. Ismail Hemi, Secretary of *Yekîtî*, cited by KurdWatch 17 September 2011. Interviews with Zara Saleh, 06 October 2012; Muhammad Temmo, 04 October 2012; written response from Abdulrazzaq Temmo, 29 September 2012.

4. The party representatives that gave speeches were, for *Azadî*, Saadoun Mahmoud Sheikho, and for *Yekîtî* Mahmoud Amo (politburo). Support Kurds in Syria 20 May 2011.

5. Interviews with Kurdish activists.

6. KurdWatch Report December 2011.

7. Only *Partîya Dêmokrat a Kurdî li Sûriyê* of Abdul Rahman Aluji, which had broken off from Dr Abdul Hakim's party, and *Rekeftin*, which was a faction of the PYD, were not included in the alliance.

8. Written response to questions, 19 July 2012.

9. The invited group did not include the PYD which, as a member of the NCB, remained open to dialogue with the regime on condition of the cessation of all violent acts against civilians. KurdWatch Report December 2011.

10. Daragahi, Borzou and Abigail Fielding-Smith 04 January 2012.
11. The party later left the SNC.
12. Support Kurds in Syria 28 October 2011.
13. Moas, Taghee 25 April 2012.
14. Interview with Abdulbasset Sieda 02 October 2012.
15. By July 2012 the number of political parties within the KNC was 16.
16. Interviews with Kurdish exiles; KurdWatch interview with Azad Muhiyudin; Adib Abdulmajid 14 January 2013.
17. Abdul Rahman Aluji died on 24 May 2012. During the party conference held on 4–5 October 2012 disagreements about leadership of the party produced a split between the groups of Dr Lezgin Muhammad Fakhri and Abdul Karim Sako.
18. KurdWatch interview with Rezan Bahri Sheikhmus 19 January 2012.
19. Ibid.
20. For example see KurdWatch news reports for 2011–2012.
21. Dr Semo written response to questions, 10 October 2012 and PCWK press release 'the Declaration of the Peoples Council of Western Kurdistan'.
22. PCWK 'The Declaration of the Peoples Council of Western Kurdistan'.
23. Barhan Ghalioun was president of the SNC until June 2012.
24. See YouTube uploads of amateur videos of demonstrations.
25. Salih Muslim interview by KurdWatch 08 November 2011.
26. Interview with Mohammed Temmo, 04 October 2012.
27. Adib Abdulmajid 08/05/12.
28. Heyam Aqil, written response to questions, 08 October 2012.
29. Text of the KNC programme.
30. Hemin Khoshnaw 16 July 2012.
31. Interview with Asya Abdullah by ANF News Agency, 27 October 2012.
32. Soner Cagaptay, 15 April 2012.
33. Alan Semo, written response to questions, 19 June 2012.
34. Salih Muslim Muhammad interviewed by KurdWatch 08 November 2011. The party has since clarified its position, openly calling for the fall of the regime and for Kurdish self-adminisation in Syria.
35. The PYD took up arms during the Syrian uprising for defensive purposes. The YPG units (*Yekîneyên Parastina Gel*/the People's Defence Units) are the only armed units and operate only within the Kurdish regions.
36. The Kurdish Globe 13 December 2012.
37. Interveiws with local residents.
38. Kafr Janna is in the region of Efrîn. KurdWatch 02 June 2012.
39. Such as the Meshaal Temmo brigade and the Salah al-Din Ayubi brigade.
40. KurdWatch 12 June 2012.
41. KurdWatch Interview with Azad Muhiyuddin 21 March 2012.
42. Interviews with Kurdish activists.
43. KurdWatch Interview with Azad Muhiyuddin 21 March 2012.
44. *Yekîneyên Parastina Gel* in Kurdish and know as the YPG. Armed units linked to the PYD.

45. KurdWatch 11 June 2012(b).
46. KurdWatch 11 June 2012(a).
47. Adib Abdulmajid 10 June 2012.
48. Hossino et al, September 2012.
49. AFP 31 July 2012.
50. Hossino et al, September 2012.
51. Minutes of the Meeting. Translation by KurdWatch.
52. Hevidar Ahmed 01 August 2012.
53. Salih Muslim quoted by Hossino et al, September 2012.
54. Hossino et al, September 2012: 10.
55. Ibid., 13.
56. Alan Semo written response 16 February 2013.
57. Hevidar Ahmed 01 August 2012.
58. Hevidar Ahmed 18 September 2012.
59. Interviews. PYD was accused of assassinating an *el-Partî* leader, Nasiradin Piro in Efrîn, and of its cadre of kidnapping Kurdish activists. Hevidar Ahmed 01 August 2012.
60. The PYD defended this action saying that it did so to prevent the provocation of local Kurds against symbols associated with the FSA.
61. Wilgenberg 05 November 2012.
62. On 15 December 2012 these parties joined in a union (*Hevgirtina Siyasi Demokratî ya Kurdî li Sûriyê*/the Kurdish Political Democratic Union in Syria which was formed as a step towards the eventual merger of the parties into a single party. The parties included were *Partîya Dêmokrat a Kurdî li Sûriyê (el-Partî)*/the Kurdish Democratic Party in Syria (the Party) of Dr Abdul Hakim Bashar; the two parties named *Partîya Azadî ya Kurd li Suryê*/Kurdish Freedom Party in Syria, of Mustafa Juma'a and Mustafa Oso; and *Partîya Yekîtî ya Kurd li Sûriyê*/Kurdish Union Party in Syria of Ismail Hemi.
63. Conversations with Kurds in Syria.
64. For example: Hossino et al, September 2012; ORSAM 2012.
65. Interview with Abdulbaset Sieda, 13 October 2012.
66. Hossino et al, September 2012.
67. Sherlok 06 July 2012.
68. Wilgenberg 20 August 2012.
69. Hevidar Ahmed 01 August 2012.
70. Interview 13 October 2012.
71. See, for example, International Crisis Group, January 2013 and ORSAM 2012.
72. ORSAM 2012: 28–29.

BIBLIOGRAPHY

Academic Books and Articles

Ahmed, Muhammad Mulla 2001: *al-Qadayah al-Kurdiyah fi Suriya* (Havîbun, Berlin).

——— 2000: *Jama'iyat Khoybun wa al-'Alaqat al-Kurdiyah–Armaniyah* (KAWA, Bonn, Germany).

——— 1988: *Safhat min Tarikh Harakah al-Taharur al-WaTani al-Kurdiyah fi Suriya* (Personal copy on file, published in Germany).

Ahmed, Muhammed M. A. and Micheal Gunter (eds.) 2007: *The Evolution of Kurdish Nationalism* (Mazda Publishers, California).

Alakoum, Rohat 2001: *Khoybun wa Thawrat Agiri* (Kawa, Bonn).

Albrecht, Holger 2008: 'The nature of political participation' in Ellen Lust-Okar and Saloua Zerhouni (eds.) 2008: *Political Participation in the Middle East* (Lynne Rienner Publishers, London) pp.15–32.

Alhamad, Laila 2008: 'Formal and informal venues of engagement' in Ellen Lust-Okar and Saloua Zerhouni (eds.) 2008: *Political Participation in the Middle East* (Lynne Rienner Publishers, London) pp.33–47.

Almund, G. S. Verber 1989: *The Civic Society: Political Attitudes and Democracy in Five Nations* (Sage Publications, London).

Anderson, Benedict 1991: *Imagined Communities: Reflections on the Origin and Spread of Nationalism* (Verso, London).

Angrist, Michele Penner and Marsha Pripstein Posusney (eds.) 2005: *Authoritarianism in the Middle East: Regimes and Resistance* (Lynne Rienner Publishers, London).

Aykan, Mahmut Bali June 1999: 'The Turkish-Syrian crisis of October 1998: a Turkish view' in *Middle East Policy*, Vol. VI, No 4, (Blackwells, Oxford).

Ayubi, N. 1995: *Over-stating the Arab State Politics and Society in the Middle East* (I.B.Tauris, London).

Barnett, Michael N. 1988: *Dialogues in Arab Politics: Negotiations in Regional Order* (Columbia University Press, New York).

Bayat, Asef 2003: 'The "street" and the politics of dissent in the Arab world' in *Middle East Report* No. 226, Spring, available at http://www.merip.org/mer/mer226/226_bayat.html (accessed 02/10/07).

——— 2000: 'From "Dangerous classes" to "quiet rebels": politics of the urban subaltern in the global south', in *International Sociology* Vol. 15, No. 3 (Sage, London) pp.533–557.

——— 1997: *Street Politics: Poor People's Movements in Iran* (Columbia University Press, USA).

——— 1996: 'Cairo's poor: dilemmas of survival and solidarity' in *Middle East Report* No. 202, Winter, available at http://www.merip.org/mer/mer202/poor.html (accessed 02/10/07).

Bedr al-Din, Salah 2003: *The Kurdish National Movement in Syria* (Kawa, Erbil).

——— 2000: *Gharb Kurdistan: Dirasah Tarikhiyah – Siyasiyah – wa Thaqafiyah Mawjzah* (KAWA, Germany).

Bodman, Herbert L. 1963: *Political Factions in Aleppo 1760–1826* (University of Carolina Press, USA).

Bou-Nacklie, N. E. 1993: 'Les troupes speciales: religious and ethnic recruitment 1916–46' in *The International Journal of Middle Eastern Studies*, Vol. 25, No. 4, (Cambridge University Press, Cambridge) pp.645–660.

Bozarslan, Hamit 2006: 'Tribal *asabiyya* and Kurdish politics: a socio-historic perspective' in Jabar, Faleh A. and Hasham Dawod (eds.) 2006: *The Kurds: Nationalism and Politics* (Saqi, London) pp.130–147.

Breuilly, J. 1993 (2nd ed.): *Nationalism and the State* (Manchester University Press, Manchester).

Browers, Michelle 2006: *Democracy and Civil Society in Arab Political Thought: Transcultural Possibilities* (Syracuse University Press, NY).

Bruinessen, Martin van 2003: 'Ehmedî Khanî's Mem û Zîn and its role in the emergence of Kurdish national awareness' in Abbas Vali (ed.) 2003: *The Origins of Kurdish Nationalism* (Mazda Publishers Ltd, California) pp.40–57.

——— 2003: 'Kurds, States and Tribes' in Jabar, Faleh A. and Hosham Dawoud (eds.) 2003: *Tribes and Power: Nationalism and Ethnicity in the Middles East* (Saqi, London).

——— 2000: 'Transnational aspects of the Kurdish question,' working paper, Robert Schuman Centre for Advanced Studies, European University Institute, Florence, available online at http://www.hum.uu.nl/medeworkers/m.vanbruinessen/publications/transnational_Kurds.htm (accessed 31/03/14).

——— 1999: 'Kurds, states, and tribes', paper presented at the conference 'Tribes and Powers in the Middle East' at London, SOAS, Birkbeck College and Iraqi Cultural Forum, 23–24 January, available online at http://www.hum.uu.nl/medeworkers/m.vanbruinessen/publications/Bruinessen_Kurds_States_and_Tribes.pdf (accessed 31/03/14).

——— 1994: 'Kurdish nationalism and competing ethnic loyalties', original English version of: 'Nationalisme kurde et ethnicités intra-kurdes', *Peuples Méditerranéens* No. 68–69, pp.11–37, available online at http://www.hum.uu.nl/medeworkers/m.vanbruinessen/publications/Competing_Ethnic_Loyalties.htm (accessed 31/03/14).

———— 1946: *Agha, Shaikh and State: On the Social and Political Organization of Kurdistan* (Enroprint).

Carothers, Thomas 2006: *Confronting the Weakest Link: Aiding Political Parties in New Democracies* (Carnegie Endowment for International Peace, Washington).

Chaliand, G (ed.) 1993: *A People Without a Country: The Kurds and Kurdistan* (Zed Books, London).

Daly Hays, M. 1992: *The Safe Haven in Northern Iraq: International Responsibility for Iraqi Kurdistan*, Woodrow Wilson Paper No. 200 (Woodrow Wilson Centre, Washington DC).

Dam, Nikolaos van 1996: *The Struggle for Power in Syria: Politics and Society Under Asad and the Ba'th Party* (I.B.Tauris, London).

Darwish, Abd al-Hamid 2000: *Aduā' 'ala al-Haraka al-Kurdiya fi Suriya: Ahadāth Fatra 1956–1983* (n.p.).

Doded, Ruth Michal 1984: *Tradition and change in Syria during the last decade of Ottoman rule: the urban elite of Damascus, Aleppo, Homs and Hama, 1876–1918* (UMI, Michigan).

Eli, Dr Mihemed n.d.: *Jabal al-Kurd: Dirasah Tarikhiyah Ijtima'iyah Tawthiqiyah* (n.p. Efrîn).

Epstein, Eliahu 1940: 'Al Jazireh' in *The Journal of the Royal Central Asian Society* (Routledge, London) pp.68–82.

Enfessar, N. 1992: *Kurdish Ethnonationalism* (Lynne Rienner Publishers, London).

Fomkin, David 1989: *A Peace to End all Peace* (Penguin Books, London).

Fuccaro, Nelida 2003: 'Kurds and Kurdish nationalism in Mandatory Syria: politics, culture and identity' in Abbas Vali (ed.) 2003: *The Origins of Kurdish Nationalism* (Mazda Publishers Ltd, California) pp.191–218.

———— 2003 (a) 'Ethnicity and the city: the Kurdish quarter of Damascus between Ottoman and French rule, c. 1724–1946,' in *Urban History* Vol. 30, (Cambridge University Press, Cambridge) pp.206–224.

———— 1999: *The Other Kurds: Yezidis in Colonial Iraq* (I.B.Tauris, London).

Gauthier, Julie 2009: 'The 2004 events in al-Qamishli: has the Kurdish question erupted in Syria?' in Fred H. Lawson (ed.) *Demystifying Syria* (Saqi, London & London Middle East Institute, London).

Gellner, Ernest 1983: *Nations and Nationalism* (Blackwell Publishers, Oxford).

———— 1997: *Nationalism* (Weidenfeld & Nicolson, London).

Gelvin, James 1998: *Divided Loyalties: Nationalism and Mass Politics in Syria at the Close of Empire* (University of California Press, London).

George, Alan 2002: *Syria Neither Bread nor Freedom* (Zed Books, London).

Gunther, Richard, Jose Ramon Montero, and Juan Linz 2002: *Political Parties: Old Concepts and New Challenges* (Oxford University Press, Oxford).

Hamo, Rashid 2001: *Thawrat Jabal Akrad: Harakah al-Muridiin* (Jamiy'a al-Haquq Mahfudhah lil-Katib, Syria).

———— n.d.: *al-Mas'alah al-Kurdiyah fi Suriyah* (private printing, n.p., Syria)

Hassenpour, Amir 1992: *Language and Nationalism in Kurdistan 1918–1985* (Mellen Research University Press, San Francisco).

————— 2003: 'The making of Kurdish identity: Pre-20th Century historical and literary discourses' in Abbas Vali (ed.) 2003: *The Origins of Kurdish Nationalism* (Mazda Publishers Ltd, California) pp.106–162.

Haywood, Andrew 2002 (2nd ed.): *Politics* (Palgrave, Basingstoke).

Heydemann, Steven 1999: *Authoritarianism in Syria: Institutions and Social Conflict 1946–1970* (Cornell University Press, USA).

Hilal, Muhammad Talab, n.d. (1962): *Darasa 'an Muhafazat al-Jazira, min al-Nawahi al-Qawmiya, al-Ijtimaa'iya, al-Sayasiya* (n.p., Syria).

Hinnebusch, Raymond 2002: 'The foreign policy of Syria' in Hinnebusch, Raymond and Anoushiravan Ehteshami (eds.) 2002: *The Foreign Policies of Middle East States* (Lynne Rienner, London) pp.141–166.

————— 2001: *Syria: Revolution from Above* (Routledge, London).

————— 1990: *Authoritarian Power and State Formation in Ba'thist Syria: Army, Party, and Peasant* (Westview Press, Oxford).

Hiwar 2008: No. 60–61 Summer and Autumn issue.

————— 2008: No. 58–59 Winter. Available on http://www.efrin.net/cms/erebi/files/hiwar/hiwar-58-59.pdf (accessed 20/03/09).

————— 2005: No.46–47 Winter and Spring issue.

Hobsbawm, Eric. 1992 (2nd ed.): *Nations and Nationalism since 1780: Programme, Myth and Reality* (Cambridge University Press, Cambridge).

Hopwood, David 1988: *Syria 1945–1986: Politics and Society* (Unwin Hyman, London).

Ismael, T. Y and J. S. Ismael, 1998: *The Communist Movement in Syria and Lebanon* (University Press of Florida, Gainesville).

'Issa, Khalil 2003: *al-Akrad wa Tashukul al-Dawlah al-Suriyyah* (n.p. Paris).

Izady, Mehrdad R. 1992: *The Kurds, a Concise Handbook* (Taylor & Francis, London).

Jabar, Faleh A. (ed.) 1997: *Post-Marxism and the Middle East* (Saqi, London).

Jabar, Faleh A. and Hosham Dawod (eds.) 2006: *The Kurds: Nationalism and Politics* (Saqi, London).

————— 2003: *Tribes and Power: Nationalism and Ethnicity in the Middle East* (Saqi, London).

Jwaideh, Wadie 2006: *The Kurdish National Movement: Its Origins and Development* (Syracuse University Press, Syracuse, New York).

Khouri, P. 1987: *Syria and the French Mandate: The Politics of Arab Nationalism, 1920–1945* (I.B.Tauris, London).

————— 1983: *Urban Notables and Arab Nationalism: The Politics of Damascus 1860–1920* (Cambridge University Press, Cambridge).

Kirişci, K. and Gareth M. Winrow, 1997: *The Kurdish Question and Turkey; an Example of a Trans-State Ethnic Conflict* (Frank Cass & Co. Ltd, London).

Klein, Janet 2001: 'En-gendering nationalism: The "woman question" in Kurdish nationalist discourse of the late Ottoman period' in Shahrzad Mojab (ed.) 2001: *Women of a Non-State Nation: The Kurds* (Mazda Publishers, California) pp.25–52.

Kreyenbroek, P. and S. Sperl (eds.) 1992: *The Kurds: A Contemporary Overview* (Routledge, London).

Lawson, Fred H. 1994: 'Syria' in Tachau, Frank (ed.) 1994: *Political Parties of the Middle East* (Mansell, London) pp.500–529.

———— (ed.) 2009: *Demystifying Syria* (Saqi, London).

Lesch, David W. 2005: *The New Lion of Damascus: Bashar al-Asad and Modern Syria* (Yale University Press, New Haven/London).

Lescot, Roger 1940/1988: 'Le Kurd Dagh et le movement Mouroud' in *Studia Kurdica* No. 1–5, (Institut Kurde de Paris, Paris) pp.101–125.

———— *Thawrah Jabal Akrad Dud al-Isti'amar al-Fransi fi Suriyah*. Above article (1940) translated from French to Arabic by Basam Kamil.

Leverett, Flynt 2005: *Inheriting Syria: Bashar's Trial by Fire* (Brookings Institute Press, Washington DC).

Lust-Okar, Ellen 2008: 'Taking political participation seriously' in Ellen Lust-Okar and Saloua Zerhouni (eds.) 2008: *Political Participation in the Middle East* (Lynne Rienner Publishers, London) pp.1–14.

Lust-Okar, Ellen and Saloua Zerhouni (eds.) 2008: *Political Participation in the Middle East* (Lynne Rienner Publishers, London).

Ma'oz, Moshe 2002: 'Middle Eastern minorities, between integration and conflict: an overview' in Ma'oz M. and Gabriel Sheffer (eds.) 2002 *Middle Eastern Minorities and Diasporas* (Sussex Academic Press, Brighton).

McDowall, David 2000 (2nd ed.): *A Modern History of the Kurds* (I.B.Tauris, London).

———— 1998: *The Kurds of Syria* (KHRP, London).

———— 1996 (1st ed.): *A Modern History of the Kurds* (I.B.Tauris, London).

Mella, Izz al-Din 'Ali 1998: *Hayy al-Akrad fi Madinat Dimashq bayna 'Amay 1250–1979* (Beirut).

Meriwether, Margaret Lee 1981: *The notable families of Aleppo, 1770–1830: networks and social structure* (UMI, Michigan).

Montgomery, Harriet 2005: *The Kurds of Syria: An Existence Denied* (Europäisches Zentrum für kurdische Studien, Berlin).

al-Mulhim, Nabil 1999: *Qa'id wa Sha'b: Saba't Ayam ma' Apo* (Dar al-Farabi, Beirut).

Natalie, Denise 2005: *The Kurds and the State: Evolving National Identity in Iraq, Turkey and Iran* (Syracuse University Press, Syracuse, New York).

Öcalan, Abdullah 1999: *Declaration on the Democratic Solution of the Kurdish Question* (Mesopotamia Publishers, London).

Olsen, Robert, 1997: 'Turkey–Syria relations since the Gulf War: Kurds and water,' in *Middle East Policy*, 5 (1997) 2 (May), (Blackwells, Oxford) pp.168–193.

———— 1996: *The Kurdish Nationalist Movement in the 1990s: It's Impact on Turkey and the Middle East* (The University Press of Kentucky, Kentucky).

———— 1991: *The Emergence of Kurdish Nationalism and the Sheikh Said Rebellion, 1880–1925* (University of Texas Press, Austin).

———— 1982: *The Ba'th and Syria, 1947 to 1982: The Evolution of Ideology, Party, and State* (The Kingston Press, Inc, Princeton, N.J.).

Özoğlu, Hakan 2001: '"Nationalism" and Kurdish notables in the late Ottoman–early Republican era' in *The International Journal of Middle Eastern Studies* No. 33, (Cambridge University Press, Cambridge) pp.383–409.

———— 2004: *Kurdish Notables and the Ottoman State: Evolving Identities, Competing Loyalties and Shifting Boundaries* (State University of New York Press, Albany).

Pênûs No 17 Spring 2005: also available on http://www.efrin.net/efrin03/penus/index/old/penus17.pdf (accessed 20/03/09).

Perthes, Volker 1995: *The Political Economy of Syria under Asad* (I.B.Tauris, London).

Pipes, Daniel 1990: *Greater Syria: The History of Ambition* (Oxford University Press, Oxford).

Posusney, Marsha Pripstein 2005: 'The Middle East's democracy deficit in comparative perspective' in Michele Penner Angrist and Marsha Pripstein Posusney (eds.) 2005: *Authoritarianism in the Middle East: Regimes and Resistance* (Lynne Rienner Publishers, London) pp.1–20.

Rashid (Sheikh al-Shabab), Muhammad 1994: *Siyra al-Munādil al-Kurdi 'Usman Sabri 'Apo'* (Beirut, Lebanon).

Richards, Alan and John Waterbury 1998: *A Political Economy of the Middle East* (Westview Press, Oxford).

Romano, David 2006: *The Kurdish Nationalist Movement: Opportunity, Mobilization and Identity* (Cambridge University Press, Cambridge).

Rondot, Pierre 1939: 'Les Kurdes de Syrie' in *La France Mediterraneene et Africaine* Vol. II, No. 1, (Lib. Sirey, Paris) pp.81–126.

Sartori, Giovanni 2005: *Parties and Party Systems: A Framework for Analysis* (ECPR Press, Colchester).

Savelsberg, Eva, Siamend Hajo and Celal Abbas Kömür 2003: 'Ausländer im eigenen Land. Die Situation staatenloser Kurden in Syrien' In Internationales Zentrum für die Menschenrechte der Kurden (IMK) e. V. (eds.) 2003: *Ausländer im eigenen Land. Die Situation staatenloser Kurden in Syrien*, pp.7–49.

Seale, Patrick 1988: *Asad: The Struggle for the Middle East* (University of California Press, London).

Shorrock, William I. 1970: 'The origin of the French mandate in Syria and Lebanon: the railroad question, 1901–1914' in *The International Journal of Middle Eastern Studies*, Vol.1, No.2, (Cambridge University Press, Cambridge) pp.133–153.

Sieda, Abdulbaset 2003: *al-Mas'alah al-Kurdiyah fi Suriyah: Fasul Mansiyah min Mu'anaah Mustamarrah* (Nina Trykeri, Uppsala).

Smilianskaya I. M. 1966: 'The disintegration of feudal relations in Syria and Lebanon in the middle of the nineteenth century' in Charles Issawi (ed.) 1996: *The Economic History of the Middle East* (University of Chicago Press, Chicago).

Smith, A. 1988(a): *The Ethnic Origins of Nations* (Blackwell Publishers, Oxford).

———— January 1988(b): 'The myth of the "modern nation" and the myths of nations' in *Ethnic and Racial Studies*, Vol. 11, No. 1, (Routledge, London).

———— July 1989: 'The origins of nations' in *Ethnic and Racial Studies*, Vol. 12, No. 3, (Routledge, London).

Snow, David A. E. Burke Rochford, Jr., Steven K. Worden and Robert D. Benford: 'Frame Alignment Processes, Micromobilization, and Movement

Participation' in *American Sociological Review*, Vol. 51, No. 4, (Aug., 1986) pp.464–481.

Strohmeier, Martin 2003: *Crucial Images in the Presentation of a Kurdish National Identity: Heroes and Patriots, Traitors and Foes* (Brill, Leiden).

Sykes, Mark 1908: 'The Kurdish tribes of the Ottoman Empire' in *The Journal of the Royal Anthropological Institute of Great Britain and Ireland*, Vol.38, (July–December) (Royal Anthropological Institute of Great Britain and Ireland) pp.451–486.

Tachjian, Vahé 2004: 'Le Khoyboun dans la Haute-Mésopotamie syrienne sous mandate français et le rapprochement kurdo-arménien' in *Etudes Kurdes* No. 6, Janvier 2004, (Fondation Institute Kurde de Paris/L'Harmattan, Paris).

Tejel, Jordi 2009: *Syria's Kurds: History, Politics and Society* (Routledge, London).

———— 2007: *Le mouvement kurde de Turquie en exil: continuités et discontinuités du nationalisme kurde sous le mandat français en Syrie et au Liban (1925–1946)* (Peter Lang, Bern, New York).

———— 2006: 'Les constructions de l'identité kurde sous l'influence de la "connexion kurdo-française" au Levant (1930–1946)' in *European Journal of Turkish Studies*, Thematic Issue N°5, Power, ideology, knowledge – deconstructing Kurdish Studies (URL: http://www.ejts.org/document751.html) (accessed 13/06/07).

Tonnies, Ferdinand 1955: *Community and Association* (Routledge and Kegan Paul Ltd, London) (Translation by Charles P. Loomis).

Torrey, Gordon H. 1964: *Syrian Politics and the Military, 1945–1958* (Ohio State University Press, Ohio).

Vali, Abbas 2003: 'Genealogies of the Kurds: constructions of nation and national identity in Kurdish historical writing' in Abbas Vali (ed.) 2003: *The Origins of Kurdish Nationalism* (Mazda Publishers Ltd, California) pp.58–105.

———— (ed.) 2003: *The Origins of Kurdish Nationalism* (Mazda Publishers Ltd, California).

Vanly, Ismet Chériff 1992: 'The Kurds in Syria and Lebanon' in Philip G. Kreyenbroek and Stefan Sperl (eds.) 1992: *The Kurds: A Contemporary Overview* (Routledge, London) pp.143–170.

Velud, Christian 1991: *Une Expérience d'Administration Régionale en Syrie durant le Mandat Français: Conquête, Colonisation et mise en Valeur de la Djézireh, 1920–1936*, PhD Thesis, Université Lumière Lyon II, November 1991.

———— 2000: 'French mandates policy in the Syrian steppe,' in Mundy, Martha and Basim Musallam (eds.) 2000: *The Transformation of Nomadic Society in the Arab East* (Cambridge University Press, Cambridge) pp.63–82.

Ware, Alan 1995: *Political Parties and Party Systems* (Oxford University Press, Oxford).

Weeden, Lisa 1999: *Ambiguities of Domination: Politics, Rhetoric and Symbols of Contemporary Syria* (University of Chicago Press, Chicago/London).

White, Paul 2000: *Primitive Rebels or Revolutionary Modernisers? The Kurdish National Movement in Turkey* (Zed Books, London).

Williams S. L. 1981: 'Ottoman land policy and social change: the Syrian provinces' in *Acta Orientalia Academiae Scientiarum Hungaricae* 35 (Akademiai Kiado, Hungry).

Zisser, Eyal 2001: *Asad's Legacy: Syria in Transition* (Hurst & Co., London).

Zubaida, S. 1989: 'Nations: old and new, comments on Anthony D. Smith's "The myth of the 'modern nation' and the myths of nations"' in *Ethnic and Racial Studies*, Vol. 12, No. 3, (Routledge, London).

———— 1993: *Islam, the People and the State: Political Ideas and Movements in the Middle East* (I.B.Tauris, London).

———— 2006: 'Religion and ethnicity as politicized boundaries' in Faleh A. Jabar and Hasham Dawod (eds.) 2006: *The Kurds: Nationalism and Politics* (Saqi, London) pp.93–102.

Zürcher, E. 2001: *Turkey: A Modern History* (I.B.Tauris, London).

Publications by Organisations

ACCORD and DIS (Austrian Centre for Country of Origin and Asylum Research and Documentation/Austrian Red Cross and the Danish Immigration Service Documentation and project Division) May 2010: *Human Rights Issues Concerning Kurds in Syria: Report from a Joint Fact Finding Mission by the Danish Immigration Service (DIS) and ACCORD/Austrian Red Cross to Damascus, Syria, Beirut, Lebanon, and Erbil and Dohuk, Kurdistan Region of Iraq (KRI) 21 January to 8 February 2010*, available on: http://www.ecoi.net and www.newtodenmark.dk (accessed 01/04/10).

Article 19 1998: *Walls of Silence. Media and Censorship in Syria* (Article 19, London).

AI (Amnesty International) 2007: *Report: Syria*, http://thereport.amnesty.org/eng/Regions/Middle-East-and-North-Africa/Syria (accessed 05/05/07).

———— 10/03/05: 'Kurds in the Syrian Arab Republic one year after the March 2004 events' AI Index: MDE 24/002/2005, http://web.amnesty.org/library/Index/ENGMDE240022005?open&of=ENG-SYR (accessed 15/03/06).

———— 29/06/04: 'Syria: unfair trial of Kurdish prisoners of conscience and torture of children is totally unacceptable' MDE 24/048/2004, available on http://www.amnesty.org/en/library/asset/MDE24/048/2004/en/c6bab194-d5ba-11dd-bb24-1fb85fe8fa05/mde240482004en.html (accessed 15/03/06).

Hossino, Omar, Ilhan Tanir and Wladimir van Wilgenburg September 2012: *Unity or PYD Power Play?: Syrian Kurdish Dynamics after the Erbil Agreement* (The Henry Jackson Society, London), available on http://henryjacksonsociety.org/wp-content/uploads/2012/10/HJS_Unity-or-PYD-Power-Play_-Report.pdf (accessed 17/01/13).

HRAS (Human Rights Association in Syria) April 2004: *The Qamishli Incidents and their Consequences in Syrian Cities* (HRAS, Damascus).

———— 16/03/04: Press Release 'The situation of Kurds in Qamishli: summary regarding the events in Damascus over the last few days' (HRAS, Damascus).

———— November 2003: *The effect of denial of nationality on Syrian Kurds* (HRAS, Damascus).

HRW (Human Rights Watch): *Reports*

————2009. *Group Denial: Repression of Kurdish Cultural and Political Rights in Syria* (HRW, London) available on http://www.hrw.org/en/reports/2009/11/26/group-denial (accessed 12/12/09).

———— 2003: *World Report 2003: Syria* (HRW, London).

———— 2002: *World Report 2002: Syria* (HRW, London).

———— 2001: *World Report 2001: Syria* (HRW, London).

———— October 1996. *The Silenced Kurds* (HRW, London), available on http://hrw.org/reports/1996/Syria.htm (accessed 15/01/03).

———— April 1996: *Syria's Tadmor Prison: Dissent still hostage to a legacy of terror* (HRW, New York), available on http://hrw.org/reports/1996/syria2.htm (accessed 15/01/03).

———— July 1995: *Syria: The Price of Dissent* (HRW, New York), available on http://www.hrw.org/reports/1995/syria.htm (accessed 15/01/03).

———— 1991: *Syria unmasked: The suppression of human rights by the Asad regime* (Yale University Press, New Haven and London).

HRW: *News and Memorandums*

———— 26/03/10: 'Syria investigate security forces shooting of Kurds' available on: http://www.hrw.org/en/news/2010/03/26/syria-investigate-security-force-shooting-kurds (accessed 01/04/10).

———— 15/04/09: 'Syria reveal fate of 17 held incommunicado: detention of Kurds and suspected Islamists for months raises grave concerns' available on: http://www.hrw.org/en/news/2009/04/15/syria-reveal-fate-17-held-incommunicado (accessed 05/08/09).

———— 23/03/08: 'Syria: investigate killing of Kurds' available on: http://www.hrw.org/en/news/2008/03/23/syria-investigate-killing-kurds (accessed 01/04/10).

———— 07/10/07 'Syria: Stop arrests for online comments' (HRW, London) available on: http://www.hrw.org/en/news/2007/10/07/syria-stop-arrests-online-comments (accessed 10/05/09).

———— 10/05/07 'Syria: a peaceful activist gets 12 years with hard labor' available on: http://www.hrw.org/en/news/2007/05/10/syria-peaceful-activist-gets-12-years-hard-labor (accessed 05/08/09).

———— 31/01/02: 'Memorandum to the Syrian Government. Decree No. 50/2001: human rights concerns' (HRW, New York).

———— 07/09/01: 'Dangerous backlash in Syria' available on: http://www.hrw.org/press/2001/09/syria090701.htm (accessed 30/03/03).

ICG (International Crisis Group) January 2013: Middle East Report No. 136, *Syria's Kurds: a struggle within a struggle* (ICG, Amman).

——— 11/02/04: Middle East Report No. 23, *Syria under Bashar (I): Foreign policy challenges* (ICG, Amman) available on: http://icg.org/home/index.cfm?id=2515&|=1 (accessed 15/02/04).

——— 11/02/04: Middle East Report No. 24, *Syria Under Bashar (II): Domestic Policy Challenges* (ICG, Amman) available on: http://icg.org/home/index.cfm?id=2516&|=1 (accessed 15/02/04).

ICT (Independent Televisions Commission) 1999: 'ITC Bulletin No.8,' available on: http://www.ofcom.org.uk/static/archive/itc/itc_publications/leaflets/bulletins/index.asp-itc_bulletin_id=19.html (accessed 09/09/10).

Institut Kurde de Paris, 21/05/04: 'Répression antikurdes en Syrie: Environ 20.000 Kurdes de Syrie seront naturalisés (général Tlass),' (Beirut).

——— May 2004: 'Damas: Des Centaines de Kurdes Libèrès des Prisons Syriennes Alors que les Américains Imposent des Sanctions Contre la Syrie' ('Damascus: Hundreds of Kurds released from Syrian jails as the Americans impose sanctions on Syria'), Bulletin de liaison et d'information No.230, (Institut Kurde de Paris, Paris).

Lynch, Maureen and Perveen Ali January 2006: *Buried Alive* (Refugees International, Washington DC).

KurdWatch (European Centre for Kurdish Studies, Berlin).

KurdWatch (European Centre for Kurdish Studies, Berlin): *Reports*

——— December 2011: Report 8. *Who is the Syrian-Kurdish Opposition? The Development of Kurdish Parties 1957-2011*, available on: http://www.kurdwatch.org/pdf/kurdwatch_parteien_en.pdf (accessed 10/01/12).

——— March 2010: Report 5. *Stateless Kurds in Syria: Illegal Invaders or Victims of a Nationalistic Policy?* (Berlin).

——— July 2009: Report 6. *Decree 49 – Dispossession of the Kurdish Population?: Commentary on the Political Implications and Economic Consequences of a Decree* (European Centre for Kurdish Studies, Berlin).

——— December 2009: Report 4 *The 'al-Qamishli Uprising': The beginning of a 'new era' for Syrian Kurds?* (European Centre for Kurdish Studies, Berlin).

KurdWatch: *News Articles and Interviews*

——— 12/06/12: 'Al-Qamishli: Further demonstrations – for the first time, the PYD constructs check points in al-Qamishli' available on: http://www.kurdwatch.org/?aid=2555&z=en&cure=245 (accessed 12/06/12).

——— 11/06/12(a): 'Afrin: Participants in a meeting of the Kurdish National Council kidnapped by the PYD' available on: http://www.kurdwatch.org/index.php?aid=2554&z=en&cure=245 (accessed 12/06/12).

——— 11/06/12(b): 'Afrin: PYD forces the construction of a checkpoint by kidnapping activists' available on: http://www.kurdwatch.org/index.php?aid=2552&z=en&cure=245 (accessed 12/06/12).

———— 02/06/2012: 'Afrin: Free Syrian Army attacks PYD and regime' available on: http://www.kurdwatch.org/?aid=2547&z=en&cure=245 (accessed 10/06/12).

———— 21/03/12: Interview with Azad Muhiyuddin, member of the Movement of the Youth in the West: 'The Kurdish Patriotic Conference is nothing more than a name. Compared to the PYD it has accomplished nothing' available on: http://www.kurdwatch.org/syria_article.php?aid=2484&z=en&cure=240 (accessed 25/03/12).

———— 19/01/2012: Interview with Rezan Bahri Shaykhmus, Chairman of the Kurdish Future Movement's Office of General Communications: 'While a people's revolution is taking place throughout Syria, the Kurdish Patriotic Conference is arguing and struggling over money' available on: http://www.kurdwatch.org/html/en/interview9.html (accessed 10/10/12).

———— 08/11/11: Interview with Salih Muslim Muhammad, chairman of the PYD: 'Turkey's henchmen in Syrian Kurdistan are responsible for the unrest here' available on: http://kurdwatch.org/html/en/interview6.html (accessed 09/11/11).

———— 17/09/11: Interview with Ismail Hemi: 'Our goal is self-government of the Kurds in Syrian Kurdistan' available on: http://www.kurdwatch.org/html/en/interview5.html (accessed 20/09/11).

———— 08/08/11: 'Interview with Samir Nashar, spokesman for the Damascus Declaration: The Kurds must receive the same rights as everyone else' available on: http://www.kurdwatch.org/html/en/interview3.html (accessed 20/09/11).

Lowe, Robert January 2006: *The Syrian Kurds: A People Discovered* (Chatham House, London).

Middle East Media Research Institute, The 16/12/02: 'Special Dispatch: Syria persecutes members of outlawed Kurdish opposition' available on http://www.memri.de/uebersetzungen_analysen/laender/ (accessed 04/10/04).

ORSAM (Centre for Middle Eastern Strategic Studies) August 2012: Report No. 1267, *Kurdish Movements in Syria*, (ORSAM, Turkey) available on: http://www.orsam.org.tr/en/enUploads/Article/Files/2012828_127%20ing%20yeni.pdf (accessed 15/01/13).

Syrian Human Rights Committee (SHRC), 17/12/02: 'Press Release' (SHRC/CDF, Syria) (fax provided by Abdul Basset Hamou).

UN CCPR (United Nations Covenant on Civil and Political Rights) 2001: 'Comments by the Government of the Syrian Arab Republic on the concluding observations of the Human Rights Committee.' Syrian Arab Republic. 08/05/01. CCPR/CO/71/SYR/Add.1. (Follow-up Response by State Party) available on: http://www.unhchr.ch/tbs/doc.nsf/(Symbol)/2297732dbf2bd41cc1256bdf004ad35c?Opendocument (accessed 25/04/05).

UN CERD (Committee on the Elimination of Racial Discrimination) 26/10/98: 'Fifteenth periodic report of States parties due in 1998: Syrian Arab Republic.' (CERD/C/338/Add.1/Rev.1.) available on: http://www.unhchr.ch/ (accessed 10/10/05).

———— 2004: 'Third Periodic Report: Syrian Arab Republic. 19/10/04. CCPR/C/SYR/2004/3. (State Party Report)' available on: http://www.unhchr.ch/tbs/doc.nsf/(Symbol)/30d6d16582a25c66c1256fce003ae238?Opendocument (accessed 10/10/05).

UN ESCWA (Economic and Social Commission for Western Asia) 03/09/07: 'National profile of the information society in the Syrian Arab Republic' available on: http://www.escwa.un.org/wsis/reports/docs/Syria-07-E.pdf (accessed 10/03/10).

USA State Department 11/03/10: *Country Reports on Human Rights Practices: Syria* (Bureau of Democracy, Human Rights and Labor) available on: http://www.state.gov/g/drl/rls/hrrpt/2009/nea/136080.htm (accessed 15/04/10).

World Bank 08/13/06 'The Syrian Arab Republic at a glance' available on: http://devdata.worldbank.org/AAG/syr_aag.pdf. World Bank, http://www.world-bank.org/sy (accessed 28/01/07).

Electronic Resources

(Including online newspapers and news articles)

Abdulmajid, Adib 14/01/13: 'Kurdish youth forces in Syria accuse parties of squeezing them out' *Rudaw* http://www.rudaw.net/english/news/syria/5656.html (accessed 15/01/13).

———— 19/05/12: 'Fear of clashes between Kurdish groups in Syria' *Rudaw* http://www.rudaw.net/english/index.php?news=4750 (accessed 29/05/12).

———— 08/05/12: 'KNC issues interim agenda that puts Kurdish rights on hold' *Rudaw* http://www.rudaw.net/english/news/syria/4712.html (accessed 09/05/12).

———— 10/06/12: 'Violent confrontations between Kurdish groups in Syria' *Rudaw* http://www.rudaw.net/english/news/syria/4825.html (accessed 11/06/12).

Ahmed, Hevidar 01/08/12: 'KNC leader: Kurds are disappointed by PYD's actions: interview with Abdulhakim Bashar' http://www.rudaw.net/english/interview/5030.html (accessed 15/08/12).

———— 18/09/12: 'PYD accused of abuse of power in Kurdish areas of Syria' *Rudaw* http://www.rudaw.net/english/news/syria/5214.html (accessed 20/09/12).

Akhbar al-Sharq 11/03/03: 'al-Assad yantaqad al-mu'ariDah al-suriyyah wa yata-hamha bil-intihaziyyah wa isaa'a fahama al-dimoqratiyyah' http://www.thisis-syria.net/2003/03/11/syria&lebanon.html (accessed 30/03/03).

AFP (Agence France Presse) 21/03/08: 'Syrian police kill 3 Kurds celebrating New Year' *KurdNet* http://www.ekurd.net/mismas/articles/misc2008/3/syriakurdistan132.htm (accessed 11/05/10).

———— 31/07/12 'Iraqi Kurdistan trained Syrian Kurds: head of KDP foreign relations' reproduced on *KurdNet* http://www.ekurd.net/mismas/articles/misc2012/7/state6397.htm (accessed 10/08/12).

Amude.net. Various articles particularly between 12/03/04 and 20/04/04 (coverage of March 2004 Kurdish uprising in Syria). Website now discontinued.

ANF News Agency 27/10/12: Interview with Asya Abdullah, 'PYD co-chair Asya Abdullah: a woman revolution' http://en.firatnews.com/index.php?rupel=article&nuceID=5275 (accessed 05/11/12).

Al-Assad, Basher Hafiz 2000: 'President Bashar Hafez Assad's inaugural speech' (Syrian Ministry of Information) http://www.moi-syria.com/_bassas.asp?Filename=20021121210936 (accessed 30/03/03).

———— 16/11/02: *'Kalama al-Sayyid Bashar al-Assad amam al-Majlisah al-Istithnaiyyah li Majlis al-Sha'ab'* (Syrian Ministry of Information) http://www.moi-syria.com/_bassada.asp?FilName=20021116163001 (accessed 04/01/03).

Aslam, Abid 15/02/06: '300,000 Syrian Kurds buried alive' available on *OneWorld US* website (OneWorld.net) http://us.oneworld.net/article/view/127600/1/ (accessed 20/01/06).

Blanford, Nicholas 20/11/02: 'As war looms the voice of Kurds is heard in Syria' in *Christian Science Monitor,* http://www.csmonitor.com/2002/1120/p07s02-wome.html (accessed 27/02/03).

Cellular-News 25/08/10: 'Syria to issue a third mobile phone Licence' http://www.cellular-news.com/story/45027.php (accessed 06/09/10).

Cagaptay, Soner 05/04/12: 'Syria and Turkey: the PKK dimension' (The Washington Institute) www.washingtoninstitute.org/policy-analysis/view/syria-and-turkey-the-pkk-dimension/ (accessed 05/05/12).

Daragahi, Borzou and Abigail Fielding-Smith, 04/01/12: 'Syria opposition groups fail to reach accord' *The Financial Times,* London.

DPA 25/02/10: 'Kurdish satellite TV overturns German ban' available on *Earth Times* website http://www.earthtimes.org/articles/news/311223,kurdish-satellite-tv-channel-overturns-german-ban.html (accessed 09/09/10).

Earth Trends, n.d.: 'Population, health and human well being – the Syrian Arab Republic' http://earthtrends.wri.org/pdf_library/country_profiles/pop_cou_760.pdf (accessed 01/02/07).

Gambill, Gary C. April 2004: 'The Kurdish reawakening in Syria' *Middle East Intelligence Bulletin,* Vol. 6, No. 4, http://www.meforum.org/meib/articles/0404_s1.htm (accessed 15/06/08).

Hamidi, Ibrahim 02/09/02: 'Syria rediscovers its Kurdish problem' in *The Daily Star,* (Lebanon) http://www.dailystar.com.lb/opinion/02_09_02_c.htm (accessed 25/04/03, now unavailable on website).

IRIN News 20/11/05: 'For many Kurds statelessness remains a way of life' http://www.irinnews.org/report.asp?ReportID=50197&SelectRegion=Middle_East&SelectCountry=SYRIA (accessed 13/03/07).

ITP.net 02/06/09: 'Mobile users in Syria boycott services' http://www.itp.net/557493-mobile-users-in-syria-boycott-services (accessed 06/05/10).

Al-Kharrat, Raed March 2001: 'Riyad Sayf: Syrian member of parliament' *Middle East Intelligence Bulletin* Vol.3 No.3, http://www.meib.org/articles/0103_sd1.htm (accessed 30/03/03).

Khoshnaw, Hemin 16/07/12: 'PYD: civil war could not take place in Syrian Kurdistan' *Rudaw* http://www.rudaw.net/english/interview/4960.html (accessed 17/07/12).

KNNTV (Kurdish News Network TV) 21/02/10: *'Miyat alaf min al-akrad fi Kurdistan suriya yukhrajun ila al-sahul wa al-wadiyan lil-ihtifal bi eid al-newroz'* http://www.knntv.net/detail.php?ID=4310 (accessed 12/05/10).

———— 12/10/09: *'Hizb al-Yekîtî al-Kurdi fi Suriya ylghi tathahirah ihtijajiyyah kanat muqarirah fi hatha al-yum'* http://www.knntv.net/detail.php?ID=3841 (accessed 04/05/10).

Kurdish Aspect 01/06/10: 'Land rights of Kurds removed in Syria' *Kurdish Aspect* http://www.kurdishaspect.com/doc060110SKS.html (accessed 10/08/10).

The Kurdish Globe 13/12/12: 'For us it is not a case of liberation,' interview with Salih Muslim, Co-Chair of the Kurdish Syrian PYD *The Kurdish Globe* No. 379, (Iraq), http://bashdar.co.uk/wp-content/uploads/2012/12/KurdishGlobe-2012-39-131.pdf (accessed 15/01/13).

Kurdistan Observer 28/04/04: 'Syria woos Kurds' http://home.cogeco.ca/~kurdistan3/1-5-04-syria-woos-kurds.htm (accessed 05/12/05).

Kurds Information (IMK Weekly Information Service) 06/0/01–20/0/01 No. 119–120: 'First meeting since 1963 between Kurds and Syrian leadership' and 'Mass detentions of Kurds in Syria' (Source: KDP-S statement 08/07/01) http://www.kurds.dk/english/2000/news76.html (accessed 20/03/06).

———— 20/06/01–20/07/01 No. 113–114 'Syrian KDP requests support' (Source KDP-S 08/07/01) http://www.kurds.dk/english/2000/news73.html (accessed 20/03/06).

Mabardi, Roueida 18/03/04: 'Kurdish unrest in Syria echoes Iraq conflict' *Middle East Online* http://www.middle-east-online.com/english/syria/?id=9312=9312&format=0 (accessed 15/04/06).

McDowall, David 1991: *The Kurds in Syria* http://www.krds.net/syriankurd.htm (accessed 30/10/02).

MEIB (*Middle East Intelligence Bulletin*) 27/09/00: 'Statement by 99 Syrian intellectuals' translated from *al-Hayat* http://www.meib.org/articles/0010_sdoc0927.htm (accessed 30/03/03).

———— January 2003: 'Arrest of Hamidi sparks outrage abroad' and 'Syrian Kurds hold rare demonstration' in *Intelligence Briefs: Syria* MEIB Vol.5, No.1 http://meib.org/articles/0301_sd.htm (accessed 30/03/03).

Miran, Dalshad: 22/01/10: *'Kharitah al-tanzimat al-Kurdiyyah fi Suriya fi 2009 al-Jz al-Ula: Tanzimat al-siyasiyyah al-Kurdiyyah fi al-dakhil'* http://ar.kurdroj.org/index.php?option=com_content&task=view&id=3565&Itemid=29 (accessed 01/02/10).

———— 16/02/09: *'al-Kharitah al-Siyasiyah wa al-Tanzimat fi Kurdistan Suriyah fi 2008'* http://ar.kurdroj.org/index.php?option=com_cntent&task=view&id=3598&Itemid=27 (accessed 10/02/10).

Moas, Taghee 25/04/12: 'Turkey caused new concern for Syrian Kurds' *Rudaw* http://www.rudaw.net/english/news/syria/4670.html (accessed 10/10/12).

Mustafa, Bassam 21/04/11: 'I did not know much about you' *Rudaw* http://www.rudaw.net/english/news/syria/3613.html (accessed 22/04/11).

Qamislo.com. Various articles particularly between 12/03/04 and 20/04/04 (coverage of March 2004 Kurdish uprising in Syria).

Rojava News 30/12/09: '*al-ahzab al-Kurdiyah fi Suriya tu'alan al-majlis al-siyasi,*' http://rojavanews.com/ar/index.php/world/kurd/707-kurd-party.html (accessed 10/01/10).

Rojhelat 31/08/10: 'Danish government launches case against Kurdish satellite channel Roj TV' http://english.rojhelat.info/index.php?option=com_conte nt&view=article&id=672:danish-government-launched-case-against-kurd-ish-satellite-channel-roj-tv- (accessed 09/09/10).

Sherlok, Ruth 06/07/12: 'Syria: united rebels grain ground as slow war comes to Aleppo' *The Telegraph,* (London) http://www. telegraph. co.uk/news/worldnews/middleeast/syria/9382582/Syria-United-rebels-gainground-as-slow-war-comes-to-Aleppo.html (accessed 06/07/12).

Support Kurds in Syria 28/10/11: 'Syria National Council leader Burhan Ghalioun talks to German TV about Kurds' http://supportkurds.org/news/syria-national-council-leader-burhan-gallioun-talks-to-german-tv-about-kurds/ (accessed 29/10/11).

————— 20/05/11: 'Friday 20 May Azadî day' http://supportkurds.org/news/fri-day-20-may-2011-azadi-day/ (accessed 02/06/11).

Wilgenberg, Wladimir van 05/11/12: 'Tensions with PYD Push Kurdish Parties to Unite in Kobane' *Rudaw* http://www.rudaw.net/english/news/syria/5380. html (accessed 06/11/12).

————— 20/08/12: 'Kurdish militias help out Syrian rebels in Aleppo' *Rudaw* http://www.rudaw.net/english/news/syria/5082.html (accessed 20/08/12).

Yassin, Selim 19/03/04: 'Syria's Hammud: 25 killed in Kurdish un-rest' *Middle East Online* http://www.middle-east-online.com/english/syria/?id=9317=9317&format=0 (accessed 20/05/04).

Yekîtî 23/03/09: 'Kurdish Newroz 2009 in Syria' http://www.wadinet.de/news/iraq/newsarticle.php?id=5192 (accessed 11/05/10)

YouTube 'Qamishlo – Qasimo Mosque – Friday of here is Kurdistan' http://www. youtube.com/watch?v=gVwfobsxdPo&feature=related (accessed 25/04/12).

Yusef, Haval n.d.: '*al-akrad al-mujridiin min al-jinsiyah*' published on *al-Tiyar al-Suri al-Dimoqrati* website: http://www.tsdp.org/al2krad%20almogrdin.htm (accessed 15/10/06).

————— 04/10/04: '*Sihadat hayat lil mujridiin min al-jinsiyyah min al-akrad al-suriyiin*' on *Amude.com* http://www.amude.net/Nivisar_Afaq_deep.php?new sLanguage=Afaq&newsId=446 (accessed 30/10/06).

Zoepf, Katherine 28/04/05: 'After Decades as Nonpersons, Syrian Kurds may soon be Recognized' in *The New York Times* (USA) http://www.nytimes. com/2005/04/28/international/middleeast/28syria.html?_r=1 (accessed 30/04/05).

Political Documents

Constitution of the Syrian Arab Republic, adopted 13 March 1973. Available on: http://www.servat.unibe.ch/law/icl/sy00t____.html

Damascus Declaration (The) 16 October 2005. English translation available on: Syria Comment 01/11/05: http://faculty-staff.ou.edu/L/Joshua.M.Landis-1/syriablog/2005/11/damascus-declaration-in-english.htm (accessed 28/11/05).

Harakat Itihad Hurriyah Qamishlo 20/03/2008: '*Bayan Harakat Iitihad Hurriya Qamishlo*' available on Gemya Kurda website, www.gemyakurda/modules.php?name=News&file=article&sid=8042 (accessed 26/07/10).

KNK (*Kongra Netewiya Kurdistan*) 2001: 'Kongra: bulletin of the Kurdistan National Congress' issue 1, (Information and Archive Commission of the KNK).

PYD 11/05/11: 'The Initiative of Kurdish national movement parties in Syria to resolve the current crisis in the county' http://www.pydrojava.net/en/index.php?option=com_content&view=article&id=63:the-initiative-of-kurdish-national-movement-parties-in-syria-to-resolve-the-current-crisis-in-the-co&catid=39:document&Itemid=54 (accessed 20/05/11).

PCWK 16/12/11: The declaration of the People's Council in Western Kurdistan. Derik, Qamishli, Syria.

Erbil Agreement, minutes of the meeting 11/06/12: translation available on http://www.kurdwatch.org/index.php?cid=185&z=en (accessed 01/08/12).

Party programmes (personal collection)

Partiya Azadî ya Kurd li Suryê 12/10/05: *al-Nitham al-Dakhili (Matruh li Munaqishah)*.

Partiya Yekîtî ya Kurd li Sûriya 1999: *Political Program Submitted to the Third Convention of the Yekîtî Party in Syria.*

———— December 2006: *The Political Program (amended and approved by the fifth conference)*, available on http://yekitimedia.org/en/index.php/the-political-programme.html (accessed 08/08/04).

Partîya Yekîtî ya Dêmokrat a Kurd li Sûriyê 2001: *al-Nitham al-Dakhiliy li Hizb al-Wahidah al-Dimoqrati al-Kurdi fi Suriya (Yekîtî)* (adopted at the forth conference).

Partîya Çep a Kurdî li Sûriyê.

Partîya Dêmokrat a Kurdî li Sûriyê (el-Partî).

Partîya Dêmokrata Pêşverû a Kurdî li Sûriyê. Kurdish Democratic Progressive Party in Syria: Political Program 1996 (n.p.).

Partîya Hevgirtina Gelê Kurd li Sûriyê. Al-Nitham al-Dakhiliy February 2001 (9th Party Congress).

Partîya Dêmokrat a Kurdî ya Sûrî (el-Sûrî). Al-Munhaj wa al-nitham al-Dakhili lil Hizb al-Dimoqrati al-Suridi al-Suri (n.p./ n.d.).

Party Papers (personal collection)

Denge Kurd /Sout al-Akrad (party paper of *Partîya Dêmokrat a Kurdî li Sûriyê (el-Partî)*) numerous issues from 2002–2013.

Hevbendi/Tahaluf September 2002: (party paper of the Kurdish alliance *Hevbendiya Dêmokrat a Kurdî li Sûriyê*) (n.p.) No. 68–69.

Itihad al-Sha'ab November 2001 (party paper of *Partîya Hevgirtina Gelê Kurd li Sûriyê*).

Newroz (paper of *Partîya Yekîtî ya Dêmokrat a Kurd li Sûriyê*) issues from 2004 and 2005.

Tariq al-Sha'ab April 2002 (paper of *Partîya Çep a Kurdî li Sûriyê*) No. 277.

Yekîtî (paper of *Partiya Yekîtî ya Kurd li Sûriya*) Nos. 63, 107, 108.

Yekîtî (paper of *Partîya Yekîtî ya Dêmokrat a Kurd li Sûriyê*) Nos. 154 and 155.

British Foreign Office Documents

PRO FO 371/5274 February 1946: 'Kurdish and Armenian communities in Syria and Lebanon.'

    3 October 1946: 'Beirut Chancery Letter.'

    14 March: 'Beirut Chancery Letter' (Ref: 50/11/46).

    19 April: 'Beirut Chancery Letter' (Ref: 50/18/46).

    5 September: 'Beirut Chancery Letter' (Ref: 50/24/46).

    11 November: 'Damascus Chancery Letter' (Ref: 95/5/46).

PRO FO 371/62145 7 February – 20 May 1947: 'The Kurdish situation in Syria' (Correspondence between Elphinstone and Sir Robert).

Interviews and Personal Communications

Academic involved in the Damascus Spring and Damascus Declaration 25/07/06: Damascus, Syria.

Ahmed, Muhammad Mulla: founding member of *Jama'iyah Wahidat al-Shabab al-Dimoqratiyiin al-Akrad*; former member of *Partiya Demokrat a Kurd li Sûriye*; author of three political histories of the Kurds in Syria, (see above). 20/12/02: Dortmund, Germany.

Ajanib Kurds group: group of four Kurds with *ajnabi* status (names withheld by author).

    11/06/07: Damascus, Syria.

Ali, Muhidin Sheikh: Secretary General of *Partîya Yekîtî ya Dêmokrat a Kurd li Sûriyê*.

    30/07/06: Aleppo, Syria.

    22/06/07: Aleppo, Syria.

Alo, Mamo: *ajnabi* Kurd and supporter of *Yekîtî* party.

    28/11/06: Sheffield, UK.

    10/12/06: Leeds, UK.

    24/01/07: Leeds, UK.

    02/02/07: telephone.

Aqil, Heyam: Kurdish activist and member of *el-Partî* of Dr Hakim.

    08/10/12: Written response to questions.

Baqi, Jamal Sheikh: leader of *Partîya Dêmokrat a Kurdî ya Sûrî (el-Sûrî)*.

    26/06/07: Damascus, Syria.

    28/06/07: Zor Ava, Syria.

Bashar, Dr Abdul Hakim: leader of *Partîya Dêmokrat a Kurdî li Sûriyê (el-Partî)*.
  12/08/06: Qamishli, Syria.
  13/07/07: Damascus, Syria.
Bekes, Kamiran: representative of *Partîya Yekîtîya Dêmokrat a Kurd li Sûriyê* in Germany.
  21/12/02: Köln, Germany.
Daoud, Khalil: Central Committee member of *Partîya Yekîtî ya Dêmokrat a Kurd li Sûriyê*.
  06/08/06: Damascus, Syria.
  10/06/07: Damascus, Syria.
Daoud, Mahammad: representative of *Partîya Dêmokrat a Kurdî ya Sûrî (el-Sûrî)*.
  20/12/02: Werl, Germany.
Deriki: representative of *Partîya Dêmokrat a Kurdî li Sûriyê (el-Partî)*.
  17/12/02: Dortmund, Germany.
Domar, Farzan: Kurdish Doctor.
  04/07/07: Efrîn, Syria.
Gelo: Kurdish intellectual.
  10/07/07: Kobanî, Syria.
Hajo, Kamiran: independent Kurdish expert.
  16/03/03: telephone interview, Sweden.
  10/04/03: telephone interview, Sweden.
  31/05/10: telephone interview, Sweden.
Hamou, Abdul Basset: former Representative of *Partîya Yekîtî ya Kurd li Sûriyê* in Germany. Currently representative of *Partîya Yekîtî ya Kurdistani li Sûriyê*.
  19/12/02: Dortmund, Germany.
  23/12/02: written account of meeting of Hasan Salih and Marwan Osman with Abd al-Qadir Qadourah, Syrian Speaker of Parliament and Isam al-Jamal, Secretary General of the Ba'th Party.
Hevgertin European branch Central Committee (four members of).
  22/12/02: Germany.
Ibrahim, Khalil Rashid: Grandson of Rashid Ibo (one of leaders of the *Muroud*).
  31/07/06: Aleppo, Syria.
Juma'a, Mustafa: leader of *Partiya Azadî ya Kurd li Suryê*.
  09/07/07: Aleppo, Syria.
Karim, Abdul: Central Committee member in *Partîya Dêmokrat a Kurdî li Sûriyê (el-Partî)*.
  29/06/07: Damascus, Syria.
Kobanî lawyer and tribal leader, (names withheld by author).
  05/07/07: Aleppo, Syria.
Kobanî resident: student in Aleppo.
  21/06/07: Aleppo, Syira.
Kobanî tribal leader.
  10/07/07: Kobanî, Syria.
Kurd from Efrîn.
  20/06/07: Efrîn, Syria.

Kurdish Lawyer (S), (name withheld by author).
05/09/02: Damascus, Syria.
20/06/07: Damascus, Syria.
Kurdish author, (name withheld by author).
04/09/02: Damascus, Syria.
Kurdish family from Kobanî.
31/08/02: Kobanî, Syria.
Kurdish family in Efrîn.
25/06/07: Efrîn, Syria.
Kurdish journalist.
21/06/07: Aleppo, Syria.
03/07/07: Aleppo, Syria.
Kurdish publisher: owner of publishing house in Damascus.
30/06/07: Damascus, Syria.
Mahmoud, Sanko: Office of the PUK representation in UK, London.
27/03/03: London, UK.
Maktum Kurd, resident of Zor Ava, (name withheld by author).
28/06/07: Zor Ava, Syria.
Maktum street trader, (name withheld by author).
Several meetings, August 2002: Damascus, Syria.
Mella, Izz al-Din: author and expert on the Kurds in Damascus.
12/08/02: Beirut, Lebanon.
Mella, Jawad: representative of the Western Kurdistan Association (WKA), London.
27/10/03: London, UK.
12/02/03: London, UK.
Miran, Dalshad: UK representative of the KDP Iraq.
08/11/02: London, UK.
27/01/04: London, UK.
Mustafa, Nazir: former leader of *Partîya Dêmokrat a Kurdî li Sûriyê (el-Partî)*.
12/08/06: Qamishli, Syira.
Naghar, Brûsk: representative of *Partîya Dêmokrata Pêşverû a Kurdî li Sûriyê* of Aziz Daoud.
17/12/02: Viersen, Germany.
Nahas, Obeida: Spokesperson for the Levant Institute which publishes *Akhbar al-Shirq*, online Syrian opposition portal.
27/03/03, London, UK.
Omar, Ismail: former president of *Partîya Yekîtî ya Dêmokrat a Kurd li Sûriyê*.
12/08/06: Qamishli, Syria.
Othman, Aziz: representative of *Partîya Yekîtî ya Kurd li Sûriyê* in UK.
11/05/10: telephone, London, UK.
Othman, Marwan: former Central Committee member of *Partîya Yekîtî ya Kurd li Sûriyê*.
10/05/03: Paris, France.
Rashid, Dr Latif: former representative of the PUK of Iraq in London and current Minister of Water Resources in Iraq.
27/03/03: London.

Rashid (Sheikh al-Shabab), Muhammad: former member of *Partiya Demokrat a Kurd li Sûriye*; friend of Osman Sabri and author of biography of him (see above).
 12/08/02: Beirut, Lebanon.
Saleh, Zara: UK representative of the *Partîya Yekîtî ya Kurd li Sûriyê* (Ismail Hemi).
 06/10/12: telephone.
Saydo, Kamal: former member of *Partiya Demokrat a Kurd li Sûriye*.
 16–25/12/02: pers.com., Germany.
Dr Semo, Alan: Foreign Affairs Representative of the PYD.
 Written response to questions: 16/07/12; 10/10/12; 16/02/13.
Sheikh: Kurdish land owner.
 22/04/10: Oxford, UK.
Sieda, Abdulbaset: former party leadership of *Partiya Palên Kurdî li Sûriyê*; Kurdish author, academic. President of the Syrian National Council, June–November 2012.
 02/10/12: Telephone conversation.
 13/10/12: Telephone conversation.
 Written responses to questions: 20/09/10; 08/08/10; 24/04/10; 26/03/10; 05/12/06; 17/11/06.
Stateless family in Dêrîk (names withheld by author).
 15/08/02: Dêrîk, Syria.
Stateless Kurdish family 1: residents of Zor Ava (names withheld by author).
 28/06/07: Zor Ava, Syria.
Stateless Kurdish family 2: residents of Zor Ava (names withheld by author).
 28/06/07: Zor Ava, Syria.
Stateless Kurd, (name withheld by author).
 14/07/07: Damascus, Syria.
Sulaiman, Haji: Representative of *Partîya Çep a Kurdî li Sûriyê* of Muhammad Musa.
 19/12/02: Hanover, Germany.
 January 2003: Written response to questions.
Temmo, Abdulrazzak: representative of *Şepêla Pêşerojê ya Kurdî li Sûriyê / Tiyar al-Mustaqbal*.
 Written response to questions: 29/09/12.
Temmo, Mohammad: independent Kurdish activist.
 04/10/12: Telephone conversation.
Yousef, Abdul Baqi: Central Committee member and former leader of *Partîya Yekîtî ya Kurd li Sûriyê*.
 19/12/02: Telephone conversation.
Yousef, Haval: independent Kurdish activist and writer specialist on Kurdish issues.
 20/08/06: Damascus, Syria.

INDEX

Note: *n* attached to a page number denotes an endnote, with appropriate number.